Tech

The publisher and the University of California Press Foundation gratefully acknowledge the generous support of the Richard and Harriett Gold Endowment Fund in Arts and Humanities.

Tech

WHEN SILICON VALLEY REMAKES THE WORLD

Olivier Alexandre

UNIVERSITY OF CALIFORNIA PRESS

University of California Press
Oakland, California

Originally published as *La Tech: Quand la Silicon Valley refait le monde*, ©
2023 Éditions du Seuil.

Library of Congress Cataloging-in-Publication Data

Names: Alexandre, Olivier, author
Title: Tech : when Silicon Valley remakes the world / Olivier Alexandre.
Other titles: Tech. English
Description: Oakland, California : University of California Press, [2025] |
    Originally published as La Tech : quand la Silicon Valley refait le monde,
    ©2023, Éditions du Seuil. | Includes bibliographical references and index.
Identifiers: LCCN 2025010558 (print) | LCCN 2025010559 (ebook) | ISBN
    9780520413740 cloth | ISBN 9780520413764 ebook
Subjects: LCSH: Computer industry—California—Santa Clara Valley (Santa
    Clara County) | High technology industries—California—Santa Clara
    Valley (Santa Clara County) | Technological innovations—California—
    Santa Clara Valley (Santa Clara County) | Computer industry—Social
    aspects | High technology industries—Social aspects | Technological
    innovations—Social aspects
Classification: LCC HD9696.2.U63 C352313 2025 (print) | LCC HD9696.2.U63
    (ebook) | DDC 338.4/70040979473—dc23/eng/20250604
LC record available at https://lccn.loc.gov/2025010558
LC ebook record available at https://lccn.loc.gov/2025010559

ISBN 978-0-520-41374-0 (cloth : alk. paper)
ISBN 978-0-520-41376-4 (ebook)

Manufactured in the United States of America

GPSR Authorized Representative: Easy Access System Europe, Mustamäe tee
50, 10621 Tallinn, Estonia, gpsr.requests@easproject.com

34   33   32   31   30   29   28   27   26   25
10   9   8   7   6   5   4   3   2   1

To Pablo and Nour . . . my New World

CONTENTS

ACKNOWLEDGMENTS

This book is based on a long investigation (far too long) on a fast-moving (far too fast-moving) topic. It was born at the crossroads of two timelines: those of new technologies and academia. Over the years I have contracted a double debt: on one hand, to the people who have given me some time in an industry where it is a scarce resource; on the other, to those who have allowed me to devote time in academia to dedicate myself to this project.

In 2013, when I was teaching the sociology of culture, media, and communication in the communication department of Avignon University in France, Cécile Cavagna, the secretary of the master, urged me to teach a new course, dedicated to digital worlds, that no academic in the department wanted to tackle. I knew almost nothing about the topic. I had no Twitter account, no LinkedIn profile, not even a Facebook page. So I immersed myself in extensive reading sessions, looking for historical works to put the subject into perspective. I was happy and relieved to find the works of AnnaLee Saxenian, Christophe Lécuyer, Randall Stross, Leslie Berlin, and Fred Turner on Silicon Valley. *From Counterculture to Cyberculture* was the intellectual starting point of this book. I'm grateful to Fred for showing me the way.

Then Daniel Cefaï, Sabine Chalvon-Demersay, Monique Dagnaud, Albert Ogien, Geneviève Pruvost, Claude Rosental, and Guillaume Braustein welcomed me to the Centre d'étude sur les mouvements sociaux (CEMS) in Paris, where media has long been seen as a social matter, from a pragmatic perspective. Bertrand Legendre, François Moreau, Philippe Bouquillon, Laurent Creton, Benoit Martin, Vanessa Berthomé, and Johanna Chollet of the Laboratoire interdisciplinaire de Recherche sur les Industries Culturelles et la Création Artistique (Labex ICCA) gave me the freedom and means to start fieldwork in Silicon Valley, and to bring my research to life on various occasions (seminars, colloquia, publications, etc.). Fred Turner and the Department of Communication at Stanford University gave me the best foothold in Northern California I could dream of.

Thanks to the Complex Networks team at Lip6/Sorbonne University (Clémence Magnien, Matthieu Latapy, Lionel Tabourier, Robin Lamarche-Perrin, Maximillien Damisch, Fabien Tarissan, and Christophe Prieur), I discovered in vivo computer sciences. They showed me how to raise the bar in professional work. I owe a great deal to my companions at the Centre Internet et Société (Mélanie Dulong de Rosnay, Francesca Musiani, Céline Vaslin, Tommaso Venturini, Ksenia Ermoshina, Jean-Marc Galan, Fabrizio Li Vigni, Simon Bourdieu-Apartis, Hélène Bourdeloie, Ramya Chandrasekhar, Axel Meunier, Ouafa Rahmani, Jean-Yves Zana, and Alexandre Gefen) with whom I've been walking the bumpy road of research entrepreneurship since 2020. Thanks to the CulturIA project led by Alexandre Gefen and Ksenia Ermoshina, funded by French Agence Nationale de la Recherche (ANR), I carried out fieldwork and gained a valuable comparative perspective on AI clusters around the world. I could not have completed this book without Centre national de la recherche scientifique (CNRS), my academic institution, which, if it did not exist, would have to be invented. I must also thank Sciences Po Paris, my second research home, where I benefited from the help and support of Dominique Cardon, Sylvain Parasie, Amélie Vairelles, Valentin Goujon, Valérie Peugeot, Pierre François, Carine Boutillier, and Florence Danton.

This book has benefited from numerous collaborations, previously published articles, presentations in various seminars, and conferences including the Association française de sociologie and the Association française de Sciences Politiques. I'm indebted to the reviewers, coordinators, and editorial board members of *Revue du Crieur, Quaderni, Sociologie, RESET, Glocalism, Réseaux, Politix*, and *AOC*. I could thank again and again Hervé Le Crosnier, Nicolas Taffin, Dominique Cardon, Larisa Driansky, Patrice Flichy, Jean-Samuel Beuscart, Sébastien Broca, Bilel Benbouzid, Gabriel Alcaras, Antoine Larribeau, Joseph Confavreux, Ludovic Ismaël, Benjamin Loveluck, Jean-Vincent Holeindre, Ana Perrin-Heredia, Camille Herlin-Giret, Charles Bosvieux-Onyekwelu, Stéphane Latté, Lionel Obadia, Sylvain Bourmeau, Hubert Guillaud, Philippe Martin, Hélène Paris, Yann Algan, Jean Beuve, Paris Chrysos, Françoise Benhamou, and Monique Dagnaud.

With the latter, we led a workshop at the Paris School for Advanced Social Studies (L'école des hautes études en sciences sociales, EHESS) on the

"Californian model" between 2016 and 2019. During the global tech craze, the workshop provided a privileged forum for academic discussion about tech. I'm grateful to the participants, coming from different disciplines, for responding to the call. As a continuation of this work, I've been running the "Digital Capitalism and Ideologies" workshop since 2020 with Benjamin Loveluck, which provided regular joyful and enlightening gatherings during the writing of this book. I would also like to thank all the contributors.

An earlier form of this manuscript was presented as part of a *habilitation à diriger des recherches* (HDR) dissertation defended in 2023 at Sciences Po Paris. I would like to thank Pierre-Michel Menger, my HDR adviser, for the openness, trust, and patience he has always shown since our first meeting in his office at the EHESS. I am deeply grateful to Christophe Lécuyer, Dominique Pasquier, Violaine Roussel, Claude Rosental, Michael Storper, and Fred Turner for agreeing to be jury members. Their remarks, comments, and individual work has served as a compass for my exploration of Northern California. I am particularly indebted to the Crunchbase Partnerships Team, Samuel Coavoux, Tommaso Venturini, and Fabien Tarissan, who produced some of the visualizations presented in this book. My colleague Céline Vaslin responded with as much efficiency as kindness to carry out many of the statistical treatments at the heart of this book.

More than once my San Franciscan life has been a confusing adventure. It has also been an initiatory and playful experience, thanks to "Uncle" Michael, Carson and Dylan, Howie and Dianne, Fred and Annie, and my "dear burner monks." I don't forget them. I'm grateful to Ted Egan and Tilly Chang as well.

This book has been like a boomerang. It was launched from Silicon Valley toward France at the beginning of the "Startup Nation" movement. My original idea was to explain to my compatriots the origins of this model along with its strengths and weaknesses. I have to thank Hugues Jallon for his interest in this project since day one as well as Le Seuil team, with a special mention for Vassili Sztil, Karine Louesdon, Séverine Roscot, Rose Nouchi, Maria Vlachou, and Marie Lemelle. The book has eventually returned to the shores of Northern California, in a revised and updated form. Several people contributed to this effort. Christo Sims introduced me to the wonderful editor Michelle Lipinski, assisted by the no less remarkable Jyoti Arvey, at the University of California Press. Edouard Isar, Birgitte Necessary, Lisa Moore, Emily Park, Emily Grandstaff and Amy Smith Bell provided invaluable support, helping me in transforming an approximative French-language manuscript into a go-to-market English-language version. I'm grateful to external and internal University of California Press peer reviewers and the production team. The improvement of the manuscript owes much to their readings.

This publication path would surely have made Howard Becker, without whom I wouldn't have gone into the field of sociology, smile. I imagine that, wherever he is, he's still doing sociology.

This research project wasn't always a cakewalk. I have to thank all those who took time out of their busy schedules to meet: Bruno Auerbach, Antonio Casilli, Daniel Cefaï, Sabine Chalvon-Demersay, Dominique Pasquier, Angèle Christin, Eric Dagiral, François-Xavier Dudouet, Cédric Durand, Jean-Louis Fabiani, Laurent Jeanpierre, Ashley Mears, Etienne Ollion, Catherine Paradeise, Antoine Roger, Jen Schradie, Yves Winquin, François Dubet, and Yvette "Yvie" Delsaut.

I owe a great deal of gratitude to my family and friends, those who didn't leave, too quickly or too late, from "the island of lost children," despite drama king and queen performances. I know how lucky I am to go through the roller coaster of life with Naïma. My only wish is that this book will one day be useful to Pablo and Nour, when they want to understand the strange world they have inherited and desire to build a better one.

Introduction

"But then," said Alice, "if the world has absolutely no meaning,
what's to stop us from inventing one?"

—APOCRYPHAL QUOTE, circulating on the internet, incorrectly
attributed to Lewis Carroll's *Alice in Wonderland*

IN TECH, ENTREPRENEURS, ENGINEERS, AND SCIENTISTS are the
ones in charge. They invent and create. Their industry represents progress,
success, and for many, the future. At the same time, some prominent tech
entrepreneurs have been exposed for fraud. The tech sector has been described
as a job destroyer. Big Tech has to pay antitrust penalties on a regular basis.
It's still unclear if AI will be an opportunity or a threat to humanity. Whether
the road to salvation or a path to perdition, Silicon Valley is the beating heart
of this ambivalence. Yet, despite its importance, Silicon Valley remains poorly
understood.

Silicon Valley has been investigated from different vantage points, from
superstars to secrets. But analysis of the industry is often reduced to a dozen
well-known entrepreneurs or companies while the inner workings of their
firms remain mostly opaque. This fosters two misconceptions. First, Silicon
Valley has not historically been the industrial domination of a handful of
firms but rather an integrated sector composed of thousands of companies. In
the 1980s there were nearly eight thousand companies.[1] More than twelve
thousand companies in the field of new technologies were listed in 2022, and
around fifteen thousand companies specializing in new technologies had an
account at Silicon Valley Bank when it collapsed on March 10, 2023. I have
identified more than 32,700 organizations involved in the entrepreneurial life
of Silicon Valley: large and small companies, firms and universities, incubators

and hedge funds, old and new economy companies. These organizations were based not only in Northern California but also throughout the world.

Second, Silicon Valley has become a model to mirror. In startups around the world, meeting rooms are named after a San Francisco neighborhood or another city in the area such as Menlo Park or Palo Alto. Celebrity investor Marc Andreessen even created a how-to guide to facilitate replication.[2] Since the late 1990s, Silicon Valley success stories have inspired policies in Canada with Justin Trudeau or in France with Emmanuel Macron. The values of "entrepreneurship," "agility," "innovation," and "disruption" have been used for modernizing sectors as diverse as agriculture, education, the film industry, and even public administration. Nearly a hundred districts around the world have made direct reference to Silicon Valley since the beginning of the twenty-first century: Silicon Sentier in Paris, Silicon Allee in Berlin, Silicon Wadi in Tel Aviv, Silicon Africa in Cape Town, and so forth.

From this perspective, Silicon Valley refers not only to an industry located in Northern California but also to a model that leaders around the world try to replicate to achieve the most likely and desirable future for their fellow citizens. It is thus revealed as a two-sided object: there is the Silicon Valley *world* and the Silicon Valley *model*. This book proposes a sociological description of both the world and the model. It does not focus on billionaires or flagship companies; instead, it looks at Silicon Valley as a system.

TECH HEGEMONY

In 2024, Alphabet, Amazon, Apple, Meta, and Microsoft accounted for 99 percent of intercontinental data traffic. The supremacy of these companies is based on their control of technical infrastructure networks, comprising 50 percent of the investment in the maintenance and development of a network of 559 submarine cables.[3] Android (developed by Google) is on 70 percent of cell phones, Apple's iOS on 28.5 percent. Google's search engine had a 91.6 percent market share worldwide. In 2023 there were 3.98 billion monthly users of one the four main services in Meta's ecosystem (Facebook, Instagram, WhatsApp, Messenger)—a number that exceeds the number of schoolchildren, English speakers, people who use the US dollar, and married people worldwide.

Sometimes presented as a rival to Wall Street, Silicon Valley has the highest concentration of stock market valuations since the 2010s, despite successive crises: the dot-com bubble burst in 2001, the 2008 subprime crisis, the COVID crisis that began in 2020, and the ongoing international climate, energy, diplomatic, and economic crises since 2022. Microsoft, Alphabet, Apple, Cisco, Intel, Intuit, Meta, Nvidia, Oracle, Salesforce, and Tesla are among the twenty-one largest companies in the world by market capitalization (the total value of a company's shares of stock). In twenty years Silicon Valley has displaced century-old groups in the energy industry (Exxon, General-Electric, Chevron), in retail (Coca-Cola, Walmart), and in banking (Bank of America, Wells Fargo). These companies are devoted to financial markets, with their capital structures and profits protecting them from stock market fluctuations. In 2021, for example, Google, Apple, and Facebook generated combined revenue amounting to $497.5 billion, with a 15 percent net profit, and invested $90 billion in research and development, all for a limited number of employees: fewer than thirty thousand employees work daily at Googleplex in Mountain View, California (nearly 182,000 worldwide early in 2023), but the company captured half of the world's advertising market. With sixteen thousand employees on its campus, Apple earned most of its profits from a value chain of forty-two suppliers, largely based in Southeast Asia.

The ability of these companies to communicate, inform, meet, and entertain in new ways has primed a growing political influence. When Arab Spring protesters, Russian objectors, Chinese youth, or the Ukrainian government seek reliable information, they turn to Silicon Valley services and foundations, such as the Electronic Frontier Foundation, the Wikipedia Foundation, the Mozilla Foundation, or the Tor Project. For many users around the world, Silicon Valley services were the path to escape from power. However, the use of Russian bots on Twitter during the 2016 US presidential campaign, the exploitation of Facebook user data for electoral purposes by Cambridge Analytica, Elon Musk's numerous provocative statements before and after the 2024 presidential election on Twitter/X, and the Silicon Valley techno-solutionist approach for reforming the federal government through the Department of Government Efficiency (DOGE) have positioned Silicon Valley as a new political power.[4] And its influence has grown over the years.

Silicon Valley companies provided the largest contributions to presidential campaigns in the United States, above those of oil companies (which until 2016 had been the largest contributors). They are also the most active lobbyists in Washington, DC, as well as in Brussels: in 2020, Alphabet, Meta, Microsoft, Apple, and Amazon spent $70 million on lobbying in

Washington, DC, and $97 million in Brussels.[5] Not content to simply wield political influence, Big Tech companies often exempt themselves from applicable laws, as numerous lawsuits involving Alphabet, Apple, FTX, Meta, Theranos, and Uber have repeatedly proved. In addition, leading Silicon Valley figures have claimed administrative autonomy from state sovereignty, assuming sovereign prerogatives such as creating a parallel education system (between EdTech, corporate education programs, and private schools), stock exchange, and monetary system. In 2017, Denmark recognized Silicon Valley as a political body and appointed a "digital ambassador" based in San Francisco.

Not only has Silicon Valley influenced politics, its influence extends to the entertainment industry, where it is now a dominant player. When the tech industry was chasing hardware in the 1980s, Luke Skywalker was selling out movie theaters by enacting a series of initiation rites that propelled his mastery of the Force against an Empire, a journey akin to a typical Silicon Valley entrepreneur's storytelling. Northern California native George Lucas infused this monomyth of the hero's journey with a mix of spiritualism and action emblematic of the Bay Area, where work is almost a religion.[6] In 1986, Apple's Steve Jobs bought Lucasfilm's Graphics Group, which became Pixar. Pixar created a whole imaginary world around technical objects turned into cartoon heroes. In the 2010s film production moved from Hollywood to the San Francisco Peninsula, and the Bay Area became one of the most represented territories on screen. Between 2010 and 2021 the number of film permits issued increased 41 percent.[7] Filming days in the city of San Francisco increased 32 percent.[8]

Lucasfilm and Pixar, two Silicon Valley companies, were bought by the Walt Disney Company. Disney bought Lucasfilm for $7.4 billion in 2006, Pixar for $4 billion in 2012. In addition, Netflix, Apple, and Amazon streaming services have been taking over movie and TV awards for a while now. Apple regularly invites stars from the film and music industries to enjoy the Apple Infinite Loop Campus design, popularly called "The Donut." In recent years Silicon Valley has been the subject of biopics like Facebook's Mark Zuckerberg (*Social Network*, 2010) and Apple's Steve Jobs (*Steve Jobs*, 2015), as well as such popular streaming hits as *Silicon Valley* (HBO, 2014–19), *Westworld* (HBO, 2016–22), *Devs* (Hulu, 2020), *The Dropout* (Disney, 2022), *Super Pumped* (Showtime, 2022), and others. The tech protagonist has made a clear U-turn from the quirky nerd (like that portrayed in *Big Bang Theory*, created in 2007) to the hubristic techie.

This twist reflects the hegemony of the Silicon Valley mentality. In everyday life, tech terms are used to describe what have become cultural norms, from posting videos on YouTube, broadcasting live on Twitch, using Instagram filters, and prompting in ChatGPT. Even sexual invitations now use the streaming moniker "Netflix and chill." Silicon Valley's data accumulation and analysis have informed disease risk assessment that predicts the development of certain troubles, self-quantification that incorporates technology into daily life to improve well-being, and optimized targeting for ads through social media. Both quantity and quality data acquisition are used in sectors as diverse as communication, advertising, health, transportation, finance, politics, and even professional sports. Baseball and basketball franchises of the Bay Area have won trophies in the 2010s based on advanced data processing, making traditional ways of recruiting, selecting, and coaching seem obsolete in comparison.[9] Some players have been offered a proportion of their salary in shares of technology companies and have proved themselves active tech investors, such as NBA champions Stephen Curry and Andre Iguodala. The tech voice also resonates in information science, claiming to disrupt the need for social science and classical knowledge to predict human behavior.

Sixty years ago, digital computers made information readable. Twenty years ago, the internet made it reachable. Ten years ago, the first search engine crawlers made it a single database. Now tech companies are sifting through the most measured age in history, treating this massive corpus as a laboratory of the human condition. They are the children of the Petabyte Age.[10] They posit that the massive processing of personal data heralds the end of our need to use human-crafted theoretical models. From space travel to surgery, mathematical algorithms will do it for us. Their ongoing efforts include refining coding by collecting, tagging, and training data techniques and improving the organization of space and time to better inform and guide decision-making. Here technology meets political philosophy. In addition to libertarianism, which has a long history in the United States, other ideological dimensions that underpin tech promises include transhumanism, techno-messianism, objectivism, solutionism, long-termism, effective altruism, accelerationism, and so forth. These ideologies have become known throughout the world thanks to Silicon Valley.

This resolutely techno-optimist view extends a typically American myth where the "valley" represents the "promised land." The "valley" invents tomorrow today and renews the hope of a better world, following in that endeavor, among other examples, John Winthrop's New England Valley, the Virginia Valley colony of agricultural reformer Pierre Samuel du Pont de

Nemours, the gold rush sparked by discoveries in the Sacramento Valley, the hydrography of the Tennessee Valley, or Dell and Texas Instruments of the Texas Valley. Silicon Valley promises to connect the infinitely distant and the infinitely small, from quantum computing to space travel, including Elon Musk's vision for colonies on Mars and Uranus.[11] Rejuvenation projects even pledging to defeat death have multiplied in recent years.[12] Silicon Valley embodies both the myth and its realization. It is the place where people come from all over the world to create the Future.

On the basis of this technological, financial, economic, political, ideological, cultural, and social hegemony, Silicon Valley has supplanted the old idea of progress inherited from eighteenth-century industrial revolutions, and instead linked the improvement of living conditions with technological innovations, interweaving individual success and collective destiny. For Silicon Valley, "innovation," "disruption," "new economy," "new organization of work," "new ways of thinking," "new experiences," and so forth are different sides of the same coin.[13] These innovations carry the promise of a better-informed, fully realized individual as well as wealthier societies. Computer tools and services provide an opportunity for individuals to join expansive networks, potentially avoiding the inefficiencies and dysfunction often attributed to both public and private bureaucracies. These are seen as underlying causes of organizational dysfunction. New technologies aim to make work freer, more creative, independent, entrepreneurial, and collaborative, to the greatest number of people at lower cost.

THE SILICON VALLEY ENIGMA

However, for a sociologist, Silicon Valley is an enigma. At the end of the nineteenth century, there was no indication that this peaceful succession of orchards would one day become a focal point for the global economy. Never before has an industrial hub been developed without a close and abundant raw resource such as cotton, coal, oil, and so forth. The area's "silicon" nickname emerged only in the 1970s when the dark mineral was used by the microprocessor industry, and it no longer justifies its location in a sector dominated by software services and AI solutions. Its geographical position did not predestine it either. Its geographical location is as difficult to access from Europe as it is from Asia, while Los Angeles, Miami, New York City, and Seattle offer simpler access to the United States.

The San Francisco Peninsula remains relatively sparsely populated compared with the major North American settlement areas. The Santa Clara County freeways, the suburban lifestyle, the impersonal avenues lined with businesses admittedly make the area less exciting than Berlin or Rio. Young tech employees do enjoy Lake Tahoe expeditions and Santa Cruz surfing sessions. But many entrepreneurs who live there complain about public services, pricy private schools, the housing market, traffic jams between Palo Alto and San Francisco, and tax rates that infamously exceed even those in Europe. In addition, soil and air pollution are now at alarming levels, drought rages for several months a year, mega-fires darken the Peninsula's skyline almost every summer, while torrential rains drench the West Coast in the winter by way of the Pineapple Express (an atmospheric conveyer belt of moisture from the Pacific Ocean). At the same time, the San Andreas Fault threatens residents with earthquakes, and corporate campuses and data centers struggle to secure a steady supply of water and energy. Another fun fact in the land of high tech: its internet connection speeds are still slower than in Singapore or in most large European cities.

For these reasons it is not uncommon to hear startup founders touting the working conditions in Austin, Denver, Miami, New York, and Portland, if not Amsterdam, Bali, Dublin, Lisbon, London, or Tel Aviv. The COVID-19 pandemic and the success of remote work have reignited the long-standing debate about the end of Silicon Valley, with most loyal employees preferring to work remotely in areas that are less expensive and more comfortable to live in. Given such unfavorable conditions, the rise of Silicon Valley, its growth and its survival, is a mystery. Research, essays, conferences, and blog posts on the subject put forward four arguments to explain the uniqueness of Silicon Valley: the role of visionaries, the concentration of capital, the presence of innovative organizations, and finally an innovation-focused culture.

Visionaries are regularly mentioned when people try to explain the rise of Silicon Valley: Frederick Terman, founder of the computer science department at Stanford University in 1965; Robert Noyce, the microprocessor virtuoso whose microchip made with silicon gave Silicon Valley its name; Douglas Engelbart, the man behind the graphical interface, the mouse, hypertext, and email in the late 1960s; Jim Clark, who made major advances in video processing in the 1980s; Larry Page and Sergey Brin, whose collaboration led to Google in the 1990s; Sam Altman, cofounder and CEO of OpenAI in 2015; and many others.[14] Beyond their profiles, common traits appear: precociousness, hard work, high demands on collaborators, thwarted filiation, and messianic discourses portraying innovation and technology as the only path to progress.

Contrary to the values of hackers, journalists have described these technologists as the "fathers," "godfathers," "princes," "kings," "masters," "gods," and often "geniuses" of Silicon Valley. In the 2010s iconic East Coast newspapers put their names in headlines, a far cry from the early short articles of the 1970s. Specialized publications such as *Wired* (founded in 1993), *TechCrunch* (2005), *VentureBeat* (2006), *Business Insider* (2007), *The Verge* (2011), and *Recode* (2014) cover technology news, while *Reddit* (2005), *Hacker News* (2007), and *Medium* (2012) based in the San Francisco area represent a growing tech reading community. However, the tech mythology overshadows the importance, and the density, of the chains of cooperation. These involve scientists, engineers, investors, lawyers, and sellers, living mostly anonymous lives among the approximately three million people who live in Silicon Valley, plus the almost 809,000 in San Francisco County.[15]

A second type of narrative highlights the abundance of economic and human *capital*. In 2020, Silicon Valley was home to 15 percent of the country's patents, 40 percent of startup investments, and 46 percent of the country's unicorn companies (i.e., privately owned companies worth more than a billion dollars—companies like Instacart, SpaceX, Canva, Discord, and OpenAI).[16] In 2024 sixty-two out of eighty-one large-scale AI models were developed by organizations headquartered in Silicon Valley.[17] From 2017 to 2022 the tech workforce of the San Francisco Bay Area grew by 23 percent, counting 407,810 people.[18] The transmission of knowledge and technical skills that began with the radio hobbyist clubs of the 1910s have been passed on generation to generation. For example, Robert Noyce took Steve Jobs under his wing. Jobs did the same with Mark Zuckerberg. Zuckerberg then mentored Daniel Ek, founder of Spotify, and so forth. This filiation is part of Silicon Valley's institutional environment. Stanford has functioned as an interface between universities, companies, government agencies, and active military funding since World War II. For instance, Fred Terman, who had run the military's secret eight-hundred-person Electronic Warfare Lab at Harvard during World War II, used his connections and knowledge to attract funds and talent to Stanford, giving a leg up to early startups such as Hewlett-Packard, Loral, and Lockheed (whose primary customer is the Department of Defense).[19]

Between 2019 and 2022 the five largest contracts awarded to major technology companies (Amazon, Microsoft, and Alphabet) totaled almost $53 billion.[20] At the same time, the State of California has encouraged business startups by keeping the cost of starting up a business at a particularly low level ($200), streamlining administrative procedures to create a variety of business and corporate structures (only one document is needed). In 2023, for example, the fee for registering a limited liability company (LLC) was $85. Fees for filing articles of incorporation to create a corporation start at $100. And the fee for registering a sole proprietorship was just $26. Right before 2020, eleven new startups were founded every week in Silicon Valley. Moreover, the California ban on noncompetition clauses makes the job market dynamic and fluid.[21] This could explain Silicon Valley's ability to shift so easily from military markets in the 1940s to civilian markets in the 1960s to service production in the 1990s and AI in the 2010s. The concentration of financial and human capital in Silicon Valley does not by itself explain Silicon Valley's ascendancy. After all, Bengaluru, Boston, London, Moscow, Shenzhen, Tel Aviv, Tokyo, and Toronto have roughly comparable assets, and some of these areas are located in countries that are even more technologically advanced than the United States. In 2023 tech workers represented less than 3 percent of the working population in the United States (a little over 171,800 million jobs).[22]

But Silicon Valley is also famous for the concentration of *startups and tech companies*. They define themselves as "innovative," "agile," "fast," and "networked." In the Peninsula, startups get everybody's attention: entrepreneurs found them, universities incubate them, investors finance them, mentors accelerate them, engineers develop them, and large companies buy them out to grow or to avoid being replaced by them. The word *startup* has an unexpected story. It first appeared in seventeenth-century England, with a pejorative connotation, referring to "upstarts." In 1976 the term reappeared in the columns of *Forbes*, in an article dealing with investments in "young companies specializing in electronic data processing."[23] Since then, the term has been applied to newly created, high-growth companies in the high-tech sector. The term became popular in the second half of the 1990s as access to technology became more accessible to more people (commonly referred to as the "democratization of technology").

The mistrust of finance and of bureaucracy in the wake of the 2008 subprime crisis reinforced the enthusiasm for this form of organization among graduates and decision-makers. However, there is no legal definition of a startup. The same word is used to refer to experiments in student dormitories (startup projects), companies recently created (startup), or companies founded fifty years ago. The word is used for companies that are either private or public, local or international. Uber and Airbnb are still referred to as "startup companies" despite their listing on the stock market. Global groups such as Meta or Alphabet demand their employees remain faithful to "startup culture." In the end, "startup" is less an organization than an ethos, as Max Weber would put it, a collectively shared but individually expressed mentality, defined by an *inextinguishable* thirst for initiative, risk, and innovation.[24]

This is why we need to look at a fourth argument: *an innovation-focused culture.* When asked about the Silicon Valley enigma, workers point more or less in the same direction—the "culture." Key elements are (1) easily started new collaborations that emerge due to a low hierarchical environment and back-and-forth loops among diasporas from all over the world, especially Indian and Chinese[25]; (2) a high tolerance of failure that promotes hyper and countercultural creativity; (3) recognition based on performance; and (4) a focus on achievements that benefit everyone.[26] However, this "culturalist" argument provides little information about the ways in which Silicon Valley culture has been built up through history and what drives the verticality of failures and successes.

A WORLD OF PLAYERS

In this book, I analyze a large social object as a whole, through its history, describing it from the perspective of the people who made it. This is not a book on sociological theory, but a social science book intended to be accessible. It lies at the intersection of several research traditions. Since the 1970s, social scientists have sought to shed light on the social forces behind science and technology. Bruno Latour's Actor-Network Theory (ANT), whereby a network exists of interactive relationships, reveals a chain of participants in the evolution of an industry characterized by innovation dynamics—many that are usually excluded from social representations. These participants include not only people but also artifacts, such as data, computers, data centers, and so forth. But if tech is everywhere, ANT does not explain it fully. The openness of Big Tech's innovation-focused culture is accompanied by doubt about the meaning attributed to each ANT stakeholder (e.g., how does a computer think?) and the significance of the associations, both in space and time. After all, when we talk about Silicon Valley, shouldn't it also be located in space within satellites, under the ocean within internet cables, in India or Africa where it has its most dynamic user population? When a German journalist, a Chinese teenager, or a Brazilian civil servant watches videos on YouTube or retweets a post on Twitter/X, aren't they also participating in the Silicon Valley economy?

This observation about space applies in a different way to time, as Silicon Valley has a far longer history than techies usually think. In some respects, it is older than the Hollywood film industry. However, the consciousness of time in Silicon Valley has very little regard for the past and an urgent duty to build the future, even five hundred years ahead, like long-termism thinkers do. In this respect, Silicon Valley history and its importance remain difficult to outline. It is possible, however, to reintroduce a principle of coherence based on the pragmatic approach defended notably by social constructionist Howard Becker, who lived for many years in San Francisco's old fishing district. He defines "world" as a collaborative network: "the network of people whose cooperative activity, organized by their joint knowledge of conventional means of doing things."[27] Nonetheless, there are a number of reasons why we can't fully adopt Becker's approach.

In Silicon Valley, people are more or less integrated, professionalized, in or out of the system. Many leave the cooperation network almost overnight. Professional boundaries are fluid, engineers regularly become entrepreneurs, and entrepreneurs turn into investors, or advisers, or conference speakers. These different hats point to the lack of a real central or clear profession. Moreover, success is very unevenly distributed. Of the half-million tech workers living in the Peninsula, only eighty-five were billionaires in 2023. Of the over twelve thousand tech companies, just over one hundred have more than ten thousand employees, and nothing guarantees their position at the top of the industry in a couple of years. When my interest in Big Tech began in late 2000, Yahoo was a triumphant and legendary company. When I began my fieldwork in Silicon Valley in 2015, you couldn't turn your gaze upon the streets of San Francisco without coming across a purple billboard promoting the company. At the time of this book's release, Yahoo is a joke among techies. A strict approach in terms of collaboration networks can hardly account for the constant changes and ruptures, regular population replacement, with failure remaining the constant.

Therefore, we could describe Silicon Valley as a "field," to use French sociologist Pierre Bourdieu's concept—that is, a distinct domain for the circulation of goods, services, and knowledge within which individuals compete for power—and where "the dynamics ... between distributions and incorporated or institutional classifications is constantly broken and restored."[28] After all, Robert Noyce, Steve Jobs, Mark Zuckerberg, and Sam Altman have been to technological disruptions what Gustave Flaubert, Charles Baudelaire, and Édouard Manet were to the nineteenth-century artistic revolutions.[29] As institutional entrepreneurs, they reconfigure their field. In the tech industry, as in many fields, the "first mover" advantage is constantly at stake. Each company aims to establish a new standard before competition moves in, similar to those in the arts who stake a claim to a new style or aesthetic philosophy.[30] Hackers in the Bay Area have been described as a bohemian community whose ethics resist the predation of Big Tech, the very same companies that have been labeled as "gatekeepers."[31]

In fact, however, large corporations, startups, and newcomers compete but also collaborate in a selective yet open ecosystem. Bourdieu explained ruptures at a given point in time but struggled to translate the dynamics of social milieus over the long term. Even the quite Bourdieusian sociologist Neil Fligstein, who spent most of his career in California, has shown how behind each new service there is a myriad of people shaping what is considered innovative.[32] These tech workers "build on the top of"—rather than disrupt—preexisting technologies: Intel's microprocessors, Apple's OS, Facebook graph, Google's Android, Nvidia GPU, OpenAI IPA, and so forth.[33] Furthermore, private companies have integrated open-source tools. The main contributors to free open-source systems like Linux or Mozilla are employees of big companies. Meta is the main proponent of an open foundation model in the AI field, along with Llama. In addition, large companies' dominance relies on the acquisition of aggressive and cutting-edge young startups. For instance, Google has, since the firm's beginnings, bought out a company on average every two weeks. So the polarization model between, on the one hand, large companies (offering big salaries to their employees, controlling infrastructures, and conferences) and, on the other hand, the culture of foundations and free open-source software—the Bourdieusian opposition of corporate and open-source—doesn't work here.

Latour semiotic, Becker pragmatism, Bourdieu structuralism—as powerful and heuristic as these models are—imperfectly reflect life in Silicon Valley. There, the idea of revolution runs through entrepreneurs' heads on a daily basis. How to explain a place so open to newcomers? How to explain a place where established firms work with newly launched companies? How to explain a place that builds products for the rest of the world, even those with life cycles that won't run for more than a few years, months, or sometimes weeks? To understand this fast space, it is enlightening to examine common Silicon Valley tropes, such as "pioneer," "rebel," "underdog," "trailblazer," "David against Goliath." Entrepreneurs aim to "make an impact," "disrupt the status quo," and "make the world a better place." This desire is reflected in their daily work, moving from a new idea to a project, from the project to the prototype, and from beta version to demo, in order to present a solution that will convince investors and users that a big change is coming.[34]

In Silicon Valley the concept of time refers systematically to a present state (described as problematic) and a future state, which will be improved thanks to a new service. In this respect innovation has "worldly" virtues, heralding a faster, more rational, better-organized, more efficient, better-informed, and better-connected world. It is mainly the purpose of semiconductors, platform services, 3D printers, the metaverse, virtual meeting solutions, cryptocurrencies, artificial intelligence, and so forth. Silicon Valley entrepreneurs are tirelessly seeking to transform the present state of the world, relying on the power of "reality distortion fields," as in *Star Trek*, to convince people around them of the necessity of their "solution."[35] To understand this state of mind and the conditions that foster it, this book proposes a detour through phenomenology—that is to say, the study of what is the experience of tech people when they target things (building General AI, going to Mars, assuring the "future of civilization" or everything else aiming to "make the world a better place").[36] Entrepreneurs, investors, and engineers seek to change the world—meaning from a philosophical perspective to bring it into play.[37]

The word *play* is not understood here in the sense of separate activities (hobbies) or ludic phenomena (entertainment) but rather as both a course of action and a goal. For these tech innovators the world is an imperfect present object and something to modify. Therefore, "play" is revered as a way of modifying a certain world order and enhancing experience for a higher, deeper, and more autonomous level of existence.[38] By "playing," they join things in a new way or give new characteristics to old objects with the goal of improving the world, making the world more connected, more joyful, and easier to navigate. At least to them, as the German phenomenologist Eugen Fink, one of the philosophers who has most questioned the implications of the act of playing on and for the human mind, put it: "In play, man transcends himself, he overcomes the determinations with which he has surrounded himself and in which he has realized himself, he makes the irrevocable decisions of freedom revocable, so to speak, he jumps out of himself, he plunges into the vital depths of original possibilities, leaving behind any fixed situation, he can always start again and throw off the burden of his history."[39]

For this reason Silicon Valley workers will not be described in this book as *agents, actants,* or *actors* but as *players*—a notion often used in Silicon Valley (i.e., "new players," "big players," or "global players").[40] The term *player* in this way does not designate a specific professional category but a mentality, an ethos, as well as a regime of action. The notion of *player* is not intended to produce a synthesis either of this area's stereotypes or the expressions commonly used there: *techie, geek, builder, maker, doer, dreamer, risk taker,* and so on. Nor is it the equivalent of a typical Silicon Valley worker. But the term does cover them in part: the *players* are most often men (74 percent of tech jobs in Santa Clara and San Mateo Counties were held by men in 2019).[41] They work in the new technologies sector. They have North American, Chinese, Indian, or European roots (note that white Americans predominate in decision-making positions). They are between thirty and forty-five years old. They are educated, with degree levels ranging from bachelor of arts to postdoctorate. If the notion of *player* partly covers an empirical correspondence to the stereotype of the "tech bro," it is above all meant to be a conceptual and narrative proposition. I offer to follow the path of this "conceptual character" in Silicon Valley.[42] This book follows his path in the tech industry, from programming interface to the streets of San Francisco. To achieve this, it is crucial to avoid the pitfalls of enchantment for which Northern California is renowned.

A SOCIOLOGIST IN WONDERLAND

During the seventeenth century, scholars used to go on a European "grand tour." During the 2010s, it was common for entrepreneurs, scientists, developers, CEOs, and managers, as well as political leaders, to "tour the Valley." During these "learning expeditions," only the smiling and happy face of the Bay Area was shown to them: the exquisitely designed tech company buildings, the startups that have just closed major fundraising campaigns, the prestigious campuses of Stanford and Berkeley, and so forth. This practice was not really new. General Charles de Gaulle himself was charmed by such a visit in April 1960. On such occasions there is much to be excited about. The Bay Area can look forward to the rapid growth of companies likely to hire large numbers of employees, as Meta did during the early part of the COVID-19 pandemic when it hired nearly thirty thousand people. But at the same time, there is trepidation. Tech companies can also suddenly lay off up to half their workforce, as Twitter did in 2022 via a simple email from Elon Musk. However, this is a region where the sun shines most of the year, and a person will be addressed as "friend" and on a first-name basis within a few minutes of meeting. Combine this welcome with the ease of meetings, the success of young people in their thirties, the tolerance of use of illegal and/or legal drugs, sexual, or philosophical eccentricities, the enthusiasm for new projects, and the "anything's possible" mentality, and it is difficult not to give in, like *Alice in Wonderland*, to both fear and enchantment.

The magic operates all the more because the time zone it is in makes Silicon Valley switch to a parallel dimension around midday, referred to in Silicon Valley as the "magic hours," when the Bay Area works and the rest of the world sleeps. The quiet of back alleys, the scarcity of skyscrapers, the proximity of forests, beaches, and mountains—these create an impression of an isolated and protected world. In the land of Ken Kesey—where many developers try LSD and hallucinogenic drugs as an initiation rite—time can either accelerate or stretch, and space expands and contracts. These alternating booms and busts are driven by traffic jams throughout the day or by the time of the year. Thanksgiving introduces a truce, for example, as does the Burning Man festival, when the Bay Area is emptied of its techies. These gaps contrast with the excitement prior to an IPO. While Big Tech employees stick most of the time to office hours, between 9:00 a.m. and 5:00 p.m., they can potentially enjoy four months of maternity and paternity leave and are often free to set their own schedules. The majority of entrepreneurs run on just a few hours of sleep. Working on a special project in a Big Tech company calls for the same level of commitment, sometimes across several time zones, to interact with team members based in Europe, India, or Japan.

In an environment where work is omnipresent, however, Silicon Valley inhabitants live in a land without factories. Dragon fruit, jujube, lychee, and many other international plants also give the Valley an otherworldly landscape, even as tech companies subcontract manufacturing to Southeast Asia and support and development functions to Asia, Canada, Central Europe, India, or Latin America. Cables lying at the bottom of the ocean, floating server projects, or even satellites relaying free Wi-Fi in the African continent accentuate the feeling of dematerialization and interconnection of an industry located there but also everywhere else. This distortion is part of the "Silicon Valley bubble," where workers can remain impervious to the brutality of social conflicts and the virulence of criticism aimed at it. As journalist Malcolm Harris pointed out in his book *Palo Alto*, eugenic, misogynistic, xenophobic, and anti-democratic claims are almost as old as the industrial cluster itself. The continuous rise of criticism during the 2010s and 2020s hasn't shaken their belief in the capacity of new technologies, innovation, and entrepreneurship to produce the right solutions for the issues of tomorrow. But this enthusiasm doesn't make it easy for foreigners to glimpse behind the scenes. Under tight control of their company's PR department, employees are instructed not to communicate with outsiders. Plus, access to companies is conditional on a "nondisclosure agreement." These agreements can sometimes last several months or even years after leaving the company. Underneath youthful and smiling faces, Silicon Valley is a well-guarded powerhouse.

THE RESOURCES OF A DUAL IDENTITY

To penetrate what looks like an oasis from afar and a fortress up close, it is necessary to overcome these barriers. Making connections, obtaining a work visa, mastering English, gaining computer skills, and finding housing when the average rent in San Francisco was $2,943 in early 2025 are just the first hurdles. Building an entrepreneurial spirit, developing the ability to create relationships, learning the local communication customs, and knowing how to quickly fill any gap in one of the above-mentioned areas, all of these are likely to discourage people reluctant to "hurry up."[43] The innovation race fuels competition, of each against all, and moreover of all against time. Lack of funding, chaotic development processes, poor maintenance, or slow customer service will certainly lead to an irreversible loss of momentum. As a sociologist, one of the main challenges has been to slow down and not give in to the acceleration logic of Silicon Valley.

For this study I needed to take the time to meet, observe, analyze, and grasp the structures surrounding and enabling this constant and relentless race. I've succeeded in being slow, since I've conducted an investigation during almost ten years (between 2015 and 2024), using observations, interviews, data analysis (on around fifteen thousand tech companies), and archival analysis.[44] Over this decade I've seen a dozen technological revolutions and the "death" of Silicon Valley three times (the Cambridge Analytica assist in Trump's first election in 2016, the onset of the COVID-19 pandemic in 2020, and the massive layoffs and slowdown of 2022). But Silicon Valley hasn't disappeared. And at the beginning of Trump's second term, it has never seemed so powerful and disturbing. For better or worse, it seems like a safe bet that Big Tech will be in our lives for a long time.

I was able to study this secretive and competitive world thanks to the possibilities offered by a double identity. On the one hand, I am a foreigner, temporary migrant, and researcher who has fostered bonds of trust with workers within the tech industry and with service workers dependent on it. This trust allowed me to interview civil servants, artists, and activists, many of whom sometimes despise techies. This initial identity made it easier to make contact with a number of entrepreneurs, particularly engineers seeking funding in the Bay Area who envision an upward trajectory for their careers from what they consider "modest" origins. During the course of this research, I moved several times (nearly ten times in two years of fieldwork)—as do many precarious workers or transient entrepreneurs. This allowed me to observe "from below" an industry whose summits and big names are the only ones who have been scrutinized. On the other hand, I benefited from the resources of a white male identity, affiliated with Stanford, in his thirties and early forties—one who is living a life between two continents, exercises several hours per week, and is fond of bike rides and cultural outings. My "researcher" status was good for fostering elective affinities within a population that is active, nomadic, cosmopolitan, elitist, highly qualified, and hungry for "brainy" people.

During my fieldwork I received three job offers, which reflects the characteristic haste and opportunistic mindset of the industry. The first was from someone who offered to hire me as a "data scientist" (they mixed up the "social scientist" and "data scientist" designations). The second was an offer to become a mentor in a tech accelerator (these are mentor-based startups with limited funds where mentors provide support in exchange for equity in the firm). This job offer came after a one-hour interview with someone who thought it was a "great meeting." The third offer was for setting up a foundation project contingent on the involvement of a wealthy heiress. My Tocquevillian endeavor allowed me to connect with the Silicon Valley world from different entry points: affiliation with Stanford, entrepreneurial networks, tech events, French diaspora, research and cultural institutions, yoga practice, comedy clubs, poetry clubs, the Burning Man festival, and so forth. I was able to establish relationships with many professionals, some of whom were well known in tech media but most of whom get little media coverage.

It proved almost impossible to approach tech employees directly though their companies, given the latter's grip on the former's communication. Finally, after a fruitless period where I was getting nowhere, I identified the fourth Silicon Valley social matrix: networks of former alumni, corporate networks, and diasporic and community networks. These community networks are based on hobbies or social proprieties, such as being identified as a woman, being identified as LGBTQI+, or being racialized in the tech industry. Following these paths, I was able to step inside Silicon Valley society, navigate between its subcommunities, participate in events a priori that were relatively out of reach for a French sociologist. I attended meetings of the Chinese Entrepreneur Association, Women in Tech, the anniversary party of the 1966 Trips Festival, a research workshop on artificial intelligence in Stanford's computer science department, and many others. There were days when I changed my clothes three or four times to fit in with the dress codes of each of these subgroups.

It is my wish that this book offers readers an experience as initiatory and unexpected about this strange part of the world as conducting fieldwork has been for me. I crossed paths in a club with a drug dealer who threatened me because he thought I was a techie. I had a lively discussion with a biker gang member high on methamphetamine. I conducted a six-hour interview with a former homeless addict, during which he told me about the daily life he had left behind. I had to stop an interview after twenty minutes when I realized I had met the wrong person—my interviewee was actually waiting for her Tinder date. I had to make a quick decision during Burning Man about whether to stay in a "cuddle tent" where the atmosphere was heating up and continue to observe what was happening for the sake of science or to get out as quickly as possible. I cycled back to San Francisco close to midnight under a red moon after a long walk on the trails of Mill Valley with technologist, smart mobs theorist, and LSD guru Howard Rheingold, along with his two dogs.[45]

In many instances this research posed a practical problem of getting around a territory that mountains, highways, entry controls, cost of living, and urban sprawl make complex to navigate. I made the most of these trips with a second-hand racing bike that I found on Craigslist and bought locally for $200 from a young designer. My bike served me well with its Italian frame, Japanese handlebars, and French saddle. It got me to computer bootcamps (2), hackathons (4), conferences (9), pitch competitions where volunteer or selected entrepreneurs present their startups in a few minutes in front of a jury that votes for the best presentation (29), meetups (46), and observations of various companies (47). I conducted observations based on the region's demographic and organizational balance—that is, according to funding categories (crossed with information from Crunchbase, a platform compiling data on companies in new technologies). I observed seed companies (most often without employees or just a few of them); A-series companies (developing leveraging capacities, which implies technical recruitments, with a few dozen employees); B-series companies (focusing on business development, with a team of between fifty to one hundred people); C-series companies (rapidly perfecting the business with a view to return on investment, with between one hundred and five hundred employees); unicorns (i.e., privately held companies valued at more than a billion dollars when new funds are raised, with between five hundred and five thousand employees); and large companies (i.e., publicly held companies listed on the stock exchange, with several thousand employees). My bike as a means of transport symbolizes the tight budget-chic mobility resources of my dual identity and went with me back to France.

I conducted in-depth interviews (161). These interviews included AI engineers (13), designers (2), data analysts (2), professional organization leaders (2), specialized lawyers (3), technology journalists (2), researchers (3), consultants for technology companies (3), communication specialists (3), philanthropic program managers (3), diplomats (3), business managers (4), chief technical officers (5), administrators (6), activists (11), developers (12), artists (13), and investors (16). And, of course, I conducted interviews with entrepreneurs (55). In addition, interviews (48) were conducted with city activists, civil servants, and artists. In order to avoid contractual commitments with their current or former employers, these interviews were conducted on the basis of anonymity. Regarding the professionals working directly in the field of new technologies, the interviewees were 89.5 percent male and 10.5 percent female, a ratio that fits the statistics made public by the large technology companies on their tech employees. In addition, nearly 50 percent were from international backgrounds, a figure that also corresponds to San Francisco Peninsula worker demographics. Finally, of all the professionals interviewed who were living in Silicon Valley in 2015, 39 percent had left by 2022, half of whom had moved to a country other than the United States, while 35 percent were still employed by the same company.[46]

During many of these interviews it was necessary to deal with the interviewees' way of doing things. Their entrepreneurial discourse often consisted of promoting themselves and their activity, or, as with investors, preserving business secrecy. Some entrepreneurs tried to transform the interview into a communication opportunity for their company. Others used the interview to find out about, through me, the situation in Europe, or at Stanford, or the quality of the technological ecosystem in France. I was offered a discount on a conference ticket in exchange for volunteer hours. These different examples reveal one of the main tech social traits: opportunism. To get meetings with other interviewees, it was necessary to go through communication managers and be recommended by common acquaintances. These revealed the ways in which networks are structured, which ones are open and which ones are mediated and selective. Here we can see a second Silicon Valley feature: its opacity.

At the same time that corporations ignored me, I often had to deal with professional speakers. I've dealt with people who try to speak as well as those who stay publicly silent. The exchange of information depends on the networking that people manipulate constantly to accumulate resources and social capital. These illustrate a third point: in Silicon Valley, storytelling is a social structure. As a communication style, narratives invite evaluation. I must have asked myself a thousand times whether my emails were sufficiently structured, synthetic, enthusiastic, and respectful of local communication customs. Efficiently researching Silicon Valley implies adopting Silicon Valley modes of communication. Meetings strictly adhered to standardized durations (fifteen, thirty, or sixty minutes), occasionally requiring an informal approach such as "walking meetings," which are particularly popular in the Valley. Some of the interviews I conducted were held on sporting trails on the Bernal Heights hills overlooking San Francisco. Some were in the vicinity of the Olympic-size pools where the Stanford water polo team trains. I was able to experience many times the Silicon Valley standard of commitment, performance, and professionalism during the fieldwork: appointments started at exactly the time scheduled (the opposite of LA's habitual lag); meetings were scheduled during the weekends, at 6:30 in the morning, or sometimes late at night; and when I was taking a break and swimming in one the Stanford pools, I was regularly overtaken by pregnant women (even if I'm a pretty decent swimmer who grew up close to the French Atlantic Ocean shore). I also had the opportunity to attend workshops and training programs in Stanford's computer sciences department located in the Gates Building, named after major donor Bill Gates.

These datasets were supplemented by monitoring social networks through Twitter/X, LinkedIn, and the specialized press (*Wired, TechCrunch, Business Insider, Fast Company, Inc., Forbes*). I reviewed fifty-four books on Silicon Valley that were published between 1988 and 2024. I collected and statistically processed information from a database on thirty-two thousand organizations (startups, Big Tech, investors, academic institutions that are part of the ecosystem, and so forth), thanks to the expert help of my colleagues Samuel Coavoux (ENSAE/Cerlis), Fabien Tarissan (CNRS/ENS Cachan), Tommaso Venturini (CNRS/Geneva University), and Céline Vaslin (CNRS/Centre Internet et Société). We analyzed the life cycles, demographics, financing networks, specializations, and evolutions of tech organizations. Finally, along with observations of debates and hearings on the impact of technology companies at San Francisco City Hall, I studied protests in San Francisco (23), part of the "anti-tech" movement.

Thus this book analyzes the space, activity, and ethos of Silicon Valley players. These players evolve within a three-dimensional space, with geographic, social, and technological dimensions (chapter 1). For them, attracting capital and resources requires weaving between the small world of Silicon Valley and the big world of finance (chapter 2). In order to do so, they need to master the communication conventions of the tech industry (chapter 3). Entrepreneurs, often portrayed as the heroes of Silicon Valley, are in fact subordinate workers, with a constant need to build, maintain, and strengthen trust on multiple fronts (chapter 4). In this configuration, growing a company is the only way to achieve success. But to reach this goal, entrepreneurs have to solve a paradox: how to stabilize an organization dedicated to disruption (chapter 5).

Following this path, developers face contiguous challenges between the fragility of their productions and the uncertainty of their careers (chapter 6). Their only conviction is tech's ability to make things better, starting with tech's impact on their own life. From this point of view the Burning Man festival offers a space of enchantment for techies, where they reinvent the self and make changing environments home (chapter 7). Faced with the uncertainty of technology, Silicon Valley players have adopted different ideologies that all include the idea that everyone should become an entrepreneur in the near future (chapter 8). However, these narratives minimize the growing criticism against Big Tech in general and Silicon Valley in particular. The protest and resistance carried out by activists and artists in San Francisco concerning an industry that has been formidably successful in its mission but has also accumulated social failures pave the way toward a politicization of tech (chapter 9). The outcome of this politicization, in Silicon Valley and the rest of the world, will be one of the key issues of the twenty-first century, for the future of this industry and the future of the entire planet.

PART I

———————

Space

ONE

What Is Tech?

Silicon Valley is a fast space.
—Interview with an entrepreneur-investor,
San Francisco, July 12, 2016

INTERVIEWEES REFER TO SILICON VALLEY as the tech "place to be,"
"Mecca," "Venice," "Disney World"—metaphors that identify an industry
with a place that concentrates resources and opportunities. For this reason
economists have called it a "cluster," geographers a "space," sociologists a
"field" enabling innovation.[1] Social scientists all agree to emphasize the whole
rather than the part, even if the latter is a multibillionaire entrepreneur.
There's a reason for that. In a pioneering study on innovation theory, William
J. Abernathy and James W. Utterback emphasized back in the 1970s the
advantages for founders and firms of being located "near rich markets, with
solid universities or scientific research institutions, and financial institutions
oriented towards entrepreneurship."[2] Indeed, privileged access to information makes it possible to orient yourself more quickly and efficiently.[3]

However, making it big in Silicon Valley requires standing out from a large
and noisy crowd. During tech conferences and technology trade shows (e.g.,
VMworld, DevConf.US, Code Conference, TechCrunch DISRUPT, AI
Conference, and others), entrepreneurs, engineers, and developers sit in booths,
side by side, and/or parade the next "big thing" on stage, cloaking their presentations in garish colors while wearing cheap T-shirts emblazoned with company
names that usually juxtapose what seems a jumble of vowels and consonants like
an ongoing Scrabble game. In the constantly changing tech environment, they
know that they can go from obscurity to the limelight and back again in a
minute. Blockchain, 3D printers, and NFTs all went through several invest-
ment-divestment cycles during the 2010s. And artificial intelligence has enjoyed
a strong resurgence since John McCarthy first coined the expression in the mid-
1950s. This value volatility is not only due to the race for innovation but also
because legal norms are fragmented, evolving in a relatively chaotic way, with

different and uncoordinated layers. When you are part of the tech industry, depending on your development stage, your political contact could be an agency; a member of City Hall; someone in county, state, or national government; or a supranational authority like the EU. From the point of view of tech players, politics is an incoherent, dysfunctional, contradictory, and sometimes corrupt amalgamation of parts. The control of professional organizations is not much more coherent. Silicon Valley companies have been hostile to trade unions since day one, and professionals have opted for flexible and nonbinding forms of organization such as associations (of venture capitalists, entrepreneurs, alumni, or expatriates). This makes stability and control an incongruity in Silicon Valley, even though they are an ideal in the history of large American companies.[4]

Tech giants know they are vulnerable. Google and Facebook , founded in 1998 and 2004, respectively, have already seen several heavyweights disappear (Yahoo, Blackberry, Theranos, and others), while young Davids like OpenAI, Anthropic, Cohere, Perplexity, Hugging Face, or Mistral have risen. This is why tech Goliaths try to collaborate with them, invest in them, control them, or buy them out, no matter the costs. From a historical point of view, the most robust Silicon Valley tech companies look like paper tigers when compared to institutions such as nation-states (which emerged in the seventeenth century), modern banks (established in the fourteenth century), or hospitals (which appeared in the fourth century). They also suffer from comparison with oil, railroad, automobile, and electricity companies, founded in the nineteenth century and still in the game. The counterpart of this tech uncertainty is risk-taking and excitement, as echoed by a consular official based in San Francisco:

> In Los Angeles, you're going to hear constantly about new film projects, scripts, etc. Here, it's the same but for tech entrepreneurship. It's a gold rush. There are plenty of signs around us . . . that echo other periods in history. When Stefan Zweig and Freud met in London and spoke about Vienna before the war, they said: "There was sperm in the air." We find that spirit here. There is a form of intellectual inebriation, of advanced interdisciplinarity, a will to test borders to the point that it becomes dangerous. There is, in this way, a spectrum of possible disasters, that one senses, from gentrification to transhumanism. The desire and ability to go beyond boundaries carries its danger within and the threat of a rupture (interview, San Francisco, February 24, 2016).

In the words of an entrepreneur-investor interviewee, Silicon Valley runs as a "fast space" where information is the key element. Change is so constant that Silicon Valley can't be reduced to a set of fixed data, a map, a table, or a graph. In the early days of PayPal, every new customer was displayed on a screen to motivate employees.[5] At the Googleplex site in Mountain View, Google's headquarters, the number of queries to the search engine was visible in real time. At Uber's headquarters on Market Street in San Francisco, recessed screens made lightly bluish white lines appear and disappear, representing the routes of rides taken in the cities where the service is located. Thus tech companies projected their success through their own tech-immersive displays. Tech is a projection.

In this respect Silicon Valley is characterized by a fundamental contradiction: it's a race against time but in a limited space. Their solutions promote remote communication, throughout the world, to save time by carrying out tasks more efficiently with the promise of emancipation from material constraints. But players in Silicon Valley compete for the same local resources. This chapter sheds light on this paradox by focusing on the way players build up services but also the way they approach space, time, and tech as a system. Every player seeks to optimize its geographical position in order to multiply relationships and more efficiently support its solution in the technological space. This social dynamic accelerates and intensifies competition, even if every entrepreneur intends to win the race in the long term.

THREE PROBLEMS

Connecting Moore and Metcalfe Laws?

In Silicon Valley the organization of time and space are based on "laws." Named after Gordon Moore, one of the original semiconductor team at Fairchild "We Started It All" Semiconductor International, Moore's Law stated in 1965 that the semiconductor complexity (i.e., the number of transistors per integrated circuit) had doubled every year at a constant rate since their invention in 1959. By extension, the size and/or cost of computers would continue to decrease and their power to increase. As the efficiency of transistors should double every eighteen months, exponential growth would follow. Indeed, the number of transistors per silicon chip doubled at a constant rate almost every eighteen months between 1965 and 2017, confirming Moore's Law. Moore went on to found Intel with Robert Noyce and Andrew Grove, and Moore's Law was confirmed by Intel's success. This law has had software equivalents since the 1990s, named after major figures in the sector: Wirth's Law, Page's Law, or Gates's Law.

Ethernet inventor Bob Metcalfe (Metcalfe's Law) takes a different angle. In 1980 this law stated that the utility of a technological network is proportional to the square of the number of users. Through them a "network effect" or "club effect" can be observed: the bigger a network is, the more its users get value from it. In Silicon Valley, Moore's Law is confirmed by Intel's success, and Metcalfe's Law by Facebook's success. Facebook's monthly active user growth trends fit the specifications of Metcalfe's Law.[6] These two laws back the transhumanist principle that technological growth is unlimited, and that it is necessary to develop solutions on a global scale—solutions that can be massively and rapidly adopted. From this perspective, thanks to Silicon Valley, the world spins faster and faster, with science and technology promising unlimited progress. You might consider that Silicon Valley workers are behaving like rational actors by considering these statements as laws. Yet both are controversial, challenged by industry representatives and researchers alike. The growth of microprocessor capability actually slows down almost year by year. For thirty years, before the arrival of China's Tencent (and its WeChat Instant Messaging service) and Facebook, Metcalfe's Law had no empirical basis. The popularity of these statements seems surprising in a world as rationalist as Silicon Valley. Moore and Metcalfe's careers provide insights for understanding this paradox.

Born in 1929 in San Francisco, Moore held a doctorate in physics and chemistry from the California Institute of Technology (Caltech). He was one of the "Traitorous Eight" who left the semiconductor laboratory headed by Nobel Prize winner William Shockley, considered tyrannical, for Fairchild Semiconductors. Many so-called Fairchildren went on to found their own companies at the turn of the 1960s. As mentioned, Moore cofounded Intel with Noyce and Grove in 1968. In 1965, Moore published an original statement in *Electronics Magazine* which he named Moore's Law. This assertion served as a management and open innovation tool to boost computer chip sales, first at Fairchild and then at Intel, while limiting competition.[7] Indeed, since Intel's ability to meet Moore's Law was dependent on other companies developing materials and manufacturing equipment, Moore and his collaborators spread his hypothesis in the microelectronics community, establishing a technology roadmap. His intention was to define the direction and pace of innovation in the domestic and international semiconductor market. This process considerably strengthened Intel's competitiveness and its dominance in the semiconductor industry until the mid-2010s, contributing to the wealth of Moore, who died in 2023, with a personal fortune close to $10 billion ($9.6 billion according to *Forbes*, which in 2021 made his the 182nd largest fortune in the world).

Like Moore, Bob Metcalfe spent most of his career in Silicon Valley. Born in 1946, he studied electrical engineering at MIT, business administration at MIT's Sloan School, and computer science at Harvard, where he worked on the Project on Mathematics and Computation (Project MAC). Funded by the Department of Defense and the National Science Foundation, Project MAC created the multiuser interface that became the basis for online communication and open-source software. Metcalfe graduated in 1973, a year after joining Xerox PARC in Palo Alto, where he developed Ethernet, a protocol for interconnecting machines via twisted-pair cables still in use today.[8] This network communication technology became operational in 1976. Metcalfe then proposed a "law" according to which the value of a communication network increases exponentially with the number of connected devices. In 1979 he left Xerox PARC to found 3Com, a networking equipment company that disappeared in 2010, in Santa Clara and later Palo Alto. The goal of the company was to provide Ethernet adapter cards to personal computer manufacturers. The solution's objective was to connect all the computers of a given company to a single, local network. Metcalfe left 3Com in 1990 due to technical issues and began writing about technology. He predicted the collapse of Microsoft. Then in 1995, at the beginning of the so-called democratization of the internet, he announced that the internet would not outlast that year. In 2001, Metcalfe joined the venture capital firm Polaris Venture. Bad timing, considering this was the very same year when the financial bubble around technology stocks burst, and the market crashed. Despite this series of unfortunate choices, he remains attached to a law considered a mantra by Silicon Valley investors since the mid-2000s. At that time the multiplication of social networks gave weight to his assertion, which was previously confidential. In doing so, the meaning of Metcalfe's Law has shifted a little bit: it went from technological domain to users.

Since the mid-2000s in Silicon Valley, investors considered that the value of a network increases exponentially with the number of connected people. In order to raise money, entrepreneurs need to show proof—rough estimates and projections—about their potential user growth. This growth is called *traction*. What investors consider as the "magic number" is in fact a doubling of users every eighteen months, overlapping Moore's and Metcalfe's Laws. When investors see this kind of momentum in a company, the projection suggests that the service will spread worldwide in no time. In this scenario the end result is a monopoly or oligopoly position, meaning a tremendous amount of money and power in the hands of a few entrepreneurs, early employees, and investors. This argument about networks is backed by economic theory. Diminishing adoption returns would prevent two noninteroperable technologies from durably coexisting in the same market segment.[9]

In other words, the field of new technologies is particularly suited to the domination of one or a few solutions. Investor Peter Thiel has shaped a mainstream narrative based on this hypothesis. Initially presented in the form of a 2012 course at Stanford, and later in a book published in 2014, *Zero to One* (a title referring to the binary code), he argues that the only path in technology entrepreneurship is to move from an outsider position, symbolized by the number 0, to a monopoly position—that is, the number 1. The way IBM disseminated DOS, Google's Page Rank ranks web pages by the number of links, or Amazon facilitates deliveries seems to confirm the theory. This echoes the economy of "natural monopolies," according to which in certain sectors monopoly is a necessity. In this scheme Moore's Law backs Metcalfe's Law and vice versa: user growth feeds a network effect, encouraging technological capacity doubling every eighteen months.

Despite their popularity in Silicon Valley, these statements are particularly controversial in the engineer and scientific communities. Regarding Moore's Law, doubling the number of transistors every two years (and by extension, processing power) represents growing costs and complexity. Rising raw material prices and the limits of miniaturization are slowing down progress in terms of production. Nvidia founder Jensen Huang declared in 2019 during the Las Vegas Consumer Electronics Show (CES), the industry's main annual technological fair: "Moore's Law used to grow at x10 every five years, x100 every ten years. Right now, Moore's Law is growing a few percent every year. Every ten years maybe only x2. . . . So Moore's Law has finished."[10] This statement is in line with many other observations. Indeed, while it is perceived as a standard, regardless of the subsector under consideration in Silicon Valley, it is relative to an era (the 1970s) and a given field (microprocessor production). Issues around the exploitation and control of rare metals, which are used for electrical and electronic component production, along with challenges related to water for data center cooling, serve as reminders that while the potential of technology may be unlimited, its development is constrained by the availability and quantity of resources. Metcalfe's Law, however, has been the subject of extensive literature since it was first stated. It has been successively described as "incomplete," "misunderstood," "false [and even] dangerous."[11] Despite these criticisms, both assertions are constitutive of the Silicon Valley development model.

Keeping Up with Innovation

Innovation in Silicon Valley is a race. Players need to create, develop, meet, recruit, post, raise money, provide superior customer service, and do it all better than their competitors. Thus speed is a value, a goal, and a way of life. An entrepreneur developing a telecommuting solution dealt with this fundamental dimension of the Silicon Valley way of life in a post:

> There are three main reasons why you want to prioritize speed. First: speed is all you really have. Your competitors have thousands of people, millions of users, billions of dollars. You don't. Yet that's often enough to win. So don't lose it! Second: speed leads to quality. This point may seem counterintuitive—most people think these two things are contradictory. But I actually think a tight iteration loop is the best way to create an exceptional product. Third, speed creates momentum, which is essential for morale. And morale is critical. I often say that startups are more likely to lack morale than money (Flo Crivello, LinkedIn post, August 24, 2022).

From this point of view, speed is not an individual parameter but a social organization. In line with Moore's Law, investors expect that companies double their size every eighteen months, aiming for an IPO or an exit. Such outcome happens after a minimum of three years, and could not materialize until fifteen years or more after the company's founding, with a peak (of IPOs) at seven to eight years of activity (like Google or Facebook). In Silicon Valley the arrow of time thus points toward a clear target, which translates into constant pressure and tactics to cope with it. As an investor points out:

> Silicon Valley is based on Moore's Law, with eighteen-month cycles. You can only survive as a company with an eighteen-month schedule.... And investors spend all their time telling you that: you, your product, it runs for eighteen months, and if in eighteen months you haven't succeeded, we'll change the project, we'll change the team, you'll end up doing something else because it's "test and learn," because it's "fail quick." ... All the Silicon Valley bullshit. When you set up your startup, the VC puts you in the washing machine, he explains to you that after your seed comes series A, in eighteen months, that you have to build your product.... And you stay in the washing machine until you've managed to get past the stage of having raised $150 million, with a multibillion-dollar company. Then you're in the club, and the club is very small (interview, San Francisco, July 8, 2016).

During my study I've seen entrepreneurs and engineers shifting their strategies: from relying on recommendation algorithms to filter and optimize their information sources; to using a personalized AI service to carry out press reviews on their topics of interest (often AI); then developing their own chatbot to answer "in a sec" the emails addressed to them. While Silicon Valley's solutions aim to free up time and emancipate themselves from material constraints throughout the planet, they lead to an acceleration of the speed race within restricted access to resources. The counterpart of this dynamic for players is that they have to deal with an innovation paradox.

Being Disruptive while Following Technological Trends

In Silicon Valley innovation goes hand in hand with the idea of progress. The Crunchies Awards' statuette was awarded annually between 2007 and 2017 in San Francisco to the "best" in several categories ("founder," "investor," "startup," "product," "application," and so forth). It depicted a Homo sapiens with a raised bone above his head, a figure borrowed from the prologue of 2001: A Space Odyssey, epitomizing the emergence of humanity through tools and technology. Yet players move simultaneously toward the same solution categories. Investment subcategories tracked between 1995 and 2024 thus make it possible to identify what one interviewee calls Silicon Valley "undercurrents." Investments have been concentrated on certain subcategories, which are considered at a given time and for a limited period as "the future," before being progressively or brutally disinvested.

Video, advertising, and music were hot in the 2000s before cooling off. Platforms were at the center of media and academic attention in the 2010s, before being relegated to the back of investors' minds. Investment in tech services applied to real economy sectors remain far from the heights reached by generative AI. The buzz around AI has a long story in Silicon Valley, starting in the 1950s when John McCarthy used the expression for the first time to, as he said, lure funders thanks to an appealing notion. The investment curve began to dip in the mid-2000s, before rising, notably in 2012 then almost continuously since then (with the exception of the COVID slowdown). Doing so, artificial intelligence has progressively overlapped with similar or related categories such as data and analytics, big data, algorithms, machine learning, and deep learning, but not robotics, which stayed pretty

TABLE I. Tech trends (1995–2022)

Types	Categories	Level of Centrality
Stable high level	Software, data, and data analysis	1
Recent decline after an upward trend	Financial services, artificial intelligence, applications, science and engineering	2
Upward trend	Clothing and accessories, food and beverages, transportation, real estate, agriculture and livestock, community and lifestyle, administrative services, consumer goods, sports	3
Stable after decline	Privacy and security, government and military, travel and tourism, sales and marketing	4
Slow decline	Hardware, digital content and publishing, video, advertising, music and audio, media and entertainment, messaging and telecom, platform, games, mobile	5
Stable low level or lasting decline	Natural resources, sustainable development, manufacturing industry, energy, biotechnologies	6

SOURCE: Crunchbase.

low in 2024. Each category thus represents highly variable investment volumes (Table 1).

The center of gravity of the technological space has thus shifted from hardware (first generation) to social applications, such as social media and web 2.0, before taking a realistic turn with what is now called the Internet of Things, referring to "smart" products like smartphones, smart medical devices, smart kitchen appliances, and so forth. AI gained an increasingly central position in the software segment of tech investments, which remains the epicenter of Silicon Valley activity, while energy and natural resource management stay peripheral. If you listen to the tech insiders I interviewed, they all say they pursue disruption and radical innovation. But if you look at investments, disruptors only lead in a dozen subcategories. Max Weber called this type of phenomenon a "paradox of consequences": an individual action is aimed at a goal (in this case innovation), but the addition of behaviors results in an opposite effect (fads and trends). Thus Silicon Valley promises a decentralized space but concentrates resources; it aims to free up time constraints but imposes a rushed pace on entrepreneurs; it seeks out innovations but is structured by trends. Accordingly, players try to adapt by making the most of resources within a three-dimensional space.

Indeed, to players, Silicon Valley *is* a three-dimensional space: geographical, social, and technological. So they have to work in an environment characterized by the interdependence between these three components. Silicon Valley is in perpetual motion because of the interactions between those three dimensions and their respective evolutions. In order to adapt in this moving territory, changing population, and expanding technological field, players try to adjust their position, seeking to multiply connections and develop new projects.

Positioning Yourself in a Shifting Landscape

Newcomers are often unaware of the complexity of the region's geography and what the landscape reveals about the industry. It provides many insights about the history of an industry built on technological layers more than cycles or waves. It has expanded since the foundation of Stanford in 1891. In the 1970s, in the midst of the personal computer boom, the San Francisco Peninsula was still far from its modern image as the cradle of innovation. An American investor and former entrepreneur in the area since the 1970s attests to the importance of this gap:

> When I arrived [in Palo Alto] in August '75, it was to go to Stanford. I arrived late in the day, a few weeks before school started. I went down University Avenue [a mile-long street that connects the Stanford campus to the city of Palo Alto], wondering if this was the right direction. . . . I went up and down. . . . I couldn't find the entrance. I walked up the avenue again. . . . There were no restaurants, no coffee shops . . . not even any streetlights. . . . I thought: *What the hell am I doing in this boondock town?* (interview, Palo Alto, September 28, 2016).

If you were to express the factors of evolution in Silicon Valley through a mathematical formula, a common trend in this universe, it could be as follows:

Mobility of Capital × Speed of Organizations / Price of Real Estate

New companies project their development based on that of older ones, relying on the resources, needs, and shortages of the latter. They try to establish themselves close to the dominant companies at any given moment. The price of rent influences this proximity strategy. But it is an unsteady hierarchy, as reported by a developer working at LinkedIn and a former Stanford graduate:

> At Stanford, the companies that students go to are no longer the same. When I enrolled in late 2000, it was Google [in Mountain View], then over the course of my studies it became Facebook [in Menlo Park], in the mid-2010s it was Uber, then Airbnb [in San Francisco] . . . because there was a lot of energy and growth and potential, and this was before their IPO. So, if you worked there early enough, you could have picked up several millions (interview, San Francisco, November 8, 2015).

The workplace is thus likely to open up not only material opportunities but also other resources, such as information, meetings, and energy. An entrepreneur, active in Silicon Valley since the mid-2000s, says:

> Where you live is super important. The first thing is the energy around you. As an entrepreneur, you need energy, and it's the people around you that give it to you. Being in San Francisco is better than being in the suburbs. When you're in the Valley, you get energy differently: nature, fresh air, sunshine . . . not people. But people are key: the access to talent, advice, and feedback on your market. The third dimension is that the place where you live will determine the access to your market. Silicon Valley is the biggest echo chamber in the world when we speak about the technology market. A product that works here will work all over the world. And with that comes access to capital. . . . After that, the question is SF or Silicon Valley. Here [Palo Alto], there's Stanford, more entrepreneurs in their forties, better schools for their kids, gardens, easier life. . . . In the end, lots of entrepreneurs end up there, but less than in SF. I'm in Redwood, so I can still get guys from SF. But if you're in San Jose, forget it. In Palo Alto, there are still bars, a bit of a night life . . . but further down, it's dead. . . . If I was twenty-five, I'd be in SF; when I was twenty-three, I thought: *Who the hell wants to move out from SF to Silicon Valley, it's all has-beens there?* And boom, fifteen years later I'm one of these fools! (interview, Palo Alto, October 28, 2015).

Within the companies themselves, place of residence follows this logic and constitutes a marker. An engineer working in one of the four largest tech companies and who spends time in international cities explains:

> At work, it's fifty-fifty, half live in SF, half in the rest of Silicon Valley; the young American or European graduates go to live in San Francisco, in the Mission, with roommates, and take the bus. The Asians are more like me, they live in Silicon Valley. And I think it sucks, especially since I'm from

Sydney, and I used to live in London and Paris. My friends from abroad think that Silicon Valley is San Francisco, and when I explain to them that I'm an hour's drive away, and that on weekends I have the kids, and that during the week I have no reason to go there. . . . They all laugh at me. And when they visit, they tell me: *You're in the middle of nowhere*. But I have no choice, with the kids, my wife . . . (interview, San Jose, March 7, 2016).

For this reason, Silicon Valley could be described as an ice core, with the oldest at the bottom and the youngest at the top. Beginning in the south, at the core's deepest, is Santa Clara County, the birthplace of Hewlett-Packard and Intel. To the north, for the most recent layer, is the epicenter of San Francisco. San Jose, the county seat of Santa Clara, owes its development in the 1950s to the transistor industry. Some twelve miles to the north, Sunnyvale became the capital of microprocessors dominated by Sun Microsystems in the 1970s. Barely three miles away from Sunnyvale is Mountain View, which was once occupied by Hewlett-Packard before Google and LinkedIn set up their offices there at the end of the 1990s, taking over part of the Silicon Graphics offices near an area that was then inexpensive because of the swampland surrounding it. About nine miles to the east of Mountain View is Menlo Park, near East Palo Alto, which has long been infamous for having one of the highest crime rates in the country. The Facebook campus is located in Menlo Park, in an area that was historically not highly urbanized, but is on the same horizontal axis as Stanford. Between the west, which is partly wooded and mountainous, and the muddy areas of the east, with its more affordable housing, lies the backbone of the region, urbanized and structured by Highway 101 and the Caltrain— the rail line and only public transportation connecting San Jose to San Francisco.

Put into service in 1987, this line served twenty-seven communities spread over 48 miles, transporting nearly twenty five thousand people a day in mid-2020. More than that, the rail line represents a spatial, temporal, and symbolic break. Only a handful of so-called express trains run every day at rush hour, stopping in strategic cities: San Francisco in the north, Palo Alto in the center, and San Jose in the south. Trains running the rest of the day stop in fewer than half of the cities that make up Silicon Valley (nearly seventy). Along this single line, the big names of the industry follow one another: in San Jose (Intel), Cupertino (Apple), Mountain View (Google), Palo Alto (PayPal), Menlo Park (Facebook), Redwood City (Oracle), San Mateo (YouTube), all the way to San Francisco (Salesforce, Uber, Airbnb, Zendesk,

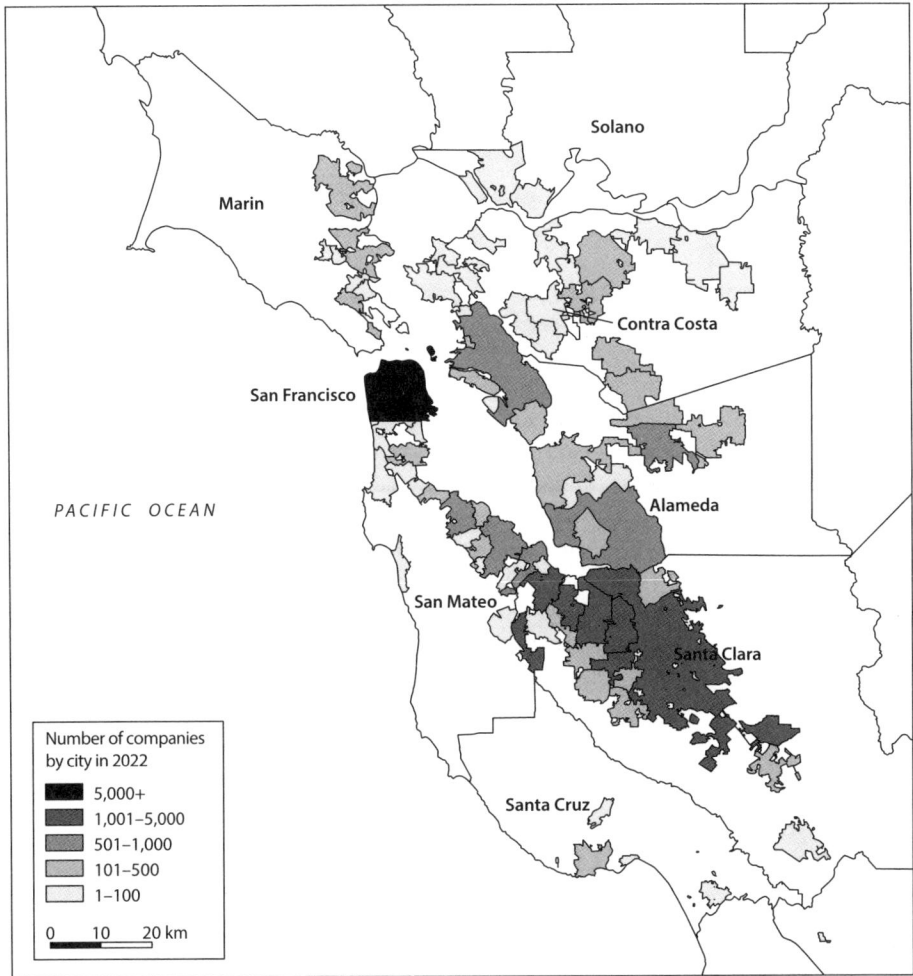

MAP 1. Geographical space. San Francisco Bay Area, number of active tech companies by county, 2022. *Source*: Data from Crunchbase. Visualization produced by Céline Vaslin.

and others). All around, a multitude of companies are trying to benefit from the opportunities opened up by these big names. The city of San Francisco experienced a technology boom in the late 1990s, and went through a crisis in the 2000s, before becoming dominant in the 2010s. At the same time as it was establishing itself as a magnet for technology entrepreneurship, investors such as Peter Thiel and Danny Rimer were highlighting the emergence of an IT "rust belt" in the south of the Bay Area.[12] Players try to cope with the elasticity of this territory and its center of gravity shifts (Map 1).

Faced with this dynamic, players are trying to optimize their "positioning" in order to stay as close as possible to the flow of information and opportunities.[13] As an investor, specializing in microinvestment and active in the region since the 1980s, reminds us:

> When you're a venture capitalist, you don't have time. Every week, I work on forty to one hundred possible deals. At my peak, I was signing forty to fifty companies a year. I've signed four hundred companies since I started. Every week, I have to decide which pitch I'm going to hear in my office on Tuesday, which is the day I string them all together, about ten. A week without a good deal is not a good week. I've settled between Palo Alto and San Francisco. Most of the deals I've done are within twenty minutes of Palo Alto. If I started today, most of them would be in San Francisco. In the 1990s what everyone was aiming for was the Stanford guys. That's why a lot of the money is still on Sand Hill Road right above Stanford. That's where the first VCs set up shop in the 1970s, to be as close as possible to where it's happening. Don [Valentine, founder of Sequoia] used to say all the time, *When I see VCs get on a plane, I know they're walking away from the best deals.* Why would I do that? The problem is, when you look at the Peninsula, it's gone in two opposite directions: hardware south, software north. So we find ourselves running out of time even faster (interview, San Francisco, August 18, 2017).

Saving time, facilitating meetings, or launching solutions—geographical considerations meet social concerns in a constantly changing population.

Multiplying Connections in an Evolving Population

Indeed, tech talent demographics constantly evolve. In the 1920s Silicon Valley had less than a hundred engineers and around two hundred technicians. Before World War II there were only a few tens of thousands of engineers and technicians in the Peninsula, mainly in Santa Clara County. In the 1950s employment in the technology field was five or six times smaller than in the Boston area.[14] But in the early 1970s Silicon Valley was considered a bastion of job-hoppers, home to a million tech workers. Between 1975 and 1990 the job supply had grown three times as much as on Route 128 in Massachusetts, Boston's tech corridor and Silicon Valley's rival tech district. In 1992, in Santa Clara County, there were 56,724 jobs in computer and data-processing services; 45,590 in computer and office equipment; 26,297 in electronic computers; 16,105 in computer programming services; and 15,247 in software, primarily.[15] Between 1990 and 2000 an average of 2,100 new technology companies were created each year.[16]

This growth has been accompanied by an increasing division of labor, multiplying titles and functions. Three activity categories have been at the forefront: entrepreneurs, investors, and engineers. Today the spectrum covers a large diversity of activities: developers, testers, product managers, designers, data analysts, lawyers, advisers, accountants, communication specialists, human resources specialists, salespeople, lobbyists, prompt engineers, and so forth (Figure 1).

An adviser describes this industry, where information, economic resources, and talent are in abundance, as follows:

> Here you see two things: smart people and money.
>
> There is a lot of money. Is it a bubble? That's not the issue. The issue is the concentration. When you go to Sand Hill Road, within a few miles, you have an insane amount of money concentrated.... Venture capital in the world is $90 billion, two-thirds of it are in the United States, and half of that is in Silicon Valley.
>
> And here, you have brains too. That means that both resources of the chemical reaction required to do great things are available here. Paul Graham [founder of the Y Combinator] says that's enough for innovation. But it's not.
>
> It's a bit like in Hollywood. You need universities cleverly playing their part in both global and local economies: there are labs doing research, specialized services, etc. In the film industry, there are luxury caretakers, people who know finding and closing large deals with A-list actors and networks, to negotiate six-, seven-, eight-figure contracts. It's the same thing here. There's this specialized service economy, which is under the surface, invisible but extremely important. That's what the ability to value a company depends on, which is to say, to value it, or to liquidate it. In every sense of the word; and it is infinitely precious. Lawyers, specialized banks, VCs, HR firms specialized in startups, etc. (interview with a consultant in new technologies, San Francisco, August 27, 2017).

This increase of tech workers is synonymous with a larger local demographic. Between 2017 and 2022 jobs for professional tech talent (such as software developers, programmers, engineers, and those managing information systems) have increased by 23 percent in the San Francisco Bay Area. The region employs the most tech roles of any market (407,810), which makes up 11.6 percent of total Bay Area employment. In such a context, to be a techie in

Startups

Bootstrap/scaling, lean/fast, cockroach/unicorn, private equity

Over 15,000

Diversity in terms of employees and location: densification in San Francisco, development of offshore teams and subcontractors

Large public companies

Listed on the stock exchange

105 tech companies with more than 10,000 employees (Google, Facebook, Apple)

Strong value capture but low job creation

Events

Conferences, meetups, pitch competitions, hackathons

About 40 international conferences per year (SF Disrupt, Lean Startup Conference, etc.)

Expertise, networking

Media

Forbes (1917), *Inc.* (1979), *Wired* (1993), *The Register* (1994), *Fast Company* (1995), *Ars Technica* (1998), *TechCrunch* (2005), *Venturebeat* (2006), *Business Insider* (2007), *HackerNews* (2007), *ReCode* (2014)

Half of these publications were born in San Francisco or Silicon Valley and are headquartered there

National networks

Including TiE (India), Silicon Valley Chinese Association, French Tech, etc.

1,900 members in the French Tech meetup Facebook group in 2020

Meeting places, support network, information exchange and mutual aid, often structured by successful "alumni"

Big companies

Research laboratories, incubators, corporate investments

Learning expeditions, labs, research and development, etc.

Universities and the public sector

Universities, city halls, counties, State of California, government agencies, diplomatic bodies

The region is the second largest metropolitan area in the country in terms of academic offerings after the New York area

Scholarships, sponsorships, programs and partnerships

Intermediates

Advisers, mentors, lawyers, accountants, etc.

Role of experts, advisers, facilitators, sometimes very expensive (US$600 per hour for the best lawyers in the region)

Investors

F&F, angels, incubators, accelerators, seed capital (100K to 1M), venture capitalists, private equity funds, investment banks, pension funds

Silicon Valley concentrates 40% of the amount invested by venture capitalists in the USA

Gig workers

"Contract employees," "gig workers," "shadow workforce," "temps," "interns"

More than 39,000 worked for technology companies in Santa Clara and San Mateo Counties

Need for expertise in a specific field, cyclical increase in tasks to be accomplished, compensation for early departure, etc.

Entrepreneurs

Founders, innovators, builders, doers, first movers

More than 30,000

Collaborative circles (CEO, CTO, COO)

FIGURE 1. Social space. The ecosystem of Silicon Valley's social and professional network. *Source:* Crunchbase, Glassdoor, SEV, WAVC, Band of Angels, Bloomberg, *Wall Street Journal,* and Quora.

Silicon Valley sounds like being a citizen in ancient Athens. Just like in Ancient Greece, only 10 percent of the population are citizens, and there are major inequalities between citizens and noncitizens.

Silicon Valley is described by its inhabitants as a welcoming land for outsiders. These newcomers come from the United States, mainly from the state of California, and from other countries, primarily China, India, and European nations. However, the region is also quick to let them go. Periods of crisis and contraction occur almost every decade: in the late 1970s, late 1980s, turn of the millennium, late 2000s, early 2020, and so forth. During the COVID-19 pandemic, at a time when Big Tech was earning record revenue, Silicon Valley experienced a tech exodus: 15 percent of new technology company employees left the city of San Francisco, and several companies closed offices or moved their headquarters elsewhere (Tesla and Oracle chose Austin; Palantir, Denver). However, worker departures have remained largely temporary, or contained within Northern California.[17] After a period of growing revenue, 2022 was a time for layoffs in Big Tech: almost fifty thousand employees of the largest companies had to leave their jobs. Beyond crises, there is high turnover in the population. One-third of those interviewed during my research who moved to the region in 2015 had left by 2022, a proportion that appears to be consistent with both the constant population growth and renewal of the region. Plus, skills, qualifications, and jobs titles evolve all the time. New titles appear; others disappear. One-third of the twenty most sought-after jobs on the Silicon Valley section of Indeed's job site in the mid-2010s were no longer listed five years later.

These changes encourage professionals to focus on networking. When the workday is over, entrepreneurs rush off to one of Silicon Valley's countless meetups. By February 2024, 140 events had been organized on the theme of AI, five per day. When you attend one of these meetings, you're guaranteed to leave with a dozen or so extra contacts. Most of these new contacts will remain buried in the depths of your LinkedIn network. And yet, for a moment, you'll be genuinely glad you met them. Why? Because social life in Silicon Valley is all about opportunities. Each new mesh in the network increases the spectrum of openings. So everybody works hard to expand their network. But players can't extend it indefinitely, nor constantly solidify it. This is why Silicon Valley is the land of what sociologists call weak ties. Weak ties are contacts and connections for professional purposes with no or few long-term emotional implications. They differ from strong ties, which are friends and lasting relationships based on confidence and reciprocal influence in their personal lives. Sociologist and Stanford professor Mark Granovetter pointed out in one of the discipline's most cited articles, "The Strength of Weak Ties," that casual acquaintances are more influential in opening up new professional opportunities than close friends or family members.[18] Weak ties facilitate access to information and intermediaries. In Silicon Valley the work culture, the obsession with networking, and the importance of departures lead people to underinvest emotionally in relationships. As one entrepreneur who has been living in San Francisco for ten years said: "I don't get attached to people I see coming in here anymore, because you don't know how long they're going to stay."[19]

An investor I used to see frequently in a Tenderloin bar in San Francisco told me how tired he was of people coming and going, insisting that if he agreed to tell me his story, I'd give him news from time to time. Another investor, with European roots, told me at the beginning of my research for this book:

> Friendship here is about doing things together. Your neighbor moves in, and you exist in relation to him, as a neighbor, even if you feel like you have a great relationship. The day he moves out, you won't see him again. But people leave regularly. They can open up sometimes, but it's not because they open up that there's an unbreakable bond. Don't forget that most of them are uprooted. I've accepted this.... But I'm always struck by the guy who had lived in Silicon Valley for years, retires, and goes straight to Montana or Florida. In Europe, people stay put, with their families, their friends.... Here, the day someone leaves, they disappear, and someone takes their place. People think it's superficial, but it works (interview, San Francisco, December 5, 2015).

In this society of weak ties, some people try to reconstitute strong ties, like one interviewee, who has lived in San Francisco for several years as an entrepreneur then as an investor. She says she has been "adopted" by an American couple:

> When you are far away, you have emotional needs, you need to reconstitute an adoptive family; I found parents here, I go to see them every Sunday, I go surfing, they watch me from the beach. ... They are my surrogate parents and I am their surrogate daughter (interview, San Francisco, October 20, 2015).

Yet the multiplication of encounters and collaborations allows for more effective evolution in the technological space.

Projecting Yourself in an Expanding Technological Space

To succeed in Silicon Valley, you need to convince investors, collaborators, and users in a preexisting space. Although technologies are understood as pure products of the imagination, with no other limit than human inventiveness, their production is neither virtual nor decoupled from material, geographical, and social constraints. You will need water, energy, computers, cloud services, brains, and money to create a technological niche with a large technological network composed of infrastructures, architectures, devices, and digital services. As one AI scientist-turned-entrepreneur told me:

> That's one of the perks of being here: technology is embedded with social. For instance, we had a group, we'd get together every Friday evening, over a bottle or two, and we'd talk, sort of rambling, about what was going to develop. And the next day, it was time for the serious stuff: we'd work on the white board, doing the math, crunching the numbers, and checking what could and would work (interview, San Francisco, September 20, 2024).

As an entrepreneur, the challenge is to convince people around you to bet on the necessity of a yet-to-be determined forthcoming solution for potential markets. Paul Graham, founder of the Y Combinator accelerator, wrote in a social media post that "start-ups usually need some time (often a year or two) to figure out exactly what their business is."[20] To get around this problem, they use labels. An eighteen-year-old entrepreneur who moved to San Francisco a few months before I interviewed him talks about how the artificial intelligence label allows him to be identified by his contacts, and his need to silence his own doubts about his solution:

> What I'm developing, I still don't know exactly what it is . . . I'm wondering . . . I could lead you on, and that's what you have to do with investors; this is AI. . . . To tell them that you're developing an AI that will completely change the way people interact, *blah, blah, blah*. . . . But the truth is that I have ideas, but I'm not convinced. . . . I'm still trying to figure it out. But if I go to a VC today, I'll say: *I'm making an AI that saves time and frees your creativity.* And what the guy will remember is the notion of AI (interview, San Francisco, September 7, 2017).

This confession is in line with the testimony of an entrepreneur saying technological categories have a more or less important pull effect:

> We just found a Japanese investor. We were pitching him what we were doing in a big trade show last week: *We're making a mobile app, all AI, to solve*

problems in real estate. . . . He directly interrupted us: *AI? OK, stop. Come to my office, Monday 10:00 a.m.* And he gave us his card (interview with a cofounder, San Francisco, November 16, 2015).

In this regard, technological categories are an interface "between things and action," enabling orientation and coordination.[21] Players interact and find each other through what they believe will be worth exploring.

It is common to analyze Big Tech through the prism of subcategories: microprocessor, algorithm, platform, artificial intelligence, spam, or meme. But when analysts do that, they isolate one piece of its network. It would be like studying a wild animal without taking its environment into account. New technologies coexist in Silicon Valley and rely on each other. Historians have shown that this interdependence is what makes technical systems operational.[22] The solutions that have received funding through a company in the region provide a representation of this technological space (Figure 2; see also "A Semantic Approach to Technological Space").

Entrepreneurs and investors are thus moving into different areas of the tech space, primarily into infrastructure or solutions. New areas for infrastructure include devices (hardware, robotics, automation, 3D technology, mobile, Internet of Things, virtual reality); IT services (communication infrastructure, cloud data services, network security, web hosting); and communication (email, web development, professional services, collaboration). New areas for solutions include sales (e-commerce, retail, delivery, restaurants, fashion); finance (mobile payments, blockchain, financial services); communication (messaging, advertising, games, photo sharing, digital entertainment); health (biotech, health care, fitness); and education (EdTech). More generally, the network of infrastructures and applications is developed around a software core.

The centrality of a software core has technical and economic reasons. Silicon Valley investors attribute much lower investment to software solutions—including AI, production costs, and development cycles—than to hardware or biotech. The latter require offices, laboratories, warehouses, abundant raw materials, and a large and well-trained workforce, whereas simple computers and a team of programmers are sufficient to develop computer software solutions. A dive into the archives of Silicon Valley innovation is enlightening in this respect. Charles Doc Herrold's first radio in 1909 required half a room. Hewlett-Packard's first oscilloscopes at the start of World War II were equivalent to a large desk in size. In the 1960s the

A semantic approach to analyzing technological space could be mobilized to recompose the chain of scientific action by following the signs produced in the course of research, from equations inscribed on blackboards to the publication of articles,[1] or to deconstruct emblematic technical categories such as the term *platform*.[2] While these might seem to indicate two directions, both orientations—that of semantic reconstruction from a situation and deconstruction of a category—rely on the idea that indexicality concerning scientific and technical activities is limited by the texts and persons that structure them and the operations of classification and hierarchization. Nevertheless, the categorization within the scientific and technical universes makes it possible to agree, represent, combine, and contract within a semantic territory.[3] For this reason we see technological categories as a relevant indicator for reconstructing the technological space. To identify technological categories, I turned to the data on Silicon Valley subcategories that have received investments. I then used network analysis: each point corresponds to subcategories of solutions that have received funding, within a company headquartered in Silicon Valley, and represents an active component regardless of the year of funding (see Figure 2).

---

1. Bruno Latour and David Woolgar, *Laboratory Life: The Social Construction of Scientific Facts* (Los Angeles: Sage, 1979).
2. Tarleton Gillepsie, "The Politics of Platforms," *New Media and Society* 12, no. 3 (2010): 347–64. The popularity of this category from the end of the 2000s could be explained by the plasticity and neutrality of a term that makes it possible to meet the expectations of actors with multiple and divergent interests (company employees, several categories of freelancers, customers, etc.) without arousing the attention of regulatory bodies.
3. Gillepsie, "Politics of Platforms."

multibillion-dollar mainframe computer SAGE took up half a large room. Today machine learning models are trained on simple laptops, and according to one of the AI leaders: "In AI, teams should be no larger than a conference room can accommodate" (interview, San Francisco, September 18, 2024). This is because most of the hardware has been outsourced and made invisible, thanks to performance gains and economies of scale. A well-known investor and longtime industry observer sums it up:

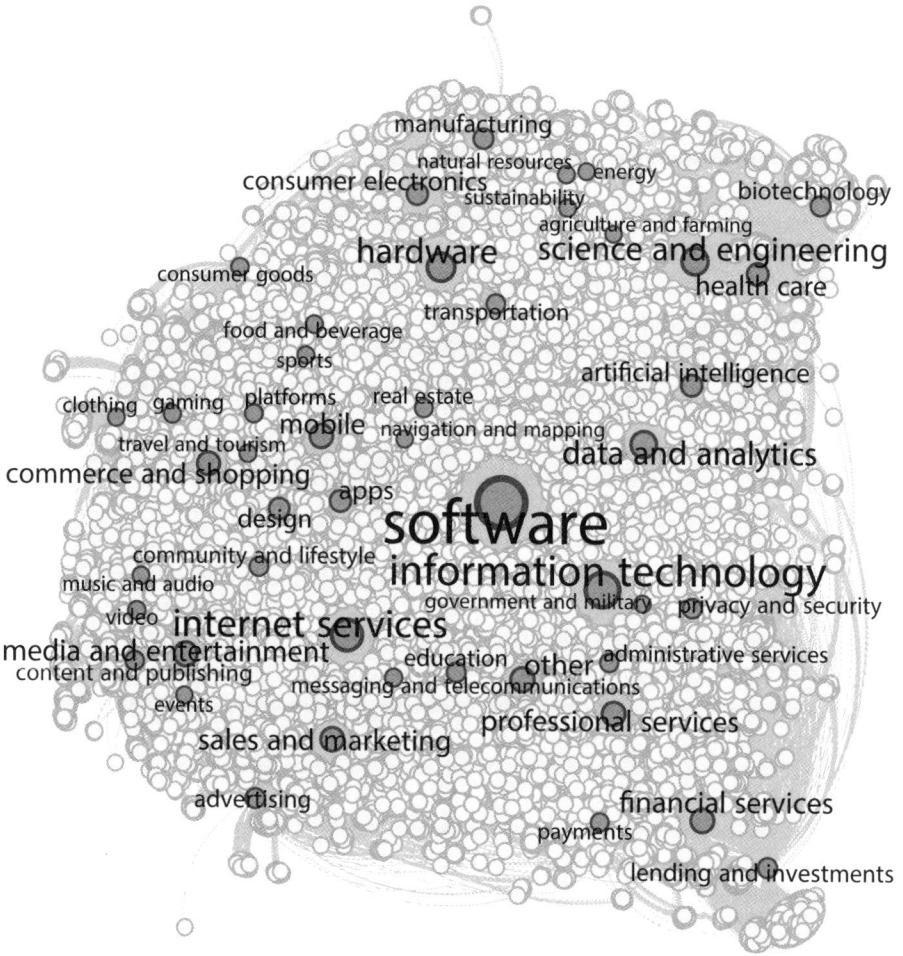

FIGURE 2. Tech space. Various sectors within Silicon Valley's tech industry. *Source*: Crunchbase (2024).

Silicon Valley has become a software business. It's a pretty different type of work, more independent than hardware was. When you produce hardware, you have to be in the office, you have to equip it, you have to test it.... When you do software, it becomes easier to test remotely. A program can also be done by several people. But the production costs are much lower. It's just the team and their computers (interview, Palo Alto, February 16, 2016).

Since the production costs of software are almost limited to the cost of labor, software is seen as a less risky investment relative to other subcategories. An early investor in Google outlines the problem facing venture capitalists in Silicon Valley:

> Venture capital firms are all measured by RR, the general return ratio: time is as important as size. For RR, it's nice to deal with size and time. But even for Google, it took from 1997 to 2004 to get there. That's still seven years. Now, most funds only last seven to eight years. So you have to raise money in the first year before you get out of the fund. Your reference signal is what we call the liquidity event. And hardware has always been a longer-term bet than software. It takes years to develop a product, whereas it only takes a few months for a software solution (interview, San Francisco, January 18, 2020).

The agility and speed of development associated with software solutions go hand in hand with the proliferation of service offerings and cost reduction in IT, as investor Mark Andreessen puts it:

> Downstream, software programming tools and Internet-based services make it easy to launch new global startups in many industries—without having to invest in new infrastructure or train new employees. In 2000, when my partner Ben Horowitz was CEO of the first cloud computing company, Loudcloud, the cost of a customer running a basic Internet application was about $150,000 a month. [In 2011] running that same application in Amazon's cloud costs about $1,500 per month.[23]

The term *cloud computing* thus indiscriminately covers functions originally performed by large machines. Their specialization, miniaturization, and delocalization encourage the design of new solutions by entrepreneurs, which can also be marketed through online services such as the App Store or Google Play. This dynamic sometimes leads players to envision tech as a space of unlimited possibilities.

This belief is fueled by three properties of software solutions: communicability, ubiquity, and computability. The ethnography of a team of computer science researchers working on an algorithm solution illustrates them.[24] Developing an algorithm involves three steps. The first step is to assemble a database that allows us to solve a clearly identified problem. Second, you have to make the writing sets sufficiently coherent to instruct computer programs. To do this, it is necessary to carry out a sequence of reductions transforming nonmathematical entities (such as texts or images) into mathematizable entities ("values") distributed in rows and columns, according to a sequence of 0s and 1s. If mastered, this operation makes it possible to match an ad hoc database with programming activities. In a mathematical form the symbols become shareable, comparable, and operable.

This series of tasks allows first of all to lift the barrier of incommunicability between humans and machines, since it becomes possible to address instructions and requests to computers. Many software solutions are designed to develop and facilitate these human-machine interactions. This is the first property of software and computer programming: communicability. Second, the mathematization of entities makes them communicable at a distance. It is common in Silicon Valley for entrepreneurs to work with technical teams located in Mexico, China, India, or Ukraine (before the war with Russia), via outsourcing (through subcontractors) and crowdsourcing (via low or unpaid microtasks).[25] Teams regularly operate at lower cost from databases, built by workers located several thousand miles away. Software solutions thus push back the geographical boundaries of work, and certain tasks can be carried out in several locations. This is the second property of software solutions: ubiquity. Then, once an algorithm matches the database and the programs, these programs are likely to perform automatable calculations within a few seconds, where a lifetime would not be enough to complete the work by hand. This is the third property: computability.

Communicability, ubiquity, computability—these three qualities explain and justify the centrality of software solutions in the tech space. They give tech workers the illusion of being free of the constraints of time and space. Like Neo in *The Matrix*, it seems possible to see and indefinitely multiply gateways between separated entities: between different software pieces, between software and hardware, between hardware and other infrastructures, and the like.[26] As a result, our world is both simplified and amplified. Tech projects the illusion of an immaterial, interconnected, fluid, and light world, with borders progressively and cumulatively pushed back. Despite the impression of manageability that the lines of computer code give it, our environment turns out to be more complex, heavier (as a consequence of the accumulation of software layers, hardware devices, and other infrastructures) and also unequal (because of outsourcing and crowdsourcing).

However, in Silicon Valley, players try to take advantage of this territory, to gain better and faster access to resources (people, companies, and capital). For the same reason they go after the hottest and most promising tech specializations, those with the highest and shortest profitability potential, to the detriment of other categories. The primacy of AI and software solutions can thus be explained for both technical and economic reasons. Players try as hard as they can to accumulate resources in a tight territory for pushing their solution in what they see as an unlimited tech space. This contradiction between a limited Silicon Valley and an expanding tech space can be described in terms of economic geography: "Capital is not perfectly mobile in any of its forms. . . . In order to produce surplus (value), firms must build a productive apparatus consisting of fixed capital, workers, land, political alliances, and so on—all with a local base. . . . The trick, therefore, is to maintain a balance between the mobility and immobility of capital, not just to maximize mobility."[27] The combination of dimensions explains why players don't see the world as a Euclidean space structured by immutable laws.[28]

In their eyes, it is an evolving and expanding universe where it is a matter of adapting, anticipating, and taking the world by storm. But the sum of individual strategies fuels a highly selective dynamic within Silicon Valley where investors play a leading role.

TWO

Surviving in an Investment Economy

We could be profitable. . . . But we're not. Right now, what we are
focused on is getting more users.

—Interview with an entrepreneur, San Francisco, September 17, 2024

GERMAN SOCIOLOGIST MAX WEBER CONSIDERED that "a capitalistic
economic action rests on the expectation of profit by the utilization of opportunities for exchange."[1] Following this definition, the players in Silicon Valley are
driven by capitalist logic. They accumulate capital. Like no else on Earth and in
the history of capitalism. The region's GDP was $497 billion in 2018, or an aver-
age of $128,308 per capita, a level equivalent to such microstates as Luxembourg,
Macau, Qatar, and Singapore. In 2024 almost 10 percent of the Silicon Valley
population (285,000) was millionaires. If you include the 630 multimillionaires
and 65 billionaires, it is the highest concentration of wealth in the world.

However, the wealthy in Silicon Valley differ from those in other economic
centers when it comes to their social origin and their occupation. Their social
origins are mostly upper-middle class and, with the exception of real estate
developers, they are all entrepreneurs, widows of entrepreneurs, technology
company executives, early-stage employees of successful companies, and venture capitalists. And their spirit doesn't really fit Benjamin Franklin's "philosophy of avarice"[2] coined as the spirit of capitalism according to Max Weber.[3]
Quite the opposite, actually: they burn a lot of cash. Tech people claim they
don't work to get rich but because they are passionate. Even if Elizabeth
Holmes, the fallen angel of Silicon Valley, already knew when she was still a
child that she wanted to become a billionaire, my interviewees told me again
and again that making money wasn't their primary purpose.[4] After all, early
2020s San Francisco had fewer billionaires (44) than New York (107), Beijing
(83), London (66), and Moscow (53), when according to *Forbes* there were 2,781
billionaires on the planet in 2024, with total wealth of $14,200 billion.[5]

Nevertheless the role of technology in the creation of wealth has influenced a number of labels: *new capitalism, informational capitalism, platform*

capitalism, surveillance capitalism, data capitalism, decentralized capitalism, digital capitalism, broligarchy, and so forth.[6] The Silicon Valley economy appears to embody a new type of capitalism, succeeding patrimonial, managerial, and financial capitalism. It is distinct from traditional American capitalism and its international alternatives (German, Japanese, French, South Korean, and so forth) where profit is paramount and based on the real economy of material goods. Instead, the economic organization of the new technology industry in Northern California is still fuzzy. Contrary to the prophecies of the 1990s, its development doesn't translate into sustained and generalized growth or massive productivity gains, nor has it solved the problem of large-scale unemployment.[7]

The technological monopolies often presented as characteristic of this model turn out to be relative. Big Tech and the so-called Magnificent 7 (Microsoft, Apple, Nvidia, Alphabet, Amazon, Meta, and Tesla) represent a handful of powerful and robust firms eclipsing the thousands of companies operating in the Bay Area, usually craving fresh cash. In the history of capitalism, evaluating the quality of companies in light of their profits is typical. However, many Silicon Valley firms, some of which are highly publicized in the media, have balance sheets that are far from breaking even, or even from their objective, profitability. A subsidiary as popular as YouTube only became profitable for Google fifteen years after its acquisition in 2006. With $911 million losses in 2019, Lyft, a well-known US competitor to Uber, became the most loss-making listed company in the country's history with a $5.24 billion deficit when it went public.[8] In 2024, OpenAI saw a loss of $5 billion on $3.7 billion in revenue. Companies can manage to reverse this trend. But when they do so, financial markets do not always react positively. Twitter/X employees can testify to this: the first financially positive quarter since their company's inception in early 2019 also came with a downgrade. After Elon Musk bought out Twitter/X in 2021 for $44 billion, cut 80 percent of the 7,500 employees, tackled the "legacy media," and won the election side by side with President Donald Trump, the valuation of X was down to $9 billion by September 2024.

Fraud, bankruptcies, and scandals prove that the tech economy rests on unsteady foundations. Theranos and FTX raised $2 billion, as much money as the most powerful investment firms in the region. These firms look for success. But success is a rare thing in the tech industry. Only 2 percent of active companies are listed on the stock market. And when they reach stock market heights, their business model is under scrutiny. The value of Tesla, for example, stood at $658.39 billion on the stock market at the height of the pandemic, almost three times more than General Motors, Ford, and Fiat-Chrysler combined. The company led by Elon Musk had not yet reached the 390,000 cars sold in the year 2019–20, compared against 1.9 million for Ford, 3.5 for Fiat-Chrysler, and 6.8 million vehicles for General Motors in 2020. This mismatch between stock market valuation and the real economy has been described as a drift. Tim Hwang, former head of public policy for artificial intelligence at Google, has warned against a financial bubble ready to burst because the efficiency of the internet ad market is well overrated.[9] Although there is no doubt that the new spirit of capitalism flourished in the minds of Silicon Valley entrepreneurs, the values promoted there go against classical theories. The four historical principles of capitalism are corporation, commodification, ownership, and profit. But in Silicon Valley, players celebrate networks, open source, free exchange, and sometimes even decommodification.

What could be seen as anomalies to accepted economic theory is understandable when you keep in mind that Silicon Valley is essentially an investment economy. The area concentrates the largest volume of investment in the country: $74 billion of venture capital funds had been invested in 2015, $107.7 billion in 2018, or 24.4 percent of the total investments in the country.[10] Venture capital spent $100 billion in Silicon Valley in 2022.[11] In addition, large companies spend nearly 15 percent of their profits on research and development, and regularly make acquisitions. This chapter presents this investment economy's organization. By following capital step-by-step, the chapter shows how players articulate different worlds (their entourage, Silicon Valley, and the finance world), under the patronage of venture capitalists.

UPSIDE-DOWN CAPITALISM

In Silicon Valley three characteristics complicate the task of accurate accounting, an exercise that Max Weber placed at the core of capitalism's analysis: the partial gratuity of services, the practice of exchange, and the proportion of failures.

A Free Economy

Contradicting economist Milton Friedman's "no free lunch" formula, a lot of things seem to be free in Silicon Valley.[12] Free meals in companies, free beer and pizzas in meetups, free time given by entrepreneurs to newcomers—these are just a few examples of what amounts to an abundance of freebies. And there is more. In the wake of web 2.0, the culture of free access was promoted all around, especially in the business-to-consumer area (BtoC). BtoC defines companies that sell to individuals, as opposed to business to business (BtoB), which sells its solutions to other companies. Employees, from small to large companies, show a strong attachment to free software. Their open access makes the Silicon Valley economy even more complex. In classical theory an ordinary commodity cannot be consumed by two people at the same time. Exchange value corresponds to use value. However, the same is not true of immaterial services, which can be consumed collectively. For this reason economists refer to intangible goods as public goods. In addition, the value of immaterial goods and services rises as their consumption increases, which is the opposite of the material goods economy. The network effect, or club effect (discussed in chapter 1), often obscures the formation of value for intangible goods. This is frequently misinterpreted as "free." The internet enables an unbridled exchange of immaterial goods at low or zero marginal cost. The popularity of Napster's Peer to Peer system, Google's search engine, Facebook's feed, WordPress tools, and LinkedIn posts raise the question of value formation. The "free" nature of these services is ambivalent because it is part of a business development strategy.

Tim O'Reilly made this point very clear in his 2005 "What Is Web 2.0" manifesto. Addressing entrepreneurs and developers, he states that "the key to comparative advantage in Internet applications is that users can enrich the data you provide. So: don't limit your participation architecture to software development. Involve your users, implicitly and explicitly, in adding value to your application." He points out that "intellectual property protection limits reuse and prevents experimentation. *Therefore:* when benefits come from collective adoption, not private restriction, make sure the barriers to adoption are low. Follow existing standards and use licenses with the fewest restrictions possible. Design for 'hackability' and 'remixability.'"[13] This credo explains heated debates about patents in Silicon Valley, particularly in the field of software. Patents have a bad reputation in Silicon Valley, with Larry Page and Sergey Brin (Google) clashing with Jeff Bezos (Amazon) on this issue in the late 1990s. In the field of machine learning, Silicon Valley dominates the production of models, far beyond China (eighty compared with around fifteen at the beginning of 2024), but the situation is reversed when it comes to patents.[14] Yet free software is part of the economic opacity of Silicon Valley, and so is exchange.

An Exchange Economy

In Silicon Valley exchange is the dominant form of economic life. In the drama series *Super Pumped*, for example, entrepreneur Travis Kalanick trades his energy, determination, and vision for the network, expertise, and wisdom of legendary venture capitalist John Gurley. But this modality goes far beyond the emblematic and partly fabulated face-to-face relationship between entrepreneur and investor. It is part of a larger economic system. An illustration of its organizational logic includes the experience of Antonio García Martínez, a controversial former employee of Facebook, who was "Facebook's first ad-targeting product manager. Literally the guy who takes your data and turns it into money at Facebook, a year before the IPO, as one of maybe 30 people on the ads team"—by doing so he provided the procedure for data collection at Facebook.[15] The targeted advertising of social network users is partly based on the acquisition and exploitation of usage data from outside the company. This data is used to sell profiles of internet user packages to advertisers, according to an efficiency criterion defined by the number of clicks made on a given content. Unlike some media, Facebook does not buy this data from specialized companies but exchanges it for services. Third-party companies are offered the possibility to use certain features of the social network. In exchange, they allow the company to collect data, which allows Facebook to improve online experience and targeting. Although apparently "free" and based on exchange, this system has an economic purpose for the various parties involved.

Exchange is also found in many acquisition transactions. Indeed, multi-billion-dollar buyout announcements correspond in part or in full to share transfers. For example, Facebook's buyout of WhatsApp for a declared $19 billion actually included $12 billion in shares offered to WhatsApp's owners, $4 billion in cash, and $3 billion in preferred shares for their employees.[16] The formation of value, associated with these so-called "free" and "exchange" schemes, thus makes measurement almost impossible in accounting terms. Deals, talent, information, and even parties—every social interaction in Silicon Valley relies on this mechanism.

An Economy of Failure

Projects, information, capital, and risk-takers flow into the region, but the failure rate is particularly high, and the majority of tech companies do not have a stable product to market. The AI boom came with a great deal of capital without any clearly established business models, including at OpenAI, which raised nearly $13 billion between 2015 and 2023 before generating $1 billion revenue in 2023. An entrepreneur-investor-researcher in AI, who has been in this field for nearly twenty years, told me this:

> Of course there's an AI hype right now. It's all nonsense. Guys [meaning investors] are signing checks with valuations of $1 or $2 billion just based on a simple spreadsheet. Lot of them are going to fail (interview, Los Gatos, September 16, 2024).

This is a constant in the industry. A serial entrepreneur in his forties put it this way:

> With my first two startups, we never found the market fit.[17] Never. And the companies ended up in a tough spot. . . . It's the Holy Grail, in the Valley. Some say you have to be willing to kill to find it. It's 99 percent of the job. If you find it, then you can screw up other stuff, that's okay, but that's the first thing you have to focus on. Out of one hundred startups, ninety won't find it. Even if there is talent, goodwill, it won't be enough (interview, San Francisco, June 16, 2016).

When startups do find their market fit, the Silicon Valley philosophy is to spend more to develop the company than to secure incoming cash revenue. Sociologist Benjamin Shestakofsky showed in great detail in his book *Behind the Startup* how investors push startups to scale as quickly as possible to inflate the value of their portfolio—sometimes without regard for the business that entrepreneurs really operate or the quality of the service that they try to build up.[18] Financial success can sometimes run counter to customer satisfaction. Indeed, customers have to deal with tech products and services that in their very architecture reflect the VC way of conducting business based on permanent updates and short life cycles. This model of growth at all costs results in a high rate of company destruction. Estimations range from 50 percent of venture-backed companies going out of business after a few years with no return for investors, to more than 90 percent of tech companies disappearing after five years, making the tech sector the riskiest industry in the United States, ahead of restaurants and finance. While these figures are approximate, this phenomenon is in line with this testimony from a blog post on startups:

> Venture capitalists fund about one in 350 companies they see, and of those funded companies, only about one in ten actually succeed (i.e., get bought

out for millions or successfully go public). To put that number in perspective, US venture capital firms invest in about 3,000 to 3,500 companies each year.[19]

Graduating from the unicorns' club, which includes companies with valuations $1 billion and above, to an IPO is also far from being a guarantee: 34 percent of those are bought, while 4 percent file for bankruptcy.[20] And for tech giants, a simple slowdown in growth metrics trickles down to stock quotes. Netflix saw its stock price devalued by 70 percent in the first quarter of 2022 after the company posted the first subscriber loss in its history. Economic life in the tech industry is thus highly intense and emotionally draining. Following the launch of ChatGPT in 2022, the race for generative AI has shaken up hierarchies. Google found itself particularly challenged because of a solution (Gemini), which was expensive ($191 million to develop) and private (while Google has always been a champion of open source), with results far from the best on the market. In 2022, Meta announced a massive layoff of more than eleven thousand employees. By the middle of 2024, Mark Zuckerberg said that Meta's AI tool was on pace to be the "most used" in the world. Value is indeed versatile in tech.

However, in Silicon Valley financial risk is socialized through capital providers, referred to as "capitalists" by economist Joseph A. Schumpeter. Entrepreneurs commit their time and labor, while capitalists provide money through specialized investors who operate as intermediaries. This threefold system leads one entrepreneur to define the Silicon Valley economy as "communist capitalism," since capital is collectivized from different sources and entrepreneurs operationalize services for the good of the common people.[21] An entrepreneur deals with an initial contact with this hybrid system as follows:

> Back then, we were all more or less PhDs at MIT. My cofounders went on the VC road show, meeting them in Silicon Valley. . . . Getting on a plane, talking about your research, getting money from rich people, who'd say: *Great, go ahead, take this money, and go back to the airport with it.* It was a lot more exciting than the rest of our college buddies' lives.
> For a twenty-five-year-old kid to have $2 million or $3 million in the bank was super exciting! We'd go to an ATM and look at our bank account's balance. . . . And we'd start planning: what we were going to need, how to evaluate the risks of what we were doing . . .
> We were starting to pay ourselves, which for a student was a pretty crazy amount of money, around $80,000 a year, compared to the $25,000 of a PhD student. And we moved to the Bay Area. . . . We thought we were super

smart and our technology was super cool, which is not the right way to do it [laughs].

In the end, one went to Google, another went back to college, and the remaining two of us started over. The VCs told us, *Okay you burned it up, but here's some money, $2 or $3 million, we believe in you.* Again . . . (interview, San Francisco, November 9, 2015).

Part of the entrepreneurship journey in Silicon Valley is to make your way in the world of capital.

THE FINANCIAL STAIRCASE

Sitting in a small café in the Bernal Heights neighborhood near Walk on the Wildside, unofficially known as San Francisco's last lesbian bar, a local radical left journalist tells me with a machine-gun flow of words: "It's very simple, if you want to understand what's going on here, you have to follow the money!" Sticking to this "simple" plan is not an easy thing. Tech companies, investors, and entrepreneurs could be extremely reluctant to open up to an outside observer. Plus, capital comes from many sources, distinct from the most common and expected: traditional banks. Indeed, few banks specialize in new technologies, including the Silicon Valley Bank. It was founded by Stanford University professor Robert Medearis and Wells Fargo executive Bill Biggerstaff, who in 1983 after a tennis match agreed that entrepreneurs couldn't rely on a financial institution that didn't really understand their occupation's needs nor took them into account. The risky and technical path of tech entrepreneurship explains the scarcity of traditional banks in the Silicon Valley financial loop. But the diversity and abundance of finance sources also explains the boom of tech entrepreneurs. Indeed, many and diverse stakeholders make it possible to start up a business in the Valley. If the metrics presented in Figure 3 are not exhaustive, they give an idea of a financial continuum, going from angels to hedge funds.

In the eyes of the players, these funding sources represent different steps of a financial staircase. And in Silicon Valley this staircase goes in one direction: upward and onward. This differs from the model found in books on management and entrepreneurship: business plans, legal procedures, marketing plans, customer base, and so forth. No Silicon Valley company follows such a playbook. Instead, the classic way of imagining the road ahead in this industry follows a funding sequence from preseed to IPO (Table 2).

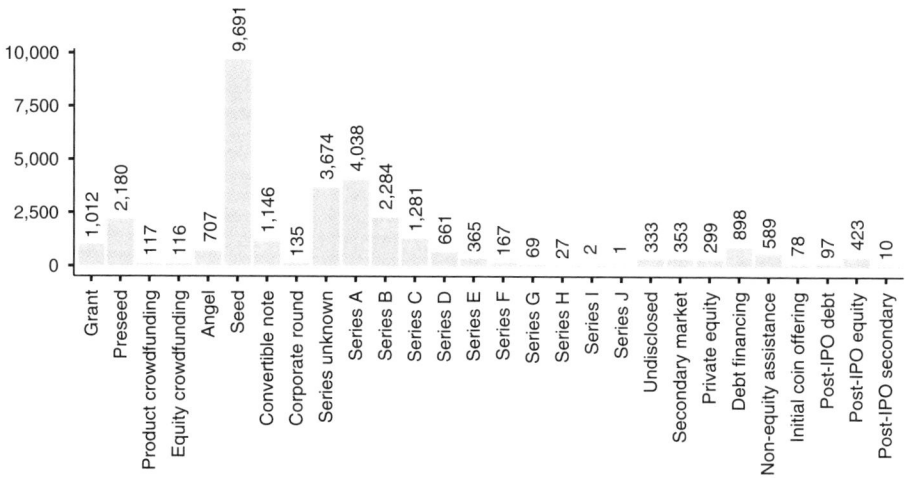

FIGURE 3. Distribution of fundings, 2011–2021. Number of deals by investor category. *Source*: Data from Crunchbase.

From a sociologist's point of view the description would be a little bit different. Indeed, entrepreneurs navigate through three different worlds: the small world of entourage, the institutional investor world, and the larger world of finance.[22]

The Small World of Entrepreneur Entourage

The first world entrepreneurs step into when starting their journey consists of friends, family, professors, colleagues, and professional opportunities. Indeed, the most basic financing method, which is legally the least restrictive, is the love money from the 3Fs: friends, family, and fools. These 3Fs are the real entrepreneurial launchpad. For instance, Jeff Bezos's first expenses as Amazon founder were covered by a $245,000 loan from his mother and adoptive father in 1995.[23] The spectrum of opportunities during these bootstrapping months extends from the home to the office: spousal income, parental inheritance, severance pay, career savings, earnings from a business sale, or income from a job that allows time to work on a side project. The entourage of early investors is more or less wealthy, supportive, and entrepreneurial.

For academics—whether they are doctoral students, postdoctoral fellows, or professors—grants are naturally providential, whether they are awarded

TABLE 2. Funding sequences

Sequences	Steps	Amount (US dollars)	Expected duration
Foundation	Preseed	25,000	9 months
Launching	Seed	100,000 to 1 million	18 months
Optimization	Series A	1 million to 5 million	36 months / 3 years
Expansion	Series B	2 million to 10 million	54 months / 4.5 years
Growth	Series C	>10 million	72 months / 6 years
Initial public offering or resale	IPO or exit	-	5 to 10 years

SOURCE: Investopia.

directly by local, national, or international universities or funded through government or private programs. Larry Page and Sergey Brin's work on web semantics during their time in Stanford's computer science department was funded by a grant from their thesis adviser. Defense programs have been the backbone of tech fields such as artificial intelligence, robotics, and satellite production since World War II. Foreign entrepreneurs who have a foothold in another country where state intervention plays a leading role (including Japan, South Korea, Sweden, Germany, France, and many others) could use it as a comparative advantage. But when it comes to technology funding, Silicon Valley is the place to be.

Entrepreneurs in the region have seen an increase in funding opportunities over time. In 1930, Stanford was already the cradle for Bill Hewlett, David Packard, and the microwave pioneering Varian brothers, whose work was instrumental in the development of radar. During World War II, Stanford's Fred Terman led a workforce of more than 850 people at the Radio Research Laboratory, dedicated to countering enemy radar and communication. In the 1970s venture capitalists appeared. In the 1980s microinvestors emerged. A 1984 a *New York Times* article referred to a "new generation of venture capitalists" who "spotted a market niche and rushed to fill it. These new venture capitalists are snapping up the riskiest deals, namely new startups, and giving them small amounts of capital in exchange for a significant amount of ownership. These new venture capitalists are taking on deals that many of their older, larger counterparts now avoid."[24] In the 1990s "angels" were added to the list, writing checks for nearly $25,000 for a few percent of the company's shares (plus or minus 5 percent). A veteran investor recalls:

The development of the VC in the 1970s left a void for seed and early stage in the 1990s. And that's when the angels came along. In 1994, Band of Angels was formed, which was a Broadway reference. . . . [J. C. Hans] Severiens started that. Drawing a parallel between the type of startup we fund here and the fact that on Broadway, when a funder came in to fund the play, he became its guardian angel. So he picked up on the expression, and in a way the mentality. Well at least it's my vision of Silicon Valley: you invest in something when you think it can be a big hit (interview, San Francisco, September 11, 2017).

The development of the internet economy has favored the growth of what is called preseed, with amounts invested close to $50,000. From the mid-2000s on, startup accelerators have been growing. Y Combinator and Techstars, two renowned startup accelerators, were created in the United States in 2005. In 2009, 500 accelerator and incubator structures existed in the country; 2,616 in 2019. The figures for Y Combinator, the best-known accelerator in the region, give an idea of how they work: in the early 2010s, out of more than 2,000 applications, 170 teams were selected for a ten-minute final interview, 64 teams were presented with the following offer, usually accepted on the spot: to join the program on the basis of $11,000 to $20,000 funding, in exchange for 7 percent of the shares of the future company that would see the light of day at the end of the few weeks of training.[25] This "small world" provides a network of support and funding for players.[26] But being in Silicon Valley offers greater opportunities, making progression to the next level more realistic.

The World of Institutional Financing

Yet the rapid growth of companies in Silicon Valley requires the support of a second world. There is a progression that players experience, highlighting the selectivity that distinguishes the "small world" from this second realm. In this context the investment path adopts a new terminology: ABC rounds. One investor described it this way:

> At first, you've got rich people who will put down $25k in a startup. $25–50k is the normal amount for a check. VCs can go from $500k to $50 million. After that, we're seeing more and more investors here who are specialized in seed, who are either VCs or super angels. And it's always institutional. Then, quite a few are doing Series A at $3–4 million, and then it's Series B, C, etc. Now we're going for $20, $30, $50 million (interview, Palo Alto, September 16, 2016).

The purpose of Series A money is to optimize the traction of production and target customers. Entrepreneurs must demonstrate the reliability of their strategy to generate long-term profits. Then Series B follows for launching a successful product in a growing market, thanks to new hires in business and technical support teams. This stage often includes investors active at seed ($100,000 to $1 million) and Series A (over $1 million to $10 million) stages. The Series C stage is for successful companies who raise additional funds to reach worldwide distribution of their service. Players in this world do not have the same weight or presence. A list of the top fifty investors in the region in terms of financing between 2011 and late 2021 shows the great inequality and heterogeneity of this world, from the Japanese multinational SoftBank Vision Fund at the top to the Wall Street white shoe Morgan Stanley firm at the bottom (Table 3).

Big Tech companies have also established integrated venture capital firms, such as Intel Capital or Google Ventures. They are now among the largest investors in Silicon Valley. A large portion of their capital revenues finance other companies, externally or internally. In 2019, for example, Google spent $16 billion of its $31 billion in revenues on this, via two levers: acquisitions and venture capital investment. The term *mergers and acquisitions* (M&A) describes a way companies appropriate solutions or recruit teams while preventing a possible competitor from emerging. Some are "killer acquisitions" for preventing competition to rise up; others "acqui-hire" to bring in high-value talent that the company would not otherwise be able to attract because of their commitment to entrepreneurship. But in this second world, Big Tech is far from the only—or even the most active—player. This second world is the realm of venture capitalists. In a field where everything is about innovation and amnesia, they've been in the loop for a long time. Some have been established since the personal computer revolutions of the 1960s and 1970s: Greylock Partners since 1965; Sequoia and Kleiner Perkins in 1972; New Enterprises Associated in 1977. Others, like Battery Ventures, were established during the 1980s. Some have made a name for themselves during the internet boom, including Benchmark, established in 1995. While still others emerged during the web 2.0 era, such as Andreessen Horowitz in 2009. Despite their historical differences, they all share a common path, mind-set, and ambition: to make it big. As an investor explains:

> Often, the VCs' ambition is to set up big funds and write big checks, because the return on investment will be bigger; there are some huge funds like that, with several billions to invest. Others have $200 or $300 million, with only ten partners and limited staff (interview, Palo Alto, September 16, 2016).

TABLE 3. Top fifty investors in the region (2011–2021)

1	SoftBank Vision Fund
2	Altria
3	Tiger Global Management
4	Andreessen Horowitz
5	Sequoia Capital
6	Insight Partners
7	Coatue
8	GM Financial
9	Saudi Arabia's Public Investment Fund
10	Silver Lake
11	SoftBank
12	DST Global
13	Ribbit Capital
14	BlackRock
15	New Enterprise Associates
16	Glade Brook Capital Partners
17	GV
18	Fidelity
19	Canada Pension Plan Investment Board, Mubadala Capital Ventures, Silver Lake
20	Kleiner Perkins
21	Accel
22	Fidelity Management and Research Company
23	General Catalyst
24	General Motors
25	Microsoft
26	Dyal Capital Partners,
27	JP Morgan Chase
28	Lightspeed Venture Partners
29	T. Rowe Price
30	Goldman Sachs Investment Partners
31	Franklin Templeton Investments
32	Intel Capital
33	Index Ventures
34	IVP Institutional Venture Partners
35	Kohlberg Kravis Roberts
36	Founders Fund
37	Counterpoint Global
38	Toyota Motor
39	Tiger Global Management
40	ARCH Venture Partners
41	General Atlantic
42	DST Global

43   Salesforce Ventures
44   Rakuten
45   Menlo Ventures
46   CapitalG
47   Permira
48   Temasek Holdings
49   D1 Capital Partners
50   Morgan Stanley

SOURCE: Crunchbase.

Many of them have a founder background and mingle with entrepreneurs in the region on a day-to-day basis. But it's not the case of some firms on the list, such as SoftBank Vision Fund, Goldman Sachs, or General Motors.

The Big World of Finance

The list of financial institutions shows the weight of big firms, including new economy giants like Microsoft and old ones like General Motors, Toyota, General Electric, and Altria (formerly the Philip Morris Tobacco Company) (see Table 3). It includes companies from the Bay Area (Intel, Salesforce) and from elsewhere (such as New York's BlackRock and Japan's SoftBank Vision Fund, which is funded in part by the government of Saudi Arabia). The list also includes older established financial players like Morgan Stanley and Goldman Sachs. These firms are able to make superinvestments, which exceed the region's investor syndicates' capabilities. There are large technology companies that are not headquartered in Silicon Valley, such as Microsoft, based in Seattle, or Tencent, one of China's largest technology groups. Key players at this stage include sovereign wealth funds (Temasek holdings, Singapore's sovereign wealth fund), investment funds (such as SoftBank Vision Fund, created in 2016, BlackRock created in 1988), investment banks (Morgan Stanley, Goldman Sachs), and pension funds (Canada Pension Plan). Their presence marks the prolongation of the investment chain in technology stocks over the past fifteen years. But prolongation also means added levels of hierarchy. As a veteran investor explains:

> The companies that were receiving VC investment were funded within the region. In the 2010s they started getting money from other sources, who come from another world. What do they do? Create unicorns, mythical creatures, artificially created. . . .

In 2015 there was $30 billion invested in VCs, but $60 billion invested in companies that VCs bet on. These companies received as much money from VCs as from non-VCs. This capital comes from pension funds, hedge funds, individual investors, and a small percentage that invest directly. For hedge funds, most of them are financiers. There are Chinese, Russian oligarchs, Saudis, people who are not going to invest at 0.5 percent return on investment. These are very knowledgeable people, who know how to structure contracts, but nothing about technology. They are betting on the fact that tech can restructure large existing markets—like Airbnb with the hotel market, Uber with cabs, energy and cars with Musk, etc. They're taking bets, but with a set of public securities.

If you're running a fund with tens of billions of dollars, the smallest unit you'll invest is $100 million. And you're not going to get 50 percent, you're going to get 10 percent of the company. This implies that the valuation will be several billion dollars. But this is an artificial valuation. And hedge fund investors are not stupid. They invest, agreeing to a valuation of × billions of dollars, asking for lots of protection clauses. For example, if the company is sold, they will be the first to receive funds. If it's sold for $100 million, not only that, but also a minimum return. For example, a 10 percent return per year ... You invest $100 million, which is 10 percent on a $1 billion valuation, with a 10 percent rate of return, that's what you invest this year, and in two years the value of the company is going to plummet and the company will be sold for $200 million. What happens if you're that kind of investor? First, I pay myself back—$100 million—after that, I take 10 percent a year—so $2 million. These are the last ones to come in, so they say: *If you want our money, you accept our terms.* If you're an ambitious entrepreneur and you're the next Facebook, no problem, but if you're just a unicorn, you might get into trouble. Because if the fund takes $120 out of $200 million, the rest is capped at $80, which everyone else has to share: the VCs, investors, founders, employees, etc. So everyone is squeezed. If you look at the financial anatomy of a unicorn, that's it (interview, Palo Alto, April 6, 2016).

This investor explains how investment activity is mainly structured. It's not with a gambling mind-set but with an in-depth expertise in two aspects: technological and financial. Legal terms are a way to formalize an unequal balance of power.

The structuration of this investment economy explains why some companies give priority to the growth and conquest of international markets, giving up on reaching the break-even point. Another investor explains how the industry deals with this iron law of venture capitalism:

Entrepreneurs who receive hedge fund investments have already received money from big VCs in the Valley. They are in a difficult situation because they are in markets where they can't play small. These are existing, large, structured markets. . . . To gain shares in these markets, you need capital. You can't do an Uber by taking on a new city every six months. You need to go after continents. So, they're on an upward trajectory, and the only possibility is hit or miss; there's not so much room for failure scenarios (interview, San Francisco, August 30, 2017).

The visualization of the financing structure of three leading companies in the Peninsula (Uber, Airbnb, and Tesla) during the 2010s highlights this upward trajectory, where members of the small world of Silicon Valley, institutional investors, and the big world of finance follow one another, to the rhythm of Moore's Law (Figure 4).

This financial chain sheds light on the links and relationship between players who are often opposed in narratives: the tech and finance industry; the heart of the Valley and internationalized investors; specialized VCs and investment bankers; large Valley companies and foreign tech companies; startups and brick-and-mortar companies. The interconnection of these three worlds—the small world of entourage, the institutional investor world, and the larger world of finance—shows the way in which Silicon Valley makes society global and hierarchical not only with tech services but also through capital. Embodying the future, the tech industry attracts capital from all over the world. But venture capitalists faithfully play the role of innovation gatekeepers, which is paradoxically reinforced as the investment chain extends.[27]

THE GUARDIANS OF INNOVATION

There is no global success in the tech industry without venture capitalists. However, they embody the antithesis of Silicon Valley in many ways. Entrepreneurs are often talkative or seductive, always smiling or in a hurry. VCs are quiet, calm, patient, and sound pretty conventional. Techies like T-shirts and hoodies. VCs wear jackets, slacks, dress shoes, white or salmon-colored shirts. Entrepreneurs scramble to secure their next round of funding. Investors weigh pros and cons, considering and comparing different variables before committing to a new deal. Waves of promising innovation are buoyed by the demographics of those in tech. Silicon Valley has a youthful face. The oldest venture capitalists are three times the age of mature companies such as Google or Facebook. Some investors still work as advisers into their eighties.

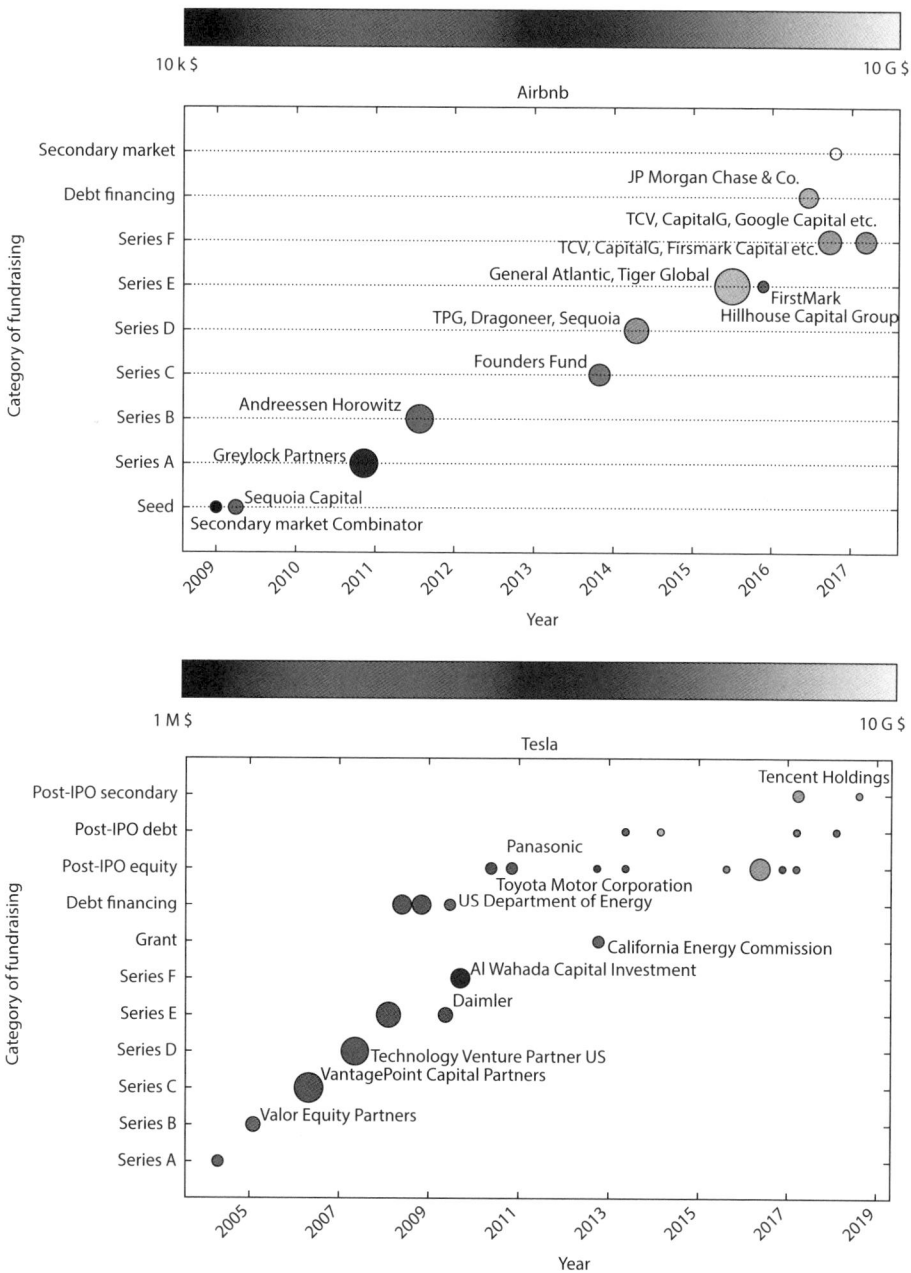

FIGURE 4. Structure and investment timelines in Silicon Valley: Airbnb and Tesla. *Source*: Data from Crunchbase. Visualization produced by Fabien Tarissan.

In addition, they are the custodians of Silicon Valley's memory. But their expression is limited by business secrecy.

The Discreet World of Venture Capital

For this research the most difficult population to get close to was that of VCs. My interview requests were often politely declined or cautiously accepted, following interviews conducted by assistants who scrupulously control questions and topics of the subsequent discussion. The scarcity of archives and the technicality of their language surround VC activity with mystery. Despite their importance, few surveys have been conducted on them, even if they are the nexus of finance, universities, Big Tech companies, tech talent networks, emergent markets, and so forth.[28] With this central position comes a constant flow of information, from different directions. This flow could be used to reduce the risks and uncertainties that come with innovation. Venture capitalists have to deal with versatile financial markets, big company inertia, high startup mortality rates, and innovation fads.

In one of the few books following a team of venture capitalists at the heart of the internet boom, historian Randall Stross described them as the financiers of "our future."[29] And he was right. According to a study on 531 nonpublic tech companies in the United States valued at more than $1 billion (unicorns)—309 in California—access to venture capital within a year of the company's creation was the main factor determining unicorn success.[30] In the mid-2000s, only 9 percent of new technology companies created in Silicon Valley received seed money from a venture capitalist. The weight of this variable on success may ascribe to VCs true entrepreneur status, using Schumpeter's model of "creative destruction," which holds that the new is built from the old by entrepreneurs who initiate productive combinations in the field of product, production, organization, technology, and the opening of a new market.[31] VCs select and shape entrepreneurs, teach them the collective know-how of the industry, integrate startups into the productive system, and give signals about the quality of companies and the merit of founders.[32] Nonetheless, describing them as a homogeneous population would be a pitfall. They do share the goal of "disrupting established research organizations and providing strong incentives for breakthroughs over other types of innovation."[33] But they don't do it the same way nor with equal success.

The National Venture Capital Association, founded in 1973 and headquartered in Washington, DC, reported 3,417 active VC firms in the country by the end of 2023, closing a cumulative 13,608 VC deals worth $170.6 billion.[34] If we cross-reference different figures circulating on the internet (such as on Quora, Wikipedia, LinkedIn, or Medium), the number of firms active in the region is between five hundred and one thousand. But the majority of newcomers and sometime experienced tech talent in Silicon Valley struggle to name more than a couple dozen. Venture capital firms vary greatly in their activity and recognition. The best-endowed ones operate with $1 billion to $2 billion, like Sequoia Capital (which has invested in Apple, Oracle, Cisco, Google, Facebook, YouTube, Airbnb, and Zappos), General Catalyst founded in 2000 (invested in Airbnb, Canva, Coda, Deliveroo, Snapchat), or Andreessen Horowitz (invested in Foursquare, Instagram, GitHub, Zynga, Skype, Slack). Others have to patiently play the microinvestment game before making a claim for access to larger rounds. In 2020 the average foundation date for the Silicon Valley–based venture capital firms was 2007.[35]

However, a majority with only one employee (called *solo entrepreneurs*) struggle to last more than a year. While the big names in venture capital are powerful decision-makers (i.e., *partners*), others are simply employees or are "entrepreneurs in residence" affiliated with a venture capital firm. The high-profile Andreessen Horowitz firm, also known as a16z, had more than 771,300 followers in 2024 on Twitter/X. Andreessen Horowitz employed more than five hundred people, with a variety of statuses: general partners, associates (partner), delegates, specialists, assistants, scouts, and so forth. Like a16z, other major companies have offices in New York, London, Tel Aviv, Hong Kong, or even in Silicon Valley itself, with split teams, the first historically based in Menlo Park and Palo Alto, and the second, younger and more software-oriented, based in San Francisco.

Despite this geographic dispersion, the quiet alley that is Sand Hill Road continues to concentrate and embody their prestige and power. Located on the hilltop overlooking Stanford's campus, this investment Olympus is the most expensive street per square foot in the country, ahead of Manhattan's Fifth Avenue. Although it is quite sparse, the entire world of technology entrepreneurship hopes to one day push the doors of one of the VC top twenty that are aligned there: Sequoia Capital, Kleiner Perkins, Andreessen Horowitz, Battery Ventures, Menlo Ventures, Draper Fisher Jurvetson, Greylock Partners, and others. This concentration in Stanford's vicinity as well as the growing presence of venture capital firms in San Francisco is significant: venture capitalists try to stay as close as possible to what they call the "deal flow." They want to see, talk to, and stay close to what they call "talent," keeping an eye on their "portfolio" and using their experience with their protégés to make their companies either fall on the right side of the profitability threshold or be ready for an acquisition or an IPO that translates into cash flow for them.

Beyond their privacy, investors are associated with grandeur: the importance of their stock market valuations, their location on the highest point of Menlo Park, and the larger-than-life statures of investors, like the dominant figures of Tim Draper, Marc Andreessen, Bill Gurley, and others. These investors are not famous beyond the tech industry, but they are the regions' main figures. Like big Hollywood producers, they intimidate, commanding fear and respect, a combination of feelings that is rare in the region and that only this small group inspires in entrepreneurs. And it's a world run by white men over fifty with a background in finance, consulting, entrepreneurship, and the world of technology. According to the first ever 2020 NVCA-Deloitte Human Capital Survey conducted by the Deloitte University Leadership Center for Inclusion, if women represent 45 percent of the total venture capital workforce, female investment partners or the equivalent on venture investment teams are only 11 percent. At the top of the firms are mostly white men. Nonwhite employees comprise 22 percent of the venture capital workforce, including 4 percent of Hispanic or Latino employees and 3 three percent of Black employees.

These VCs find themselves in the midst of a thriving economy, yet one that remains vulnerable to uncertainty. The first venture capital firm was established in the 1930s, but venture capital did not become an organized form of financing in the United States until the late 1970s. A change in federal legislation allowed pension funds, traditionally risk-averse, to invest in venture capital.[36] Indeed, while newcomers in Silicon Valley see them as moguls, VCs work with money raised from a network of partners, including rich people, pension funds, and institutional asset managers such as BlackRock. While many media and researchers have focused on the theoretical wealth of billionaires (which amounted to $14,500 billion at the start of 2025), this represents just 13 percent of global market capitalization. Since the 1970s, a silent capital revolution has been under way, leading to the formation and subsequent multiplication of vast collective savings schemes in the United States and in the rest of the world: pension funds, investment funds, life insurance plans, insurance policies, and so forth. Venture capitalists have benefited from this financial revolution, ensuring the link between capital and technological labor. In the 1990s the development of the internet came with a large influx of money, increasing the overall percentage of venture capital–backed startups. As Randall Stross described about the dot-com boom:

> It was easy for the financial world to fall in love with venture capital in the late 1990s: the average return in 1998 for venture capital funds that focused on early-stage startups was more than 25 percent, and the top funds had annual returns well over 100 percent. This was a world in which the investment criteria used by the venture capitalists themselves were calibrated not in percentages but in multiples, as in: *ten times our money*.[37]

The dot-com bust was followed by crisis and stagnation until the 2010s, which marked a clear recovery for venture capitalism. The amount of money invested rose from $10 billion in the wake of 2001 to nearly $95 billion twenty years later. During this period VC investments in Silicon Valley as a proportion of total US investment ranged from 30 to 50 percent.[38] And as management scholar Patricia Thornton reminds us, the VC model is based on "the assumption that investing in entrepreneurial companies, while carrying a higher risk, can offer higher returns than conventional investments."[39]

A Portfolio Mentality

Venture capitalists rely on a portfolio mechanism.[40] Until the Second World War the financing of technological promises was provided by banking and financial institutions as well as large fortunes: Morgans, Vanderbilts, Rockefellers, and Dupont de Nemours supported projects that they considered useful for the development and internationalization of their businesses, without expecting immediate profitability.[41] New technologies benefit marginally from this, finding support in universities and the research and development departments of large companies, as well as the army, state agencies, and public funding programs. The venture capital model took off in the aftermath of World War II, a development often attributed to the figure of Georges Doriot.

Born in Paris in 1899 and passing in Boston in 1987, Doriot's career was three-pronged: influential professor, pioneering venture capitalist, and architect of internationalization. He was the son of one of the founding partners of automobile manufacturer Doriot, Flandrin & Parant. His father sent him to the United States after World War I to study at MIT. There he developed an interest in the emerging discipline of management. In 1920 he enrolled in the

MBA program at Harvard University. He worked for a while in the investment bank Kuhn, Loeb, and Company, where he discovered the subtleties and mechanisms of the investment industry. He returned to Harvard Business School in 1926 as a professor, where he taught industrial management for forty years, with the exception of five years of service in the US Army during World War II. Gaining American citizenship in 1940, Doriot served as the Military Planning Division director for the Quarter Master General within the US Army. After the war he returned to his teaching position at Harvard. In 1946 he created the American Research and Development Corporation (ARD) with several political leaders, businessmen, and academics from the region.

The creation of this organization could be presented as the birth of venture capital. However, similar structures had appeared before or in conjunction with it. At the same time, MIT's former director, Karl Compton, created a company of the same type, intended for the financing of technological projects. Doriot's structure encountered many difficulties in its early days, but his "father of venture capitalism" nickname has stuck. It is valid to see him as this model's main theorist. Doriot laid down three principles. First, the money invested by ARD must come from fundraising with investors, independent or institutional, with no prior relationship or common interests either with each other or with the organization's founders. Second, the professor ensured he retained control over investment decisions, without interference from partners. Third, while Doriot's original idea was to encourage private investors to invest in military companies once the war ended, after a series of bad investments he decided to steer ARD toward financing young companies specializing in the technological and scientific fields. He planned to make ARD profitable within four years. It would take six years, with significant local support and investment.

In the mid-1950s two engineers by training, Ken Olsen and Karlan Anderson, worked on the TX-2 computer at MIT. Faced with technical difficulties, they decided to found their own company in order to devote themselves fully to the project, after working in various laboratories in the Boston area.[42] But investor reluctance made them give up their initial project. They opted for the development of small computer modules that were more easily marketable. In 1957, Doriot decided to invest $70,000 in the Digital Equipment Corporation (DEC) via the ARD, in exchange for seven hundred of the company's one thousand shares. The company became profitable and started to produce its computer, the PDP-1, in 1961. This was followed by other models, which were considered to be superior to IBM's machines in terms of quality and price. In 1964 the production of the PDP-8 (the first mini-computer) was a great commercial success. On this basis DEC's management planned an IPO, which was completed in 1968.

In nearly ten years, the $70,000 initially invested by Doriot yielded a return of $400 million, five thousand times the initial investment. Doriot emphasizes the importance of profit to support his model: a focus on longer-term but more promising returns. In fact, the returns on investment are higher than those of the Dow Jones, but in a limited way, and remain contingent on a big success: 14.7 against 12.8 for the Dow Jones. Without the presence of DEC, the rate of return falls to 7.4 percent.[43] Still, it disrupted the financial paradigm of innovation. This model takes the opposite view of political economist Jean-Baptiste Say's Law of Markets, which postulates the equilibrium of savings and investments through the interplay of interest rates, and which, according to John Kenneth Galbraith, was considered an act of faith in American business circles for more than a hundred years.[44] In this model the economic rationality of capital relies on extending time horizons, with the anticipated benefit being higher returns. This approach is especially suitable for financing technological assets due to the uncertainty surrounding their success and the length of their development cycles. But, to work, venture capitalism needs "breakthroughs."[45]

Pursuing Breakthroughs

Doriot praised the merits of the VC model to several generations of students. At a time when Harvard and the MBA were the undisputed leaders in the country's graduate system, he taught a course known for its difficulty but nonetheless popular with students, called "Manufacturing." Despite its title, the course neglected the topics of factory organization or production methods, focusing instead on the entrepreneurial mind-set and how to build one's own success. Moving away from the case studies that dominate business school methodology, Doriot conducted his courses in the "French style," using lectures to explore how to analyze a sector, a company, and potential collaborators. He emphasized the importance of paying attention to details such as clothing, speech, and behavior in interactions. By the time he retired in 1966, after founding INSEAD in the Paris area on the Harvard MBA model, nearly seven thousand students had taken his course.[46]

Two former students became particularly famous in Silicon Valley: Don Valentine and Thomas J. Perkins. Valentine cofounded Sequoia Capital in

1972 and soon after made an investment in Apple. Perkins was an executive at Hewlett-Packard when he left the company to cofound a venture capital firm, Kleiner Perkins. He went through several stressful years before making a substantial return on the investment in the early 1980s with Sun Microsystems and Lotus Development. Despite the rivalry between Valentine and Perkins, they made a joint investment in Google in June 1999, at the initiative of microinvestor Ron Conway, for 5 percent of the company's shares. This investment would have earned the two firms' thirty-one partners an average of $7 million after Google's IPO in 2004.[47]

The great successes of Silicon Valley were built on this venture capitalism model. VCs are funded by a pool of third-party investors and build portfolios that are often unspecialized in new technologies. They aim for returns on investment over nearly five years, driven by the potential for "breakthroughs." Indeed, the touchstone of this system is a "breakthrough"—that is, financial success through an IPO allowing the resale of the company's shares. An investor sums up this arithmetic logic:

> For us here, out of ten investments, five companies lose, three or four break even, and one booms. In the last fund, we only lost money twice, made a modest profit five or six times, and four times, a more substantial profit. When you make an investment, you have to be able to convince your partners that you have a reasonable chance of a tenfold return. If there's a small market, it is not possible. So there being a big market is the necessary condition (interview, Palo Alto, October 22, 2016).

In this model, investors push players to "think big or go home."[48] An entrepreneur reflects on the sometimes necessary mind-set adjustment for individuals coming from countries or social backgrounds where modesty is highly valued:

> I'm from France, but I've totally immersed myself in the mentality here, thinking *big*, I believe in it more and more. You have to really believe in your project and when you really believe in it, you can move mountains. Before, I used to say to myself: *I only have a 5 percent chance of succeeding*. I had to completely change my mentality: I aim very high and I hold on to that (interview, San Francisco, December 12, 2015).

In this configuration multimillion-dollar buyouts and IPOs are an industrial purpose for venture capitalists, who own 15 to 40 percent of the company.

To make such a "breakthrough," venture capitalists mobilize their know-how. Indeed, while some may claim that they are visionaries, they claim to have forged expertise over the years. When they invest, it is not only a question of making a commitment but also of providing advice on recruitment, strategy, communication, sometimes energy, and support. Activating their network is a crucial aspect of their work, guiding them to seasoned professionals not only in technical fields but also in areas often less mastered by entrepreneurs, such as financial management, legal advice, and sales. They introduce entrepreneurs to potential suppliers, industrialists, and potential commercial partners likely to develop market opportunities, including financial intermediaries in the case of a stock market listing. This follow-up can go as far as replacing the management team, as in the case of Eric Schmidt, who became CEO of Google in 1999, replacing Larry Page. Investors wanted a more experienced manager than the two young computer scientists, Page and cofounder Sergey Brin. It's only a short step from there to consider VCs as the real entrepreneurs. After all, behind every great success there are VCs behind the scenes: Valentine for Apple, Perkins for Sun Microsystem, Peter Thiel for Facebook, John Doer for Google, and others.

But venture capital is not just about success or celebrities. Many venture capitalists make what one venture capitalist calls "active financing" claims:

> We've been here [Palo Alto University] for fifteen years. If entrepreneurs want to get active funding from people who are going to help them build a company, they know where to find us. And active funding, generally, is not so much about technology. It's more about reviewing the go to market, pricing strategy, packaging, etc. Entrepreneurs often don't have a complete understanding of the field and the competition. We've been seeing a thousand companies a year for the past fifteen years, so we have a good understanding of what's going on (interview, Menlo Park, September 11, 2017).

Every entrepreneur-VC relationship in Silicon Valley relies on a "deal." This emblematic concept of Silicon Valley designates the contractual act by which a sum of money is exchanged for shares in the financed company and a place on the company's management board. This contract opens up a set of reciprocal expectations. As one investor puts it:

> The classic model here is *ABC rounds*. Which is a specific mentality that allows entrepreneurs to get bigger and bigger. But that's not followed in the rest of the world. If you're a startup and you get your first funding, you're going to get money, but you're also going to get a lot of signals and information that will get you to the next round; if you screw up, you're out. But you're lucky enough to be told what to fix; therefore, the ABC model is about help-

ing entrepreneurs grow from one funding round to the next (interview, San Francisco, September 11, 2017).

This collaboration proceeds from a convergence of interests but also exposes the expression of divergent expectations. Entrepreneurs want their company to develop properly, while investors aim for breakthroughs. In this scenario entrepreneurs operate as production factors as well as speculative capital. However, VCs access what the Austrian economist Rudolf Hilferding, who lived at the crossroads of the nineteenth and twentieth centuries, called the "founder's profits."[49]

Hilferding built his analyses of capitalism on Marx's theories. He tried to shed light on financial dynamics in the economy. He especially wanted to explain the fundamental trend toward replacing sole proprietorships with joint-stock companies. According to Hilferding, with the latter, capitalists double their power. Indeed, they only need to conserve half their capital to retain full control of companies. With the capital they've saved (and replaced by the sale of shares to third parties), they can find subsidiaries using the same process. So possession of a third or even a quarter of a company's capital is enough to guarantee its total control. In this new configuration small shareholders have the illusion of sharing ownership of the joint-stock company and participating in its management. But the capitalists are those sitting in the driver's seat. In Silicon Valley, VCs get this benefit. A seasoned investor states: "On my desk, I have a statuette: two pigs with a farmer. I named them Victor and Charles. Same initials as venture capitalist. Between the two, the happy idiot. I'm the Silicon Valley idiot."[50]

The asymmetric role in the relationship between VC and entrepreneurs structurally fuels misunderstandings and frustrations for both parties. The often-used metaphor of "wedding" to describe it hints at the potential for disagreements, which players rationalize and reduce through binary categories of understanding, separating "good" and "bad" or "real" and "fake" entrepreneurs, investors, companies, and so forth. An eighteen-year-old entrepreneur-developer describes some of the frictions:

> It's easy to see if an investor knows their place. The bad ones feel superior because they have a lot of money to invest and talk to you like crap. They send you emails, talk to you like spammers. It's like: *Use our solution for $150 a month.* I'm exaggerating, but in the spirit, it's: *Go ahead, sign up!* So you don't answer because the email is badly written, in a passive-aggressive way. And then, after a day, they call you back, saying: *You didn't answer?!* And then it's:

You know we're a $2 billion fund, we've invested in blah, blah, blah, blah. And they show their roster. That's a really poor relationship. . . . We're often told here that your investor has to be a little bit like your wife. Okay. Well, I don't want my relationship with my wife to be like that (interview, San Francisco, July 27, 2016).

A seasoned investor is even harsher about this system:

VCs take advantage of people who don't have wealthy family, wealthy friends, or a large enough network. They basically take half your wealth. It's not a bank asking you to pay back at a discounted rate. You see all these kids come in who don't have a big bank account or an old-boy network. YC Combinator makes money that way. And VC means learning how to do deals, anticipate taxes, go to meetups. . . . That's the beauty of Silicon Valley: you can network from scratch. But you have to do the whole circus of meetups, events, becoming a brand, going to startup weekends, workshops, meeting what's-his-name from Google, meeting what's-his-name from Apple, every week, growing your network by five hundred people. . . . Who on earth does that? When boutique VCs look at the returns, they see that entrepreneurs who are over forty are more profitable. With my friends, we don't need that, we do business together, we just need to sit at a table, we don't need to pay a fortune to my lawyer. . . . But it's hard to have a network like that when you're just out of college (interview with an entrepreneur-investor, San Francisco, February 4, 2021).

If this relationship is so frustrating, it's because venture capitalists aim to accommodate both capital and labor. Indeed, VCs' playbook is multilevel.

In addition to entrepreneurs, they need to find, enroll, and report to limited partners, who have their own timetable. In fact, their capital comes from sources other than their own funds: pension funds made up of employee savings, private investment funds, public agencies or programs, sovereign wealth funds, or large fortunes seeking to diversify their assets. The funded pension system in the United States explains why the California Public Employees' Retirement System (CalPERS) and the California State Teachers' Retirement System (CalSTRS) are two historical sources of funding for Silicon Valley venture capitalists:

Most of the closing in venture capital here comes from sovereign wealth funds, investment funds, some of it comes from insurance, some of it comes from wealth management companies, and that sort of thing. That's the bulk of institutional funding. Wall Street doesn't come into play until the IPO. The Californian Public Employee System [CalPERS, with $360 billion invested] and CalSTRS [California Teachers' Pension Fund, the eleventh largest pension fund in the world with a portfolio of nearly $224 billion] are among the top two limited partners (interview with an investor, Palo Alto, June 2016).

Plus, investors have to respect funding cycles, which have a short horizon. As one San Francisco investor explains, "As a venture capitalist, you're always looking at the future. No one can tell you if you're right or wrong about the future. All you can do is make a bet. But for me, I have to make ends meet for next year. Some of us wonder about the next five years. . . . But no longer."[51] The VC horizon is thus woven with several timelines and constant conjectures. Stress comes from the intermediary role of venture capitalists ensuring the coherence of three agendas: their own, the entrepreneurs', and the partners'. This triple-layered agenda guarantees a minimum of economic rationality to the business.

VCs therefore play the role of gatekeepers on three levels: people, capital, and technological markets. VCs operate as points of contact placed as close as possible to innovation in progress, committing funds belonging totally or partially to others. In this way VCs are like Hollywood producers, and Silicon Valley is similar to the organization of cultural and creative industries, where the high degree of uncertainty weighing on production chains is compensated by three types of strategies: the deployment of intermediaries at the margins of powerful production organizations, overproduction, and the differentiated promotion of new products.[52] In the tech industry venture capitalists thus act as intermediaries. Overproduction strategies have to compensate for the high mortality rate of organizations. And startups are worthwhile as novelties to be promoted and developed. The professional trajectory of venture capitalists reflects their hyphenated condition, as VCs are most often converted to investment after a stint in the new technology sector (former founders or employees of a technology company).[53]

The questions of overall value creation, social utility, or the economic efficiency of this system take a backseat when pursuing breakthroughs. In this sense they are the bridges between the technological past and future, labor and capital, investment opportunities and those yet to be picked. The quality of interactions between players means more or less access to information, capital, and talent. Socially and culturally, this is why Silicon Valley seems both inclusive and selective, open and closed.

THREE

——————

Making Culture a Universal Variable

Discussion between two men, thirties, wearing T-shirts, sitting
side by side on the Caltrain (the commuter rail line that serves
the San Francisco Peninsula). One says to the other: "A lot of the
talks about the Valley have common cultural traits and it pushes
you to adopt them."

—FIELD NOTES, June 7, 2016

*TECHIES, TECH WORKERS, IT GUYS, makers, doers, builders, dreamers,
trailblazers*—there is no shortage of designations for the *vectorialist class* or
the *coding elite* within the *tech community, tech industry, tech ecosystem.*[1] For
all the similarities among the techie elite, however, Silicon Valley's population
remains diverse, from different perspectives: ancestry, profession, gender, age,
beliefs, standard of living, racialization, and so forth. Half of the workers in
new technologies were born in another country. Entrepreneurs work daily
with investors, lawyers, accountants, data analysts, designers, developers,
product managers, salespeople, communicators, service workers, and others.
The list is almost endless, because it is constantly evolving. At tech conferences billionaires cross paths with people living below the poverty threshold.[2]
Unicorn founders who frequently attend institutions like Stanford, Berkeley,
and Harvard are joined by engineers, developers, and designers who have
graduated from foreign schools and universities and have varying levels of
training and degrees. Such diversity should lead to fragmentation and
babelism, considering the absence of a common language and culture.

But instead, there is a strong element of social stability. As sociologist of
organizational behavior Arthur Stinchcombe explained, socialization has a
stabilizing influence in common organizations: "If new organizational elites
are socialized into an elite culture, by attending academic schools with other
elite members, by participating in parliaments, by common ideological indoc-
trination in a dominant political party, they are more likely to accept common
norms governing competition for organizational wealth, prestige, and power."[3]
In the case of Silicon Valley, disparities in background, education, nationality,

78

and activities should lead to a differentiation of norms, endless quarrels over values, and a form of ambient social chaos. Yet numerous books, courses, conferences, and online publications extol the "Silicon Valley culture." Those I interviewed emphasize its coherence and homogeneity. This chapter explores the roots of this culture, highlighting how it has been historically constructed within the region, and how embedded professionals produce and disseminate a set of conventions and principles to increase the volume of opportunities.

THE CULTURES OF SILICON VALLEY

If there is one place on the planet where new technology is second nature, it's Silicon Valley.[4] In an informal discussion a Stanford professor says, "Technology here isn't even really an object. It's just something like [she holds up her hands and waves her fingers] . . . the air." Those I interviewed report that in Silicon Valley there is a shared interest in new technologies and a belief in their beneficial potential. This is reflected in the daily monitoring of the latest solutions, but it is also reflected in the all-out practice of objectification, measurement, and quantification. Techies keep an almost constant eye on the tables and dashboards that summarize in real time the activity that reports performance. These activity reports on tech solutions follow trends, develop models, and collect data based on a series of indicators, which they also produce, organize, and analyze. If techies claim to be objectivists—a philosophy that posits reality is objective, that it exists before its observation "just as the North Star existed long before all astronomers," and that human beings perceive reality through objective observation—they do so without acknowledging they are actually acting out and transforming these "observations."

Computer science, psychology, and economics share the characteristic of being both empirical and nomological, stating universally applicable laws based on this objectivist illusion. Techies and others make their so-called objective observations through the use of statistical apparatus and, while statistics themselves are neutral, they are also socially oriented and constructed. Thus such observations introduce political and moral elements to data.[5] Research from the Brookings Institute notes that "substantial socioeconomic harm" can result from Machine Learning "through failures in fairness," for example.[6] Some people, therefore, see the rising field of Fairness in Machine Learning (FairML) as a good example that techies are coming to understand that politics inform statistics. Nevertheless, a taboo on constructivist thinking—that is, that human beings construct knowledge—seems to carry undue weight in Silicon Valley, relegating history, sociology, and anthropology to a secondary status in the scale of knowledge. For example, historian Randall Stross has shown that Stanford humanities graduates, despite their ability to adapt to the business world, found themselves devalued in terms of salary in comparison with engineers, whose profile and status remain higher within Silicon Valley's larger companies.[7]

Techies crave great universalizing narratives—arguments that illuminate the entire mystery and history of the world—like those proposed by Nicholas Negroponte,[8] Chris Anderson,[9] Nassim Nicholas Taleb,[10] or Yuval Noah Harari.[11] Despite this taste for objectivity and uniqueness, the history of Silicon Valley culture has different roots. Three lineages can be identified from this perspective, each based on a relationship between culture and a secondary concept: culture and action; culture and freedom; and culture and communication.

Makers: The Art of Doing

In many places around the world culture is related to art and cultural industries. But in Silicon Valley, culture has rarely been associated with these industries. Unlike New York with theater, publishing, and journalism, or Los Angeles with film and television, or Miami with music, Silicon Valley has not historically been identified with a specific cultural field. On the contrary, since the end of the 1990s it has been presented as the source of an economic crisis in the creative sectors. Several interviewees pointed out the weakness of the region's artistic offerings, which put it far from the cultural standards of London, Los Angeles, New York, Paris, or Shanghai (Table 4).

But for techies, this is an asset. As one AI entrepreneur-AI researcher told me:

> If you live in New York, which is an incredible city, the tech industry is just one sector among many. Here, it's all about tech. There's an incredible concentration of people working in the field. You always end up at a party, in a big house, chatting with some weird guy, who's walking around barefoot, and you find out that he's the owner and has a very high position at Google (interview, San Francisco, October 9, 2024).

To understand this entrepreneur's enthusiasm for the place, it is important to get back to another meaning of the term *art*, aligning with what ancient

TABLE 4. Global cities' cultural scenes (2017–2018)

Cities	Movie Theaters	Bookstores	Art Galleries
Austin	181	45	112
London	911	360	478
Los Angeles	1073	474	279
New York	374	814	1475
Paris	1107	1251	1142
San Francisco	38	77	98
Shanghai	767	3800	770
Toronto	32	365	433
Sydney	377	258	170

SOURCE: According to data from World Culture Cities Forum.

philosophers referred to as *technè*, from the Greek word for *art* or *skill* and meaning "practical knowledge." But for techies the issue is not *about* technical objects; it's about *doing* them. This mentality is close to what French sociologist Michel de Certeau called the "arts of doing."[12] Groups of amateurs ("hobbyists") were tinkering with radio equipment as early as the 1910s. Between 1944 and 1950 three quarters of all computer models were developed by users.[13] Robert Noyce, cofounder of Intel, was recognized as a child for his early skills as an inventor or, in the vernacular of the Valley, a *maker*. In 1968, Donald Knuth published a book (*The Art of Computer Programming*) that became the computer science bible for many generations, just before joining Stanford for the rest of his long career. Steve Jobs attended Homebrew Computer Club meetings, a circle of passionate amateurs, where he presented the Apple 1 in 1976, designed with Steve Wozniak and Ronald Wayne.

In 1978 several makers, including Apple employees, founded the Survival Research Laboratory (SRL), for building giant machines for the only purpose of demonstrations, performances, and fun. Many hacker and maker spaces are active in the region, starting with Noisebridge in San Francisco.[14] Their members claim to be part of a *do-ocracy*, meaning a democracy by doing. In this do-ocracy each participant is expected to "make" technical objects in the form of collective and participatory projects. The Burning Man festival presented itself in the same way during the late 1990s. Its founding members defined it as an "arts community" and a federation of makers.[15] If creativity is a key element in the life of these collectives, legitimacy and social status are largely based on technical virtuosity and mastery. Multiple connections and intersections exist between makers and Silicon Valley companies, all of which are linked to values of independence and freedom in the workplace.

Freedom at Work

In the 1990s the "new economy" was characterized by a focus on projects, creativity, open collaboration, networks, and initiative-taking. These principles and values were aimed at overcoming three of the main contradictions of capitalism—a system that promises to everybody freedom, individual enrichment, and global growth, but that causes disenchantment, exploitation, and alienation. Indeed, at the beginning of the twentieth century, Max Weber considered that capitalism had no other purpose and meaning than the accumulation of money for its own sake, which by definition takes as profit the surplus value of work resulting in the exploitation and alienation of workers.[16] This he defined as a social organization without transcendence, doomed to collide with the steel cage of pure reason and calculation. Those I interviewed often expressed a certain weariness with Silicon Valley, a world where everything is transactional and subject to opportunistic exchange. However, many interviewees also described their journey in the Valley as extremely transformative and, even, a philosophical experience.

During the 1960s sociologist Daniel Bell observed that the development of cultural industries and leisure time had compensated for the loss of meaning in capitalism. But he worried that the rise of leisure societies would threaten people's ability to get work and stay employed.[17] In Silicon Valley work is an obsession. "Work hard, but play harder" is one of its mottos. It's common to meet entrepreneurs or programmers who sleep only four or five hours a night to devote themselves to their projects. Pictures of Twitter/X employees sleeping under their desks just after Elon Musk took over the company are a symbol of this religion of work.[18] But leisure is never far away. Startup foosball, the big red slide at YouTube's headquarters, or the beach volley ball court in the center of the Googleplex are not just empty promises.

In the mid-1990s two French sociologists, Luc Boltanski and Eve Chiapello, examined the question of capitalism's survival.[19] They questioned its ability to overcome the deep economic crises and social protests of the 1970s. Logically, capitalism should have collapsed or been profoundly transformed at the time. Yet it has thrived since then. To Boltanski and Chiapello, the explanation lies in the evolution of work organization. From this period on, the service sector grew dramatically, with more and more jobs in communication, advertisement, cultural industries, and so forth. This transition is embodied by the iconic hero Don Draper of the drama series *Mad Men*, who left his job as a fur salesman to work for a prestigious advertising agency. In a digitalized economy, work is organized around projects, creative inputs, networking, and a blending of leisure time with work time, along with the individualization of career paths. In this economy it is no longer merely a matter of exploitation but of succeeding through personal projects and enjoying work to the fullest. In many ways the tech economy represents the most direct extension of this new form of capitalism. In the early 2000s sociologist Andrew Ross described the companies in New York's Silicon Alley as places that were "non-conformist in their organization and liberal in their culture."[20]

Employees were encouraged to think outside the box, to assert their convictions and ideas, even the oddest of them. This organization of work is directly linked to the development of networks and communication services. It would accompany the rise of an economy considered as open, with almost unlimited potential. The paradox is that this culture spread from urbanized organizations and spaces, which concentrated the decision-making population. Entrepreneurs, investors, developers, and engineers have increased the number of semiopen meetups dedicated to networking.[21] There, interactions follow particular codes, and respecting those codes grants individuals access to crucial resources, such as information and talent. In an industry where workers are called upon to be entrepreneurial and independent, even when they are employees of large companies, these spaces are emblematic and decisive places for the evolution of projects and career paths. They require a sense of communication, a theme that is in line with the third tradition.

Communication System

To better understand how culture is identified with interactions in Northern California, it is necessary to take a detour through communication theory, starting with one of its main figures, Norbert Wiener. Even though Wiener spent most of his career at MIT, he has influenced several generations of Silicon Valley technologists. Published in 1948, his book *Cybernetics: Or Control and Communication in the Animal and the Machine* critiqued the information theories of information science pioneers Ralph Hartley, Claude Shannon, and Warren Weaver. These early thinkers examined the flow of information from sender to receiver. Wiener proposed an alternative theory of signals circulating in communication systems. According to him, the amount of information accessible in a system shows its degree of organization. The higher this level, the more efficient the system is. Wiener's ambition was to develop a general theory of information systems. In his eyes the development of better communication systems could prevent a new world war catastrophe.

This thesis finds ramifications in the fields of computer science, biology, and in the group of theorists known as the Palo Alto School. Also called the "invisible college," the Palo Alto School brought together thinkers such as Ray Birdwhistell, Gregory Bateson, anthropologist Edward Hall, sociologist Erving Goffman, psychologist Paul Watzlawick, and others. Indeed, Hall, Goffman, and Watzlawick were some of the most influential social scientists of their time. They developed a series of hypotheses based on Wiener's retroactive circular model. For them, communication had to be studied according to a systemic and multidisciplinary approach open to linguistics and logic. This approach allowed scholars to better understand, describe, and theorize interaction systems. From this perspective communication is equivalent to an information system constantly fed by human behavior. Attention to the horizontal and vertical interaction contexts reveals a logic. This orientation has found concrete applications in Silicon Valley, through several entry points and at different periods of its history.

Stanford professor Adrian Daub points to the Esalen Institute in Big Sur, founded by Dick Price "as a counter-cultural rebellion against mainstream psychology and organised religion"[22] to create a "religion without religion."[23] Price regularly invited theorists such as Gregory Bateson, anthropologist and theorist of the "ecology of mind," the German psychotherapist Fritz Perls, father of Gestalt therapy, and Brave New World philosopher Aldous Huxley to discuss his research on drugs and ways of pushing the limits of consciousness. Their discussions were the starting point of the Human Potential Movement, based on the idea that the development of each individual's potential is a path to a happy existence that includes an abundance of creativity and personal fulfillment. The Esalen Institute became a retreat center for wealthy techies seeking to reconnect with life in the 2010s. The people who connected there were also behind Stanford's d.school, "where people use design to develop their own creative potential and make positive change" (founded in 2005 by David Kelley, CEO of IDEO, after the first program was launched in 2004).[24] The program has become one of the most highly sought-after academic programs at Stanford, nurturing the future of product design, public policy, and medicine. In a loft-like building where almost everything is modular, nearly seven hundred students attend each year to learn how to place the user at the heart of the creation process, all while keeping costs low. Big Tech employees attended the program, helping them to implement design thinking to the app economy in the 2010s.[25]

This lineage, here schematically and partially exposed, illustrates how in Silicon Valley, tech is not second nature but something constructed. This construction is based on three foundations: doing, working, and communicating. These three elements are the breeding ground for innovation, localized but with a global claim.

A SO-CALLED OPEN SOCIETY

A Variable of Hospitality

In 2018, 40,185 and 11,811 workers arrived in Silicon Valley—in Santa Clara and San Mateo Counties, respectively—to work in private sector technology jobs. Arriving from the rest of California, other states, and foreign countries, especially Taiwan, India, and Europe, these transplants typically ranged in age from twenty-five to forty-four years old.[26] Silicon Valley's diversity is often contrasted with the lack of diversity in China's technology districts, noting that Silicon Valley's diversity includes mostly Asian transplants (Table 5). Many young people come to study and find their first jobs in long-standing communities. Their presence has grown steadily over the 2010s. In contrast, there are few representatives of Hispanic and African American populations in the tech industry. Decision-making positions remain frequently occupied by the white population. According to the 2024 Silicon Valley Index, the region "is attracting more tech talent in the core working age group than other top US tech centers, especially among those already residing in California. Combined with San Francisco, more than 64,000 employed, college-educated adults in technical occupations relocated to the region in 2022, with 68 percent relocating from within the state."

TABLE 5. Talent recruited into the new technology sector in the main working
age group (25–44 years), by ancestry

Santa Clara and San Mateo Counties, 2018	
Asian (including Indians, Chinese, and Southeast Asians)	67%
White (including Hispanic)	30%
More than two ancestries	2.0%
Other ancestry	0.9%
Black or African American	0.4%

SOURCE: Silicon Valley Institute for Regional Studies.

This influx is part of a Northern California tradition marked by migratory movements that began with the gold rush of the mid-nineteenth century. Those I interviewed frequently celebrated this welcoming culture. One female entrepreneur I interviewed described the welcome as "really nice":

> I live in Palo Alto. It's a place that's used to welcoming people. New people are really welcomed. . . . Neighbors come over with a plate of cookies, they block off the street on Sundays for everyone to meet. My daughter at Palo Alto Public High School painted with the local kids, they reserved a table to eat with her. . . . It's really nice (interview, Palo Alto, September 16, 2016).

Working in an extremely competitive professional environment leads them to overinvest in their careers, while their age and life circumstances drive them to seek friends and romantic partners. This is particularly relevant in a region that attracts many young newcomers and has the highest divorce rates in the country. This dynamic was illustrated by the most popular groups on the social network site Meetup in 2022: "20 & 30-something friends and fun in SF" with over 19,465 members; "New to SF/Bay area" with 9,312 members; "SF Area Young, Wild and Free Singles" with over 5,000 members.[27]

Silicon Valley appears to be a cosmopolitan and tolerant space. The prevailing sentiment is one of being part of one community. This sense of belonging is rooted in shared industry connections, international backgrounds, tolerance for extravagant ideas, and a search for new collaborations. The industry offers entry points and ways to socialize, notably through meetups organized at the end of each day throughout the region, with San Francisco and Palo Alto as the main meeting places. These meetups are listed on specialized websites and are physically accessible with a free online registration or for a few dollars (prices charged during my research ranged from ten to eighty dollars). An entrepreneur coming from Europe testifies:

> When I arrived, it was even cooler than I thought, I had contacted entrepreneurs, everyone welcomed me with open arms, TechCrunch was already a thing, as soon as there were people of my country, I contacted them, and they replied to me: *Let's have a coffee*. They told me that life here was cool, that it was easy to network and get in touch with the right people. They told me: *You can be out every night*. Then they gave me a lot of tips, about school because I had my six-year-old daughter, health.... All the things you underestimate when you're not from here. For me, coming from Europe, it was completely new, there were no meetups over there, just competitors (interview, San Francisco, October 8, 2015).

Some respondents mentioned or expressed signs of xenophobia, underlining the difficulties of working or being neighbors with people from other countries. Others told me they debate time to time, "on the basis of scientific arguments," about the inferiority of women's performances at work over men's. But workers who have experienced religious or gender discrimination in other states or countries highlight the open-minded mentality in Silicon Valley, as one former manager in Big Tech told me:

> Here, it is very easy to be a foreigner. They don't care what color your passport is, they don't care what color your skin is. It is easier to be Black or Muslim here than in London or Paris; it is easier to be gay than in the rest of the country. Tolerance is sometimes even a little rigid in its implementation. (interview, Palo Alto, August 27, 2017).

Even though support for Donald Trump in 2024 showed cyberlibertarian influence, libertarians have historically been a minority in the region.[28] The values of openness and empathy had been defended and promoted. Internally, Google highlighted studies revealing the improved productivity of teams with a higher proportion of women and minority workers. Entrepreneurs in new technologies who come from Europe, India, or China, knowing what authoritarian regimes mean, frequently defend values of progress, contrasting with the conservative orientations of more established elites (such as those in the energy, construction, textile, and similar sectors).[29] During many years diversity, equity, and inclusion (DEI) initiatives were developed in such companies as Google, Facebook, Apple, and Microsoft to avoid discrimination based on race, gender, sexual orientation, or disability.

In 2016 the election of Donald Trump was the source of a moral shock for Silicon Valley. The MeToo movement had resulted in a wave of layoffs at

Uber. In 2018 the Google Walkouts demanded equal pay for men and women. The Tech Workers Coalition organized climate actions in 2019. Employees of Amazon, Microsoft, and Alphabet mobilized against their companies' military programs and collaboration with the Israeli army, on several occasions from the late 2010s until 2024.

Since the reelection of Trump in 2024, several leaders of major companies who had cultivated the values of openness, progressivism, and inclusion have put an end to DEI initiatives. Silence seemed to prevail in Silicon Valley after the presidential election, at least on the surface. Some LGBTQ+ employees have expressed their dissatisfaction internally and sometimes even resigned. This movement is not public, for several reasons: lay-off pressure (Meta cut its workforce by a further 5 percent in January 2025), management (CEO of Alphabet S. Pichai asked Google employees not to talk politics at work before the election), moderation (internal content moderators have since been deleting political messages and suspending access to newsgroups for those who break the rules), and so forth. The noisy and influential libertarian figures such as Elon Musk, Peter Thiel, or Keith Rabois make people forget that they are a minority in Silicon Valley and that they themselves have targeted the latter for its "so-called wokism," preferring to live in Florida, South California, and Texas. In 2024 more Silicon Valley billionaires backed Kamala Harris than Donald Trump. The same applies to the electorate of the three Silicon Valley counties.

SILICON VALLEY VALUES

Since the end of the nineteenth century, Silicon Valley has oscillated between conservatism and progressivism, pacifism and warmongering, war and peace. But since the beginning of the 1990s, thanks to the election of Bill Clinton and the development of the internet, it has been most often associated with progress for different reasons. First, considering work organization, it's true to point out the historical "disdain for hierarchical communication models."[30] Its work culture is horizontal and collaborative, unlike the vertical and hierarchical work structures on the East Coast. Access to management positions is also different. In Silicon Valley individuals with modest backgrounds can rise thanks to hard work and opportunities, whereas birth privilege—validated and consolidated by serial and selective access to preschools and Ivy League campuses—opens doors to management positions in large corporations and consulting firms for East Coast executives.[31] Silicon Valley, however, benefited from an early migration to the West, for some as early as the beginning of the nineteenth century, that allowed immigrants to form a new elite type, one that was attracted to and characterized by novelty. Two poles thus oppose "outsiders" and "insiders," the "social genius" to social heritage.[32]

Success in Silicon Valley is not based on control of administration, mastery of good manners, or the transmission of economic capital from family to family. Entrepreneurs in the region often express a sense of disconnect or even opposition to institutions, viewing the creation of a company as a way to break free from the inertia of both public and private bureaucracies.[33] Historian Fred Turner has shown that this distrust of institutions is historically consistent with the counterculture of the late 1960s, and among Northern California technologists this distrust is displayed through a focus on the emancipatory potential of new technologies (rather than New Left and/or campus protests).[34] This countercultural orientation contrasts sharply with the student clubs, corporate organizations, and political parties of an East Coast "establishment" represented by the interests of a culturally homogeneous elite.[35]

While attendance at selective private institutions has enabled the great families of the East Coast to secure access to the highest positions in the political and economic world, in most of Silicon Valley entrepreneurs do not come from "great families," nor do they make their careers within institutions. They often claim to be independent-minded thinkers and innovators known for their cosmopolitanism, even their atheism. In 2019, 35 percent of the adult population in Silicon Valley said they are "nonreligious," compared to 26 percent in the rest of the country.[36] Juxtapose this freethinking Silicon Valley attitude against Wall Street or Boston, for example, where the Episcopal Church has been a reference point for values and socialization. This is even truer for countries with nondemocratic regimes, as one entrepreneur told me:

> I come from [a Middle East country]. I have worked there, in England, Japan, Canada, and the United States. I've never found what exists in Silicon Valley. What makes it impossible to duplicate elsewhere: culture. Here, I was able to meet people I admired in my field. A simple email or an invitation at a barbecue and boom, I was at Stanford or Berkeley, talking with giants in the field, but with no ego, judging you only on your ideas. You won't find this openness and freedom elsewhere, especially in [my country]. The [authoritarian and religious] regime there was even one of the reasons why I got involved in AI in the first place: to show that it wasn't God behind creation, but that human beings could create (interview, Berkeley, September 11, 2024).

However, being less religious than the rest of the country has not prevented the expression of a work ethic, focused on performance and demands.

More broadly, lifestyles and purchasing habits are quite distinct from those of both East Coast high society and the nouveau riche of Gulf countries in the Middle East.[37] In Silicon Valley barbecues are the ritualized social form of Sunday get-togethers. As an interviewee who advises several governments on AI matter told me, evoking the Valley's combination of high-level expertise and laid-back culture: "Here, you're turning a sausage while talking about quantum physics." I observed the same irony for networking sessions, with sometimes very technical and advanced presentations with access that is either free or subject to a charge of ten or twenty dollars. Beer, pizza, and packaged raw vegetables from nearby supermarkets are served in self-service containers alongside paper plates and napkins. When it comes to business meetings and lunches, salad, pizza, and ramen make up the bulk of the menu, and this is what is also on the menus at the restaurants in Palo Alto, Mountain View, and San Francisco frequented by young entrepreneurs, including some of the most prominent. For example, Theranos founder Elizabeth Holmes, before being convicted of fraud, was a regular at Coupa Cafe, where patrons could get certified fair-trade coffee along with organic food from nearby family farms. The casual family-run bistro was founded in Palo Alto in 2004.[38]

As with many local spots, the menus offered here are far from sophisticated and cost the same as admission to the movies or a train ticket between the south and north of the Valley. In Palo Alto and Menlo Park, where many of the world's leading investors are concentrated, the single-story houses and their standard-sized garages and gardens are architecturally homogeneous with long, low open plans close to Frank Lloyd Wright's modernist housing aesthetic. These postwar houses were most often built on former farmland to accommodate professionals attracted by the region's job market and growth opportunities. Given the cost of living, one Google employee living with a partner declared that he couldn't afford furniture for up to a year after buying his house.[39] For the same reason, furniture for new arrivals, particularly those from abroad, is purchased from supermarkets or bought secondhand to meet the most urgent needs.

The resulting not ostentatious ethos is expressed through the tech uniform: T-shirts, hoodies, and sneakers. This self-consciously antistyle attire is the norm among new technology workers, including top executives. In November 2023, Sam Altman presented OpenAI's latest innovations during a "dev day," a demo event showcasing new applications to developers, data analysts, and designers.

To promise "superpowers for all," the superstar entrepreneur took to the stage as usual, embodying Silicon Valley style in jeans, a sweater, and tennis shoes. This low-key normcore fashion has become the signature for Silicon Valley icons. Consider, for example, Mark Zuckerberg's flip-flops, Paul Graham's sandals (Y Combinator founder), Reid Hoffman's cargo shorts (LinkedIn founder), and Steve Jobs's jeans. Several respondents said they focus on work, at the risk of showing up for business meetings wearing "pants that are too long" as Evan Williams, the cofounder of Twitter, did in that company's early days.[40] Clothes that would be considered unkempt in Boston, New York, or Paris give Silicon Valley the appearance of equality, even though it is the world's leading source of wealth. The preferred modes of transport for professionals are bicycles, electric scooters, and buses, and many corporate employees commute to work via Caltrain, the only rail line that crosses Silicon Valley from north to south. The region's emblematic cars are not sports cars or even self-driving cars, but hybrid or electric vehicles, and during the 2010s Priuses were as popular with Uber and Lyft drivers as with the founders of Google.[41] Ostentatious displays of wealth are uncommon and likely to be socially sanctioned.

Those I interviewed said they like what they called "mainstream" leisure activities, such as playing video games, watching Netflix programs, listening to Spotify, using social media, frequenting San Francisco's dive bars, enjoying outdoor activities, plus traveling and dining out when money and time allow it—a far cry from the eccentricities of some tech celebrities. None of the respondents reported going to the city's opera house. Literate culture, in terms of its formats and content, receives less investment by the tech crowd compared to the natural sciences, engineering, science fiction, or geek culture. While students at an institution like the famous private Saint Paul School in New Hampshire learn, embody, and show their privileged status by exercising the codes of high culture, in Silicon Valley meetings and conferences borrow nontechnical references from comic book culture.[42] For example, the technology director of one major company illustrates his presentation on artificial intelligence at a data-processing conference with an image of Superman taking flight, to emphasize the power of the solution being discussed; a designer uses a photograph of herself posing next to Captain Kirk from *Star Trek* as a way of introducing her talk; two entrepreneurs go to a specialized conference dressed as Captain America; at the now defunct Theranos headquarters, a quote from Yoda could be seen on the wall; Uber employees named their San Francisco headquarters "The Death Star," invoking a reference to *Star Wars*.

In the quiet town of San Bruno—the soft, residential, and impersonal heart of Silicon Valley—YouTube employees use screening rooms whose names are borrowed from the history of American television. At YouTube's 1000 Cherry Avenue building, employees pass daily in front of a giant screen covering the entire wall of the entrance hall. A multitude of built-in screens also line employees' paths, from corridors to staircases to kitchens. Content from the recent history of web creation and the internet is constantly broadcast, along with an uninterrupted series of memes. In her study of the late 2000s social media scene in San Francisco, the communication scholar Alice Marwick demonstrated how YouTube led to a renewal of the canons and pathways to fame, disrupting traditional notions of celebrity as managed and controlled by the cultural industries.[43] In this regard, Silicon Valley appears to be driven by "classless elitism," having no ideology other than work, openness, and progress.[44]

A 2017 Stanford study of more than six hundred "elite tech executives and founders,"[45] mostly millionaires active in philanthropy, revealed that 96 percent supported same-sex marriage, 82 percent advocated universal health care even if it meant raising taxes, 82 percent wanted strict gun control, 79 percent supported abortion, twice as many as Democratic supporters considered fighting climate change "extremely important," and only 8 percent of the sample voted for Donald Trump in the 2016 US presidential election. Funding from the leaders (CEOs and senior executives) of the 175 largest Silicon Valley companies to political parties and foundations between 2015 and 2016, along with their public statements, further supports this progressive orientation.[46] Despite particularly high-profile cases, such as Peter Thiel (a Donald Trump supporter who contributed $5 million to his 2016 campaign) and Robert Mercer (an artificial intelligence figure and influential investor who founded the far-right website *Breitbart News*), the majority of this sample supports the Democratic Party, as in the case of Facebook cofounder Dustin Moskowitz, who contributed $18 million to the Democratic Party's 2016 presidential campaign, and almost $39 million in 2024.

The 2024 election seemed to mark a political shift, with a significant wave of support for Donald Trump. In fact, and as in other countries (in Brazil, in England during Brexit, in France or in Germany), a division within economic and tech elites is rising. The Trump support faction is still a minority but is better structured, put more money on the table, and is more active in the media (new and old ones). The progressive faction is larger but less organized and more discreet. Reid Hastings, Dusting Moskovitz, Vinod Khosla, Sheryl Sandberg, John Doer, Laurence Powell Jobs, and many others gave money ($55 million for Hoffman as well as Moskovitz) to the Democrat candidate in 2024. This Silicon Valley progressive elite faction is distinct from Elon Musk–Peter Thiel's network of influence, authoritarian elites in Brazil who advocate a racialist vision of society, in France where republicanism masks social stratification, in India where caste organization reinforces conservative principles, or in China where navigating the Communist Party is a necessity.[47]

In addition, the LGBTQI+ tech workers who met with me during the survey all celebrated the freedom and welcoming environment they enjoyed. As one European-born gay entrepreneur put it: "It was even hard to be gay where I was before. It's just that here, it's far away and there's a lot of freedom. So, it was a great liberation, from codes and obligations—a bit like a rebirth."[48] According to a 2021 UCLA Law School study, the San Francisco metropolitan area, with 6.7 percent of its population identifying as LGBTQI+, has the highest percentage of LGBTQI+ residents in the United States.[49] Gay tech workers had their own organization (High Tech Gays) from 1983 to 1997. There has been gay activism in Silicon Valley since the 1970s with prominent role models like Rick Rudy, founder of High Tech Gays in 1982, gay rights activist Kim Harris at Hewlett-Packard, and his husband, Bennett Marks, who started Apple Lambda in 1986, a gay employee group at Apple. And several of Tech's top bosses and investors are openly gay, quite far from construction, military, or oil sector standards. The lesbian, queer, and trans communities are smaller but still represented.

For these different reasons, players are invited to integrate an open, welcoming society that values diversity. However, this culture is not a natural and spontaneous phenomenon. It is the result of a construction process, with underlying purposes. The limitation of external signs of wealth partly covers a strategic dimension. In the 1940s and 1950s the general increase in salaries and the reduction of differences were implemented in transistor companies in order to strengthen team cohesion and limit turnover.[50] The erasure of differentiation thus encouraged collaboration.

MAKING CULTURE A VARIABLE

In many social worlds access to conventions and ways of doing things is conditioned by high entry and information costs. Mastering the rules of the game not only facilitates entry, maintenance, and advancement within the reference milieu but also represents an asset to be preserved and defended, even fiercely if necessary. The etiquette of Louis XIV's court, the "rules of the game" in the literary world, the aesthetic standards of the Academy of Painting in nineteenth-century Paris, the norms of the university mandarinate, the "laws" of gangs in Chicago's South Side, or the mores of Paris's exclusive Sixteenth Arrondissement—all are variations of what the classical German sociologist Georg Simmel termed "secret societies." According to Simmel, such societies are concerned with the protection of ideas, activities, or objects they value. Members seek this protection by controlling the distribution of information on the elements that are valued.[51] Secrecy confers value to hidden knowledge, and revelation demonetizes it. Revealing and spreading secrets is therefore considered a form of betrayal by members of the group. Simmel thus considered that there is a fixed "quantum" of secrets in each social group.

This quantum seems extremely low in Silicon Valley, an industry based on information. Books, lectures, classes, tweets, blog posts, social media posts, journalist investigations, and advice are exchanged informally. Making explicit what is usually implicit is commonplace in the region, as an English investor points out:

> I arrived in 2010, and then I found myself in a kind of speakeasy in the Tenderloin, there was a group of four to five entrepreneurs, on a Thursday, and what immediately struck me was that they were discussing what they were doing, they were talking without hiding, sharing information, describing what they were doing, they were talking about their business. . . . People who for me were competitors. . . . Where I had been, in London, in Paris, in New York, you had to stay hidden. Today, I've been here for seven years, I know now that this is a typical cultural trait of this place. If you compare it to elsewhere, in terms of cultural, psychological traits, here there's this ability to say things (interview, San Francisco, September 9, 2017).

This openness reflects a desire to integrate people from diverse origins, countries, and backgrounds as quickly as possible.

A Culture to Integrate

Embedded professionals spend a large part of their time meeting with newcomers, explaining how things are done in Silicon Valley, what practices they need to adopt, who they should contact, and what they need to work on to increase their chances of success. The director of a coworking space recounts his advice to newcomers: "Here, I see a lot of people come in, they come to me and I tell

TABLE 6. Silicon Valley work etiquette

Be on time	People don't know much about you, if anything at all. To overcome this problem, they will use any signal to infer something about you. And people are hungry for signals. Late? In one fell swoop, you send three messages: (1) You're not organized. Would you do business with unorganized people? And don't pretend that the traffic was horrible on the 101. Of course it was. Use Waze! (2) You don't respect me. "Sorry, my previous meeting took longer than expected." Which basically means "You probably have a meeting right after me, but I don't care about *your* schedule." This is not appreciated. (3) I can't trust you. When we set up the meeting, we had an agreement. You just broke it.
Email response the same day	Signals sent: You are in control, you are fast, and that's a good thing. What the sender had to say matters to you. You made them feel important.
Intro	An introduction must be beneficial to all parties, the "introducer" (nodes in a social network have value) as well as the "introduced parties" (successful people can only afford to trade some of their limited time for value). You can't force someone to make an introduction, or to be introduced to someone else. It's counterproductive (you risk bringing suffering instead of value).
Communication rules	People have very limited time. Your communication should be succinct (three points, five lines maximum), clear (readers shouldn't need a PhD in philosophy to understand you), and precise (data). A three-point rule for emails: What do you do (two lines); Why is this exciting (two lines); What do you want (one line).
Potlatch	This is the essence of Silicon Valley culture. It means that if you do something good, something good will happen to you. This is the foundation of the "pay-it-forward" attitude. It translates into that question that anyone you see for the first time will ask you, "How can I help you?"
Time frames	15/30/60. The difference is in the substance of the item(s) to be discussed. If things and decisions can be settled in thirty minutes, why ask for (and block) a one-hour slot in the other person's schedule? If you ask for a "thirty-minute meeting," you show that you likely know how the system works. You earn free points.
Language	An accent is fine. Not speaking English is not acceptable. To thrive, you must be able to express yourself correctly, with nuance and precision. Improving your English should be a priority from day one. Otherwise, you will face discrimination at some point in your journey (quite quickly, in fact).
Data	Nothing is better, clearer, more objective and comparable than data.
Storytelling	The most effective way to connect with people and raise awareness. A way to sell. A good story connects your message to something bigger. It can be about a mission, an emotion, or a journey. But whatever it is, it must engage the other person. A story is a well-crafted script. It's a missile with a specific target.

SOURCE: Romain Serman, "Silicon Valley Etiquette, Manners Matter" blog post, October 3, 2016.

them … [*gasp*]. I have a whole speech, I tell them about Silicon Valley, I tell them it's hard, it's ultracompetitive, not many are going to make it, but it's cool, go have fun!"[52] Beyond these discussions, professionals spend time clarifying and formalizing guidance on best behavior. Table 6 summarizes Silicon Valley communication conventions, and how they are communicated to newcomers.

Other principles regularly mentioned throughout Silicon Valley seem to be validated by half a century of economic sociology: accumulate weak links to access information and opportunities[53]; associate talent according to potential and performance[54]; imprint the values and expectations of the environment in which a company originates[55]; multiply weak signals to optimize product return and its quality ("Don't worry, be crappy," according to Guy Kawasaki's formula); pair selectively (player A collaborates with players A, according to Steve Jobs's mantra); open windows of opportunity through social capital ("Go out and reach out"). The dissemination and valorization of these mottos illustrate the region's philosophy of action, aiming for efficiency, through quantification and formalization. Sociologist Arthur Stinchcombe identified three characteristics of successful formalization: abstraction, transparency, and feedback.

> First, formalization must be based on abstractions that are useful representations of the problems and solutions in question—that achieve *cognitive adequacy*. If abstractions do not map well to real situations, they will not be useful guides to action. Second, formalization must be communicable. It helps if rules are transparent, and if they are written in the *lingua franca* of those subject to them (legalese for lawyers, physics terminology for physicists). Finally, rules must have feedback systems (a *trajectory of improvement*) that allow them to be updated.[56]

Yet in Silicon Valley, despite the population diversity, professionals rely on a set of communication rules and formalization-oriented norms borrowed from the three culture traditions mentioned at the beginning of this chapter: doing, working, and communicating. They are openly spread, to make professional integration and collaboration easier and faster. As one entrepreneur-investor explained:

> It's been five years since I've been here. I've changed my life. I've learned to understand the ecosystem, to understand its codes, which are very simple, very basic: there's one way to pitch, not two, a specific number of slides in presentations. … This is due to the fact that we're a big melting pot so the lowest common denominator becomes the culture of all (interview, San Francisco, November 12, 2016).

As Table 6 shows, the principles made public aim to optimize the procedural efficiency of collaborations within an open professional group. These principles include time-saving, symmetry of communication formalism, objectification, dataism, and rhetoric that combines personal life trajectories with professional missions, among others. They are conventions in the sense given to this term by sociologist Howard Becker—that is, rules that govern professional practices and that must be "known by all or almost all."[57] If newcomers don't know them yet, they have to learn them very quickly.

A Culture to Select

In Silicon Valley professionals face an intense and increasing flow of people, capital, and information. By communicating the norms and rules to follow, they intensify this flow and give themselves more chances to benefit from it. A European entrepreneur-investor claims that alignment with Silicon Valley communication standards leads to optimized work efficiency:

> When you're only with people from your country, you can use humor, metaphors . . . but it's only with your people. I've been here for six years. I stopped that here. Because people from different countries don't have the same humor. French people, for instance, are cynical and ironic. The only French humor that works with Americans is to make fun of themselves, to make fun of the French; they love that. They don't really understand English irony. Or Indian metaphors. Likewise, I'm very careful with metaphors. I don't have the cultural background to make American metaphors or sports references such as drawing an analogy between the situation at the end of the game between the 1970s Boston White Sox and a Bears final or whatever. I'm not going to try to do that. . . . Here, I go straight to the point (interview, San Francisco, February 12, 2016).

Faced with an increasing flow of projects, players seek to evaluate and arbitrate between the different options for allocating the time and money available to them. During the dot-com bubble, the most sought-after venture capitalists reported receiving two hundred projects and funding requests per month, or about twenty-five hundred per year.[58] In the mid-2010s interviewees working as investors said they received about one hundred requests per day.

Unlike traditional economic and political elites, the Valley's various professionals cannot rely on a culture learned through attending the same school. In doing so, professionals adopt two seemingly contradictory practices. On the one hand, the explicitness and publicity of norms offer a practical and cognitive resource to professionals in the region. On the other hand, they evaluate potential partners and collaborators on their speed of learning, compliance, mastery of openly publicized norms, including not being late. For instance, a lawyer being three minutes late to our meeting told me how sorry she was. I told her that apologizing for three minutes was really nothing. She directly replied: "That's because you don't live here!" While the publicity of standards increases the volume of opportunities, attention to their mastery offers rational criteria for orienting oneself and knowing with whom to collaborate. Always arriving on time will thus be perceived as a sign of seriousness, rigor, being in control, and so forth.

This is why, in Silicon Valley, social relationships are less about intimacy and more about professional friendships, carefully nurtured and constantly reassessed. These practices are based on what economist Oliver Williamson defined as opportunism—that is, "self-interest seeking with guile."[59] Indeed, professionals produce and disseminate a culture like a variable, allowing for better partnership sorting and selection. As a fixed and objective entity, it serves to judge the value of stakeholders during interactions, conferring an objective, almost scientific dimension to particular, socially constructed and historically localized ways of doing things together in this innovation cluster. It is similar to a set of sharable and rational traits. The standards disseminated stem from the generalization of decontextualized practices; their historical context is disregarded. They prevail based on measurements, comparisons, and evaluations, with the aim of increasing the efficiency of interactions.[60]

Silicon Valley is an industry that produces services, equipment, and infrastructure on a global scale. The region's "culture" plays a key role in integrating workers from around the world. Through it, players resolve the conflict between two goals: integrating and selecting. People look nice, open-minded, and friendly. But it's partly instrumental: players try to increase the flow of information, capital, and people, while expanding the spectrum of opportunities for themselves. Identifying, objectifying, and disseminating the most appropriate working convention reduces opportunity costs. In this way "culture" is turned into a sharable variable: it allows newcomers to adapt efficiently and quickly to an unfamiliar and evolving world by respecting stable conventions. The prevalence of terms like *Valley, Peninsula, Bay Area, ecosystem,* and *tech community* illustrates the dual nature of this cluster: both localized and globalized. It seeks to integrate new entrants into opportunities while being selective and Darwinian, reflecting a production system oriented toward breakthroughs.

PART II

Work

FOUR

Geniuses at Work

Entrepreneurs are very special animals. But real entrepreneurs
are wolves—they are both solitary and move in packs. They
sometimes have huge egos, great strength, and big balls.

—Interview with an investor, San Francisco, February 12, 2016

ENTREPRENEURS IN SILICON VALLEY are referred to as *wolves, lions,
beasts,* or *unicorns.* When they are not compared to mythical animals, they
are qualified as *visionaries, risk takers, rebels, rock stars,* or *underdogs.* Full of
energy, able to get by with little sleep, they seem to be gifted with superior
strength and intelligence. Silicon Valley entrepreneurs embody a desirable
and enchanted modern image of individualism. They can build empires and
make a fortune in a few years. Eight of the world's ten biggest fortunes belong
to tech entrepreneurs. Several preeminent figures have similar profiles: challenging childhoods (orphans, immigrants, victims of harassment, children of
divorced parents); significant parental investment during their youth and
early careers; training as engineers and computer scientists; and a rapid rise
from anonymity to the top of Wall Street. They have helped turn IT into a
mass-market industry, bypassing the bureaucracies deemed dysfunctional
and liberticidal by libertarians. Tech entrepreneurs are celebrated for the
same reason. Governments grant them tax cuts and seed-funding. These cel-
ebrations and social status seem a far cry from the daily life of ordinary entrepreneurs, who often start their own business midcareer following a career
break or for lack of any better opportunity or because they want to be their
own boss. The majority of ordinary entrepreneurs in the United States create
few jobs, marginally participate in innovation, and earn less than they would
in a salaried position.[1]

Some tech entrepreneurs turn into generous philanthropists, especially in
health and education.[2] Coming from intellectual professions, tech entrepreneurs see information, education, and technology as the only ways to reshuffle the deck. Their ethos is to challenge the established order for the benefit

of the many. They are the eternally youthful faces who have risen through the ranks to push back the frontiers of the future. In a nutshell they are like modern-day knights, overthrowing the status quo.[3] However, the reality of entrepreneurship in Silicon Valley is different. The population is far more heterogeneous than the tech entrepreneur stereotype. But this heterogeneity is forgotten, disappearing behind the image of geniuses who started from almost nothing before rising to the top of the industry. This chapter examines the mythology surrounding the Silicon Valley genius, demonstrating how it supports entrepreneurial activity and how it is utilized to develop the bonds of trust that are critical to success in Silicon Valley.

THE GENIUS MYTHOLOGY

The Information Revolution

Silicon Valley's history doesn't begin with the exploitation of silicon in the 1960s and 1970s. Nor did it start with computers, despite the impression a hasty visit to Mountain View's Computer History Museum might give. It goes back to the nineteenth century. This story is not synchronous with the Industrial Revolution. It's a consequence of it. The history of Silicon Valley starts with the engineering of information systems developed to solve to a very specific problem. In the second part of the nineteenth century, new agricultural technologies like the combine harvester increased farm production. The major problem facing farming in California was how to get these goods to market. With new and improved methods of transportation, particularly trains and cars, surplus farm produce could be transported to a national market and beyond. But there were countless incidents: accidents, blocked roads, switching problems, delays, lack of information on directions and timetables, and so forth. These problems meant losses for producers and carriers. With systems that produced better information, producers and carriers could improve coordination, reduce loss, and increase wealth.[4]

One man played an important role in this story. During the gold rush a young lawyer in the Midwest, Leland Stanford (1824–1893), made his way to the West Coast along with his five brothers. They did not come to dig for gold in 1852. They came to sell mining equipment to those seeking it. Stanford's case gives weight to the famous business school mantra: "The gold rush millionaires were not the diggers but those who sold them shovels and picks." He moved to Sacramento in 1856 and was one of the four merchants who invested in chief engineer Theodore D. Judah's plan for the Central Pacific Railroad, incorporated in 1861. After a failed first run for governor in 1859, Stanford was elected governor of California in 1861. In 1868 he became president of the Southern Pacific Railroad. Then in 1874 he moved to San Francisco as president of the Occidental and Oriental Steamship Company. As governor, Stanford helped to create the state's first normal school in San Jose (a teaching college that became the future San Jose University). He and his wife funded a new university, to honor the memory of their son, who died of typhoid fever in 1884, donating nearly $40 million. It opened in 1891.

If Stanford University could be summed up by a shape, it would be the square. The university is based intellectually, architecturally, and spatially on four pillars: engineering, humanities, law, and math. It is between these four points that the entrepreneurial model typical of Silicon Valley was born. Up until today the university's heart has been its main quad, an open space designed by Frederick Law Olmsted (who also designed Central Park) for meetings, exchanges, and projects among people from these four different horizons. One idea has grown with each generation of engineers: that improving information supposes developing better information systems, systems that help solve problems and produce prosperity. Information innovations have multiplied in Northern California, initially with telegrams and telephones and then with radios, televisions, transistors, processors, routers, graphics processing units, and applications. From radios to generative artificial intelligence, new entrepreneurs come along at a steady pace (almost every ten years) to reshuffle the increasingly more sophisticated and complex technological deck (Table 7). But all these innovations have the same objective: improving the quality of information.

Over the course of this history, a magic trick has occurred. Systems have expanded, but their visibility has shrunk. The first radios in the late 1900s were the size of a room. The computers of the 1950s sometimes required an entire building. But their distant cousins, cell phones, fit into a jean pocket. The physics of technology has changed, with improved versions further away from users' eyes. However, two things haven't changed: the philosophy behind these information systems and the embodiment of entrepreneurship. Indeed, information technology and history go hand in hand with a kind of philosophy notably formalized by Norbert Wiener in a time of war: information enables better organization; poor information systems lead to entropy (a measure of randomness) and a loss of energy that could extend to chaos. The more open and information-dense a system, the more efficient it will be—whether you're

TABLE 7. More than a century of Silicon Valley information revolutions

Year	Organization	Technology
1909	Federal telegraph	Radio
1927	Farnsworth	TV signals
1939	Hewlett-Packard/Varian	Electronics
1956–57	Shockley Lab/Fairchild	Transistors
1968	Intel	Semiconductors
1976	Apple, Cromemco	Personal computer
1984	Cisco	Internet service
1994–95	Amazon, Yahoo	Internet consumer
2005–6	YouTube, Twitter, Facebook	Social Media
2015	OpenAI	LLM

talking about IT or international relations.[5] In short, according to Wiener, the development of better information systems allows the world to avoid chaos. For Wiener, information systems exist as islands of progress, offering hope for a better future. These systems are produced by engineers and scientists, entrepreneurs at heart, in and around universities. But while technologies have never stopped their evolution, the embodiment of tech entrepreneurship has stayed the same. From the outset tech entrepreneurs seem to have been male, white, trained as engineers, from highly educated classes, and freethinkers with a tendency toward atheism. This embodiment has remained unchanged—from radio pioneer Charles "Doc" Herrold to OpenAI's Sam Altman.

Ordinary Tech Entrepreneurs versus Super Entrepreneurs

In Silicon Valley, as elsewhere, there's a wide gap between tech stereotypes and sociological reality. When asked who best embodies Silicon Valley, people think about Steve Jobs, Larry Page, or Mark Zuckerberg—men who are white and wealthy, American citizens, considered masters of all trades, and eternally young as exemplified by their juvenile faces. In this, they look a lot like the Philadelphia WASP elite as described by sociologist Digby Baltzell in the 1950s.[6] Baltzell believed that an upper class must reflect the ethnic makeup of the country as a whole in order to stay legitimate.[7] However, this tech entrepreneur stereotype reflects neither the American population nor the population of Silicon Valley entrepreneurs. Of a population of 2.7 million including 1.6 million workers, only 0.5 percent of the global Silicon Valley population has started a business.[8] Every year, 13,500 people set up their own business in the Bay Area. The number of active entrepreneurs in the tech industry alone is close to forty thousand. This group presents certain similar sociological traits, but it is also more diverse than people might think.

While most entrepreneurs in the tech industry are indeed men, there is also a significant proportion of women. In 2022, 19 percent (4,808) of the 25,000 entrepreneurs I monitored in Silicon Valley were women; 79 percent (19,993) were men.[9] Silicon Valley is associated with a youthful image. However, the average age of founders is around forty-five years old—in a country where the average age was 38.8 in 2021.[10] During the survey I came across a number of profiles far from the entrepreneur stereotype: a seventy-year-old doctor trying to develop a diabetes measurement solution; an African American nutritionist mother and her business school graduate daughter developing a balanced-meal service platform for teenagers; a Cameroonian-born entrepreneur, father of two, promoting a meditation app to, in his words, "change the way we live and work"; and a cofounding couple, with a Rwandan-born husband who fled his country during the 1994 genocide, developing a real estate sale and rental platform; among many other examples. In a land where people associate technology with becoming rich, income levels also show significant differences. In 2017, Silicon Valley had seventy billionaires and over seventy-five thousand millionaires. But 75 percent of Silicon Valley entrepreneurs earned less than $75,000 a year and 66 percent less than $50,000. By comparison, the average income of entrepreneurs was $72,363 in Australia and $30,208 in India.[11]

Similarly, these tech entrepreneurs are not monolithic soloists dedicated to a fixed idea that would justify confusing them with inventors.[12] They launch, pivot, fail, change their title or profession—and start again. It is common for a company's name to change at various stages of its life, either at the request of its board of directors or its current leaders. Silicon Valley CEOs have gained notoriety from a position of designated manager (such as Eric Schmidt at Google and Jeff Wiener at LinkedIn), while renowned entrepreneurs have left the company they cofounded, either of their own accord or under duress, or went hands off—among them, Steve Jobs and Steve Wozniak at Apple, Larry Page and Sergey Brin at Google, Larry Ellison at Oracle, and Travis Kalanick at Uber. In this respect the tech entrepreneur cannot be reduced to the figure of the founder. This is especially true given that the renowned companies like Hewlett-Packard, Cisco, Apple, Yahoo, and Google often began with friendly duos or small teams. These teams can include up to six people, with three members the most common number. Formed during their studies, or even during their children's school outings, these entrepreneurial collectives stabilize for a handful of years, usually the time it takes to set up a company. During this time they develop a solution and, most of the time, fail.

Nevertheless, from time to time, entrepreneurs fit the stereotype.[13] I refer to them as *super entrepreneurs* because they have specific characteristics fitting the unicorn founder population. Most unicorn founders have no direct professional experience in the sector they disrupt. Neither are they the first to commercialize the idea that made them successful: 60 percent were individuals who had already started a company and sold it for more than $50 million. This level of success applies to only a limited proportion of the population: the executives of only 540 of the 12,000 Silicon Valley companies active in 2021 (4.5 percent). And 30 percent won't go through to IPO. A sample of 531 companies founded in the United States (including 309 in California) and valued at more than $1 billion[14] revealed that of the 1,322 entrepreneurs who founded unicorns, there were 485 bachelor degrees, 359 masters, 236 MBAs, 286 PhDs, and only 56 dropouts.[15] These degrees were awarded by prestigious universities (mostly Stanford, Harvard, Berkeley, and MIT) to an overwhelmingly male population (95 percent) that averaged about thirty-five years old. The majority of them were from the United States (56 percent). Their foreign counterparts were, in decreasing order, Indian, Israeli, Canadian, English, Chinese, Taiwanese, German, French, and Ukrainian.

Despite this diversity, the new technologies industry is described as dominated by white young men, and this stereotype has a direct impact on startup culture and service design, as various studies have shown.[16] In fact, contrary to the position of some of the most controversial tech voices to back Donald Trump's campaign in 2024—Silicon Valley investors such as David Sacks, Chamath Palihapitiya, Andreessen Horowitz, and Elon Musk—the new technology industry is proving to be far more willing to embrace inclusive leadership and diversity than the oil or finance industries. Inequalities are high, and signs of misogyny and racism real, but many of the people I met also said they benefited from a more open, tolerant, progressive, and accepting working environment. To them, Silicon Valley is hierarchical but also meritocratic and inclusive—certainly more so than what they had experienced in their home countries or previous jobs.[17] This progressive paradox is not easy to break down.

Actually, the higher up the corporate ladder, the more obvious the white dominance. According to a 2016 study by the Center for Employment Equity, which analyzed a sample of 177 large tech companies based in Silicon Valley, white men accounted for approximately 39 percent of tech professionals, 47 percent of managers, and 59 percent of executives. Asian men made up 16.3 percent of tech executives, while Asian women represented 4.5 percent. Hispanic men accounted for 2.1 percent of executives, and Hispanic women 0.8 percent. Black men comprised 2.1 percent of executives, and Black women 0.4 percent. During my study I was able to conduct interviews with founders. Access to women was harder because they are rarer, but it was still feasible. I was able to approach female founders by following communities and networks of women entrepreneurs, all run and managed by white women. I was only able to interview one African American woman entrepreneur. She stated that she never experienced direct racism during her entrepreneurial journey in Silicon Valley, but also said that is was difficult for her to grow her network. Nevertheless, in 2024, of the forty-two hundred companies specializing in artificial intelligence, and excluding individuals from India and China (the two main diasporas in Silicon Valley), only twenty-five companies were founded by Black people.[18]

In Silicon Valley the higher up the ladder of success, the more the entrepreneur fits the stereotypical tech genius profile: a young white man trained as an engineer. You can better understand this gap between ordinary entrepreneurs and super entrepreneurs, and the way the gap widens at the top of the hierarchy, by looking at the way intelligence and entrepreneurship have been valued throughout Silicon Valley's history. This paradox of diversity can be understood if we look back at the reasons why intelligence has been celebrated in Silicon Valley.

Revenge of the Geniuses

Sand Hill Road. Located on a hill overlooking Stanford University in Menlo Park, Sand Hill Road is close to Silicon Valley's budding geniuses. The most powerful names in venture capital are found here. It's the most expensive street in the United States, along with New York's Fifth Avenue. A stroll along Fifth Avenue is full of things to see. On Sand Hill Road the street is empty most of the time. Investors are elsewhere during the week, hunting for deals at cafés, restaurants, meetups, and conferences. On weekends and holidays they might be golfing, playing tennis, sailing, attending barbecues, or even going to Burning Man. They are always engaging with entrepreneurs.

When asked about this unconventional approach, investors explain that rather than sitting behind a desk analyzing financial plans, this is the best way to get to know entrepreneurs. This typical Silicon Valley routine sheds light on why success remains associated with the trait of white male dominance.

Looking back over 150 years of Silicon Valley history, many of its founding fathers defended social Darwinism and even eugenics. When Leland Stanford decided to found a university in 1885, he hired several academics trained by and working at Indiana University, a state where racism and eugenics has had a lasting influence. (Eugenics laws were on the books in Indiana from 1907 to 1974.) For these academics, coming to California was an opportunity to rethink social organization by placing order and excellence in the heart of the system. Stanford first hired David Star Jordan (1851–1931) for the position of university president. He was a biologist from Indiana University and a renowned specialist in fish reproduction who had authored nearly two thousand academic papers.[19] Like many biologists of his time, Jordan drew conclusions about human societies from phenomena observed in the natural world. He had lost his brother in the Civil War, and throughout his life worked for peace and prosperity. He tried to develop a social theory holding war responsible for chaos and decline.

In an influential book, *The Blood of the Nation: A Study in the Decay of Races by the Survival of the Unfit* (1901), Jordan argued that war led to the passing of the "fittest," the strongest, and the most intelligent people. Their disappearance therefore caused a loss of quality in the human population and the country's reproduction potential. As Stanford's first president, Jordan pioneered the tradition of offering support to tech entrepreneurs, funding the Federal Telegraph Company (FTC), which Cyril Frank Elwell founded in Palo Alto in 1909. Admittedly, Jordan's eugenics views were part of an intellectual climate with Darwinist overtones that emerged in Europe and the United States in the second half of the nineteenth century and in California especially that included the anti-Chinese movement. In 1862, Governor Stanford declared "that the settlement among us of an inferior race is to be discouraged by every legitimate means."[20] But at Stanford University scientists were going to shift the question of the superiority of race to the question of individual superiority. The emerging social sciences played an important role in this shift.

Edward Ross (1866–1951), a major figure in American sociology and criminology, was hired by Jordan, his friend whom he met during their time at Cornell University. Ross was a professor at Stanford between 1893 and 1900, then had to leave the university because of a eugenics scandal. He had defended the "race suicide" doctrine—that the white race would fade due to its diminished birthrate in the face of the fertility of other races. Ross also objected to Japanese and Chinese immigration. In a public speech he declared that "it would be better for us if we were to turn our guns upon every vessel bringing Japanese to our shores rather than to permit them to land."[21] Ross was pushed to resign by Jane Stanford, Leland Stanford's widow (Ross had been critical of the railroads and their use of Asian labor). The same year, Ross published *Social Control: A Survey in the Foundations of Order* (1901), which investigated the causes for order and disorder within societies. In his view societies that thrive and prosper are those in which new men emerge, men he called "social geniuses." These men assert their values, not because of their lineage but thanks to their moral and intellectual superiority, to the point of instituting new social religions.

Valuing intelligence in this way may seem natural, especially in Silicon Valley. But at the time intelligent children were perceived as "conceited, freakish, socially eccentric, and [insane]."[22] Basically they were seen as freaks. This perception stands in contrast to the historic attribution of intelligence, knowledge, wisdom, and even sophistication to "great men." And in the nineteenth and early twentieth century, doers and men of action were at the top of the country's heroic representations. But in a country founded on anti-aristocratic principles, intellectualism and refinement (or any qualities that assumed superiority over others) have often carried negative connotations, even in science.[23] Great scientific minds like Robert Oppenheimer in the United States and Alan Turing in the United Kingdom suffered from lack of understanding and judgment about their lifestyles, despite their tremendous contribution to the war effort. So, at the turn of the nineteenth and twentieth centuries, seeking out and enshrining intelligence were not common practices in the United States.

Yet it was to this endeavor that Lewis Terman (1877–1956) devoted his entire life. He joined Stanford University's faculty as a professor of educational psychology in 1910 and served as the psychology department chair from 1922 to 1945. The Indiana native began his career with a doctoral thesis based on the comparison of two sample groups—one made of seven individuals considered "stupid," the second with seven "bright" people.[24] Terman's conclusion was that intelligence could not be radically influenced by one's environment and was largely hereditary. This led him to redirect his work from pedagogy toward the testing and assessment of intelligence. Believing that intelligence is inherited before it is cultivated, Terman joined and led several eugenics organizations. To this end, he imported and adapted the Simon-Binet Test of Intelligence and applied it on a very large scale to World War I soldiers; 1.7 million of them were IQ tested. Examiners scored tests on a scale ranging from *A* through *E*, and respondents achieving *A* scores would be trained as officers. After the war Terman argued that his test could be used in American schools to improve the educational system's efficiency. Starting in 1921, he initiated the Genetic Studies of Genius, a longitudinal survey conducted on "gifted" people. This study followed children with extremely high IQs over several years. The results didn't fit the original negative stereotype of intelligence. They were neither sick, nor failing, nor isolated, nor deviant, but generally taller than average, less often divorced, and more often successful in their careers. In this way Terman did much to promote the social value of intelligent people and argued through his findings that intelligence should have better recognition and more power in the United States.

Lewis Terman was the father of Frederick Terman, considered one of Silicon Valley's founding fathers. Fred was a living contradiction of his father's biological theory of intelligence, since he could be seen as a pure product of his social environment. Indeed, Fred Terman grew up on the Stanford campus and was interested in all kinds of disciplines, starting with engineering sciences. Then he went to MIT and earned a doctor of science in electrical engineering in 1924. The influential inventor and engineer Vannevar Bush was Fred's adviser. Fred eventually got tenure at Stanford, worked on radio engineering, and directed the Radio Research Laboratory during World War II. He was renowned for acquiring government funding that dramatically improved Stanford's financial base. He constantly pushed for faculty and students to focus on what he called the "steeples of excellence," striving to recruit the "finest faculty in the country."[25] Fred also believed in the benefits of cross-disciplinary work and encouraged its development, working on developing statistics within the university with the Applied Mathematics and Statistics Laboratories and the Institute for Mathematical Studies in the Social Sciences. He restructured the university's entire engineering department and inspired several generations of researchers to take the entrepreneurial plunge through the Stanford Industrial Park that he launched in 1951. The university leased portions of its land to high-tech firms such as Hewlett-Packard, Varian Associates, Eastman Kodak, Lockheed Corporation, General Electric, and many others (including Tesla Motors, Nest, and Skype).

At the same time, another man was also convinced of the importance of individual ingenuity and talent: George Doriot. One of his nicknames was "the East Coast's Frederick Terman" and, as discussed in chapter 2, Doriot was the main architect and theorist of venture capitalism.[26] During his time as head of the Military Planning Division, Doriot repeatedly observed how inventions could make a difference in the military field and criticized bureaucracy as an obstacle to their implementation. During the nineteenth and early twentieth centuries, several German theorists (Friedrich Hegel, Max Weber, Otto Hintze) claimed that bureaucratic organizations were laying the path to rationalization, respect for law, and progress, both in the public and private sectors. But to Doriot, administration and bureaucracy were the organizational evils of the time. For him, bureaucracy stifled talent and curbed human intelligence in the name of meaningless rules.[27] Doriot believed it was necessary to move away from bureaucracies, foster lean organizations, and place trust in the brightest people.

Doriot promoted scientific talent as the key to the new postwar world. However, one of the challenges lay in identifying the brilliant minds who possessed the most ingenious and resilient forces of character. To spot them, Doriot observed men during informal interactions. To him, getting out of the office and away from the accounting books was essential to finding "superior men," distinguished by their "personality, intelligence, and moral strength." Before investing in Digital Equipment Corporation (DEC), Doriot even questioned the wives of the two founders, Ken Olson and Harlan Anderson, to find out how they behaved at home and whether they were hard and dedicated workers. Through this selection process, Doriot intended to develop innovation, limit the range of influence of bureaucracies, and put the best minds in charge. The history of the tech industry is thus also the history of rational intelligence legitimatization, of lean organizations versus bureaucracies. But this story has its dark side: racism, eugenics, social Darwinism, superiority complexes, and radical libertarianism.

In 1995, Peter Thiel and David Sacks published *The Diversity Myth,* in which they criticize multiculturalism as "dumbing-down" admissions standards at Stanford University.[28] Elon Musk condemns what he calls the "woke virus" on Twitter/X and criticizes "unvetted immigration at [a] large scale" as "a recipe for disaster."[29] Marc Andreessen argues in his "Techno-Optimist Manifesto" that societies are "like sharks, they grow or die." The influential transhumanist Nick Bostrom has also more than flirted with eugenicist and racist thinking. Outspoken tech voices such as these show how this history has left a deep mark on Silicon Valley's philosophy. If it is coherent at its core, it has also spread, secularized, and detached itself from its envelope to silently influence ways of hierarchizing people, organizations, and interactions in Silicon Valley. But mostly in an indirect and diffuse way.

Venture capitalists like to meet entrepreneurs at cafés and barbecues. They say they pay little heed to diplomas, race, or social background. They claim they focus on intelligence, modes of reasoning, logical and argumentative speed, mastery of quantification, and the ability to project. They also purport to believe they test so-called moral qualities through punctuality, knowing how to bounce back after a failure, managing a dispute, and so forth. Most VCs despise bureaucracies and regulations, because they advocate entrepreneurship and lean organizations as far more efficient ways to tackle public problems. This way of thinking seems purely rational, backed up by reliable, statistically accurate indicators. However, even when they consider themselves faithful progressives, many investors more readily see talent in men than in women, in people in their twenties than in those in their fifties, and in white Americans than in racialized people from other countries. By doing so, investors reveal their talent fetishes—social traits that seem to them to embody talent (such as being an American, a graduate, a white man)—and ignore the fact that the goal of entrepreneurs is not to outsmart everyone else but to build trust.

A STRATEGIC MIND ON FIVE FRONTS

Entrepreneurs must simultaneously seek financing, hire and fire employees, promote products, report to regulatory authorities, and monitor the impact of the product for users—all of which involves giving demonstrations, keeping up to date on industry news, following the competition, meeting with suppliers, preparing financial projections, paying taxes, and knowing how to speak, listen, decide, and trust.[30] The success of one task often determines the success of others. For example, the development of solutions at the technical level is interdependent with the development of the product at the commercial level, just as hiring depends on financing, and so on. Entrepreneurs are multitaskers. Success—when it is achieved—also opens up a series of material and symbolic rewards on the five fronts of entrepreneurship: personal enrichment (investment front), professional recognition (employee front), notoriety (media front), political alliance (regulators), and social impact (user front). Entrepreneurship in Silicon Valley therefore involves entrepreneurs positioning themselves on these five fronts.

Addressing a Problem

To do this, they need to start by doing one thing: addressing a problem. In Silicon Valley entrepreneurs are primarily judged by how they make visible an issue that was previously unsolved and how they plan to market an innovative solution that can address this issue. Pitch competitions are thus structured around these steps: problem, market, solution. The pitch necessarily includes the team gathered to solve the problem. This problematization is not very far from that observed in scientific circles: formulate problems, ask questions, and identify a set of actors who must necessarily use the proposed solution.[31] The problems do not exist in themselves but are *constructed*. To effectively construct a problem, entrepreneurs need a significant amount of information—information that cannot be dissociated from the environment where the problem is built up. They can then collect, produce, and communicate this information. An entrepreneur I interviewed recalls the original context in which he shaped his problem regarding traffic measurements on websites:

> The advantage of being here in the early 2000s was that the Valley was the epicenter of everything that was being done in the internet space, the data being generated on the internet. We use all that to understand behavior. Our idea was to create audience measurement indicators for this new medium, offering them to our clients, mainly internet companies, so that they could monitor their own activity. We met many of these new clients directly here. It's very useful to know them, to see them. . . . The way we built our business was directly influenced by our presence here, by the discussions we had with our friends, with our clients, who had consumer internet startups and who were complaining about not being able to understand and measure their audience, and present it to a third party, whether it was investors or advertisers (interview, San Francisco, October 7, 2016).

Once the solution has been defined, the entrepreneur must promote it on different fronts (investment, employee, media, regulator, user). This military metaphor illustrates the adversity encountered, as well as the need to constantly progress, to set up new alliances, while maintaining minimal unity.[32] Indeed, the progress made depends on the level of resources allocated: capital from investors, work from employees, advertising by the media, authorizations granted by regulators, money and feedback from users. Faced with this, entrepreneurs and their partners can easily feel lost or like they are drowning, both inside and outside the company. The risk is high that they will be seen as an idle deserter, a disorganized jack-of-all-trades, or a manager whose actions spread anxiety and suspicion. An early PayPal employee described how at a crucial early stage of the company, CEO Peter Thiel was increasingly absent, meeting with investors in secret before announcing the company's merger, much to the surprise and disappointment of employees.[33] Founder Elizabeth Holmes was often described during her years at Theranos as distant from its research laboratory's reality, deaf to the technical deadlocks encountered.

The complexity of the task is all the greater because these different fronts do not require the same knowledge, skills, and in a way, intelligence. An entrepreneur thus accounts for the specificity and diversity of the interlocutors in the field of regulation:

> In the US there are different levels of government, you have to go to them, negotiate face to face, the technologies you use, the growth of the number of users, our market presence in other countries, our driver record systems, how we verify that the vehicles are in good condition, our insurance and employee insurance, and that there's money in the company. And it's political too, because it's really negotiation. We are trying to obtain the right for citizens to use this type of service. It's democratization, something that was supposed to be free, and that has been monopolized by the government. The government says: *It's new, so it's illegal* (interview, San Francisco, February 11, 2016).

Thus entrepreneurs develop military thinking to overcome an almost infinite series of obstacles, each more unpredictable than the previous one. A founder I met with gives the following account of his journey to promote an interactive gaming solution in televisions:

> With my previous startup, we started dealing with Turner Sports. Let me tell you what happened to me. We tried to sell our solution to the network. But they didn't understand, they said: "No, it's free." I replied: "But wait, I need to live!" And they retorted: "We're Turner, it's a great opportunity to work with us.". . . So I thought, *We're not going to do that, we're going to take the money from advertisers through them.* I said to the broadcaster: "I'll become a sales agent for you, I'll make a product that you'll sell for me to the advertiser, at a higher price." They said: "Okay, that's interesting."
> So the salesman from the broadcaster walks away with his product, plus the one you dumped on him when you left. It's the equivalent of the guy who goes to sell his chickens in the next city, and on top of that you give him six pounds of potatoes. He'll tell you: "That's a lot of potatoes." You think: *Work it out.* But you don't tell him; you're cheering him up. He is commissioned to

sell the chickens, not the potatoes. If he doesn't sell his chickens, he's in deep shit. So he goes and it turns out that every time he sells a chicken, he sells a potato. And your service is the potato. So the price of the chicken is more expensive. The guy who is used to buying chickens, that is to say, the advertiser, says to him: "But why are you selling it to me for more?" The broadcaster replies: "Well, you didn't see, there's a potato with it." The advertiser replies: "But I don't give a damn about your potato!" And then, the thing that happens, and it's wonderful, is that he says: "You know what? If you get me two chickens with potatoes, I'll sell you the second chicken for less."

So the network comes back from the market delighted and tells you: "I sold all the chickens!" You: "Great! But the potatoes?" "—Ah, well, you know what, they didn't want them. I had to give them away." And you: "But wait a minute, the potato was our product!" So I told them: "You don't want to buy it, you don't know how to sell it, but you sell it like an extra. . . . So, we're going to take part of the advertising revenue that will be generated by the interactive program." And then they react as if you were pulling off a major heist, stealing Rome's treasure. They replied: "You, stinking barbarian, that has never happened; nobody has ever touched that money. And it won't start with you." This is my experience (interview, San Francisco, July 12, 2016).

In this configuration entrepreneurs should think and act as military strategists. They have to be both Caesar and Alexander the Great—that is to say, a cold-blooded leader and one who follows the most rational action possible. Twenty-three-year-old Musk compared himself to Alexander the Great when he was trying to raise money. The entrepreneur is one who both pushes his luck and doubles down on risk-taking.[34] Whatever the inclination, the goal is to become trustworthy.

Demonstrating Your Trustworthiness

Investors, employees, media, regulators, and users are exposed to a multiplicity of solicitations. Large companies provide known services. New solutions seem random and risky. So entrepreneurs must convince people of their relevance, guarantee the reliability of the production process, and distinguish themselves from competing offers. They must therefore make up for the lack of information on the quality of their solution by amplifying positive signals. Everything becomes a pretext for evaluation. Trust is important for people who must rely on each other as they encounter complex entities on these different fronts. As systems theorist Niklas Luhmann points out, the more a social organization is driven by heterogeneous motivations, the more trust is needed.[35] The world of technologies imposes constant change regarding solutions, people, and information. In such circumstances individuals cannot rely on routines, familiarity, or habits to establish trust. But in order for solutions, people, and information to align, entrepreneurs must present themselves as worthy of trust. Entrepreneurs have to provide a minimal level of safety in a highly uncertain process. Trust is thus demonstrated by the entrepreneur-investor relationship.

Because of the accelerated turnover of projects and solutions, potential partners cannot rely on reputation, awards, or prizes.[36] Backers don't know the quality of the solution under development. Entrepreneur reputation is not a reliable indicator because in Silicon Valley entrepreneurs are numerous, from different countries, from different schools, come and go and mostly fail. But what they have done before says little about what they are going to do next. In addition, they attempt to solve problems in a sector where investors cannot be experts of new technological trends. One investor I interviewed summarizes the task's difficulty as follows: "People come to apply for a job that you don't know, don't understand, and don't necessarily know much about, and it's up to you to say whether you buy it or not."[37] This is why investors fall back on low-key psychological and behavioral indicators. They look silently for reasoning patterns, adaptability, work stamina, learning speed, execution speed, communication skills, and stress resistance. Everything is likely to become a decipherable sign, even though interactions often seem casual. One investor I interviewed described himself as a psychologist:

> On seed, I only invest in people. On a guy. I mean, a team. Only on that. If I like the team, if it has resources, vision, if they are strong with each other, if they won't fight. . . . That's one of the reasons why I love my job; today, I only do psychology. VCs, in early stages, are great psychologists (interview, San Francisco, November 4, 2016).

While Silicon Valley is associated with relaxed modes of sociability, interactions there are in fact like serial sequences of professional evaluation governed by a double language. On the one hand, there is a procedural side, relating to respect for Silicon Valley communication codes; on the other, a personal side, which refers to the moral, psychological, and intellectual qualities of the entrepreneurs—qualities deduced from their gestures, posture, mimicry, manner of speaking, and way of doing things. And if entrepreneurs are often beginners, experienced investors have learned the art of neutrality to assess these signals for themselves. A novice investor thus reports on the effectiveness of this poker-face attitude:

> Last year I had a deal with a big investor who was setting up his fund. I wanted us to put $7 to $10 million in it. He doesn't know me; I don't know him. We had lunch in Palo Alto. I worked for one of the biggest executives on the planet who called me an asshole ten times a day in his office. So I'm experienced. But that was the worst lunch of my life. I spent an hour and a half with someone who didn't show anything. Until the end. He laughed when I paid the bill. It took him thirty seconds to figure out I didn't totally master the subject. He scrutinized me constantly. And he gave me nothing. Not an eyebrow. Not a word (interview, San Francisco, October 5, 2016).

In the Silicon Valley interaction system, each person's support is analyzed. Professional relationships are frequently established in private spaces, such as a dorm, garage, home, café, or restaurant. Sociability, such as using first names or calling someone "friend" after just one meeting, commonly blurs the boundaries between the professional and the private. If a quick glance could lead you to believe that Silicon Valley is the friendliest society on Earth, the reality is that in fact it is a marketing relationship, with every attitude and behavior evaluated for economic motivations. What is experienced as a social and proxemic blurring between the private and the public, the intimate and the professional, can be understood from the perspective of trust. Each interaction is likely to be transformed into observation and evaluation in an effort to reduce uncertainty. Behaviors become indicators. This explains the importance of face-to-face meetings in the region.[38] Becoming a trusted support within a growing network is an essential part of the entrepreneur's work.

A NETWORKED SELF

In Silicon Valley, networking appears to be second nature. The ubiquity of business cards, LinkedIn profiles, and networking sessions (some people do two in a row) prove it. At the start of my fieldwork in 2015, an adviser I met at the Marriott Hotel bar in downtown San Francisco pointed to the number of contacts on my LinkedIn account, which at the time was *only* four hundred. He remarked: "Here, we start playing at +five hundred"—the limit beyond which LinkedIn no longer displays the number of connections. Another investor told me that he had reached thirty thousand contacts then stopped "playing." However, the meaning and science behind this approach to networking is not always conscious.

The Uses of Networking

Networking allows an exchange of information. This exchange increases the availability of resources. These resources are now available when they are needed to respond to an opportunity. In this respect the social network does not appear to be a political ideal but rather a social organization based on informal transactions. Players have to increase the number of professional connections—aka "weak ties" (strong ties being those with the emotional resonance of friends and family)—because fostering trust on various fronts makes it possible to access new resources. But the connection between network and resource is not automatic. One interviewee mentions that entrepreneurs must sometimes show the patience of a gold miner:

> Here, there are meetups all the time, opportunities to pitch to people, etc. Angels go to these things. They go, watch, and sometimes sign checks, and they like to do it two, three, four times a year, because they're retired, or they're successful. I used to do that at the beginning, I used to go to these things. You start, then you have a bigger network, deeper, you know tech billionaires. You have the opportunity to get one or two investors who know people higher up, who get an introduction done. It's a snowball effect . . . but it takes a lot of sales work, and networking all the time. . . . Once you have the money, you can drop out, but the day will come sooner or later when you'll need money again. And the thing is, you never know what's going to happen (interview with an entrepreneur, San Francisco, February 26, 2016).

This is why entrepreneurs strive to expand their networks with daily zeal. To play their cards right, they need to accumulate at least a rudimentary kind of social capital—social capital they can build into a system of guaranteed trust. In this the introduction is key. It consists of introducing a person C to a person A via a person B. If C is unknown to A, C and A are members of B's network. Professionals exchange one introduction for another, in an extended system of bartering small services (such as office loans, advice, or invitations). According to sociologist Michel Ferrary, VCs reason that their network will lead them to worthwhile projects: "The operating principle of venture capitalists is to only consider projects that have been recommended by someone they consider reliable (lawyers, university professors, etc.)." For example, John Doerr (partner at Kleiner, Perkins, Caufield, and Byers) says:

I never look at a project that is not warmly recommended by someone whose judgment I respect. If you don't have an introduction, a way to get co-opted, there's no way I'm going to fund you. I receive more than 200 projects per month, that's almost 2500 per year, while I make about ten investments in the same period. I don't materially have the time to analyze them; it all depends on who recommends you.[39]

The way the network is developed in Silicon Valley is based on this three-way game, an interactive triangle of people sharing knowledge. It replicates the triad identified by sociologist Mark Granovetter in what has become the most cited article in sociology on how people find a job, "The Strength of Weak Ties":

Agent A who seeks a job solely on the basis of his or her strong ties will be less likely to find a job than Agent B who draws on both his or her strong and weak ties. Indeed, within the same social network, using only strong ties does not give agent A any advantage in the job search compared to agent B: A and B mobilize the same strong ties, and therefore the same information provided by these strong ties. On the other hand, agent B, by mobilizing his weak ties, has an advantage over agent A. Insofar as the weak links are simple knowledge, they are not systematically shared by agent A. As a result, agent B potentially has more information than agent A about job opportunities.[40]

Thus compounding weak ties is greatly useful where the speed of development and population renewal prevent coordination such as professional control or corporatist organization. In this respect Silicon Valley is a transactional society, as one entrepreneur put it:

Look here [pointing to the people in a downtown café near San Francisco City Hall, half of whom are typing on their laptops]: there are only smart people, it's hard to sort them out. So what do we do if they want to raise money? Well, they're not going to raise money unless they've been introduced by a VC. So what do you do? [shows me his phone—and reads aloud:] messages from Mike who I saw yesterday and who is writing to one of his contacts about me. *I want to introduce you to my friend and total badass*—this is important—*Reid Hoffman, just joined the team as an adviser.* That's validation! Because Reid doesn't care about me alone. On the other hand, he knows Mike, whom he respects, who tells him that I'm a good guy. And if Reid ever thinks Mike is a moron, Mike will know it. Because everyone here knows very well what their sphere of influence is. Everybody knows the intros they can do and nobody is going to have fun doing an intro if they think it's going to put them in danger. So they're only going to make an intro to people they have influence with. Or because you have influence that could benefit the guy. So somewhere along the line, he's giving you a gift (interview, San Francisco, March 4, 2016).

Players develop, maintain, and improve their network, following a job-matching philosophy prosaically stated by Steve Jobs: an *A* player must associate with an *A* player.[41] Although the expression *networking* maintains vagueness about what is at stake, it is in fact a matter of expanding your potential transaction net thanks to reputational guarantors. Each move is a call for an exchange, possibly deferred, probably asymmetrical, but inscribed in a broader potlatch economy. This is why players in Silicon Valley try to make weak ties seem stronger than they really are. To observe this, we can look at the semantic nuances common in the region: casual acquaintances are often labeled as "friends"; colleagues might be called "brothers" or "bros"; members of the same company may be referred to as "family"; and a network of former colleagues might be described as a "mafia." This systematic amplification of links and the exaggerated impression of solidity that emerges from it testifies to the practicality of the network.

Networking through Communities

Although Silicon Valley emphasizes natural networking, the experience of networking is different for each individual. What appears to be a universal network actually encompasses a variety of forms, structures, and temporalities, each with different degrees of openness, density, and supportiveness. The value of the network varies greatly depending on initial position, quality of the interconnected parties, and strength of the connections. In Silicon Valley, it operates through four matrices: universities, companies, diasporas, and socioeconomic traits (gender, race, class, and so forth).[42] The network is a key element of entrepreneurial success, but it operates through channels of varying influence, as demonstrated by the story of an early investor in Google:

> I started interviewing all the people who had PhDs at Stanford and were still working there in the engineering departments. That was about fifty people. They were the best and the brightest. I asked each one of them: *Who is the best with the best idea?* Almost all of them said: *The two guys who worked at Google.* And what's interesting about this story is that this way of doing things is exactly the same as Google's algorithm (interview, San Francisco, October 11, 2016).

In the academic field Stanford University and its computer science department attract more attention than any other. There, several famous solutions have been developed from projects launched within the university.

Researchers, external contributors, and students openly collaborated on projects such as Arpanet (Stanford Research Institute), Cisco (study engineers), Coursera (professors), Google (PhD students), Instagram (students), the internet (professors), LinkedIn (former graduates), Snapchat (students), Sun Workstation (Stanford University Network), or Yahoo (former students). In the department, machines or documents that have made the history of computer science are displayed like in a museum. Students benefit from industry-integrated socialization in an environment conducive to interaction (only 17,529 students at Stanford in 2023's commencement, compared to 45,307 at Berkeley). One former student-turned-entrepreneur reflects on the benefits:

> You have more interaction with your professors than at other universities, a lot of professors work part-time. My first instructor worked almost full time at Facebook and taught a course at Stanford, another worked at Apple, another founded his startup to expand his research. They can really give you career advice. My brother was at the University of Maryland. I guess he got career advice from his professors, too [laughs]. . . . But when your instructor works in these companies, they can tell you what team to go to, what they do, how they do it, introduce you to them. And they know what it's like to work in this industry (interview with an entrepreneur, February 25, 2016).

The life story of a former Stanford University graduate, now CTO of a world-renowned company, highlights the importance of this access over time:

> I went through the process that became typical of going from a good East Coast high school to a West Coast university, because at the time Stanford was mostly attended by West Coast people. I wasn't a super bright student, my first choice was MIT, I was in a selective high school, with quotas that made getting into the Ivy League hyper competitive. Stanford was not the name it has become today. But in 1997, as an undergraduate, I ran into some of the people who have become world leaders today. The CTO of Facebook was in the same dorm as me. Marissa Meyer was the girlfriend of a good friend of mine; I was in the same electronics class as Elon Musk. The web was providing a lot of opportunities for computer geeks. . . . I remember Elon putting a map on the web with a browser for the first time (interview, San Francisco, September 24, 2016).

In the 2010s students attended a program involving former graduates, who became employees of prestigious or trendy companies, providing success tips and setting benchmarks for recruiting the cream of the crop. At one of the sessions two employees of a company valued at more than $1 billion presented a series of slides titled: "You are the product of your environment"; "You could have learned everything you know from Wikipedia and Coursera, why Stanford?"; "Keep looking for the best people and teams"; "Make friends with people who are strong in areas where you suck"; "Seek out real mentors"; "Develop a growth mindset"; "Remember what it's like to learn a new skill"; "Build an ever-evolving identity model"; and so forth. In an interview following this session, one of the developers reflected on the changing landscape, and through it the incentives and opportunities to get into entrepreneurship:

> I came to Stanford in 2010. It wasn't as exuberant as it has become, but there was a big startup scene in Palo Alto. *Hacker News*[43] is one of the ways I got into that world, people I was interacting with who were on campus, people I was meeting and who invited me into their little offices, talking to me about what they were doing, offering me to do little freelance things, because I was a freshman and I needed the money. Plus, there was a group, with a $500,000 budget that came from different VCs who gave $10,000 every year, that I joined; a group of twenty or thirty people that became a platform of people who knew each other, talked about their projects, their startups, offered to come and work there. . . . And tech became a cool thing, something that people had to do when they were at Stanford. . . . I remember realizing this, when I ran into a freshman in my dorm. I was wondering what major I was going to take and he said, "Yeah, me neither, I don't know, I was thinking I might take the startup option." Everyone wanted to start their own startup, were looking for a cofounder, or wanted to partner with a startup (interview with a developer, San Francisco, February 25, 2016).

Going to Stanford opens windows of opportunity in many ways: practical advice, early access to resources, and the most promising networks. In this way the university acts as a bridge to business.

Companies offer a second matrix. A CTO who cofounded a well-known company with a member of the PayPal mafia (the founders and former employees of the original PayPal group) illustrates the dynamics of resource collectivization within an alumni network:

> When we started, TechCrunch was already there, we shared their office at one point; they started using our service very early, in 2007. In the more mainstream dot-com articles, there was a lot of talk about people who were in our very close environment. After doing PayPal, my cofounder stayed very connected with the whole PayPal mafia; they talk to each other, still often, have done many projects together, with models and technologies that have evolved and that have been a way for us to feed our roadmap. The PayPal

mafia, some of them are friends, others not, but they all respect each other, have quite brilliant backgrounds, and share a lot in common. My cofounder started a student fund with a PayPal alum; he also joined Peter Thiel's fund. But they don't all get together every year for a big party. The term *mafia* is a misnomer. It's a network, a very small one, in which they exchange information and share their projects. When you look at our investors, there are three members of the PayPal mafia, all of whom are on the board. It's a microsystem of financial and information sharing that's very hard to replicate (interview with a CTO, Paris, January 13, 2020).

Those without privileged access to top-tier companies, basically the majority of Silicon Valley entrepreneurs, use the companies they have been involved with as a way to build what Bruno Latour called their "credibility capital."[44]

The third network matrix is diaspora. Faced with the trials of expatriation, expats see diaspora as a primary resource and shelter. They find a wealth of advice on hiring, firing, tax optimization, local professional conventions, cost of living management, competition, and more. In addition, they can enjoy the comfort of their mother-tongue, their home country's cuisine, and a sense of humor shared among compatriots. It can be the source of practical advice (where to stay, where to eat, what to do on weekends, where to enroll your children in school), recommendations, and entry points into the industry ("You should meet . . .").

Finally, being a woman, a minority, identifying as gay, lesbian, queer, trans, or coming from a certain social background are also the means to feed a network.[45] An AI researcher tells me at a downtown café:

I'm often the only woman at meetings, meetups, etc. So I'm very active in creating a community of women in tech, where we can talk, meet, and help each other. It's vital for us if we want to gain visibility and progress (interview, San Francisco, September 13, 2024).

Social properties can be activated and solidarities build up differently. For example, male-centered networks differ from female-centered ones; US nationals differ from foreigners; graduates of major universities differ from those with less reputable training; and so forth. A woman entrepreneur talks about how she sought to turn a property originally seen as a liability into a moveable asset:

It took me two years after my master's degree to master what I was doing when I was networking. Before, I was doing what I had been advised to do during my studies at Berkeley: reaching out to alumni. Someone is paid full time at the university to network with alumni and help students, so emails are exchanged once a month, summer programs are organized with alumni. . . . It's very formal. I had my eureka moment when I came back from maternity leave. People had seen me pregnant, so right away it was a chance to talk about something other than work, and that's when I understood what networking is: not talking about work but making connections, and nothing better than kids for that. Having kids here has been a professional advantage. Because it becomes so easy to connect (interview, Berkeley, January 26, 2016).

University, company, diaspora, and other socioeconomic variables thus constitute the four matrices of one's network in Silicon Valley. However, they converge toward a common organization: the community. As one immigrant entrepreneur told me:

It's never easy to create a company, even harder when you're not at home. Foreigners all suffer from that. The codes are different. But you need to understand them. It's useful to meet someone who says: "You're not crazy, I have exactly the same problem and I think that . . ." It took me four years to understand, first, that I shouldn't try to mimic Americans, then that I won't change them. They come and tell you: "I love pizza, I love latte . . ." And you tell them: "Wait, I'm from Europe, you're too stupid, I'm going to teach you about food, gastronomy, taste . . ." After a while, you stop. You're not going to change them. So second step, you go back to the starting point which becomes the third step: *I'm going to adapt.* But it still doesn't work. So you arrive at a fourth stage . . . You have to get beaten up, and you understand as you go along . . .

An American finally explained it to me one day like this: "Here everything is about community. I don't care if you're Chinese or Indian and live in the same building as me. My problem is if you're not in the building, that you are a stranger, in the sense of a stranger in the house. I don't care if there's a Chinese guy living on the second floor. On the other hand, a Chinese guy who rings my doorbell at 6 a.m. and whom I don't know: that's a danger. And I'm not going to make a deal with him. If you're my neighbor, even with your shitty accent and your stupid style, I don't give a shit, as long as you're in the building, that is to say that you respect the rules of the condo."

People mock Middle Eastern guys who go to business meetings in traditional garb. But foreigners here are the same. Europeans come wearing a tie . . . Have you seen people wearing ties around here? You have to accept it. You're like a Senegalese arriving in Paris, Black, with a shitty accent. You don't dress like them. But you can't go back to the village, because if you do, you will be the shame of the village. In Silicon Valley, as foreigners, we are beacons of our countries; when you realize that, that you're actually a projected dream, well, you reboot.

Everything I did before doesn't count. It's not an Italian renaissance. It's an American *rebirth.* I have to build a new project and a new identity (interview, San Francisco, March 4, 2016).

For newcomers, initial euphoria gives way to disenchantment, reality sets in, and their outsider mentality evolves into a player mind-set—for example, starting to be the architect of one's own network and career. Up or down, this path exposes entrepreneurs to intense highs and lows in experiences.

THE ENTREPRENEURIAL EXPERIENCE

Entrepreneurs describe business creation as an incomparably fruitful and transformative life experience. However, it also implies overwork, sacrifices, and deprivations. You are exposed to failure, overconsumption, and unfortunate allocations of time and money.[46]

The Roller Coaster

The entrepreneur's Stakhanovist daily life—that is, a life of intense productivity—turns out to be as dull as it is unappealing, and quite distant from Elon Musk's pop eccentric lifestyle, as one entrepreneur shared:

No movies, no sports, no going out [laughs] . . . I haven't been to a restaurant in eight months, I can't. Every dollar I have, I have to put into work, calls, sponsoring, meeting startups, my team, etc. I have no leisure time. You can't give yourself any distractions. You have to go fast, get up at 5:00 a.m. The first thing I do is look at everything that happened overnight in relation to the product on my feed: *what happened, the feedback, my team, did they struggle, etc.* Then I answer the emails. At 7:00 a.m., I really start working on the product. I take the app, I throw it on the grill, and I look at everything that doesn't work in relation to the feedback I've got. Because we ask users: *What doesn't work? What can we change?* And as a user yourself, you ask yourself: *What can I improve?* I do this until 12:30–1:00. I stop for fifteen or thirty minutes. I eat. . . . Right now, I'm in a granola phase. I'm excited about it too [laughs]! I make myself a bowl of granola, and then I go for a walk around the neighborhood [Fillmore in San Francisco], fifteen minutes, I come home, I start again around 1:30-2:00 p.m., and then it's the acquisition part. I contact landlords. I tell them what we're doing. I ask if we can call each other. I explain the service. I call them right away. They tell me if they're interested, if they know what we do. . . . If they want the full presentation, I send it to them again.

It didn't work? Okay, why? Anyway, you talk to them. And I do this all afternoon. Until 7:00 p.m. If everything is fine, I eat a little bit. A little salad, if not ramen [laughs]. Good entrepreneurial food! But we [his wife and cofounder] don't eat together. No, no, no. Oh, she goes to meetups, we meet afterwards in the evening, she gives me direct feedback, so I know right away. At 8:30 p.m., I open Slack, because our teams are starting to work in Europe. I check the bugs, the things that don't work, the devs who are on vacation, I explain, etc. So, you finish at 1:00 a.m. (interview, San Francisco, September 20, 2015).

Entrepreneurship thus feeds ambivalent feelings: enthusiasm, excitement, exhilaration but also disappointment, discouragement, depression. It echoes philosopher John Dewey's definition of learning from experience, which is "to make a backward and forward connection between what we do to things and what we enjoy or suffer from them in consequence."[47] This intense flow of interactions contributes to the richness of entrepreneurial life, according to the interviewees, due to its effect on learning. A former trader who became an entrepreneur says: "I work between twelve and fourteen hours a day, maybe ninety-five hours a week. And I feel great. I couldn't work that hard in any other industry."[48]

Entrepreneurship means alternating periods of euphoria and despondency, often referred to as the "entrepreneur roller coaster." At a café in Palo Alto, the founder of three companies, who has lived in Silicon Valley since the late 1990s, explains why:

In reality, when you have a company, it's an emotional roller coaster. When you go up, you struggle with your product. You're disgusted. Your money, you see it melting away. You lose a lot of energy. . . . Then, you go for it, and it's *wooooowww*!!!! It's cool!!! Except when it doesn't work. Market reception is not good, your product is not good. . . . So you go to raise money, and there you go back up. . . . It's complicated. . . . But you raise some money, and here you go again! You can burn all the money and launch. . . . This first sequence takes a year, with a small team, and then you have to talk to as many people as possible to confirm your problem.

The key question is: Is it a problem that really exists? Then you confirm your solution: Does your solution answer the problem? This is the product. You do different iterations. Then what counts is the difference between the number of features and the speed of development of each of them to reach what we call here the minimum valuable product. Basically, the question is: What is the production of value? So the procedure is: You pay $500 in advertising on Facebook, you can do a little targeting . . . finding different problems. Then it becomes your guide. Do you have a product? Okay. If it doesn't work, you stop and do something else. That's really the quantity aspect, the size of the market.

And then there's the qualitative aspect: What's clicking? You go deeper, then you test the solutions. If it suits you, you enrich . . . and it's the market that gives *you* ideas. No matter how great you are, you'll never be as great as the market. You take the stuff, you continue improving your product. For the minimum valuable product, the first thing to do is a prototype, with a nice design, it's super important. You get a guy to do it, and you pay him $15,000, $20,000, or in shares of your company. It's expensive, but it's worth it.

After the prototype, you look at it. You make a list of the problems you solve, via features, and then you can do focus groups. You identify your population, its demographics. You get feedback, and then you decide on the priority. Then, you talk to VCs to maintain momentum generated by features, feedback from users, number of clicks on ads, etc.; and as soon as you have momentum, it's easier to get money. And there the timelines are: in one to three months, definition of the minimum valuable product; three to six months of development; and then you make the product in one year; then you launch. And then, there's a big chance that it won't work, even if you've done the thing well, because it's not well done on a technical standpoint, or a guy comes along before you and destroys your idea, or you encounter a whole bunch of problems you hadn't foreseen (interview, Palo Alto, November 3, 2015).

This intensity reflects the ever-present risk of failure and the potential for organizational disasters in entrepreneurship.

However, interviewees in Silicon Valley highlight that failures are dedramatized and instead are even valued as opportunities for gaining experience. This is possible due to several reassurance mechanisms: moral (putting failure into perspective), social (the collective valorization of entrepreneurial experiences), economic (opportunities to restart a project), and even geographical (returning to one's city, region, or country of origin). As one entrepreneur told me:

What's good here is that you're in a sector with a social Darwinist aspect, but we know that those who succeed could have failed. So whatever happens, you're part of the ecosystem. If you fail, we'll support you. You've contributed to the system. If you succeed, you give back. And when you fail, you try again (interview, Palo Alto, August 30, 2017).

But for those who experience failure, it can still be a traumatic experience.

When you fail, it's a big slap in your face. It can take a few years to recover financially and psychologically, because running a startup means pushing yourself all the time, working days, evenings, weekends, etc. So, afterwards you feel the emptiness. You lose a sense of control, and the feeling of having missed things sets in. You wonder what you did wrong. We talked about this for two years with my cofounder, so maybe it's also a kind of therapy, a learning process, accepting and knowing what you can learn from it (inter-view with an entrepreneur, Stanford, February 15, 2016).

In this case, entrepreneurs tend to take responsibility for failure, even if they see themselves as part of an ecosystem. Consequently, entrepreneurs must navigate numerous crises. During these entrepreneurial storms they need to demonstrate moral virtues.

Virtues of Simplicity and Sincerity

Entrepreneurs are said to be driven by a "need for achievement"; their com-bativeness is seen as the expression of "individual traits" that demonstrate almost innate qualities.[49] However, Silicon Valley offers them an environ-ment where it is expected of entrepreneurs to demonstrate qualities that are socially controlled and sanctioned. For this reason I will speak of virtues. These are not abstract entities or intrinsic moral qualities. They are relational and behavioral expectations aimed at fostering trust. They are valued as benchmarks and minimum guarantees for stakeholders. In this respect they blur the lines between what French philosopher Vladimir Jankélévitch described as two categories of virtue: those characterized by an underlying self-interest and self-expression (*quidditatives*) and those characterized by self-forgetfulness (*quodditives*).[50] Indeed, entrepreneurs present themselves as resources that can be exploited by others, a posture that is understood in an apparently extremely classic Silicon Valley phrasing (and *Godfather*-style): "How can I help you?" Surprisingly, in a world that has adopted the formula "fake it till you make it," two virtues are particularly emphasized in profes-sional interactions: simplicity and sincerity. Simplicity is valuable because it reduces the cost and volume of information to be transmitted by the entre-preneur on various fronts.

As the tech marketing pioneer Guy Kawasaki said to me during an interview, with a weary tone: "I started the ten-slide presentation, because I couldn't take it anymore after listening to tons and tons of bullshit."[51] Simplicity is championed in communication but also in production and organizational matters. An ideal is pursued: the alignment between communication, solu-tion, and organization. This industrial pursuit makes Silicon Valley firms quite different from the multiservice company model, which has been the reference for capitalism in the United States.[52] A serial entrepreneur explained this virtue:

When I started here, the way I thought about everything was super complicated. The thing I've quickly learned here was to monotask, stay monofunc-
tional, and maintain focus. . . . And at the end, I've realized that a company
is a product, a distribution channel. When you have a big company, you can
become multiproduct and so on. But to do this, you need to have a product,
which is a brand, which has the name of the product, with a buyer or a type
of buyer. If you already have two types of buyers, it will be too complicated
(interview, San Francisco, August 29, 2017).

This virtue of simplicity must be maintained throughout different stages and
must be accompanied by sincerity.

Sincerity helps address uncertainties and information asymmetries
wherein someone has more (or better) information than another. The reasons
for not being entirely straightforward are plentiful, as the spectacular case of
Elizabeth Holmes demonstrates. Holmes used a deep voice in public and
with employees to project her authority, avoided blinking in front of the
media to emphasize her conviction, and wore black clothing to enhance her
credibility, all while she manipulated figures sent to investors.[53] Hiding,
omitting, or modifying information are powerful temptations in Silicon
Valley, with the Theranos and FTX court cases as reminders. Entrepreneurs
may feel as though they are walking on the edge of a moral precipice due to
the complexity of their position. They must constantly carry a promise,
which has by definition an uncertain outcome, while reassuring stakeholders
of its feasibility. This ambiguity is particularly evident in the entrepreneur-
investor relationship, as described by a Silicon Valley veteran:

Entrepreneurs rarely know what they're going to do and what they need to
do, but you still have to express confidence and some form of certainty in
front of VCs. I remember when I was in front of the Kleiner Perkins committee, with John Doerr pitching with me, because the VC who backs you
is standing in the room with the entrepreneur to present the project to the
investment committee. We were presenting the financial projections, and we
were saying it would be a $5 billion company within five years. And then John
turned to me and said, "We go with what? 60 percent of that?" And I said:
"Huh . . . What do you mean John . . .? 60 percent No! We're going to go
home, do the math . . . What are you doing to me?! Is that a trick question or
what?" I could feel the blood pumping in my head. Standing up in front of
the whole committee with John Doer cutting my projection by 60 percent . . .
I wish I had a good answer. . . . In fact, he was trying to say to me: "That's just
not realistic. You know we're going to have to lower your numbers. So where
do we start?"

Then you learn that's part of the process. You commit to investors and then three months later, *whoops*, you realize you're not going to be able to sell at the price you said you would; you're not going to get the set of customers that you were planning to get. And no entrepreneur *knows* [changing his voice] that. . . . The whole point of being an entrepreneur is to be in the fantasy while thinking you're realistic. You spend your time in this very heavy cognitive process. . . . Because it's *suuuuuuper* important to show that you are not wrong. And in relation to that, there are several layers: the personal layer, basically your integrity, your team's integrity, your investors' integrity, and this very last layer which is if you're really wrong, you'll get kicked out [laughs]. When I started my investment fund, what we tried to do was get the investors close enough to the entrepreneurs that the entrepreneurs would trust them and tell us the truth (interview with an investor, Palo Alto, October 11, 2016).

Sincerity is expected in order to maintain quality of information. Social sanction testifies to this collective expectation. Glenn Mueller is a good example. In the early 1990s, Mueller funded Jim Clark, a Stanford professor who founded Silicon Graphic. Taking advantage of the entrepreneur's naivety, the venture capitalist obtained a larger share of the company's capital than was customary. When the company went public, only the venture capitalist truly profited. Clark then started another company, Netscape, and refused funding from Mueller. By then a well-known figure in Silicon Valley, Clark spoke out about the greed of venture capitalists (it was he who popularized the term *vulture capitalist*). The consequences for Mueller were tremendous. Many entrepreneurs refused to be financed by the Mayfield Fund and Mueller's associates blamed him for failing to invest in the promising Netscape company. On April 4, 1994, when Netscape was officially incorporated, Mueller committed suicide, shut out of the deal and rejected by the social networks vital to the economic, social, and psychological lifeblood of Silicon Valley.[54]

This story shows how trust is a fundamental principle of the relationship between contractors. In a world of "promises," "cheaters" risk sanctions, ranging from jail to ostracism. The scandals involving notoriously fraudulent entrepreneurs should thus be seen as an expression of a systemic quest to preserve trust within an industry based on information, projects, and networks of weak ties. To demonstrate the virtues of simplicity and sincerity, to overcome daily challenges, and to excel on multiple fronts, entrepreneurs need a great deal of energy.

Energy Capital

In January 2025, Mark Zuckerberg caused a stir by celebrating "masculine energy" in a Joe Rogan podcast. If the masculinist tone of this declaration put him on the spot, energy optimizing is a widely shared concern in Silicon Valley. Some interviewees mention energy not as an autonomous bodily quality but as a form of capital. The level and quality of energy capital depends on adopting a particular lifestyle. Entrepreneurs are particularly attentive to maintaining, feeding, and increasing their energy capital, as it allows access to other kinds of capital (economic, informational, and relational).

Silicon Valley is famous for launching new diets and spiritual trends. It's because the self, mind and body, is seen as an object to shape, adapt, and nurture. Since the early 2000s, transhumanists have been advocating the integration of technologies into the body. During the course of my research I met engineers who were monitoring everything they absorbed—liquids, solids, and drugs. Others were carrying out longitudinal studies on their microbiota using new technologies. For $2 million a year, American millionaire Bryan Johnson employs a team of thirty doctors to help his body and organs regain their youthfulness. Without reaching this level of investment in self-transformation, most of the entrepreneurs I met were thinking about how to maintain and improve their energy.

In this respect energy constitutes a characteristic of human capital, which economist Gary Becker defines as the combination of physical and intellectual resources. Entrepreneurs use different techniques to enhance their energy capital. Some advocate such diets as Keto, intermittent fasting, and cleanses. Others champion super drinks, such as green juices (favored by Elizabeth Holmes), salt juice (favored by Jack Dorsey), and açai beverages.[55] Still others rely on yoga, training at the gym, or outdoor sports like cycling, cross-country running, surfboarding, and kitesurfing. Some enhance their energy by dating, partying, and drugs. Others, just the opposite. They go on dopamine fasts by cutting out dating, partying, drugs, and sex. Others strategically aim at recharging energy levels through meditation, prayer, or time spent with family. Various approaches coexist in a region that is conducive to syncretism between the West and the East.[56] As one entrepreneur explained:

> When you are an entrepreneur, the main issue is to take away the stress. Because stress thrives when something is not sure. . . . When you are an entrepreneur, nothing is sure: Will my code break? Will my server hold up? Will

the market take my product? Is anyone going to screw me over? Plus, while you're building your company, you're not making any money. So it's ... wow [takes a step back and widens his eyes] ... A lot of stress. For that: I do ten to thirty minutes of meditation a day; yoga in the morning; and sports, gym, at night. When I was young, I used to party a lot, because it takes away the stress (interview with an entrepreneur, Palo Alto, November 18, 2015).

Encounters are regularly presented as an energy source by interviewees, an observation that is in line with the hypothesis of American sociologist Randall Collins, for whom energy constitutes one of the main purposes of interactions: "In a rite of interaction, two or more people are together in the same place and affect each other with their common bodily presence, whether they pay attention or not."[57] This quest for energy is based on eminently individual practices and logics, while at the same time proceeding from resolutely collective approaches promoted by prominent entrepreneurs. Entrepreneurs aim to survive in a world that is inclusive with values but selective in practice. The cumulative disparities in placement, trajectory, and opportunities explain why an open environment produces such hierarchies. Those I interviewed work to counterbalance the inequalities of opportunity by putting their identity into play, modulating their reactions to stress, promoting healthy physical habits, and remaking their self in order to heighten activable resources. Thus the articulation between the individual and the collective tends to be reversed: entrepreneurs become the imprint of their environment rather than impacting it. The company is the main vehicle for this dialectic.

FIVE

Evolutionary Companies

Change is inevitable. Of everything...
—Interview with a product manager, San Francisco, January 28, 2016

IN EARLY 2025, ELON MUSK and the "DOGE kids" (a cadre of young tech workers within Donald Trump's so-called Department of Government Efficiency) set about an overhaul of the federal state, deemed dysfunctional by the entrepreneur, based on a techno-centric approach. Seeing the tech industry and work organization as a means of economic and political revival is not a new idea. In the 1980s the American economy was hit hard by a severe recession and competition from Japan. Former California governor Ronald Reagan was elected in 1980 largely on the promise of making America great again by following new economic paths. Technology companies were already presented as the new solution. The *New York Times* described Apple and Genentech as the "technological elixir" for a flagging American economy.[1] Published in 1982, *In Search of Excellence* became an international bestseller, a book written by two San Francisco–based McKinsey consultants about "America's best run companies." The book praised Silicon Valley companies for their positive bias toward action, customer proximity, employee autonomy and initiative, and productivity. Silicon Valley productivity, in particular, stood out—attributed to the added value of its people and its sense of pragmatism. This sense of pragmatism evolved out of key Silicon Valley principles: focusing on a core business, implementing a simple organization with small teams, and combining flexibility and rigor.[2] Intel, Apple, Microsoft, Dell, Oracle, Sun Microsystems, and Lotus embodied the hope of an industrial renaissance for the country.

These companies are different from classic American firms, characterized by economist Ronald Coase in the 1930s as enabling a reduction of the cost of information exchange: "a firm will tend to expand until the costs of organizing an extra transaction within the firm become equal to the costs of carrying out the same transaction by means of an exchange on the open market."[3] In

Silicon Valley the exchange of information was nimbler. To understand how, its work organization warranted particular attention. Cisco was praised for its ability to make the company a home away from home. In the 1990s the "new economy" fascinated people with its ability to combine family values and a rock 'n' roll spirit.[4] In the 2000s Google intertwined workspace and playground, becoming the antithesis of the streamlined atmospheres found in soulless bureaucracies, dehumanized factories, and retail chains. This dichotomy between the great companies of the past and those of the future echoed in several disciplines, creating two polar opposites. The first is based on rationality, even if limited, via control of work, pace acceleration, and marginal cost reduction (Charles Taylor, Henri Fayol, Peter Drucker, James March and Herbert Simon, and others). The second one relates to evolution, valuing change and constant adaptation to the environment.[5] Adaptation focused on teamwork and group projects, which, although more random in their development, were more efficient in providing access and information-processing services to a broader audience. Silicon Valley epitomizes this second tradition. Production and data processing are at the heart of its activities, and organizations are presented as "collaborative," "agile," "fast," "lean," and "learning."[6]

These companies seem to have found an answer to historical critiques of capitalism: exploitation and alienation. Adam Smith and Karl Marx shined a light on alienating labor division and repetitive tasks, the unfortunate arrival of machines in cotton, linen, and wool mills where women and children worked, and the "despotism of capital"—that is, the need "to produce in an ever-decreasing time an ever-increasing quantity of value."[7] All around the world, students hoping to join the tech workforce send in applications. For example, twenty thousand application letters came in for an internship in 2015 at Google France, whereas a job opportunity gets an average of twenty applications in France. Employees of new technology companies say they are passionate about exploring and pushing the capabilities of the solutions they develop. Developers, designers, and data analysts enjoy a hedonist but challenging work environment. At work, these tech workers smile and collaborate, fulfilling their dream of working in the tech industry. In sunny Stanford and tech campuses, which sometimes feels like summer camp, I have witnessed firsthand that hedonism can go hand in hand with high standards. Close by, during a visit of Google's headquarters, I wrote:

> It's 4:00 p.m. A beach volley 2-on-2 is starting on the court at the center of the campus. It's weird that they put it there. An employee joked that the peo-

ple playing there were hired actors. A group of thirty-somethings, more than twenty strong, is heading to the soccer field adjacent to campus. Just crossing "Google Avenue." Walking leisurely. I'm sitting under one of the parasols adorned with company colors. Weather is mild and sunny. The atmosphere makes me think of a summer camp, rather than the heart of the tech industry (field notes, February 23, 2016).

In addition to their high salaries, Big Tech employees get access to sports facilities, daycare centers, laundry services, team retreats, free food, open bars with DJ sets every week, free medical services, and massages. In 2014, Apple and Facebook even offered their female employees an egg-freezing service.

However, tech companies are numerous and heterogeneous in terms of capitalization, structure, workforce size (Table 8), and geographical location. Teams either grow or shrink. Facebook peaked in 2022 with 87,314 employees, up from 12,691 at the beginning of my research period in 2015. In 2024, Facebook claimed 44,942 full-time employees, spread across twenty-three teams in its eighty-two offices worldwide. However, one-third of the region's tech companies had no more than ten employees. Furthermore, the tech industry's employee turnover rate is the highest. In 2023 median tenure at Amazon was only one year. One year, one month at Google; two years at Apple; and two years, three months at Facebook.[8] While the world sees Silicon Valley as a land of giants, it is full of seemingly unfaithful employees and small companies with limited life expectancies.[9] Small tech companies seek to leverage the money, power, and service ecosystems of Big Tech, while Big Tech aims to capture innovation emerging from these small companies.[10] Beyond this interdependent relationship, organizations are on a continuum, and becoming a larger company implies going through several development stages.

This is why teams frequently change in terms of management, projects, size, location, name, image, logo (often daily for Google's search engine), and more. The belief of Silicon Valley entrepreneurs, managers, and investors is that change is "inevitable," as the manager in the opening quotation of this chapter puts it. Routines, standards, and processes fade away when faced with "evolutionary scenarios."[11] Companies must evolve. Employees jump from project to project and management frequently changes. Thus Silicon Valley companies are characterized by a protean ability to constantly evolve. This ability comes with a series of organizational challenges: remaining effective despite change, maintaining coherence despite evolutions, and preserving a structure beyond adaptations. This chapter analyzes the ways Silicon Valley

TABLE 8. Active tech companies with headquarters in Silicon Valley, 2020

Number of employees	Companies
1–10	4,338
11–50	4,931
51–100	1,318
101–250	801
251–500	358
501–1,000	267
1,001–5,000	177
5,001–10,000	76
10,000+	105
N/A	2,197
Total	14,568

SOURCE: Crunchbase.

responds to these challenges. To adapt to inevitable change, tech companies strive to retain employees and integrate them quickly by continually shaping their company culture, often personified by the CEO.

HIRING THE BEST

The management history of Silicon Valley could be summed up by three fears: the fear of top employees leaving the company; the fear of top employees joining direct competitors; and the fear of employees departing to start their own ventures, potentially replicating the company's business. Companies are therefore obsessed with hiring and retaining the best people. But this objective takes on different meanings depending on the stage of a company's development. Usually founders start their business in their home.[12] Nolan Bushnell programmed his first *Computer Space* game in his daughter's room before creating Atari. The whole garage startup imagery illustrates it. These modest and relatively solitary beginnings are extremely important for innovation. Innovative products are often developed in the early days of a company, before creativity slows down. Even though returns and profits typically increase later due to a more structured market, the initial innovation occurs early on.[13]

Building a product, developing new features, and investing in a novel niche within a large information system—while stabilizing the product amid setbacks, competition, and challenges—requires hiring technically skilled workers. The next development phase is described in sociologist Arthur Stinchcombe's examination of the challenges of information processing:

> Maintaining the quality of the information flow is usually done through constant monitoring by people who know what uncertainty needs to be analyzed, where information about it needs to be obtained, what causal units determine which units are subject to that uncertainty, how to trade off timeliness of information for noise reduction, what is the temporal scope of the decisions, what is the degree of uncertainty in the different types of information and how to properly indicate the level of uncertainty, who is motivated to distort the system, what auditing or control procedures will work, and who are the other experts to consult on all of these issues.[14]

The company is then ready to engage a third phase. This one sets it apart from traditional sectors: an operating technology; an extensive, structured, and clearly identified market; and a substantial means of production but with a slower innovation dynamic. In fact, once a market niche has been identified and invested in, teams often systematize procedures and tend toward bureaucratization. Tech workers usually look down on these big yet slow-moving organizations because their learning potential would be stunted if they worked for them. Large companies can of course grow externally, by hiring people or buying other companies. Apple made 100 acquisitions between 1976 and 2020, Microsoft 225 in forty-five years, Amazon 88 in twenty-five years, Facebook 82 in fifteen years, Google 236 in twenty years—an average of one acquisition per week. Throughout these three phases the fate of organizations and the lifespan of innovations in Silicon Valley continuously depend on the human factor.

Chasing Talent

In Silicon Valley, being innovative also involves finding new way to identify, attract, and retain tech workers, often referred to metonymically as "talent" or "brains." Their merits are conceptualized in a hierarchical manner. Strategies and procedures vary, organizational needs evolve, available capital fluctuates, and so does the type of talent sought. Small startups must compensate for a lack of human resources by diversifying tasks performed by employees. Companies with the highest capitalization can attract the most sought-after specialized profiles, provided they act quickly. Faced with the cost of labor or the difficulty of attracting the best talent, growing companies are likely to outsource technical teams, trying to arbitrate between remuneration, skills, and ease of communication according to time zones, linguistic gaps, and so forth. An experienced product manager talks about how to handle this conundrum:

> I manage a team of four people working on the company's scalability. Customer support is a big issue for us. We have to be available twenty-four hours a day, seven days a week, everywhere in the world, so we have people in Mexico and India. They have hourly shifts, without geographical zoning, to be able to reply quickly, no matter where the request comes from. I had already experienced this type of relocation when I was at Google in the 2000s, with India, but it didn't work very well, because of the time zone, the culture, the language. . . . The other problem with India is the absence of middle management. In short, it's a huge hassle and the quality of the work is not so good. There are brilliant people in India, that's not the problem. But the logistics don't work. We wanted to open in Europe, but it's too expensive, too many taxes. . . . So we gave up. But Mexico is extraordinary. We have a team of fifty people there, which reminds me a bit of a Google team, with highly trained people who went to US universities, young, hungry, intelligent, driven, and in the same time zone. . . . A real treat! And we pay them half as much as in the United States! Basically, it's 100 for an American, 50 for a Mexican, 17 for an Indian (interview, San Francisco, August 29, 2017).

An entrepreneur who manages two companies with several dozen employees spoke of the trade-off between hiring within the region at a high cost or relocating but with the increased cost of coordination:

> You look at what people are asking for in terms of salary, what they want. . . . You try to bring the teams together, asking yourself if it makes sense for you. . . . I'd like to have all my developers in San Francisco, because I need them to develop the product. . . . But in reality, only Google, Facebook, Uber, Airbnb can afford it. For the others, it's too expensive, and people are not loyal. In Silicon Valley or in India, people are always on the move. In the beginning, I had several overseas teams. If you can show that the profitability/price ratio is good, investors are fine with it. When I split my company, I set up a team in Ukraine and one in India, which streamlined things for both companies. I learned how to do that in Silicon Valley. But it's problematic when it comes to raising [funds and growing]. If there are too many overseas centers, in terms of management, distribution, it's too complicated (interview, Paris, January 16, 2020).

To handle this problem, recruiting young engineers is an option. Not because they are computer geniuses but because their salary and learning curve make them look like good investments. Big companies hunt them on university campuses by funding programs, organizing training sessions, and financing job fairs several times a year. A former student in Stanford's computer science department reports:

> At Stanford, in the computer science department, in the third year, companies come to you: *Do you want to come work for us?* It was the late 2000s, the economy was suffering, but tech companies put up a big tent, two or three times a year, in front of the Gates Building [financed by Bill Gates, housing the computer science department], and for big events, it was in front of the bookstore. Each firm pays $20,000 per booth. I know because afterwards I was part of a team to go there; because it's a never-ending cycle [laughs]! The idea is to send Stanford alumni because they will have more connections with the students. Every quarter end, the companies set up their little booth, with goodies, saying: *Hello, we are Google, Facebook, Uber, how are you?* All the students give their résumés, the courses they took, and the internships they did in computer science. And people from the company discuss with them. Usually it's the engineer, unshaven, smells a little bit bad, and the recruiter, a pretty cute girl (interview with a developer, San Francisco, November 11, 2015).

After two or three years of work, employees are considered experienced and are subject to nearly daily solicitations. A Facebook data analyst says:

> Usually I don't answer, because there are too many requests and they are not targeted: it's a recruiter sending feelers to all the valley's data analysts. But if it's a manager who took the time, I respond by saying: "So far, so good." Airbnb, last week. Uber contacts me all the time. I think I must have talked to all their managers there [laughs] (interview, Menlo Park, March 10, 2016).

Others choose to train talent themselves, like this researcher-entrepreneur:

> Do you really want to pay kids just out of school that you're going to pay $250,000? Of course they're good. But they're not worth that price. You don't even know if they can stand on their own or if they're going to have to take it all back. So what I'm doing right now is looking for PhDs, in disciplines other than computer science, in biology, physics, etc., and I'm looking for people who can help me. The best are math researchers. That's the dream. And then I train them. They cost much less and are much better! (interview with an entrepreneur, investor, and AI researcher, Los Gatos, September 16, 2024).

The difficulty of attracting tech workers in high demand on the job market explains why elaborating, preparing, and conducting recruitment procedures is a job of its own. Regardless of the company's level of development, members spend a lot of time on hiring. The technical and cultural criteria used to assess engineers and developers is commonly composed work ethics, communication style, behavior, and so forth. Recruiters also try to determine the "culture fit" between the employee and the company. Technical skill and culture are entangled. A Googler, who has been involved in many hiring processes, explains the process in his previous company:

> A committee is made up of several recruiters who fill out an evaluation form, which must say what we thought of a candidate. Then, we discuss. The interviewer scores them from 0 to 4, which mimics the American system: 4 meaning, *If you don't hire them, I quit*; 3, *I think we need them*; 2, *I'm not sure*; 1, *I don't think we should hire them*; and 0, *if you hire them, I'm out of here* [laughs]. If you only have 3.5s or 4s, you don't question it. But if you see 2.2, 1.9, then you have to read in detail, and then. . . . It's called raising the bar. Basically, it's where do you set the bar? Do you raise the bar with this candidate or do you lower it? The other day, we turned down a guy even though he had extremely good technical scores. But all the feedback was consistent after the five to six interviews: no one wanted him on their team. So we didn't hire him (interview with a software engineer, San Francisco, March 4, 2016).

Although Google's method is a standard in the Valley, managers or employees regularly try to find a different angle.

> With a buddy of mine, we're working on our recruiting process, because we weren't getting enough signals from our candidates, our drills weren't very high quality. . . . We took three days to redo it. We just asked for permission from the personnel department (interview with a software engineer, San Francisco, March 6, 2016).

This alignment between employee and firm often comes with a fundamental divergence in purpose. In economist Albert Hirschman's terms, "loyalty" in Silicon Valley is an extremely important value for companies, not for workers. Although tech may have been known for employee loyalty in the 1980s (e.g., IBM offered lifetime employment until the 1990s), staying with a company for a long time has become a negative indicator of worker value.[15] It supposedly reflects a weak entrepreneurial mind-set. As one eBay employee confessed in the late 2000s, "staying in the same company for fifteen years, people don't do that here."[16]

Moving from company to company as often as possible gives workers the opportunity to confront new problem sets, expand their networks, and improve their earnings. Moreover, the path of contestation (strikes, unionization, collective mobilizations) is rarely taken. The uprising of Uber drivers in California in 2016 and 2019, the Google Walkouts where almost half the employees protested the inequalities suffered by women within the company in 2018, the internal opposition to military contracts signed by Microsoft and Alphabet in 2019, the Alabama union organization initiative in Amazon warehouses in 2022, the UK DeepMind workers', unionization attempt in 2025 against the contracts between Google and defense groups, including the Israeli military—all were resolved by these companies' management in the same way: by dismissing the organizers and spokespersons of the protests.

An organization like the Tech Workers Coalition, which was established in 2014, still exists but wields very limited influence. This position finds a form of historical coherence. Since the 1930s, Silicon Valley companies have done everything in their power to prevent the development of trade unions. Despite a few lawsuits, the most common way to solve workplace conflicts is through outright dismissal or settlement with compensation. The result is a structural infidelity of workers to their companies. Companies fight this infidelity through various types of rewards, given that employee loyalty is optimal for the development of these companies. Rewards include learning opportunities, potential impact of the service developed, working conditions, and both current and future compensation.

Valuing Talent

In a professional world dominated by science, computing, and engineering, gaining knowledge through the work environment is a form of compensation. So techies take that dimension into account when they need to make a choice, as a manager explained:

> Working in a startup is complicated. There are a lot of companies, you don't know if they will fail or not. The only thing that's guaranteed is what you'll learn. Where I was before, we were tackling a big problem. We had to create a business graph from big databases. When you tackle big challenges, you're going to learn a lot: data engineering, scaling up machine learning. . . . The most important thing for an engineer, if you don't already have it, is experience. That's what you will be able to monetize. The more experience you have, the higher your salary will be. Here, to be considered good, you need two or three years of experience.
>
> But these years won't have the same value of years if you are in a startup or in a big company. There is a big difference. When you have worked in a

startup, you will have done many more things, you will go faster, it is an accelerated process. You can manage to do two or three times more in the same amount of time. Of course, Google and Facebook don't hire bad developers; they're premium companies; after spending two or three years there, people won't necessarily look for a completely new startup. It's not the same clientele. But someone who worked at Oracle or Cisco, slow-moving companies, for two or three years, they won't have developed anything new, just maintaining some code, done few features here and there, and in the end, they haven't learned much (online interview with a senior manager, Palo Alto, December 2, 2020).

From this perspective, demanding collaborators and complex problems are attractive:

A VP contacted me after I wrote a tweet. I was interviewed. They told me how, at my level, I was going to contribute and how they were going to give back to me, drawing a line between my past, present, and future aspirations, as a network engineer with a background in product and looking forward to doing something else. Which is a question I ask myself all the time; what do I want to do. . . . And at the end of the interview, I told them: "Your open project will never work, but it's such a great challenge that I'm excited to do it" (online interview with an engineering manager, San Francisco, April 2021).

Similarly, companies value and try to offer training and learning opportunities. At Google, where 20 percent of work time is allocated to "free" projects, employees can host workshops on a voluntary basis.

We have an online site that lists all the learning resources. You have literally hundreds of workshops with guys like me who are good at something, who'd love to give back to the community, and who will schedule seven to eight sessions. You can get colleagues to do rehearsals, and if people like it, you offer your knowledge to other people. I've done classes with three hundred people, on deep learning, and others with five or six people. And there are classes on everything: programming, meditation, welding (interview with a software engineer, Mountain View, August 29, 2017).

In addition, companies aim to deter employees from leaving by addressing their health concerns, educational needs, and other personal issues.

I've witnessed it since my beginnings at Google. When people need support outside of work, Google is always there for them, for family problems, health issues . . . I had a back problem. I had a physiotherapy follow-up at the office. They were there for me, and I was able to continue working. . . . On another note, we have top-of-the-line hardware, with great computers; it's smarter than paying less to buy equipment that's slow. An extension of that: if some-one needs to take time off because they're not doing well, you have to be there for them. It's a kind of social contract. Because we're going to spend time together. When we hire, we ask ourselves: *Will we be able to help this person progress in their career?* If not, we're not doing them a favor (interview with a developer, Mountain View, February 23, 2016).

By doing so, Big Tech companies appear to be a positive counterpoint to what sociologist Erving Goffman referred to as a "total institution," which he defined as "a place of residence and work where a large number of individuals in similar situations are cut off from wider society for a substantial period and lead an enclosed, formally administered life."[17] If tech campuses are far more enjoyable than asylums or religious boarding schools, there are still strategic maneuvers behind their cheerful atmosphere. The tactics used to retain employees go from work conditions to salaries.

In *Making Silicon Valley*, historian Christophe Lécuyer traces the history behind this model.[18] Problems at tech companies in 1930 and 1940s were almost the same then as today: attracting good engineers and avoiding unioni-zation. In Santa Clara companies three corporatism approaches emerged: the Varian approach, the Hewlett-Packard (HP) approach, and the Fairchild approach. In 1939, during their time at Stanford, Russell and Sigurd Varian invented the klystron, a vacuum tube that amplified radio frequencies. The klystron tube was especially important for the development of radar and later for satellite communication, among its many uses. The Varian brothers grew up in Halcyon, a utopian community in California. The company the brothers founded in 1948 shares principles inspired by utopian socialism. They wanted the company to remain the property of its employees. Therefore they refused money from Boston and New York investors and distributed stock options to all their workers, including technicians. Employees elected representatives to the board of directors. An egalitarian work environment was promoted.

Emerging almost at the same time, the HP approach had different roots. It was originally shaped by anti–New Deal Republicans. It placed the com-pany at the heart of an economic and social model aimed at securing employ-ment and financing employee pensions. Within HP, recreation areas for engineers had been set up. Management acquired an estate in the Santa Cruz mountains for their entertainment. It also gave them important responsibili-ties. Employees were involved in the company's strategic decisions. Employees have shared company ownership since the 1950s.

Fairchild Semiconductor was founded in 1957 by eight "traitors" who left the Shockley Semiconductor Laboratory in revolt against the autocratic management style of adamantly antiunion Nobel Prize–winner William Shockley. To rebuff the creation of workers' unions and limit their influence, Shockley adopted several measures to improve working conditions: the creation of company sports teams, an "open door" policy, autonomy for engineers, managers sharing lunch with employees, human resources departments focusing on career development, and the introduction of stock options. And it is a valuable approach that has been a key management tool in Silicon Valley ever since. But its legacy is not associated with Shockley, as these policies were conceived by Robert Noyce, one of the "traitorous eight" who had left Shockley and gone to Fairchild.

The approach has had a tremendous influence on Silicon Valley. At Fairchild, Noyce and Fairchild's director of human resources implemented policies aimed at addressing the industry's greatest threat: that the best engineers would leave to start their own companies and directly benefit from their innovations. To retain them, Fairchild offered, after two years, options on the purchase of company shares at a price fixed at the time of offer. If the company grows and the value of its shares increases, the potential for significant capital gains is substantial. The top forty engineers were offered the opportunity to take these stock options. However, decision-makers at the company's East Coast headquarters were concerned that engineers would become mere capitalists and direct competitors. So they limited the number of options, offering so few that men left Fairchild to found their own companies, nearly fifty in total; these "Fairchildren" were inspired by Fairchild's management techniques. In particular, they systematized stock options, laying the foundations of a valuation system that has become emblematic of Silicon Valley. Indeed, following new accounting rules put in place after the stock market crash of 2000, stock options were systematized. The financial successes of Google and Facebook have made early recruitment by a company one of the primary paths to wealth.

Beyond accumulated capital, this approach socializes and temporalizes capital within the firm. In doing so, it aims to distance itself from unions. In addition, a bond of solidarity is maintained within teams. At the same time, this approach encourages employees to invest themselves in developing the company, right up to its stock market listing. Each company builds employee loyalty through gradual stock options (25 percent in their second year, 25 percent in their third year, and 50 percent in their fourth year). If all goes well, employees can make a fortune of this investment for the company. Wendy Brown is a surprising example. She was fresh from a divorce in 1999, answered an ad for an in-house masseuse at Google, then a Silicon Valley startup with forty employees. After five years of kneading Google engineers' backs, Brown retired, cashed in her stock options, and became millionaire. This profit-sharing logic is so widespread in Silicon Valley that in 2024 an agency specialized in connecting parents and nannies sent to an entrepreneur a list of expectations that included "equity in your startup" for the future hired nanny.

In companies, this sharing plays the role of an employee loyalty policy, as a founder explains:

> At our company everyone has shares in the company's capital, stock options, a significant amount even, it's important for us, so that people feel that they are part of the company, and that there is an advantage to that (interview with an entrepreneur, Burlingame, October 13, 2016).

The spirit of the system is to align the worker's development, in terms of learning, skills, and investment, with that of the organization. To business leaders, this is a zero-cost strategy, as the burden will pass on to existing or future shareholders. The flip side is that it introduces a tension between shareholders and employees. Silicon Valley's companies have a history of distributing wealth internally while limiting redistribution to external entities, such as unions, shareholders, or governments. Stock options, Dutch auctions, tax optimization, and lobbying efforts to limit taxes on wealth are all part of this approach. The prospect of an IPO becomes a key factor in a company's attractiveness to employees. The promise of a stock market flotation strengthens employee loyalty because it offers the potential for significant capital gains when shares are resold. Becoming an early employee of a small startup that rises to dominance is synonymous with recognition and becoming wealthy.

A dialectic is thus observed between the hierarchization and equalization of conditions. Not all companies respond in the same way. Amazon, which is based in Seattle but runs a research lab in Silicon Valley, combines statutory gradation of employees (levels) and a gratification system of salary plus bonuses.

> At Amazon, we have a pretty extensive hierarchical system, with at least ten levels. At the very bottom, there's the people in the warehouses. Higher up, there's the software engineers, the devs, who start at grade 4 and go up to

grade 6; they often come from universities. At this level you also find the managers. Levels 6 and 7 are a higher barrier. They came to me about joining level 7, and when they look for people, they take great care of them, it's really a unique experience. For a level 7 or higher recruit, they give you the royal treatment, bring you to the headquarters, put you in the Fremont, send you the car, the secretary takes care of everything. . . . They had approached a while ago . . . and they made me an offer; I couldn't believe it. My salary before was $230,000 a year, I still had stocks, but the bonus and profit sharing were gone. Amazon offered me the maximum salary they offer, which is $170K. But with a $300K first year bonus, and then a $260K bonus per year (interview with an engineer, Sunnyvale, July 9, 2016).

If individual rewards are not deemed sufficient, employees consider leaving the company. Interviewees made ironic comments about that: "Engineers have this culture of independence; but they take the check anyway!" or "Here, if you give them an extra 100 bucks, they'll cross the street" to work for the competition. As a sales manager explained, companies try to keep their teams together:

At Google, my manager buddies spend their time on save opportunities: it has become 50 percent of their work. Engineers come to them saying: "I've been contacted by such and such company, they're offering me much more, I want to leave." And they tell them: "No, no, we're going to have lunch, we're going to talk," etc. Sometimes they ask Sergei and Larry to call directly and say: "We'd like to keep you, give you shares, increase your salary," etc. (interview, San Francisco, September 30, 2015).

But their ability to retain employees is closely tied to the company's financial capacity and outlook. An engineering manager explained it this way:

There are companies you can't align with. So you inevitably lose high profiles. Where I was before, we had raised quite a lot of money, because the CEO had been the first intern at Facebook, so he had made a fortune, was very well connected, with an ability to raise money. They had money from Peter Thiel and raised more than $125 million. So we didn't have the problem of classic startups; we could pay well. The good engineers were paid between $150K and $200K per year, and we stayed in that range. But we had limits too. When I started, there were 45 of us. When I left, we were 150. In almost two years. We hired good people, not juniors. We needed smart people, asking them to do things quickly. At the level we were at, the young graduates, even smart ones, it's going to take them a while to do things professionally, because there are things you don't learn in college: quality code, good design, correct architecture, proper processes. . . . You don't learn that in class or at home (interview, Palo Alto, September 23, 2016).

As competition is strong, and loyalty is low, managers try to find other ways. One entrepreneur of a company of about twenty employees said:

> I make sure devs work in the best conditions, that they're happy at the office. My goal is to see them at work and not at home doing nothing. So I put a TV in the office, a fridge, pizzas, and I hire a hottie, so they get a hard-on. Anyway, you need a girl in the mix, otherwise it's just a bunch of males who are not good with girls. I give them free food, have eggs made in the morning, so they come at 9 o'clock and not 11 o'clock. Since they can't make their own food, it forces them to get up (interview with an entrepreneur-investor, San Francisco, July 28, 2016).

This gendered logic shows how companies differentially value employees, but it also emphasizes the importance of corporate cultures.

CORPORATE CULTURES

Silicon Valley is characterized by the diversity of social, educational, national, and organizational backgrounds, which is usually seen as a downside due to the lack of shared references. An Apple employee explains how he finds it difficult to speak with a colleague newly arrived from a different county:

> When we go to lunch. . . . First of all, we just say who's available now; and when I eat with my Chinese colleague who just arrived, we talk about work, or if he's found a place. . . . It's never a big deal. At work, it remains very technical, otherwise it's: *You have to call him, to do this, etc.* (interview with a manager, Sunnyvale, March 3, 2016).

However, Silicon Valley has been a reference for corporate culture design and management since the 1980s, during a time of crisis for the US economy when comparisons (between countries, sectors, cultures, and so forth) were multiplying.[19] But in fact, in Silicon Valley each company tries to develop its own culture. For this reason the question of corporate culture should be considered only in the plural, since these cultures correspond to a set of explicit guidelines aiming to frame work and cooperation within the company. They are sometimes presented as a source of rewards by employees, because of their coherence or inspirational force. In some organizations inclusion and mutual aid are tightly controlled and sanctioned. In others competition and aggressiveness are encouraged. A comparison of testimonies

TABLE 9. Plural cultures

Culture at Pixar	Culture at Uber
"It was very hard to get a job at Pixar, it had Ivy League acceptance rates. . . . Pixar had been around for a while, it was early 2010, everyone was working hard, and everyone was nice to each other, with respect for each other's jobs, which is not so common. The idea was that everyone was working for the good of the movie and that's what should come first. Most of us, we really had to fight to be here and we loved what we were doing. . . . The other thing is that at Pixar they were very concerned about team culture, how people worked together, and they were very quick to fire people who made others look inferior or feel bad—like being hypercritical, or acting like an asshole, making people cry, or just not sharing nicely. The idea being to foster a critical culture without criticism, prejudice, negativity, or aggression. As soon as something threatened that, they made decisions super-fast: they hired fast, fired fast too. They made the right decisions to keep the team healthy. When there are deadlines, if someone behaves like an asshole, in many companies, we keep them, because we need them. But here, they were fired right away. I have several friends who didn't last there." —Online interview with a software engineer, former Pixar employee, San Francisco, January 2020	"When I joined Uber in early 2015, it was like being choked, it felt like a slap in my face. . . . I really liked it. I was twenty-four years old; I had founded a first company that didn't work out, and then I had only worked at a startup in the Valley. But when I got here, there were five thousand people in the office. Yet, it was like a startup, or even more than a startup, because it moves very, very fast. . . . One of our values was fierceness. Basically: you have to go for it, not asking, even internally. Uber had this reputation in the Valley [smile]; we were seen as the bad boy of the Valley. A VC said that Google was *Don't be evil* but that at Uber it was more like *Be a little evil and don't get caught*. I think we had a kind of contempt for rules, both external laws and regulations, that is still healthy. We tend to apply this attitude internally as well. One of our other values was *toe stepping*. When you are five thousand people, you have a space full of feet—that is to say, various and varied initiatives—and it becomes hard not to step on the toes of others. But you can't move forward without disturbing people. Externally, it's the cabs; internally, it's the same. You can't come up with innovation without annoying people." —Interview with a software engineer, former Uber employee, San Francisco, February 2016

by former Pixar and Uber employees highlights this organizational dissimilarity (Table 9). Violence is present in both organizations (each has faced issues related to sexism) but manifests differently: at Pixar it serves as a tool to delineate boundaries, whereas at Uber it is central to core management values. This cultural design within organizations can be explained from various perspectives.

First of all, the isomorphism hypothesis and its variations (institutional isomorphism, mimetic isomorphism, and so forth) posits that every company reflects the characteristics of its activity sector, through its management style.[20]

This is to better bring into play the comparative advantage of its technology: openness and the circulation of information at Google, networking at Facebook, competition at Uber, design at Apple, and so forth. However, it is common in Silicon Valley for several companies to jointly position themselves in the same market segment, such as Uber and Lyft, without adopting identical cultural traits. In the 2010s Lyft was building a brand by promoting a culture of openness and inclusion, which was quite the opposite of Uber. Culture could therefore be seen as a means of comparison for investors, users, and employees. Sociologist Harrison White emphasized that comparability is a condition for competition.[21] From this perspective culture facilitates the organization of competition between companies. But such a hypothesis does not provide an answer to the question of how these corporate cultures are developed.

According to imprinting theory, companies are influenced by their original environment.[22] They remain faithful to the problems and, by extension, the values, and the cultural context that justified the creation of these organizations. However, in Silicon Valley companies and problems from different generations exist side by side. Intel, for example, has significant cultural differences from Airbnb, founded forty years later. The former operates in the microprocessor subsector. The latter emerged during the app era. Nevertheless, their employees emphasize a common point: the fact of belonging to the same innovation-focused industry, beyond affiliations with this or that company. It is therefore necessary to look elsewhere to find the roots of such diversity.

Stories in Action

Silicon Valley companies operate in a world of change and uncertainty. In order to cope with this shifting environment, players use narratives that can provide reference points and guide decision-making. Indeed, stories survive the chaos and uncertainty of relatively stabilized identities. People and organizations present themselves as units, crossing periods, past and future. Narrative thus transcends the instantaneous nature of interactions, inscribing identities in a longer and wider horizon. In this way telling stories makes it possible to influence the world perceived, anticipated, and planned by interlocutors.[23] In private entrepreneurs see their businesses as completely random. But in public they emphasize their ongoing "missions"; the strength of their "values"; the singularity of their "visions"; and the uniqueness of their "stories." Like mythology, traditions, or folklore, these narratives are symbolic constructions, feeding each other, changing over time. These representations are intended to counterbalance entrepreneurial chaos. Indeed, narratives possess a valuable quality: they provide meaning and direction to a trajectory that would otherwise remain uncertain and indeterminate.

The entrepreneurship course given at the Stanford School of Engineering by investor Roelof Botha provides an illustration.[24] In discussing strategies for managing uncertainty, the investor refers to the work of Viktor E. Frankl, a pioneering psychoanalyst who distanced himself from the Freudian tradition. In *Man's Search for Meaning*, Frankl recounts his experience in the concentration camps of Nazi Germany.[25] Clearly establishing a mission enabled him to muster the strength and energy to endure horrific circumstances, helping him put suffering into perspective and thus make informed choices. Even if not as harrowing, entrepreneurial life exposes you to deep uncertainty. Staying focused on a mission helps you navigate the chaotic course of action. Like political activism shows, storytelling helps in compelling people to collective action.[26] Innovation evangelist Guy Kawasaki presents it as the condition for "effective discourse."[27] Although it can be found in many sectors, storytelling is a skill defined as vital in Silicon Valley. Entrepreneurs learn how to execute their strategies effectively through books, workshops, rehearsals, and pitch competitions. Children who grow up in the region are trained in this manner throughout their school years, a significant departure from Chinese, Indian, or European educational styles:

> In middle school, my kids have pitch nights, in front of investors, entrepreneurs.... Students come and present their business projects. Even in kindergarten, they pitch. They prepare reports, about nature, about this party or the other, you take pictures, and on Monday you present that in front of everyone (interview with an entrepreneur, San Francisco, March 4, 2016).

Entrepreneurs need to learn how to tell their story in different ways (pitches, decks, demos, alternating oral and written, physical and online) and formats (a few seconds for elevator pitches, a few minutes during pitch competitions, twenty minutes in front of investors in offices). Each situation relies on different standards.

This art of storytelling—acquired, developed, and modulated over time—addresses the need to convey abstract data and to evaluate nearly limitless potential through a standardized medium. Execution and level of mastery provide valuable insights. As one investor points out, mastery of the narrative is often viewed as evidence of inherent quality:

TABLE 10. Big Tech missions

Company	Mission
Intel	"Delighting our customers, employees and shareholders by relentlessly delivering platforms and technological advances that are becoming essential to the way we work and live"
Apple	"Delivering the best user experience to its customers through its innovative hardware, software and services"
Google	"Organizing information from around the world and making it universally accessible and useful"
Facebook	"Empowering people to share and make the world more open and connected"
Airbnb	"Belong anywhere"
Uber	"We create opportunities by setting the world in motion"

In Silicon Valley there's a lot of people who don't know what they are talking about and they show it right away. The speech is incoherent and they don't know how to express what they are doing in a precise way. It's the first sign that they're going to screw up. They don't know how to explain in a concise paragraph what they're doing. It's not just a problem of intellectual coherence. Oral and written communication are fundamental skills of a successful entrepreneur. An entrepreneur must be able to raise money. If he can't articulate clearly, concisely, what he's doing, why it's interesting, and how it's new, he's not going to get there (interview, Palo Alto, February 4, 2016).

To be more convincing, entrepreneurs are thus called upon to transform themselves into professional storytellers. However, it takes time to distinguish among different types of stories. Interviewees sometimes admitted that they were still searching for their mission, and confused "vision" with "mission" or "values"—and uncertain about how to use these notions effectively. Some companies make their values and missions public, while others keep them confidential (Table 10).

But employees are supposed to use them as guidelines. Facing changes, growth, or team restructuring, employees rely on these guidelines to decide how to proceed. This explains variations from one company to another, at the same time that the guidelines also reflect the company's history. Company cultures are regularly reset, updated, or refined according to the organization's growth and needs. The cofounder of a stock exchange–listed company highlights the importance of this work, both as a task and as a management tool:

We are feeding nearly six hundred people, with a salary; intellectually too, through the projects; and in their lives, because we make them dream about what the company will become, through their stock options. It forces them to change a lot, personally, and to think about the team, its organization, to ask themselves if everyone is in the right place at the right time. . . . We try to identify the problems early on, in order to solve them. We have to make sure that the strategy is clear, that everybody understands it. . . . And we think about employees and users. We have to make sure that our values are in line with what we tell them. So we work a lot on branding what we are as a company; about the image we want to have with users, internal people, how to organize it, how to transcribe it in forms, design, in the colors we use. . . . There is an organizational part, a visual part, a communication part. . . . We just spent six months redoing our branding, to find the right words, our values (interview with a CTO, Paris, December 8, 2020).

Through these revisions to a company's story, companies stay relevant and offer an element of cultural continuity and stability. It thus fits into what sociologist Howard Becker refers to as "culture"—that is, "the sum of shared expectations that individuals use to coordinate their activities."[28] Pitches, values, vision, stories, and mission are different parts of the same narrative system.

At the macrotemporal level, the "mission" sets a sufficiently precise course to guide the actions of company members, while leaving room to adapt the strategies and initiatives of employees who must deal with a number of technical and commercial uncertainties. On an intermediate time scale, employees refer to the company's "values," which are explicit within the organization and which must be known and applied by all to better orient work and coordinate activity within teams. At the project level, the "vision" sets a goal over a few weeks, ensuring consistency despite the back-and-forth of some employees faced with the need to manage emergencies. In this respect culture should be considered less on the basis of shared beliefs than as "a series of acts of communication," meaningful in a specific work environment.[29]

The Work Environment

In Silicon Valley architecture encapsulates corporate cultures, and sometimes becomes another and different way to do public relations. For instance, communications scholar Christo Sims describes Apple's corporate headquarters as "an object of public fascination for its technical marvels and green magnificence."[30] In his article on "technologies of enchantment," Sims claims the headquarters is "designed to counter growing disenchantment with neoliberalism, its technologies, and its environmental defilements."[31] However, by doing so, Silicon Valley companies haven't invented anything new. The gardens of the Palace of Versailles were already intended to demonstrate the supremacy of French royalty by immersing visitors in a journey through art, architecture, and engineering. In this, royal architects sought to echo the grandeur of the Roman empire. At the court of Louis XIV, social rank was expressed through the type and style of seating and furniture (stool, back seat, armchair, and so forth). In a completely different context, New York's Museum of Modern Art's exhibitions in the 1950s aimed to create "democratic personalities" in contrast to the authoritarian personalities associated with fascist regimes. All designed architecture manifests social and political intent.[32]

However, in Silicon Valley, working environments are more or less controlled: from the myriad sublet garages to the campuses of large companies where art installations, interior decoration, and the careful organization of space reflect thoughtful considerations of company design. In the 2010s dedicated teams at Facebook collaborated with artists on pieces reflecting incompleteness, movement, openness, and self-expression. Some of these infused Facebook offices with an air of leftist activism. The idea was to cultivate creativity in a constantly changing environment.[33] The black-and-white decoration of Uber's offices echoes the values of the high-tech aggressiveness promoted by the founders' team. In the early 2020s Google promoted a modular office layout, mirroring their server development strategy. Apple's headquarters combine transparency and mystery, reflecting the company's culture and its flagship products. As one former employee explains:

> At Apple you don't know who does what, there's no organization chart, the guy can be VP [vice president], it's not marked anywhere, if you're careful you can get the information, but otherwise. . . . There are people who work next to me, I don't know what they do. In the companies and sectors where I worked in before, you had charts, photos, titles, etc. At Apple everything is hidden, and it's on purpose. It's a tradition: *don't document what you don't need to document.* And outside the company, I'm not allowed to say much, not even to my wife (interview, San Francisco, July 19, 2016).

An EdTech company offering online services helping teachers and students interact, located in downtown San Francisco, adopts a décor akin to a modernized classroom, with giant paper airplanes hanging from the ceiling. In Dropbox's offices elevators lead to an airlock, the company's nerve center, where employees pass each other, greet each other, and start or end conversations before entering or leaving the office. Opposite the elevators are paintings illustrating the company's values through allegories: a boat at sea, a group of six skydivers gathering in a midair circle, a medieval castle under construction. They represent values such as "be trustworthy," "we not I," "attention to details," and so forth. These illustrations are to employees what standards are to jazz musicians: a framework known to all that allows for improvisation.[34]

In a similar vein, but with radically opposite conclusions, other tech companies are choosing a resolute economy of means, such as this company's retirement services, located not in San Francisco but in one of the ordinary cities of Silicon Valley:

> The work culture has become kind of a cliché in the Valley. Here, as you can see, the walls are . . . white. We're an adult startup. Which means: no massages, no crazy stuff. I've experienced having toys everywhere, giant pillows to sleep on, etc. I don't want people to be distracted. I want them to be focused on the product, the creativity, not on their environment (interview with an entrepreneur, Burlingame, August 25, 2017).

The WordPress company, which develops a free open-source content management system, took its call for flexibility and adaptability to the extreme by completely eliminating its offices in the late 2010s. Whether saturated or minimalist, the environment serves a performative purpose, materially reflecting and embodying the company's core principles. Beyond their specificities, the purpose of these environments is to optimize the circulation, processing, and quality of information. While factories are located in the heart of offices or assembly lines, several Silicon Valley organizations are built around open spaces, which, according to sociologist Ronald Burt, can be seen as "structural holes" that invite encounters and interactions to fill them.[35] Stanford's quad, Google's forecourt, Pixar's lobby—all these spaces rely on the same design philosophy. However, to stay efficient, these environments need to be embodied.

In the rationalist corporate tradition, organizations have to be anonymous. The dissociation between rationalization and individuality is connected with industrial modernity. Capital management must be dissociated from dynastic control, family interest, or an almighty ruler. Asset management and informed decision-making must prevail. In modern capitalism bosses have evolved into anonymous managers, causing the prominent names and dynasties that once symbolized economic power during the Industrial Revolution to fade from collective memory. However, in Silicon Valley companies remain personified. The company's identity is often closely tied to its CEO.

The Company Personified

Companies are most often run by several executives, with members frequently changing due to investors' decisions, board of directors' actions, media pressure, legal issues, retirements, shareholder demands, and other factors. Nevertheless, they remain personified, sometimes even several years after the departure of an entrepreneur: Apple's Steve Jobs (CEO for twenty-two years of the company's forty-five years of existence), Google's Larry Page (CEO between 2000 and 2001, then again from 2011 to 2019), Uber's Travis Kalanick (after his resignation in 2017), Amazon's Jeff Bezos (after leaving management in July 2021), and others. Of course, startups haven't been around as long as the sometimes century-old companies in sectors like energy, oil, or finance. However, identification processes serve a purpose. Maintaining a connection between the organization and individual leaders provides coherence to an otherwise random, unilinear, and chaotic development process. The interweaving of various narrative actions finds unity through strong personalization.

The identity of a "person" turns out to be like any other, both constructed and subject to variation. The individual does not create this identity alone, and for good reason. The personality of founders is thus the result of a collaborative process of construction and representation, both within and outside the company. This identification of a collective with an individual person begins at the very first legal stage of the company. While entrepreneurs use specialized services and are supervised by their investors, supported by managers, and collaborate with engineers, their name sits on top of the legal "incorporation" documents. In fact, an individual embodies an organization based on property rights. This person represents the company to various stakeholders—investors, media, regulators, and so forth—giving a distinct identity to an otherwise contingent process.

Entrepreneurs will use stories to narrate more or less authentic eureka moments, such as a lack of cabs in Paris for Uber's Travis Kalanick or a need for money for rent, which Airbnb's founders raised by renting out air mattresses in their apartment when local hotels were sold out for a conference. A simple revelation of personal intimacy would be remarkable in a world that venerates control and professionalism. Life stories often do not warrant a confession or a biographical twist. They are sometimes purely invented, regularly modified, and always shaped over time. The aim is to prove the entrepreneur's motivations and to hold their audience's attention. However, as Guy Kawasaki points out, when a story feels personal and embodied, the audience is far more engaged.[36]

In addition, during the lifespan of a new organization, management is expected to collect information, sort it, synthesize it, give it meaning, and communicate it to the collective. Thus employees regularly turn to management to reduce the uncertainty surrounding an organization's evolution. Entrepreneurs institute specific, ritualized moments for speaking out. On these occasions they share information, answer questions, provide benchmarks, and react to current events—those of the company or sector and also events of broader importance (such as presidential elections, the Black Lives Matter movement, COVID, remote work, and so forth). Weekly Q&A sessions with executive teams are a Silicon Valley classic. Here, leaders physically embody the company (usually standing with a microphone in front of a seated audience), respond to uncertainties expressed by employees (who ask questions), and encode the meaning of information. CEOs stand up, keeping a central position. They introduce the sessions, react to questions, and close the sessions. Each of these communication acts is part of staging and scenography (lighting, sound) such that mastery in the CEOs' performance determines employees' feeling that the business's growth is under control.

A former employee of Square, a company founded by Jack Dorsey, explains the importance of these meetings as rituals that stabilize the organization and perform a collective through the CEO:

> Every week, there is "Time Square," a meeting with the whole company, reviewing what happened during the week, in a room with three hundred peo-

ple. There's a stage, and a live broadcast to the other offices. You can find out what worked and what didn't, from the support people who spend all day with people who have problems, telling you what function is driving users crazy. . . . Then the business team talks about the expansion in the current state, the specific problems in each region. . . . It gives you an overall picture of the company. And in closing: there's an open mic, employees ask questions, and usually the CEO answers or refers to a VP. Jack [Dorsey] is on stage with a microphone (interview with a software engineer, San Francisco, March 4, 2016).

Like in this testimony, CEOs give coherence both spatially and symbolically to disparate actions and topics.

The CEO as an Information and Gratification Matrix

This process extends within a company's walls through the visibility of the individuals who embody it. At Google founders participated in projects developed by employees during the 2000s. At Facebook this centrality is serial: the centrality of the engineers' building on the Menlo Park campus, the centrality of the open space within this building, and the centrality of Mark Zuckerberg's desk within that open space. Netflix's former CEO Reed Hastings had an opposite strategy, with no fixed workspace at the company's headquarters: "You see Reed all the time in the hallways because he doesn't have an office. So you can see him on a couch when you go on a break."[37] The death of the company is also a moment when the founder-director crystallizes attention and responsibility. The Theranos and FTX scandals illustrate perfectly how a collective process ends up being totally reduced, embodied by one person, in this case Elizabeth Holmes and Sam Bankman-Fried.

The birth, maturity, and death of the company thus constitute three moments during which a collective is represented by its leaders through the staging of their person, working to give an impression of controlling random processes. In these three sequences the identification of a collective with a person tends to reassure employees. CEOs are the central point of an extensive network. Success depends on how effectively they leverage this position for the benefit of the company and its employees:

Management gathered all [European employees] of the company at the time when they were going to launch Netflix [in that country]. We were talking about a subject I know; I spoke up. I said two or three things to explain the landscape. As I was talking, I saw a notification on my phone pop up: a LinkedIn invite from Reed Hasting [Netflix's cofounder and historic CEO].

It's not super common that right when you're having a discussion with the CEO of your company, you get an invitation.... You figure it's because you have something interesting to say. I avoided looking at my phone like he did, but I thought: *This is gratifying....* What you say can be echoed all the way up the pyramid.... The company is really like it says it is (interview with a manager, Paris, November 17, 2020).

This type of information loop and symbolic rewards are similar to the logics studied in the systems of social organization attached to a personality, in the manner of the governments of old order. An investor proceeds by exaggerating the comparison: "Facebook is the best company in the Valley. It has a leader. An ideology. *Ein reich, ein.* The company is very well managed, with a boss who is a real nerd, who can read and write. There aren't that many here."[38]

In this respect CEOs are the central element of a system of information, narratives, and rewards, both economic and symbolic. Despite the collective dimension of entrepreneurship, the company is highly personified. An individual is presented as the embodiment of the collective, acting as a stabilizing factor for activities, managing the flow of information, and ultimately guiding the entire organization. Conversely these personification strategies encourage workers to consider themselves as entrepreneurs, a trend that is particularly noticeable among programmers.

SIX

Programming Uncertainty

One of the challenges in any AI and digital life cycle is this: as an engineer, you're preparing, cleaning, orientating, labeling, creating the model. . . . And I can get 98 percent accuracy. Then you're deploying it. But there is a huge gap between the data that I have used to build the model and the real-world dynamic changes.

— Online interview with an AI engineer, Mountain View, September 2023

IN SILICON VALLEY MOST TECH WORKERS deal with code. As an investor puts it, programmers are "indispensable to the global economy." Another one described programmers as "the new skilled workers" of the 1950s through the 1970s, playing a central role in the production system. But another investor warned me: "programmers are weird animals." Some reports predict their disappearance, while others claim they will be the big winners of the AI revolution. Like entrepreneurs and investors, they are players who primarily play via programming interfaces. In Silicon Valley they are mostly young (thirty-five years old on average), socioeconomically advantaged (overrepresented by individuals from major cities and those with careers requiring advanced degrees), internationalized (including a high percentage of foreign-born workers[1]), and heavily male-dominated (with 80 to 90 percent men). Many programmers recognize that they have better living conditions and opportunities than their parents and previous generations. In addition, they often reject conventional education, work organization, and regulation standards. In their field there is no unified training system and no real trade association. They often declare that they learned programming on their own, through a friend or a family member during childhood or adolescence, especially via video games. Some attended only short programs lasting as little as two months or even two weeks, in contrast to the four- to six-year educational systems found in European, Chinese, or Indian engineering schools. Other programmers, however, attended the country's most prestigious computer science schools and departments at Stanford, MIT, Caltech, or Carnegie Mellon. One programmer I interviewed declared: "Here, no one knows what *programmer* really means."

In Silicon Valley programmers move from one task to another, sometimes from coding to product development, from teaching to management. Programmers value logic and analytics as a work organization method but also "velocity," "agility," "lean," "flow," and "serendipity." Due to the relatively rapid pace of technological evolution, titles and specialties are constantly renewed without any institutional control. Job titles have evolved over the years, ranging from *dev op* and *software developer (SD)* to *software engineer, software architect, data analyst, data engineer, data scientist, computer scientist, algorithm architect, machine learning engineer, AI engineer, AI architect,* and so forth. Job ranks have also expanded: junior (no experience); I (with a degree in computer science); II (with several years of experience); III (project manager); senior (team leader); manager; chief technical officer (CTO); and up to VP of engineering, the highest technical position. In this context, being a programmer takes on a double meaning, not only to write code but also to constantly develop professional skills, experience, and know-how.

Studies on hackers have focused on ethics and politics, dealing with freedom, disinterested exchange, community, and free collaboration. So, even if hacking was carried out in the San Francisco Peninsula, hackers have little to say about the professional stakes of programming.[2] In the 1980s, it was considered a disclaimer among hackers to regard programming merely as a profession. Even today, programmers emphasize their mind-set, projects, pleasure, challenges, and what they can learn or achieve, rather than their job title or salary. Nonetheless, programmers are now Silicon Valley's essential workers, sometimes referred to as *gods, kings,* or *rock stars.* The fact that so many high profiles in the Bay Area were former programmers (Larry Ellison, Mark Andreessen, Larry Page, Sergey Brin, Mark Zuckerberg, etc.) strengthens their status.

Yet programmers often feel powerless, regardless of their skill level. All day long, they encounter bugs, version conflicts, and/or security breaches without knowing whether those are a brief hiccup or a permanent dead end. In addition, they must learn new languages, programming frameworks, standards, architectures, and paradigms at a pace in line with Moore's Law (i.e., that semiconductor complexity doubles every year at a constant rate). For many programmers, the development of AI services has accelerated this pace, with product launches touted as "revolutionary" almost every week. Their continuous learning process is hampered by such organizational constraints as team restructuring, strategy changes, buyouts, or business closures. And in the end they often have to deal with the prediction of a deep transformation, or even the death, of their activity due to the widespread of no-code—that is, the ability provided by tools and AI services to do IT development without knowing how to program. For these reasons developers are aware that the projects they embark on are likely to fail. Therefore, addressing technical, organizational, and professional uncertainty is central to their work.

It is important to note here that what economists call "uncertainty" is different from "risk." Risk pertains to known and probabilistic (involving chance variations) distributions of states, while uncertainty arises from situations where the distribution of future states is unknown and cannot be determined.[3] To manage uncertainties, programmers seek footholds "among the surrounding entities." These footholds provide a position from which to orient themselves.[4] After evoking the magic in programming, this chapter addresses the inherent fragility stemming from the numerous unforeseen events and the instability of associated entities. Programmers cope by adopting three types of strategies, relating to three action sequences: programming sessions (short term), projects (medium term), and careers (long term). During the programming sessions, they rely on support to deal with the unexpected. To execute their projects, they employ a range of tools not only to minimize production and information costs but also to navigate uncertainties more swiftly and effectively. To mitigate the uncertainties of the companies they work for, programmers ultimately seek to create pivotal changes in their career paths.

SOFTWARE MAGIC AND PROGRAMMING DRAMA

Software Has Eaten the World

"Any sufficiently advanced technology is indistinguishable from magic," declared science fiction author Arthur C. Clarke.[5] Computing is often regarded as magical and mysterious, both enchanting and unsettling, a black box as much as an extension of the mind. Its hidden power, with its impenetrable operating systems, is seen as capable of predicting behaviors, replacing human work, and fueling numerous dystopian visions. The tipping point of these utopian or sometimes dystopian visions is known as "singularity" or "superintelligence," the point where machines will surpass human capabilities. *Software, big data, algorithms, machine learning, deep learning, neural networks, artificial intelligence*, Artificial General Intelligence (AGI), and so forth. These subcategories have become central to this industry. Beyond all the trends, software has historically been the broadest and most structuring category.

"Software is eating the world," Marc Andreessen wrote in an op-ed published in the *Washington Post* in 2011. Netscape's cofounder emphasized the growing dominance of software in the tech industry, the assertion of Silicon Valley's importance in the North American and global economy. Technology stocks, according to Andreessen, were still largely undervalued.[6] The investor presented software as an almost autonomous and uncontrollable force, exactly as AI in the mid-2020s. However, this field has a history shaped by human choices and the dynamics of organizational power. For instance, the fact that software is hidden from user view is the result of technical decisions. The supercomputers of the 1950s showed their wires, functions, and motherboards. Personal computers, tablets, and cell phones do not. On the contrary, they project the illusion of objects existing in themselves and by themselves. This seeming autonomy supports the "mind" and "intelligence" metaphors used for computer science by such foundational figures as Alan Turing, Jeff Wiener, and John von Neumann.[7]

This concept is reflected in the French term *logiciel* ("software"), a term derived from the Ancient Greek work *logos*. Under its various names the field has maintained two (rival) promises: automation (performing tasks on behalf of humans) and augmentation (enhancing human capabilities). Since the beginning of computer history, with every new technological breakthrough, the very same question arises: Will technologies replace humans, or enable them to develop their capabilities? But behind this controversy between Promethean and Humanist view on technology, there are prosaic applications. The solutions observed in Silicon Valley during my research period aim to aggregate, measure, and process data-sets in the most coherent ways possible. In this regard computer programs aim, like other information management activities, to reduce uncertainty so that "what is uncertain at a given moment [becomes] predictable (or a calculable risk) at another moment when new information arrives."[8] Despite the historical consistency of this software function (organizing information), *software* has never quite solidified into a single, cohesive discipline.

The term *software engineering* first emerged in 1967 to describe a diverse array of techniques and know-how, though these skills fall short of meeting the standards of a scientific discipline.[9] At that time the accumulated knowledge from "numerical control" was focused on enabling and optimizing complex systems within R&D departments of major corporations, military research units, and a few university departments with computer facilities, such as MIT in the Boston area and Stanford University in Silicon Valley. The interplay between engineers and significant funding through the Defense Advanced Research Projects Agency (DARPA) gave rise to collaborations among the esteemed technologists at IBM, hackers at MIT, and graduate students in the engineering departments at Stanford. From the 1970s on, projects conducted at the interface between electrical engineering and the emerging field of computer sciences became an established part of academia and the technology industry. Historian Michael Mahoney argues that "the dual nature of the computer is the result of its two origins: on one side, the hardware, encompassing devices from the Pascaline to the ENIAC,[10] [and on the other side] software in the series of investigations that reaches from Leibniz's combinatorics to Turing's abstract machines." Mahoney goes on to explain that "between the mathematics that makes the device theoretically possible and the electronics that makes it practically realizable lies the programming that makes it intellectually, economically, and socially useful."[11]

Activities and functions once performed by workers, related to memory and calculation, which were mechanized from the eighteenth century on, have gradually been consolidated and integrated into computerized electronic functions. The power of microprocessors reduces the size of machines while it increases their memory and calculation power. In doing so, they perform increasingly diversified, complex, and automated tasks faster. Machines gradually emerged from universities, companies, military, and civil aviation sectors in the 1950s and 1960s. These machines were introduced to an expanding audience of students, researchers, and computer enthusiasts in the 1970s just as software became an independent field of activity.[12] In Silicon Valley software initially developed as an extension of hardware production. During the 1980s computer hardware companies remained dominant in the region. As one former executive recalled:

> When I arrived [at a large, world-famous computer company] in the early 1980s, I knew more about software than many of the people in the company, who came from semiconductors. Semiconductors and software are related, but software was a big mystery to them. At the time people were making technical objects, computers, but not so much logical objects—that is to say, software. But the industry was moving towards mixed objects with Apple, Oracle (interview, Palo Alto, March 4, 2016).

The apparent rise of software from the 1990s on is in fact the result of growing specialization of the computer industry, with programmers becoming particularly sought-after workers.

When I enrolled at Stanford in the mid-70s, my degree was in electronic engineering. The year I left grad school, Stanford was launching the computer science program, distinguishing computer science from engineering. I started my engineering career as a software engineer, when in fact I was trained as an electronics engineer. Basically, I was designing microprocessors.... The perception at the time was that the intellectual value was in the computer's hardware design, whether it was microprocessors or the design around them. You needed a little bit of software, but it was considered secondary.... From that point of view, things have completely turned around. The world has turned 180 degrees. Most people who are doing software today have only a vague idea of what makes it all tick. They're not really aware of it. They're at levels of abstraction, in terms of production, where they have only a very vague idea of how the hardware works that they need to do their work. There is only a very small percentage of people in the sector who have a transversal vision of this whole.

I'll give you an example: one of the big problems in the industry is managing performance, because when you had an app in the 2000s, your app was running on your server down the hall. Today, what makes these apps work no longer has a physical existence for developers, they're running on servers in farms as big as soccer fields, and no developer has any idea what's running on the server next door, nor where it is located. And if you're wondering where it is located at a t moment, at $t+epsilon$ it's somewhere else. So nothing to do with what was going on. And bringing this up, understanding it, finding solutions to optimize it—it's not a small problem, and that's the kind of problem we're interested in (interview with an investor, Palo Alto, February 25, 2016).

In the region programmers are symbolically described as *builders, makers, innovators*, or *architects* and are valued accordingly on the job market. In 2024 the average salary for a machine learning engineer was $140,000, and $127,000 for software developers. In contrast, a graphic designer earned $80,400 on average.[13] Programmers also enjoy higher status than their counterparts in other countries or industry hotbeds. Sitting in a juice bar in downtown San Francisco, an Indian machine learning engineer under thirty working for one of the biggest tech companies told me with enthusiasm that:

When you do AI, the Valley is the place to be. When I was in India in college, then doing my PhD in the US, I used to read articles. Here, at the office, some of my coworkers sitting right behind me have written some of these articles (interview, San Francisco, September 16, 2024).

A Big Tech employee who has worked in New York City and Paris explained the status of computer science in Silicon Valley compared with other countries and industry:

TABLE 11. Code professionals in the San Francisco and New York regions

Profession	San Francisco	New York City
Application developer	**53,050**	39,970
Systems software developer	**48,440**	11,140
Computer network architect	**6,200**	4,860
Research scientist	**2,900**	420
User support	18,350	**21,760**
System administrator	14,760	**15,270**
Computer programmer	12,400	**15,880**
System analyst	11,410	**24,740**
Web developer	5,970	**7,140**
Network support	5,490	**6,130**
Database administrator	2,890	**4,780**
Security analyst	2,290	**4,400**

NOTE: Numbers in bold represent higher values.
SOURCE: According to data for 2015 from the Bureau of Labor Statistics.

In France, when you say you do computer science, people look down on you. You're seen as ... the *IT guy*, part of the people who didn't manage to help them in the IT department of the companies they've worked for. We talk about IT because it's a support function, not where the value is created. Here, it's the other way around: IT is not a support function but where value is created. If I was in marketing, I would go to LVMH. But I do IT, so I want to be at Google, Facebook, Apple, companies whose core business is IT (interview with machine learning engineer, San Francisco, March 4, 2016).

A comparison between the Bay Area and New York City illustrates Silicon Valley's preeminence as the leading tech hub. In the Bay Area the distribution among categories of coding professionals shows a dominance of such roles as developers, architects, and scientists. In contrast, maintenance occupations and IT support functions, including administrators, analysts, and support staff, are more prevalent in the New York City area (Table 11).

Programming, once viewed as confidential and cryptic, is now enshrined as mainstream. The cultural codes of the programmer predominate within Silicon Valley companies. For example, Silicon Valley valorizes the casual, collaborative spirit of programmers right down to their T-shirts and hoodies—a standard dominated by heterosexual white men. The standard has become a Facebook *brogrammer* cliché,[14] taking the form of an agonistic ("rivalry among comrades"[15]) mind-set and normcore fashion. Women, Black, and Latino/Latina workers are underrepresented in tech departments, and are even more likely to be excluded from decision-making leadership positions (see "Is the Programming World Masculinist?"). This limits their contributions to the form and function that shape new technologies.[16] Many studies have shown how this bias is reflected in technologies: facial recognition systems flag Black people more often than white people as possible matches for criminal suspects; most voice assistants have female voices and struggle to understand ethnic accents; voice enhancers exist to make people's phone voices "whiter"; and so forth.[17]

As sociologist Susan Leigh Star has shown, these examples illustrate how the norms of a specific social group can become naturalized and embedded within technological standards.[18] More than once, this set of norms and values is presented as the common good. For instance, in July 2024, Sam Altman and Ariana Huffington endorsed the new AI health startup Thrive AI Health, stating their aim to "improve health and productivity." This implies a consensus on what constitutes "health" and "productivity" and suggests that these concepts are inherently aligned and mutually reinforcing.[19] Programmers are eager to reflect on their beliefs about what is real and valuable. They view their conceptions as inherent to their work and a model that applies to every activity in their life. An influential Asian AI engineer explained this rationalist and universalist philosophy to me as follows:

> I'm an engineer by training and at heart. I believe that there is no afterlife, and that the dead do not live among us. No gods, no ghosts. All we have to do is make the best of the time we have between our birth and our death: in our work, our family life, community, and so on (interview with machine learning engineer, San Francisco, September 17, 2024).

At a party a machine learning engineer at Facebook said to me that for him statistics become a way of seeing the world. Some techies see them as a way to train and control their environment, sometimes even their own mind and body. An engineer-entrepreneur tells me he has created his own AI tool to manage the flow of information and emails, providing him every morning a summary, and the most interesting messages addressed. A developer at Facebook showed me on his phone the quantities of vitamins, caffeine, drugs, and sleeping pills he took on different days of the week to help him "maintain his balance," along with the precise times of their consumption. This health tracking mirrored the promises of the Altman-Huffington AI health assistant. Computer science, in this context, represents not just a technical practice but also a mind-set that believes technology can shape the world.

Given the statistical domination of men over women in Silicon Valley, the gender gap, and cases of sexual harassment in Big Tech companies, the question comes to mind. In 2022 only 26 percent of tech jobs in Santa Clara County were held by women, according to Silicon Valley Index. In the Bay Area men with a college degree earn 42 percent more than women with similar degrees. Cases of harassment at Uber and Google were revealed in 2017–18, while a company like Facebook has often been described as masculine and demeaning toward women in its early years.[1] Yet women have played an important role in the history of computing. Ada Lovelace is now considered the inventor of the first computer program (1843). The "ENIAC girls" (Jean Jennings Bartik, Marlyn Wescoff Meltzer, Ruth Lichterman Teitelbaum, Betty Snyder Holberton, Frances Bilas Spence, and Kay Mauchly Antonelli) programmed the ENIAC computer in 1945.

During the rise of modern computing, women often took on tasks considered repetitive and boring. Back then, programming was perceived as a menial job, not requiring qualifications or providing prestige. From the 1970s on, however, programming's status changed: Donald Knuth presented programming as an art in a book used for teaching all around the world, top engineering schools opened up to software programming, engineers began to see it as an autonomous activity, and investors saw it as a potentially profitable market, above the hardware layer. Self-taught women mathematicians saw new graduates coming in, the latter became their managers and team leaders, and the gender ratio started falling. There were more women in the big IT nations in the 1970s and 1980s than in the 2000s and 2010s.[2]

Today, in Silicon Valley, women are primarily employed in "support" functions: accounting, marketing, human resources, public relations, and so on. In the field of artificial intelligence they account for less than 10 percent of the workforce. The women in technical positions I interviewed rarely mentioned cases of overt sexism or sexual harassment (unlike female entrepreneurs or marketing professionals). On one hand, they declared feeling that their colleagues had tried to make room for them. On the other, they often pointed out that

---

1. Soraya Chemaly, "Facebook's Big Misogyny Problem," *The Guardian*, April 18, 2013.
2. Isabelle Collet, *L'informatique a-t-elle un sexe? Hackers, mythes et réalités* (Paris: L'Harmattan, 2006); and Janet Abbate, *Recoding Gender: Women's Changing Participation in Computing* (Cambridge, MA: MIT Press, 2012).

(continued)

they were assigned to a gender (women by men) daily, and that this gender was identified as isolated (a minority of women compared to a majority of men). Some of the phrases I heard during my research period include: "I've often been the only woman in the room"; "When I go to an event, people point out that I'm the only woman"; and "I've never had any women to identify with in my field, AI, because I've simply never come across any." Several studies show how the underrepresentation of certain social categories, starting with women, impacts how services are designed in the IT field and beyond.[3]

To remedy this, authors Catherine D'Ignazio and Lauren Klein have defined seven principles, constitutive of data feminism: examine power, challenge power, elevate emotion and embodiment, rethink binaries and hierarchies, embrace pluralism, consider context, and make labor visible.[4]

---

3. Donna Haraway, "A Cyborg Manifesto: Science, Technology and Socialist-Feminism in the Late 20th Century," in *Simians, Cyborgs, and Women: The Reinvention of Nature* (London: Routledge, 1991), 127–48; and Caroline Criado Perez, *Invisible Women: Exposing Data Bias in a World Designed for Men* (New York: Vintage Books, 2019).
4. Catherine D'Ignazio and Lauren Klein, *Data Feminism* (Cambridge, MA: MIT Press).

However, the production of software solutions is particularly difficult to plan and uncertain in its outcomes. It remains constantly subject to various hazards, which programmers frequently experience as dramatic setbacks.[20] A single bug can cause the work of several days or even months to collapse in a matter of seconds.

Bugs, Contingencies, and Dead Ends

Programming entails computation, problem solving, app development, data management, testing, debugging, security control, product management, sometimes even design, all while collaborating with developers, designers, data analysts, product managers, contractors, and users. Programmers must deal with multiple stakeholders on a daily basis, while ensuring the service's consistency. In the course of their work it is crucial for them to reduce the psychic noise of irrelevant details, systematic errors, and the uncertainties that develop over different periods of time or through unreliable information.[21] Indeed, programming does not tolerate approximations.[22] However, the complexity of entities tends to increase the number of potential errors, including calculation errors, misalignment of lines and values, conflicts between different versions and programs, extraction problems, poorly structured databases, or failure to comply with recently updated standards. These problems, which are sometimes retroactive, interfere with the work of programmers and expose them to constant downtime. Programs crash for no obvious reason and problems may remain unresolved. This dimension explains why programming sessions can be emotionally intense. Those I interviewed describe programming tasks as tedious, time-consuming, intellectually arduous, and often emotionally taxing. Programmers can become deeply engrossed in complex and challenging problems in their drive to "solve a puzzle."[23]

The daily life of developers is haunted by those kinds of enigmas, most of which remain unresolved. In fact, problem resolution was no more than 10 to 15 percent in the early 2010s, according to an analysis of the support forums for Facebook and Google Map developers.[24] The inability to solve problems could be the result of environment challenges or it could come from a lack of skills.[25] But even success in resolving technical problems does not mean the end of problems for programmers. In Silicon Valley the abundance of solutions and the competition among programs make the fate of each and every technical solution uncertain. A former Facebook employee revealed that 90 percent of new features and products developed by the company are abandoned because of a lack of users.[26] This high rate of abandonment reflects a broader trend in Silicon Valley. Only 10 percent of projects, products, and companies are expected to succeed. Indeed, failure is often seen as an inevitable part of the business culture and landscape of Silicon Valley.

Moreover, programmers have limited knowledge and control of operating systems and material innovation. Part of their technical environment, and sometimes their own machine learning solutions too, stays mysterious to them. From this point of view, things haven't changed much in Silicon Valley since the beginning of Silicon Valley. Studying microchips, Christophe Lécuyer and Hyungsub Choi highlighted the fact that this industry has been faced with three types of uncertainty: cognitive uncertainty, material uncertainty, and prospective uncertainty.[27] They indicate that in the 1960s "techniques were ahead of scientific knowledge and physicists and chemists did not understand why certain devices and production methods did not work, while others worked perfectly." Their study recognized that "for a long time, engineers and scientists did not accurately know all the properties of the crystals" newly used in industry, such as silicon. Finally, "it was often difficult to know which projects and techniques companies should focus their resources and innovation capabilities on." This description is not far from the day-to-day experience of contemporary machine learning engineers.

Faced with the high likelihood that solutions will crash, products will flop, or companies will fail, programmers are left grappling with uncertainty about which path to follow. The uncertainty that weighs on programmers is therefore overwhelming, especially for those working alone:

> I started by myself, I was staying in my apartment. . . . You spend your days, your weekends, with no feedback from anyone, wondering if it's going to work. . . . And it crashes. You follow different leads that go nowhere because someone else already did it. . . . You're struggling with your app, with no money, with no exit. You wonder what you're going to do, if you're going to make it, what's the point. . . . Plus, San Francisco is expensive, a lot of people here make money a lot easier (online interview with a former entrepreneur-developer turned investor, San Francisco, December 4, 2020).

Seeing a project fail can sometimes feel devastating to programmers. A crash, for them, is dramatic. Sociologist Everett Hughes has pointed out that such professional dramas result from technological changes, organizational shifts, mismatched timelines among stakeholders, resource asymmetries, and differing objectives within the same organization. According to Hughes, "part of the drama lies in the fact that what is daily and repetitive work for one is an emergency for another."[28] Programmers are regularly confronted with this type of discrepancy. This is understandable because of the very purpose of their work: to create gateways, to automate tasks, to set up functions that did not previously exist, to modify the way things are done. With stakeholders multiplying as the process unfolds, programmers try to transform them into resources.

Reaching Out for Support

In fact, to get out of the deadlocks, programmers reach out for various forms of support.[29] These programmers did just that when developing a sports app for network TV:

> With television, during commercials, people are doing something else. Advertisers pay, but there is a big attention problem. Studies show that 80

percent of people do something else during commercials. We developed a solution to keep people in front of their screens. We got a deal with a media network, broadcasting baseball playoffs. It had twenty million viewers, one of the biggest audiences of the year. The deal was $800K, twenty-one games, over three weeks. The problem was that our app only ran on iOS. So, we made special APIs for the network, and we subcontracted the Android version to Colombians, great guys. They did what they could but everything was buggy. It was a disaster. During, before, and after the games, adverts were shown to download the app; during the game the anchorman was telling people to use the app, with real-time feedback, and at the end of the games, there needed to be top five players ranking of our game.

It was the end of 2011 and Instagram had just been bought for $2 or $3 billion, so we thought: *This is it! We're making it! It's great!* You don't sleep much, you're really into it, you don't touch the ground anymore . . . and then, disaster. Everything collapses. When the twenty thousand simultaneous users mark was passed, the architecture couldn't support the traffic. So we had to pull all-nighters, and we brought in two guys who were specialists in scaling. The guys took days off, we paid them a lot of money as consultants, paying an overpriced fixed rate of $30,000; they did a quick audit and told us: "Wait guys, the technology you have is not scalable, you have MySQL and PostGreSQL relational databases, they can't handle the load." . . . It was such a mess that they had to go through another guy, who had helped Instagram to scale (interview with a CTO, San Francisco, October 21, 2015).

From this example three types of support can be distinguished: direct and personal support (colleagues, acquaintances, and peers), intermediate and contractual reinforcements (those hired for a mission), and indirect and collective reinforcements (users).

Developers constantly seek out the opinions and advice of their colleagues. Their expertise is valuable and swiftly mobilized—and it comes without immediate financial compensation. Companies adapt their organizational structures to facilitate this type of support. They ensure the availability and accessibility of workrooms, provide freely accessible blackboards, allow writing directly on walls with chalk or pens, develop internal forums and communication systems, and establish specialized teams for emergency interventions, often with distinctive squad names. A developer emphasizes the value of this type of support:

As an engineer, in terms of know-how, I learned a lot from the people around me, which was not the case in the other countries where I have worked. It's really nice to be able to reach out to a champ when you're freaking out about a problem. In my company they had a very pretentious thing, a team they called the "tiger squad," four engineers, who had no specific assignment and who were in charge of helping blocked projects; there were always projects that were in a dead end or on a critical path, because the guys were no good, because some bullshit happened, etc. In those situations they sent these engineers. They're not good at everything, but they have a huge base. When I found myself going crazy with my team, and this happened several times, I went to them; they stood next to me, *boom, boom*, showed me things and then you say: "Oh yeah . . . ." And you go back to work. It's a type of skill building that I've never seen anywhere else but Silicon Valley. When you work elsewhere, you read articles. . . . Here, you end up working with the guys who wrote the articles and explain things directly to you (interview, San Francisco, March 4, 2016).

In addition to this intracompany support, programmers frequently turn to their personal network, following the logic of collaboration and exchange emblematic of Silicon Valley.[30] They also use external resources. In particular, they hire advisers, consultants, or subordinates for short assignments. The high cost of these services encourages companies to outsource support functions as soon as their financial and logistical capacities allow it. Programmers make extensive use of open-source documentation and online resources. One interviewee mentions their importance as follows:

The fascinating thing about programming is that you don't necessarily need a high level of training, and frankly, I didn't learn much in college that helped me as a developer; what mattered was being able to learn, read, and use tools online. It's free and available. When I was building applications, I would ask myself: *What are the limitations of this or that environment?* The documentation is there. If you build an app for an Apple product, Apple shares all the documentation online to help you. It's boring to read, but it's there. You find it and then you build (online interview with a developer-entrepreneur, San Francisco, October 28, 2020).

Finally, the community of users, especially when they are themselves programmers, represents a resource in its own right for information, corrections, suggestions, and what an interviewee calls visceral feedback:

We wanted to have shorter sales cycles than product cycles. I'm in software, in a company where the sales cycles were so long that selling didn't give you a good return on the product. Interaction with the market, how you can use it, improve it, is super important. When you have short sales cycles, you start to get visceral feedback and you can see how your product is developing (interview with an entrepreneur, San Francisco, March 10, 2016).

These three types of support (direct and personal, intermediate and contractual, indirect and collective) constitute a continuum for programmers. The development of Twitter (now X) shows the importance of iteration within a network of developers, internal and external to the company, including users.[31] These exchanges are an opportunity for a dual operation, both collecting information on technical and strategic options and forming alliances with various entities (organizations, technologies, and professionals) that can test, evaluate, and validate the choices made. Beyond the cliché of the lonesome programmer bending over a computer screen, this twofold process gives us a glimpse of the social depth of programming activity—all the more since these feedback loops maintain the excitement and enthusiasm of the developers. The entrepreneur-developer thus becomes an international reference point that testifies to the early years of a startup as programmers do their best to mobilize resources to solve problems and avoid drama.

PROJECTIONS

Project-based organization has its roots in the capitalist economies of the Industrial Revolution where new machines increased productivity and brought in new business methods, including a professional *project manager* to oversee teams of workers. As the industrial economy gave way to the service economy, project management underwent changes from managing teams by function to organizing multifunctional teams around a particular project. In management manuals of the 1970s, the term *project* has the highest number of occurrences.[32] Silicon Valley developers do not view the project as just a preferred type of work organization but rather as an implicit part of their activity.

Computer Surgeons

One of the first classics in software management helps us understand the logic behind it. In 1975, Frederick Brooks, the engineer in charge of the OS/360 project, an operating system developed for IBM's new 360 mainframe, published a book presenting the takeaways from his trying experience as an IBM team leader. In *The Mythical Man-Month*, Brooks presents software design as an almost anarchic series of versions.[33] Starting with a prototype or beta version, computer engineers develop new functions relying on feedback and iterations between engineers, and then users, without being able to anticipate the properties of the final version. From a problem, team members work to develop solutions in the form of schemes and scenarios. The goal is to produce a stabilized version of the solution, within approximate end points that are rarely, if ever, reached. Brooks points out that this mode of operation leads to multiple tracks that end up threatening the conceptual continuity ("unity") of the software. The addition of workers to the team cannot act as a resource, since each new worker is likely to open up new avenues of work in an uncoordinated way, taking the collective further away from creating a coherent version. Therefore, "adding manpower to a late software project makes it even more later" (this is known as Brooks's Law). Series production, hierarchical organizations, and a strong division of labor are inappropriate from this perspective.

These conclusions lead to overturning the model of work organization associated with large companies in the United States. Historian Alfred Chandler highlighted the way in which the centralization of information and decision-making by head managers, at the top of separate divisions, had been a comparative advantage for the flagship transport, energy, and communications companies that emerged in the nineteenth century.[34] Managers prevail as empowered intermediaries between producer-providers and customer-buyers. They embody and concentrate power for functional reasons, because they allow information and decision-making to circulate coherently, hierarchically, and vertically within firms. Through the writings and conclusions of Brooks, an opposing model is also apparent. According to him, in order to give free rein to the iteration processes necessary for software production, work must be coordinated horizontally, to boost support and ensure the continuity of software development. Brooks argues in favor of small teams structured around a central worker, comparable to a chief surgeon. This central worker is not positioned in a higher position or as an overseer, as in the large companies Chandler analyzed. They are instead at the heart of the action. This mode of organization aims to fit the specificity of software services.

Programmers start engaging with a project without knowing the outcome, the time required, or the final properties of the production process.[35] Software design thus necessarily proceeds via projections, without guarantees of feasibility. Although developers can rely on scenarios, visions, and diagrams, these do not allow for lasting coordination, unlike scripts in cinema or scores in music.[36] This is why managers in Silicon Valley don't focus on the circulation of information between different division heads to control the work of sub-ordinates. Rather, they manage teams' workflows and project timelines:

> I am an engineer manager. There's something very important that someone explained to me when I became a manager: *You think that being a manager means doing what you were doing with more responsibilities? In fact, it's just a different job.* It's not that you're above or below. You're on the side. You have a different job than the people you work with. Your job is to carry the vision. To remove all the obstacles in their way so they can express themselves to the fullest of their abilities (interview with an engineer manager, San Francisco, February 13, 2016).

Since developers cannot rely on support from continuous downstream processing, they mobilize a series of tools upstream in the production process.

Computer Tools

Silicon Valley developers frequently speak about their dedication to innovation. However, they never stop using preexisting tools, such as programming languages, text editors, compilations of ready-to-use routines, versioning, database management, operating and integration systems, servers, cache systems, monitoring systems, and development frameworks (variously referred to as "frameworks," "development infrastructures," "programming environments," or "application bases"). They also use performance measurement tools, content delivery network systems, and package managers to automate software installation/uninstallation and update processes. In addition, they must know how to use bug tracking systems. This number of entities explains the success among programmers of software development kits (SDKs) that group together some of these tools developed by Big Tech companies.

Most programmers have limited knowledge of these tools' history. Digital culture scholar Bernhardt Rieder explains the reason for this limited flow of information: "Programmers or companies freeze some of their own techniques in modules or libraries in order to code faster and build more reliable programs, but never share these elements. Copyright, patent law, and technical procedures such as compilation or obfuscation are some of the strategies for limiting the flow of techniques."[37] However, it is imperative for developers to establish and maintain a personal repertoire helping them to navigate efficiently in a changing technological environment. The programming tools inherited from school and humanist culture plays an important role in this respect, since these tools correspond to scripting technologies.[38] Programmers use "libraries," "chapters," "scripts," "repositories," "translators," and "interpreters" to translate and link a program with the interpreter running the program. "Linkers" combine different modules and libraries of routines into a single executable file. To manage sets though modular architectures, programmers employ concepts such as "lines," "syntax," "archives," "code," "predicates," and "paradigms." Paradigms can be imperative, declarative, logical and functional, object-oriented, semantic, textual, and so forth. On the one hand, programmers evolve in a preconstructed environment, full of tools structured by operating systems. On the other hand, programmers need adequate training and the appropriate mind-set for accessing and using these tools properly.

In Pierre Bourdieu and Jean-Claude Passeron's critique of French schools, they describe the "inheritors" as those who distinguish themselves socially, culturally, and economically by mobilizing knowledge accumulated outside the school system from their culturally privileged backgrounds.[39] Programmers in Silicon Valley, however, rely on a school culture to make them professionally successful and thus extend their mostly middle- and upper-class social status. Although they regularly describe schools as dated or unconnected with the industry needs, their success depends on their acquisition of disciplinary knowledge (grammar, linguistics, statistics, and so forth) and their ability to learn skills related to managerial, social, hermeneutic, and topological competencies, such as accepting criticism, building bridges to others, analyzing hidden agendas, and logically synthesizing different mathematical spaces (Table 12).[40]

Despite the solitary image often associated with coders, their own development is shaped through community: equipment provided by family; programming with friends met at school—often through shared video game practices; books recommended by close relations; and so on. This socialization often follows masculine lineage. Older brothers, cousins, uncles, fathers, neighbors, or classmates lay the first milestones of programmer homosociality (meaning social bonds between persons of the same sex).[41] This socialization goes without the performance pressure of sports, music, or sciences.[42] Respondents willingly embrace the "geek" label, emphasizing their pleasure in discovering and building computers, devices, or programs. Moreover, very few of them report having experienced the bullying and stigmatization associated with the media stereotype of the computer geek, especially since they never view this practice as exclusive or vocational. Their experience of computing emerged between school and family, work and leisure activities,

TABLE 12. Programming skills

Skill	Description
Intrapersonal	Accepting criticism; correcting oneself; taking care of oneself; the art of balancing speech in a community of exchange; not resorting to personal accusations, violence, or insults; knowing how to express disagreement with a superior.
Interpersonal	Openness to otherness; seeking heterogeneity in encounters; varying one's relational universe; being able to find resources in others; building bridges.
Hermeneutics	Ability to insert oneself into a language game; to correctly decipher documentary sources; to analyze power games and hidden agendas.
Topological	Knowing how to explore and adopt logical reasoning; "stroll," and Euclidean geometry; tension between these two lines; computer skills; knowing how to dialecticize them.

SOURCE: Nicolas Auray, *L'alerte ou l'enquête* (Paris: Presses des Mines, 2012).

without a focus on competition. For many of programmers, viewing computing as a credible professional path came later in their educational journey, as one interviewee explained:

I came to Stanford in the 2000s to become a traditional engineer. Even though I loved computers, for me it was a hobby. In high school I was trying to learn C++ to understand computers ... because it was related to video games, not something you learn seriously, even though I spent a lot of time on it. But for the first time, at Stanford, I saw people who were seriously considering it. Stanford is a very lecturer-based teaching system, and a lot of the people who teach are not professors. They're not academics. They don't necessarily have PhDs, but they're still great professors.... They love teaching, it's not a career-driven thing, they're really super passionate. A girl who had worked at Apple was telling us about the Mac, about Steve Jobs returning in 1997–98. She witnessed it. So there's a strong connection to the industry with people who love it. So it gives you a great desire to join the industry, and at the second class, I thought: *Okay, you have to do this*. It clicked. I thought: *It finally fits: it's not just a hobby; it's my passion.* And you can make a living out of your passion. I started in biology with one class in computer science, and I ended up doing more than just computer science, and that was pretty cool. And then it all just kind of came together (interview with an entrepreneur former data analyst, San Francisco, February 25, 2016).

But this path doesn't always look the same. As sociologist Ethel Mickey showed in her work on gender and work organization in the tech industry, there are obvious asymmetries between men who can build professional relationships on informal relationships with other men through masculine activities and women who feel marginalized and uncomfortable because they can't ensure the same social continuity between work spaces and leisure time.[43]

Programmer culture is simultaneously open, tolerant, playful, and collaborative. It is shaped by school encounters and a network of connections. However, it is also masculine, influenced by disciplinary logics and an objectivist conception of knowledge. From this perspective the skills described in Table 12 are the link between playful and collaborative and objective, certain, and accurate knowledge. Programmers value these qualities and actively seek them out. They are considered assets and potentials. In Silicon Valley the pinnacle skill is often regarded as the ability to learn how to learn.[44] Paradoxically, programmers view confronting problems as a means to enrich their skills.

Making Progress by Facing Problems

Indeed, developers in Silicon Valley orient themselves according to problems they identify and the learning potential those problems represent.

> It was the early 2010s, I wanted to make mobile apps, but I couldn't think of anything that wasn't just a derivative of 4chan, Foursquare, etc. It was hard to find something really original. I wanted to invest in something new, but I was spending my time reinventing the wheel.... And then finally, I came across something that I had a problem with, that I couldn't find a solution for anywhere else, and I decided to try to solve it (online interview with a developer-entrepreneur, San Francisco, November 8, 2020).

Most of the time problems are dead ends. But sometimes they are gateways. In mathematics "basic problems" are distinguished from "atypical or open problems." Programming problems can be categorized around these two types. In some cases programmers work on problems based on preexisting solutions or those known by their peers. When they are confronted by "atypical or open problems," they need to generate ways to overcome them. In Silicon Valley players crave this second type of problem because it entails a greater learning curve, both quantitatively and qualitatively, and it can be monetized directly or indirectly. When it comes to choosing between different professional opportunities, this matters the most.

> A company that's six months old is a mess. Because you're just going to spend your time programming. In a big company setup, you inherit a big cathedral, which has been built for years and years. . . . That's the joke about Google: It's

all very beautiful . . . and very calcified. In a way you'll learn a lot about reading code, but you don't need to write code that much. You're just visiting! But
it all depends on what you expect: is it your level of professionalism, your time
off, etc. (interview with a developer engineer, San Francisco, July 18, 2016).

The type and volume of problems encountered also depend on the size of the
organization and its technical architecture.

At the old startup I was at, there were twelve of us; here at Uber, we're five
thousand. I'm a senior, I have a team of three people. Even though it's a much
bigger company, I have more flexibility and room to maneuver. So more
autonomy, and the impact is much greater. It's a completely different model
from what I've known: working on an app that has several million users a
day, it's nothing like an app that's trying to grow its user base (interview with
a developer engineer, San Francisco, February 3, 2016).

Programmers consider problems from the point of view of possible rewards,
whether material (financial compensation, services, opportunities), symbolic
(meetings, recognition), or cognitive (learning). They tend to anticipate the
skills that will be acquired during the resolution process. Developers, unable
to predict the sector's evolution, nevertheless resort to probabilistic anticipations of chance variations. Beyond the projects themselves, programmers try
to orient their careers in the long run by initiating turning points.

TURNING POINTS

Before even mentioning their career choices, interviewees emphasize decisive
events in their career path.[45] These might include the purchase of a computer
within the family, an introduction to coding by a third party (friend, brother,
cousin, or neighbor), a chance meeting at university, a first job in Silicon
Valley, the possibility of working on a project, the opportunity to join a company, a eureka moment, and so forth. Sociologist Everett Hughes stressed the
importance of the temporal dimension of working life.[46] The "cycles of social
life" are matched by the "cycles of work." These cycles are marked by transi-
tions through educational institutions and influenced by historical arbitrariness, such as wars, economic crises, and demographic changes. Events are
usually sudden and random. But programmers claim to consciously engage
in turning points, which they aspire to master and control.[47] To them,
they are not tipping points in the past, evoked retrospectively, but desired,

anticipated, and intentional turning points, committed in the present with a more or less distant horizon. The search for certification, the creation of widely adopted solutions, and the founding of companies are three types of programmers' turning points.

Obtaining Certifications

As mentioned, programmers often adopt a critical discourse with regard to school training, while still praising the side roads that enabled them to learn about coding. Nevertheless, programmers in Silicon Valley are most of the time highly qualified and specialized. During my study I interviewed thirty-eight programmers, trying to replicate Silicon Valley's demographic reality: thirty-five men and three women, sixteen Americans, twenty-two foreigners, with an average age of thirty-eight years. Of them, 95 percent had a master's degree, and 92 percent have completed their training in the field of computer science. Their initial training was conducted far from the prestigious and historic training centers such as MIT, Stanford, Caltech, or Carnegie Mellon. This is partly why in Silicon Valley they sought out certified training, even if it can be redundant, time-consuming, and expensive (nearly $25,000 for a full graduate certificate in computer science at Stanford University, where tuition was more than $65,000 a year in 2024). This was the case for nearly half of the sample.

To obtain these certifications, programmers in the tech industry are not only turning to universities but also to large companies and code schools. More than a dozen code schools are listed in the Bay Area. And in 2021, 28 percent of programmers said on their LinkedIn profile that they had obtained a certification issued by Microsoft, Amazon, or Google. Incubators and accelerators are also likely to offer certifications, which programmers believe can have a positive impact on their career. Motivations are diverse: obtaining a visa, developing one's network, on-boarding in a field regarded as the future. The lack of international standards and benchmarks between different schools partly explains this attempt at converting the value of foreign educational credentials in the Silicon Valley job market. An engineer explained it this way:

> The definition of what is an engineer in Europe and in the US is very different. In the United States, there are computer science departments, which produce guys who specialize in computer science, guys who know how to do algo

and deep learning, which is the closest thing to what a European engineer is. But the Americans don't have many schools with a standardized curriculum, like in Germany, England, or France, where you have institutions, with certain rules, courses, fundamentals. In addition, in the United States, you have more and more guys who do three months of online training and sell themselves as engineers. It's exploding so fast here that anyone can become one; there are no rules (interview with an engineer manager, San Francisco, January 28, 2016).

Programmers explain the paradox between their criticism of school and academic training and the desire to better position themselves on the job market. Some spoke about resetting their résumé or getting a "stamp," to make their profile more attractive:

I learned to code early, but I have flaws and holes in my training, so I wanted to fix that, and that's why I wanted to be a coder and not a product manager. I wanted to go deep. So I read a lot of books, I specialized in backend, because it's supposedly better, and the projects are more interesting, like not doing iPhone but data infrastructure. I did many MOOCs [massive open online courses], about ten. And now, I'm applying for a $4,000 course at Stanford. Today I wonder if I'm not going to continue my studies. I want to reset my résumé. Because here, there are two ways to make yourself known when you're an engineer: the company you work for, and mine is not bad, it works, we're the world leader in what we do, but it's a niche. So there's no buffer. And then your school degree. Stanford, Berkeley (online interview with a developer-entrepreneur, San Francisco, November 23, 2020).

In the absence of a regulation, jurisdictions, or unions, these certifications operate as a guiding principle in the labor market.[48]

Creating Solutions

A second way to initiate a turning point is to produce solutions that will become standard. The history of computer science provides a few examples of designers who have become references, honored in particular at the Mountain View Museum of Computer Science or the computer science department at Stanford University. This staging of memory gives them lasting recognition, but as one respondent explains, it is relatively rare and limited:

In computing, it depends on the specialty. . . . There are things in common, then branches, by communities. . . . In the Linux community Bill Gates has no place and Steve Jobs, who didn't invent anything, is a nobody. The people who worship him are into marketing or entrepreneurship. Otherwise, in CS, in the mainstream, there's Turing, Knuth . . . that's the top. There aren't thousands of greats, I would say it's between thirty and fifty people. . . . And maybe a dozen or so who are gods. Guys who made modern computing. There's a bit of a divine, mysterious side, because you don't understand where it comes from, so there's blissful admiration. But it's an admiration limited to the computer field. If you see Knuth eating at McDonald's or promoting a brand, you don't give a shit (interview with a developer, San Francisco, October 11, 2016).

While it is rare for developers to reach such a position, many seek to produce highly ambitious solutions, as the success of certain software products brings significant social recognition within their professional community, in addition to a sense of personal enjoyment, accomplishment, and gratification.[49] "The beauty of solving problems, producing solutions that people will use, it's really an amazing feeling."[50] They also consider achievements as an element of comparison and objectification of their value. However, achieving a high level of recognition requires a high level of technical mastery, usually referred to as virtuosity.

Indeed, virtuosity is often presented by programmers and in dedicated literature as an elective criterion. Brooks argued in the 1970s that an application was three times easier to create than a compiler, itself three times easier to develop than an operating system, while the productivity of the best computer engineers would be five to ten times higher than that of their most mediocre colleagues.[51] As a former executive specialized in the field puts it: "What's striking about software is that the performance ranges from one to twenty-five. There are magicians, Mozarts, who used to say: *Music comes out of me like milk comes out of a cow.*"[52] If the analogy between developers and artistic creators is common in Silicon Valley, it is because mastery of production and style are indicators of quality. Through these, programmers compare and rank themselves within their community. In Silicon Valley many produce applications, features for platform services, maintain programming interfaces, feeding a technological environment built on the top of older and deeper technical layers. In the group of interviewees only two had been part of ambitious projects: one worked on the Android operating system and the other on the Swift programming language. They were members of teams composed of dozens of people, led by renowned project managers—Andrei Rubin for Android and Chris Lattner for Swift, a language Apple developed for apps and services like iCloud, keychain, and others.

If creating a tool that significantly changes how a large user community operates is rare, many programmers are nonetheless keenly attentive to opportunities presented by emerging technologies or pivotal services.[53]

Initially, my vision was to work on the idea of generations. I had seen the different generations, from the time I was at Oracle: I worked on mainframe computers, web, apps, mobile. . . . When apps came along, it was clear that it would be the equivalent of the browser for the web. The channel through which things would be made accessible. Apps were going to be the vessel, the container to give people access to new service features. When I saw that, I asked myself: *How or how much of enterprise software is going to go mobile?* My conclusion was that CRM was going to be the best place to innovate (interview with an entrepreneur-developer, Berkeley, January 26, 2016).

This testimony raises the question of the profitability and usefulness of time invested in projects or companies. In order to optimize it, some programmers found their own company.

Founding Startups

Loyalty to one's company is a rare thing in Silicon Valley. Those I interviewed had changed companies at least once and some up to eight times between the first quarter of 2015 and the first quarter of 2023. Starting one's own business, however, represents a more significant commitment. A majority of the developers tracked in the survey had made the leap from freelancer to employee to entrepreneur. By 2021, 55 percent of them had become business owners. This transition to entrepreneurship is paradoxical, considering the treatment developers receive in Silicon Valley companies and the low chances of leading a company to success. According to investors' criteria, success is typically defined as a resale or an IPO after five to ten years. For those who work for Big Tech, quitting to start their own company means giving up a high salary, bonuses, health insurance, free food and transportation, maternity and paternity leave, childcare, gym memberships, and so on, for a greater amount of work for an undetermined period of time. From this perspective entrepreneurship does not appear to be a rational choice for programmers committed to objectivity, measurement, and logic.

If many mention Silicon Valley's entrepreneurial culture to justify this change of course, they also emphasize the desire to retain control of the value that can be generated. Indeed, for developers, starting a company is not the surest way to get rich, but it offers the greatest potential. A programmer explains the dilemma that young professionals in the region face between being a salary earner and a business founder:

> Working for a big company like Google, or a good, mature startup? My feeling is that I'm too young. I think, *I'll try a startup again for the third time.* And then I'll go work for a Big Tech company. When you have just graduated, the trick is not to go straight to Google. Because sure, you'll have a good salary, you'll have $200k, shares, and lots of perks. But you'll have almost the same thing all your life. I know one guy who got hired to work in a startup, a European, he took four months to get his visa. In the meantime the company raised $20 million. It's become a medium company. It's not interesting anymore because there is no economic potential for him.... He can't become rich.
>
> But if you get into a company early, get a few percent back, you can really become rich and make an impact. Even more so if you start your own company. Once fundraising is done, you're going to end up in a position of responsibility to mentor new employees, and a lot of money. So a lot of young graduates want to work or launch small startups; you get a lower salary, but you can earn a lot of money, several millions, or even more, compared to Google's $200,000 per year. Afterwards, when you are an entrepreneur, you also have a personal deadline. I can't stay an entrepreneur for ten years, earning $1500, in *early stage*, working fifteen hours a day.... The goal is to develop, raise, recruit, be less in charge and enjoy a bit (interview with a CTO, San Francisco, September 26, 2016).

The potential reward difference explains why some people prefer to abandon a better situation in favor of a particularly uncertain position. Entrepreneurship offers the possibility to access "founder's profits"—that is, the capital gain from the resale of shares.[54] Indeed, as the company grows, the value of the shares the founder controls increases, and can be sold at the price that investors, and then stock purchasers, are willing to pay in the highly dynamic technology investment market. From this perspective creating a company requires maintaining an alignment between work and value, time and capital, technological and professional shifts.

PART III

—————

Spirit

SEVEN

Burning Man, the Spirit of Silicon Valley

Burning Man is the Silicon Valley's carnival.

—Informal discussion with a Stanford University
professor, Stanford, February 5, 2016

THE FACE OF BURNING MAN has changed significantly since about twenty friends gathered in 1986 to celebrate the summer solstice and set a larger-than-life human effigy ablaze on a San Francisco beach near the Golden Gate Bridge.[1] The first Burning Man sculpture was built out of scrap wood by landscaper Larry Harvey and carpenter Jerry James. Harvey recounts: "When he was lit he simply incandesced, and for a moment it turned night into day."[2] Over the past thirty-plus years the modest "family picnic" has transformed into a giant event attracting eighty thousand people every year to the Nevada desert. Burning Man now occupies a special place on the international festival map, and episodes of *South Park*, *The Simpsons*, and *Doctor Who* have paid homage to it. In fact, many series, films, and advertising campaigns borrow its aesthetic. Though its theme changes from year to year (Renaissance in 2016, Rituals in 2017, Robots in 2018, Metamorphoses in 2019, Multiverse in 2020, The Great Unknown in 2021, Waking Dreams in 2022, Animalia in 2023, Curiouser and Curiouser in 2024), the promise remains the same: a festival where, for a week, the boundaries between artworks and spectators vanish. (During the COVID pandemic the 2020 and 2021 events took place largely in a virtual world.) Burning Man features psychedelia and participants include cyberpunks, naturists, survivalists, makers, shibarists (afficionados of consensual rope bondage), and positive sexuality adepts, to name a few. A large contingent comes each year from Silicon Valley.

During the 2010s more than thirty thousand people left the Bay Area for Black Rock City, the home of the festival in Nevada. Big names have endorsed Burning Man as an explicit source of inspiration, including Sergey Brin and Larry Page (Google), Jeff Bezos (Amazon), Mark Zuckerberg (Facebook),

Garrett Camp (Uber), Drew Houston (Dropbox), and Matt Mullenweg (WordPress). The festival directly influenced the visions of Philip Rosedale, Elon Musk, and Tony Hsieh, inspiring Rosedale's *Second Life* (a game dedicated to random interaction, play, and creation, launched in 2003), Musk's SolarCity (a company aiming to power entire cities from a system of solar panels, founded in 2006), and Hsieh's Zappos (an online retailer famous for its communal work organization and way of life, founded in 1999). Of all the Silicon Valley companies, Google maintains the most organic relationship to the festival.[3] It became the majority shareholder for the nonprofit Burning Man Project in 2019.

Both a pilgrimage and an initiation rite for young techies—and wilder than the musical festival Coachella—Burning Man is a living painting of the tech industry's culture and player mind-set. It's common to hear discussions and gossip about fundraising, company launches, buyouts, and entrepreneurs both in and out of the convoy. By the mid-2010s Silicon Valley represented half of the camps, a proximity that led the Valley to strongly identify with Burning Man. In 2014, Musk invoked the festival's unbridled creativity in a criticism of HBO's *Silicon Valley* series:

> I really feel like Mike Judge [the series creator, who worked in Silicon Valley during the 1980s] has never been to Burning Man, which is Silicon Valley. If you haven't been, you just don't get it. You could take the craziest L.A. party and multiply it by a thousand, and it doesn't even get fucking close to what's in Silicon Valley (quoted in Tess Townsend, "What Elon Musk and Other Tech Executives Say About Burning Man", *Inc.*, August 28, 2015, www.inc.com/tess-townsend/tech-titans-love-burning-man.html).

This feeling is shared in Silicon Valley. A LinkedIn developer told me while sitting in a downtown bar in San Francisco: "Ask anyone on the street, and they can tell you about their Burning Man experience." A manager at Google similarly stated: "When I first came to Google, there was nobody in the office. There were five thousand Googlers who were at Burning Man, plus five thousand from Facebook; so, two companies represents one-seventh of the attendees."

In Northern California the Silicon Valley–Burning Man symbiosis spawned feelings of hatred for the festival. In bars, restaurants, and social media, you are likely to hear from residents fed up with the idolization of the festival: "Don't tell me about Burning Man or I'll burn you"; "If you spend your week in Black Rock City, stay there!"; "One more word about Burning Man, and I'll scream." The annoyance marks a symbolic boundary between participants and nonparticipants regarding a gathering that celebrates "radical inclusion." Nonparticipants, as well as journalists and even some participants, like to point out the festival's contradictions. The festival has ten constitutive principles: *radical inclusion, gifting, decommodification, radical self-reliance, self-expression, communal effort, civic responsibility, leave-no-trace, participation*, and *immediacy*. For each principle, however, there are notable contradictions. *Radical inclusion*, for example, is at odds with the festival's social selectivity, attracting a majority of residents from the San Francisco and Los Angeles areas who work in tech or media, including even billionaire entrepreneurs.[4]

Gifting is contradicted by the fact that admission prices range from $400 to $3,000. *Decommodification*, which forbids the use of money except for purchasing coffee and ice cream from the festival organization, is championed by high-income individuals who spend the rest of the year commodifying information and communication.[5] *Radical self-reliance* is undermined by some participants who pay for amenities such as chefs, Wi-Fi, and air-conditioning (including Plug 'n' Play camps, where arrangements for sleeping accommodations, showers, food, and the like are set up for you). *Self-expression* is challenged by the fact that certain outfits, initiations, and behaviors are repeatedly showcased year after year. *Communal effort* is contradicted by the fact that half of participants attend as "independents," and incidents of incivility and food theft increase toward the end of the festival. *Civic responsibility* is challenged by the fact that authorities (including the Reno police, the State of Nevada, and the FBI) monitor issues such as drug use, vehicle speed, and assaults. While *leave no trace* is an enduring mantra, many festival-goers leave behind glitter, pistachio shells, and even bikes, contributing to a growing carbon footprint. *Participation* is difficult due to stringent access conditions, and *immediacy* is compromised by the fact that the event requires several weeks, sometimes months, of preparation, especially for art creation.

In addition to these contradictions, commentators regularly complain that Burning Man is no longer what it used to be—despite the fact that evolution and adaptation are part of Burning Man's identity. Notably, the number of participants has steadily increased, with a few exceptions due to the financial crises of 2000 and 2008. There were 20 participants in 1986; 350 in 1990; 4,000 in 1995; 25,400 in 2000; 35,664 in 2005; 43,558 in 2009; and 67,564 in 2015. After two years of being organized online due to the COVID pandemic, the gathering is now capped at 80,000 people. The sculpture placed in the center of the Black Rock Playa, the flat created from the bottom of a dried-out lake in the Black Rock Desert, is built for the festival's needs. The sculpture changes each year and is ultimately burned on the last night of the festival (with the temple constructed for offerings during the festival being burned the day before). This tradition is inherited from the San Francisco wooden boat builder community and its summer solstice celebration.[6]

Despite criticism, the festival remains unique in many ways. It does not award prizes, ranks, or any hierarchical status. Nor does it promote a specific territory, discipline, or artistic genre. Participants transcend the traditional divide between artists and audience, as well as between artworks and spectators. At Burning Man interactions between art and nonart, as well as body and spirit, are ubiquitous. As a result, there is limited space for anticipation. Immediacy becomes a fundamental aspect of social life. Communities are celebrated, including survivalism, which contributes to ongoing ambiguity about the relationship between progress and modernity, ideals embraced by the festival.

Since the end of the 1990s there have been various expressions of the festival's relationship with modernity, the past, and the future, from detaching from commercial logic for a week to better understand it[7] to participating in an anarchist gathering to enhance organizational sciences.[8] Thus the festival helps participants distance from the world in order to better shape the cultural infrastructure they seek to organize.[9] Tech professionals during the year, but Burners for a week, organize activities around projects, work in teams, and pool knowledge and resources, interweaving private and professional lives. Individuals must serve the community. Contributing to the common good yields both material rewards (such as donations, services rendered, connections, access to information, and professional opportunities) and symbolic rewards (like a positive reputation and opportunities to make a name in an often forgetful innovation industry). Burning Man shapes the mindset of players and reflects Silicon Valley society, where the exchange of information functions as a social matrix.[10] These aspects are foundational for the Silicon Valley ethos. As tech journalist Sarah Buhr writes: "It's all part of that spirit of challenging the status quo, innovation and autonomy that embodies startup culture."[11] A San Francisco attorney confirms this spirit:

In New York, even though I was working at Morgan Stanley, as far as I could go there were places that were off-limits to me: probably a bit like in Europe, if you didn't go to the right schools, in the right city, and you're not from the right family. . . . But here it's different. If there is something that is a little bit close to the way the VC and entrepreneurial world works, it is Burning Man. That is to say, it's not so much being a member of a club that gets you recognition. It's more fluid. . . . By the way, if you want to find a gathering that

[they] attend in numbers, it's going to be Burning Man, much more than an association meetup or school's secret society. . . . It's a society, but more open (interview, San Francisco, July 25, 2016).

Black Rock City, a temporary city built from scratch in the middle of the desert, serves as a surreal backdrop for profile images on Facebook, photos on refrigerator doors, and even the décor found in startup offices (including Burning Man and third-eye imagery, representing inner vision and enlightenment). According to interviewees, attachment to the festival is due to its ability to reveal (their "real" self) and to amaze (through "magical" experiences). For many attendees the festival represents more than a moment of jubilation. It provides new meaning to the lives of two-thirds of the participants, encapsulated in the oft-criticized phrase: "Burning Man has changed my life." The rationale behind this transformative effect is particularly challenging to understand as it involves paradox and detachment from conventional logic. Burning Man is experienced, not analyzed. Among the most common feelings I noted after speaking with participants are "It's very difficult to explain"; "It was crazy"; "It was magical"; and "I'm not the same person." These sentiments echo up to 60 percent of respondents to a Black Rock City survey organized in 2001.[12] This festival is marked by the enchantment of participants who nevertheless spend the rest of the year disenchanting the world through the creation of digital tools and measurement instruments that rely on processes of objectification and rationalization.[13]

This paradox serves as the starting point of this chapter and seeks to illuminate how Burning Man functions as a matrix of enchantment for its participants. It proposes an analysis of the festival from the Burners' perspective through three temporal phases: before, during, and after. First, I explore how the festival is part of a lineage that sets expectations for transformative experiences. During the festival Burners undergo a series of trials that lead to shifts in mind-sets, the enhancement of multiple talents, and displacements in their self-image.[14] After the festival Burning Man continues to influence social life and embody the spirit of Silicon Valley.

BEFORE: "I GO TO THE DESERT FOR THE MAGIC . . ."

The festival presents itself as a space of interactions—interactions between artworks and participants and among participants themselves. Information about music, works, experiences, exchanges, solicitations, and proposals of all kinds saturates the festival. The sheer volume of spontaneous expressions and interactions creates an environment that promotes the "fun madness of creation," as one Burner describes it. This orientation is rooted in the unique history of San Francisco and Northern California as pivotal crossroads of counterculture.

A World of Interactions

Every member of the audience is expected to be creative, whether through a work of art, a costume, a word, an act, or other form of expression. However, the indeterminacy of roles, complicated by the increasing number of *virgins* (i.e., new participants), is a counterbalance to individual creativity. In 2014 new participants amounted to 40.69 percent of Burners.[15] Participant experiences are defined by several boundaries. A physical fence encloses the expansive areas of the playa and the city. Temporal boundaries include day and night. Linguistic boundaries emerge around specific terminology and advice. Ritualistic boundaries exist around questions like "What did you see?"; "Where did you go?"; "How was it?" And finally boundaries occur because of preexisting social connections among participants.

> At my camp some have known each other for a very long time, but most don't. So there are questions that come up: *How many times have you been at the Burn? Are you a virgin? How is your Burn going? What did you see? Yesterday, it was great; today, it was really hard.* There was a day where I suffered from dehydration. I was really scared to be in Reno [the nearest city, two hours and fifteen minutes away by car]. I couldn't drink. It was anxiety (interview with a software engineer, San Francisco, September 28, 2015).

Part of the experience is simply wandering. During the many moments of wandering, participants fully embrace spontaneity and the unexpected, including surprising encounters with cosplayers, drag queens, and naked people. Despite this apparent spontaneity, the festival is far from unstructured. Each year, around sixty artistic projects selected by the executive committee receive financial and logistical support, based on their ability to foster interactions between artworks and participants. Burning Man's approach is fundamentally different from festivals like Basel, Cannes, Bayreuth, or Coachella, which maintain a clear separation between the public and artistic works. Burning Man fits philosopher John Dewey's approach to art as a potential for experience that invites action, emotion, and interaction—and it embraces the possibility of failures, misunderstandings, minimal interactions, unsuccessful performances, and incompleteness. However, interactions can also resemble scenes from a movie. For example, I observed participants watching a sunrise from a western-style bar, taking a collective shower in a place with no water, dancing spontaneously in a tornado, running a marathon across the desert, and two strangers sharing a long, languid kiss during a sandstorm that limits visibility then parting without a word. Other performances included a drag queen dressed in pink, perched on stilts at forty-five degrees and handing out cotton candy. There was also a showdown between a DJ and a band of trumpeters on an open-air bus.

These sometimes-surreal snapshots maintain the festival's enchantment, as illustrated by this excerpt from my field diary:

> Shirtless. White pants. Bulging muscles. In the "default world" Chris is thirty years old, lives on an island, is a gallery owner, DJ, dance instructor, yoga teacher, went to Stanford and MIT, worked in Big Tech and is a millionaire since he sold the startup he cofounded with his friends at the end of his studies. Today? He travels. Most of the time. In the last six months: Iceland, Paris, Bali. . . . He is an active member of the camp where I stay. In the supply tent, he comes to drink water and isolate himself from the giant sound systems around. Jim, another member of the camp, wearing a pair of Ray-Bans, calls out to him, without moving his head.
> - "Eh . . ."
> - "What?"
> - "You're right."
> - "About?"
> - "One drop . . . is enough."
> Chris laughs mechanically, then repeats:
> - "One drop is enough . . ."
> Next to him sits Jane, perched on a cooler. She is wearing a pink 1930s-style negligee with dusty boots. She gazes straight ahead, her expression blank. Then, a flash catches my eye—the rhinestones on Milo's full-body suit. A systems engineer in Silicon Valley, he's preparing a water bottle: half vodka, half juice. Outside, sounds and lights emanate from all directions; I glance at the window of the van parked in front of me. In bold red letters, the inscription reads: "Burn Baby burn!" (field diary, third night of Burning Man, September 2017).

The modes of coordination are not heavily oriented toward history. However, participants can rely on a lexicon, premade lists, and maps. As a participant told me:

When you receive your ticket, there is a little booklet, a map, with a zoom on the Central Camp where you can come and get ice, where there is an emergency area, detailing all that. There's a lexicon too . . . A newcomer is a *virgin*, a newcomer who has adopted all the codes, a *vet-virgin* [*veteran* and *virgin* contraction]. They are brand-new, but it feels like they've been here fifteen times. *Moop* are the things that don't belong there, that are kinds of pollution. Some people talk about DJs playing and to go see. With every year rumors, legends. Daft Punk at the deep playa comes up every year. . . . I think they never played there. . . . I'm sure they've attended, but not as public figures. But every year, it is said that they're playing (interview with a data analyst, Palo Alto, November 9, 2015).

The main rituals seem to have no origin stories. Burners make few attempts to learn about the history of Tutu Tuesday or the origin of the Bunny March when festival-goers, wearing fake rabbit ears, meet at the foot of the temple for an ear-stealing brawl. For most of the participants these practices are not associated with any historical significance but have everything to do with situational meaning. A dive into the history of countercultures nevertheless shows the historical coherence of interaction-centered festivals.

A Platform for Countercultures

The term *counterculture* can seem like an exaggeration as it implies a linear and homogeneous movement while in reality it encompasses a variety of groups and experiences that are distinct in time and space. In Northern California the term *counterculture* refers to a series of groups and events connected through a few key individuals. Many of these originated at the Berkeley, Stanford, and UC San Francisco campuses in the 1950s, evolving through classes, shared housing, and student community support (such as the crash pad tradition). At the time Northern California became known for readings, parties, stores, cafés, concert halls, secondhand shops, and various happenings. Beginning in 1955, a series of readings was held at the Six Gallery in San Francisco's North Beach neighborhood featuring Beat writers Michael McClure, Jack Kerouac, Allen Ginsberg, and others. Creative writing workshops emerged as an expression of the Beat Generation's rebellion against the conformity of postwar America. At Stanford's Creative Writing Center, Ken Kesey began writing his bestseller *One Flew Over the Cuckoo's Nest*, which was published in 1962 and adapted into a movie in 1965.

After moving to La Honda, just a stone's throw from Stanford in the Santa Cruz mountains, Kesey invited friends, Stanford alumni, artists, and bohemian writers like Neal Cassady (who inspired the main character in Jack Kerouac's *On the Road*) to weekend parties at his secluded getaway. Through parties and performances, a burgeoning psychedelic scene began to take shape; Kesey played a significant role in this development after trying LSD at the Palo Alto hospital as part of a CIA-funded experiment searching for a truth serum. In 1964, Kesey's followers named themselves the Merry Pranksters and bought a school bus to take a trip to New York City, inspired by *On the Road*. A trip on Kesey's "Further Bus" included multiple occasions for acid tests. This journey earned mythical status after the release of Tom Wolfe's book *The Electric Kool-Aid Acid Test* in 1968. The author, a pioneer of the literary style of New Journalism, highlighted two key phenomena: *synchronization*, which refers to the interconnectedness of the acid trips experienced by various members, and *religion*, denoting the establishment of shared references among those participating in these events. Kesey summed up this distinction with the phrase: "You're either on the bus or off the bus."[16]

Locally the Merry Pranksters initiated and engaged with other groups. Under their influence the Grateful Dead began in 1965. The Trips Festival held in San Francisco on January 20–22, 1966, was the first public gathering of the psychedelic scene in the country, and it was followed by increased regulation of LSD.[17] Stewart Brand, who had been one of those on the Further Bus to New York City, was an active member and organizer of these events. In 1968 he oversaw the publication of *New Games*, a collection of noncompetitive games. Between 1968 and 1972, Brand became the editor of *The Whole Earth Catalog*, which offered do-it-yourself items available for order. Modeled after early mail-order catalogs, the catalog included summaries of books and resonated strongly with the back-to-the-earth movement, selling over a million copies by 1972 and earning the National Book Award. In the same 1960s period, the San Francisco–based group the Charlatans held their first concert in 1965 at the Red Dog Saloon in Reno, Nevada. Drawing on various American popular music styles, they dressed in the late nineteenth-century style of saloon dandies and refused to produce records or sign onto record labels. They performed in Northern California until 1969.

The Diggers, a street theater troupe active from 1966 to 1969, founded the Artists' Liberation Front and staged numerous street shows and performances throughout San Francisco. Several of its members joined the Communiversity, an open university project initiated in 1969 that promoted education and fun for all. This group served as the foundation of the Suicide Club, a secret society established in 1977. Its members engaged in adventurous explorations of San Francisco, including climbing the Golden Gate Bridge, hosting costume parties in parks, and conducting expeditions in the sewers, among other activities. Several members of the Suicide Club went on to form the Cacophony Society. Over time, the core group from the Cacophony Society became the organizing committee for Burning Man, including key figures such as Larry Harvey, John Law, Michael Mikel, Kevin Evans, and Crimson Rose, among others. In this history Kesey, Brand, Law, John Perry Barlow, and Howard Rheingold have been key network entrepreneurs. They were efficient in their roles due to the influx of student communities since the 1960s. Each new generation of newcomers contributed to a culture oriented toward practice within local networks. This culture values DIY ethics, fanzines, art houses and clubs, blending art with craft and professional with amateur. It is characterized by strong opposition to mainstream industry and big corporations, standing apart from Hollywood, Miami, or Broadway in terms of values.[18]

These countercultural groups were structured as networks—dense at their core yet open and dispersed at their peripheries. Over more than half a century they interconnected various communities dedicated to experimentation and connections. They emphasized free participation, the rejection of formal hierarchies, minimalist rules, autonomy, and the valorization of immediacy. Unlike its counterparts in Paris, Vienna, Chicago, or New York, San Francisco's bohemia was neither supported by nor directly opposed to institutions such as the Academy of Fine Arts, the New Bauhaus, or the Modern Museum of Art (MoMA). These more or less ephemeral collectives expressed defiance to authorities—such as San Francisco's City Hall, the police, the administrations of Stanford and Berkeley, and even the CIA and FBI—by occupying spaces conducive to a practice that can be described as *outsiding*. This means engaging in experiences that intentionally deviate from norms. Instead of targeting institutions to subvert them, they have invested in border zones like neighborhoods near campuses, the areas surrounding the Golden Gate Bridge, Alcatraz Island, San Francisco's beaches, abandoned warehouses, wharfs, Sequoia forests, and even the sewers, extending all the way to the Nevada desert.

This lineage also covers technology: the *Whole Earth Catalog* became a reference for many back-to-the-land communities, and for many technologists through today, including Steve Jobs, who considered the catalog an ancestor to the internet.[19] In his commencement speech at Stanford University in 2005, Jobs described the catalog as one of the most important documents in internet history. He presented as a philosophical mantra for the tech world the *Whole Earth* epitaph reportedly used in its final publication: "Stay Hungry, Stay Foolish." Shel Kaplan, who would later become Amazon's first employee, was part of the team managing the *Whole Earth* publishing site in Menlo Park.[20] The large-scale custom-built robots first created in 1978 by the performance artist group Survival Research Laboratories are closely related to those that can be seen at Burning Man. Others in the maker spaces of the region included John Perry Barlow, who founded the Electronic Frontier Foundation in 1990 and wrote the cyberlibertarian manifesto "Declaration of Independence of Cyberspace."[21] A Burner from 1994 to his death in 2018, Barlow was elevated to the rank of "semi-official co-founding member" of the Burning Man Project. In the same spirit, the art cars—painted, decorated, and altered into sharks, rockets, insects, or pirate ships (to name but a few of these designs)—extend the ethos of Kesey's Further Bus. Similarly, cobbled-together bicycles, radio broadcasts, costumes, and fanzines reflect this spirit.

As Stewart Brand put it:

> Burning Man has far surpassed the various initiatives we were exploring with the Acid Tests and the Trips Festival. It has achieved a depth, originality, and scalability that we only touched upon. With minimalist yet functional rules, Larry Harvey has truly brought to fruition what we were only experimenting with. I don't think this would have happened without passing through the spectrum of the 1960s—the vibrant prism of colors and ideas that we embraced during that era. The Internet and subsequent computer-related booms amplified everything, but I believe they also significantly shaped the fundamental nature of Burning Man. Its initial Hellenistic inspiration evolved over time, much like how the Hellenistic Period was influenced by Alexandria, ultimately leading to a more refined outcome. I think this analogy holds to some extent in this case.[22]

In this sense its coherence is grounded not in theories but in practice: making, networking, organizing, happenings, detours, expressiveness, and so forth. For those I interviewed, the real uniqueness of Burning Man lies in its practice, which the media often oversimplifies by focusing on influential participants or shocking behavior. Participants emphasize that the festival embodies the ideals envisioned by internet pioneers: free expression, knowledge, and information sharing. As Fred Turner suggests, Burning Man serves as a physical platform facilitating exchanges, connections, and transactions among different communities.[23] From this point of view it is remarkable that the term *connection* is an emblematic word at Burning Man, even if takes on multiple meanings there: connecting with others, reconnecting with oneself, connecting with the festival, connecting the different stages of one's life (or as Jobs put it, "connecting the dots"), or even taking Ecstasy/MDMA/Molly or LSD to "feel the connection" (with people or the environment). These experiences ultimately challenge established habits and ingrained representations, including those related to self-representation.

DURING: "I DON'T KNOW WHO I AM ANYMORE . . ."

Participants go through a series of trials related to body, space, time, and self.[24]

Body Trials

Participants are confronted with a series of physical and mental trials. They face numerous challenges, including sleep deprivation, dehydration, construction site injuries, sunburn, and acidic desert sand that can burn skin. They contend with poor nutrition, fatigue from covering long distances, and working in extreme conditions—both high heat and cold—while setting up and dismantling their camps. Hardships include the omnipresence of lights and sounds at night, the thermal variation between daytime temperatures (more than 110°F) and nighttime temperatures (40°F), sandstorms that can last from a few minutes to several days (known as the Big White), and suffocating gusts of dust and wind. In addition, participants may encounter unwanted interactions. The 2023 festival included rain episodes and mud. The festival's intensity can be gauged by the number of forced repatriations due to physical issues (such as dehydration or minor injuries) or psychological reasons (such as nervous breakdowns). According to the euphemism used by the Black Rock Rangers—volunteers responsible for the smooth running of the event—there is a notable increase in the number of "disoriented people."

The physical trials are closely linked to the spatial challenges participants face. The city emerges and vanishes at the end of each summer. Camps are set up and dismantled, often involving several weeks of preparation. Structures must be transported and stored. And the central statue (The Man)—around which the city is organized—is built over several months only to be burned. The continual renewal of themes and artistic creations each year prevents the establishment of permanent landmarks despite the map and the rudimentary signage designating each alley by a letter and a number. The space remains loosely divided between the city, the playa and its constant show (art cars, art pieces, bikers and walking Burners), and the area further, with less people and art, which is known as the deep playa. Many Burners return to their camps at dawn without a clear recollection of where they have been or how to get back. Directions exchanged to locate a point of interest ("You should check this out") are often vague, inaccurate, or poorly followed. This spatial confusion is evident in next-morning stories, where directions and sometimes even days become mixed up. Accounts are often reduced to brief expressions of vitality, such as "It was life" or "I'm alive."

Even before this spatial trial comes a temporal trial. First, everyone must purchase a ticket, which involves several hours of waiting through the official online site in March. This is especially challenging for those who are less socialized to the festival procedures, and acquiring a ticket can be anxiety-provoking as there are often twice as many requests as available tickets. Then preparation can span several months for the most dedicated attendees (although preparation can take just a few hours for those who are less organized). The six-hour drive from San Francisco to the gates of Black Rock City when the road is perfectly clear can turn into at least twenty-four hours at the time of the festival because of traffic jams leading to the ephemeral city's entrance. Once past its gates, setting up camps can take a variable amount of time depending on the complexity of the setup—a few hours for lighter equipment or over a week for more elaborate structures. Then the return—known as the exodus—can be even more challenging, often involving extra fatigue and frustration. It is followed by a period of decompression, a phase of varying duration during which participants readjust to normal life.

The geographical distance, lack of information and communication tools, along with the harsh conditions amplify the sense of time's weight and the feeling of separation from the rest of the world and loved ones. The search for immediacy, sociability within one's reference group, and ongoing experimentation provide ways to cope with this sense of distance, initiating a process of reflection and adjustment to your environment. As one Burner described it:

> Just the transfer, for seven hours. . . . It's like going into a cave with a flashlight to discover a whole world. It made me think . . . about what a community is about, how to connect with people. . . . When I was a kid, I preferred computers, because people are irrational, impulsive. . . . Using a computer is

much easier, because it always does what you tell it to do; but at Burning Man, I looked differently at how a community is built, and how you can do things together through simple steps, how you make people feel safe, how you make them share things, going from gong healing to meditation (interview with an entrepreneur-programmer, San Francisco, August 25, 2017).

This renewed and altered experience of space and time serves as a trial for the self. Physical exposure, including nudity, is one aspect of this challenge. According to a study from the Black Rock City Census, 5 percent of participants walk completely naked throughout the festival. Many more are partially undressed, with some women walking bare-chested, using only small pasties to cover their nipples. Masks, costumes, and especially mirrors—ubiquitous on structures, artworks, and attire—create a reflexive environment. The goal is not merely entertainment but the exploration of alternate selves through various displacements and perceptual distortions. From this perspective the proliferation of interactions and their inherent uncertainty tend to undermine previously stabilized self-representations. The week's peregrinations serve as a playground for identity exploration, involving choices in clothing (costumes, clothing exchanges, and gifts based on what "suits you"), naming (the "playa name" chosen by oneself or assigned by others), and associations (new relationships, whether platonic or sexual, including potentially lasting "playa couples"). All this occurs within an environment of constant change:

> Actually, there are moments at Burning Man where you drop the masks. You realize that you've been playing roles all your life: you've been playing the role of the kid, the role of the brother, the boyfriend, the friend, the network guy, which is the most important role in Silicon Valley: *What are you doing? When did you get to San Francisco . . .?* And here at Burning Man, you feel like you're talking to real people, in their truth, and so you can make deep connections with people. Talking about very intimate things . . . without being afraid (interview with a software engineer, San Francisco, February 12, 2016).

The flow of representations, both of yourself and of the world, is intensified by the use of various psychedelic drugs such as THC, DMT, LSD, mushrooms, and Ecstasy/MDMA. LSD, in particular, stands out as the most emblematic drug. Since initial testing at the Palo Alto hospital during the Cold War period in the 1960s, LSD has become more deeply rooted in the San Francisco Peninsula than anywhere else in the world. Many people have written about LSD. However, as essayist Howard Rheingold, a Burning Man participant since 1986, summarized with irony: "trying to explain LSD is like dancing to tell the weather."[25] Burners present it as an initiation drug that introduces a rupture in the way you sees the world. The molecule initially equalizes senses that are usually hierarchized (with sight at the top of the pyramid), resulting in either exhilarating or destabilizing experiences. Constant framing and unframing occurs in space and time, where each detail becomes a world, and the world gains the presence of a detail, oscillating like a rubber band.

Participants I interviewed describe similar temporal loops. A minor detail elevates to the rank of a scene, and time dilates. At this point it is far from certain that the normal flow of consciousness will resume. Immersed in the colorful and loud vortex of Burning Man, they say they seek to temper the chaos of perception by focusing on their "own path," "inner voice," "inner thought," or "deep desire." A Burner described it this way:

> It makes the experience even more intense. It overwhelms you at the beginning, coming up is quite violent, you have to hold on, physically, it's kind of terrible: you shake, your heart rate increases. . . . But as there is art everywhere, it increases your interactions with art, it increases interactions with people, it develops empathy and allows you to see the person in front of you even more. It makes you more aware of what the art was doing to you. . . . It's emotional, and intellectual too, you're aware of it and you can analyze it. You can see how the connections are made in your mind, your present and your past; it allows you to make connections; to identify the connections you make implicitly in life (interview with a developer, Paris, November 9, 2018).

The experience is initiatory. Spatially you perceive yourself as a component of a whole. Time becomes dramatized. Once the come-down is over, the contrast between hallucinated time and sober time causes you to reflect on how life is brief, monochrome, and finite. You are prompted to undertake what you realize is most important, starting from preestablished connections and the life paths that take shape. Not every interviewee gave a comparable account, but many emphasized how Burning Man had led them to question their habits, routines, and modes of representation. From this perspective the festival challenges norms and the self.

Putting the Self into Play

The relationship between norm and deviance is reversed here. Deviance becomes a zone of knowledge and realization distinct from the social rules prevailing in social space. A machine learning manager said:

It's the biggest art event in the world, people spend thousands of dollars just to put art in the middle of the desert for no profit. So there are a couple of interesting things: people who are self-managing, self-organizing, no one is giving up their freedom for security, and by doing that, they realize they don't need it. The other thing is the absence of money, which makes you realize more what is important, which undermines the question of status. Here, it can be the social status linked to your house, the car that projects your importance; but in the desert, it is what you build. What structure? Its beauty, its grandeur, how cool your friends are. . . . So hierarchies and values are turned upside down (interview with a machine learning manager, Paris, September 18, 2019).

Individual consciousness is symbolized by the sculpture of The Man in the heart of the playa. Burners constantly circle around it, turn their back to it, and return to it. The free expression of desires is evident: cuddle tents in camps, spankers who ensure consent before any interaction, BDSM workshops, and the "orgy dome" with its spaces for couples and a "welcome to join" side. These elements encourage exploration of homosexuality, polyamory, sadomasochism, and more. This series of experiments tends toward discovery and acceptance, both of the individual and of others. Spectacular in the case of sexuality, the cumulative acts of separation from the norms of the external world (the "default world") introduce a detachment from a subjugated identity in which you sacrifice yourself to please others. Instead, participants embrace revealed, borrowed, or chosen identities. The role of costumes and mirrors echoes the modes of identity construction analyzed by sociologist Anselm Strauss: "[Identity] is linked to evaluations made by oneself and by others. Each person sees himself reflected in the judgments of others. The masks he presents to the world are shaped by his anticipations of judgments."[26]

During the festival, masks multiply and shift, and the anticipation of judgment is suspended or modified through a sequence of positive judgments ("It suits you," "I like you a lot," "You are very beautiful like that"). Dedicated workshops play a specific role in this process:

There are lots of workshops at Burning Man, some of them explore the human side, like the identity workshop; it's lots of people who get together in a tent, with a master of ceremonies who asks you to walk and then stop and look at the person who's closest; and then look into their eyes for ten minutes, which is kind of . . . weird. And then, they ask you to say what you share with that person. And in the end, you realize that you're always looking for the same thing: love, security, recognition. . . . You have this common ground and the differences are in the way you get there. A second important experience I had there was in a workshop where six people stand in a circle. One person stands up and the others have to say what they look like, what they do in life, their personality (interview with an engineer manager, San Francisco, February 24, 2016).

For participants who fully experience these displacement processes, the term *burn* takes on new meaning: *burn* the superfluous and get rid of the limits and barriers that were previously integrated and respected.

At one point there is no more frame at Burning Man, the walls in your head fall down. Because all your life, you're in a frame: family, school, work, your group of friends. . . . And there, what is extremely powerful as experience, is when there is no more bullshit, and that you realize: *Man, you're in the middle of the desert. Why do you live for? You live for what? You don't owe anybody anything.* . . . You really realize that at Burning Man. Because who is there to impress? What's there to do? And it's not really a moment . . . but a gradual realization. I think that's what Burning Man is about. That's what changes you. And that you can try things, that you wouldn't have done because of the way what's-his-name was going to look at you, or the way you were going to judge or censor yourself (interview with a developer, San Francisco, August 26, 2017).

Testing the body, experiencing space, altering time perception, and challenging norms and self-representation create a divide between the external "default world" and the discovery of new identities. Such discovery invigorates Burners once they return to their normal life. A developer I interviewed explained: "Professionally, when I came back, I felt much freer to do what I wanted to do, and to drop everything else; as they often say over there: *Live your life in your own terms.* I think *Am I allowed to do this or not* way less often. If you think it's the right thing to do, do it."[27] This idea is powerful and useful for entrepreneurs, techies, and investors engaging in extremely ambitious projects. For participants the "default world" ends up representing a world of conventions, routines, and useless certainties. Burning Man encourages constantly readjusting and going beyond these norms.

This explains the many profound questions that arise during or after the festival, prompting significant life changes. Interviewees reported a strengthened resolve to pursue their projects and follow their instincts, as well as to develop new skills and a capacity for change. Established habits, routines, and representations are thus challenged in favor of plasticity, adaptability, and openness to the new. Their old habitus appears outdated, with a focus on what the Ancients would call metastasis—displacements and changes in space and time.[28] This highlights how the festival functions as a social structure for some participants.

For participants who live in Silicon Valley, Burning Man extends beyond the festival. It provides an opportunity to develop skills tailored specifically to the tech projects that are worked on throughout the year.

Skills Development

One iconic event elevated Burning Man to a founding myth for Silicon Valley workers. In 1999, Larry Page and Sergey Brin raised $12.5 million from the investment firm Kleiner Perkins Caufield & Byers. To reassure their investors, the two young founders agreed to hire an experienced director to replace Page. After reviewing about fifty applications, they found out that Eric Schmidt, a renowned software engineer who had worked at Bell, Xerox Park, and Sun Microsystems before becoming the respected CEO of a major software company, was a former Burner. Fans of the event, which *Wired* magazine had already featured on its front page in 1996, invited Schmidt to spend the week at Burning Man to assess his management skills, mind-set, and ability to grow a company that had only eight employees at the time. A group headed to Nevada, notifying users of their absence by changing Google's logo. While the search engine encountered unusual bugs, a night of "navigation" in Black Rock City convinced the two founders. They were impressed by Schmidt's behavior, particularly his ability to establish discussion principles to solve problems effectively, whether related to spatial orientation, temporal organization, or improvement of camp life. This experience laid the groundwork for the enduring connection between Google and Burning Man, evident in the participation of thousands of employees, the substantial donations to the organization and artists, and the numerous references and nods to the festival scattered around the Mountain View campus.

Beyond any particular festival, Burning Man represents a rich source of learning that is applicable to participants' professional lives. The festival aligns closely with Silicon Valley's entrepreneurial ethos, emphasizing creativity, adaptability, resourcefulness in changing environments, reflexive action, energy and body managment, openness to opportunities, trusting his instincts, seeking to learn new things, overcoming taboos, and rule bending.[29] Extreme activities like a thirty-one-mile ultramarathon, the Mad Max dome, or the Bunny March push physical and psychological limits to sharpen the spirit of competition and of surpassing yourself. At the same time, activities like meditation, yoga, and the use of psychedelic drugs enhance stress management. Thus the festival and Silicon Valley companies develop a dialectical relationship that mutually reinforces each other's principles and practices.

Organizational Skills

The modes of organization of Silicon Valley's high-paid workers in companies and at the festival overlap in three key areas: optimizing collective functioning ("group flow"), aligning individuals with the collective ("culture fit"), and fostering network-based development ("network organization"). Those I interviewed noted that their Burning Man experiences influenced their approach to group dynamics. Groups include introductory ceremonies, for example, and focus on balancing free and structured time. Retreats and playful discovery-oriented workshops are common. In addition, limited yet widely accepted rules are established with the goal of fostering creativity. Plus the judgment of individuals is suspended to focus on evaluating proposals and contributions to the collective. In this vein, tools, solutions, and individual knowledge are considered communal assets. The tests and experiments carried out in the Nevada desert are likely to find extensions in the companies of Silicon Valley, and vice versa.

Moreover, the structural instability of companies, like the significant turnover each year of Burning Man's camps, leads to the formalization of behaviors and associated values. Members can choose a collective that aligns with their values and then navigate within it. This approach is illustrated by Burning Man's ten principles (radical inclusion, gifting, decommodification, leaving no trace, radical self-expression, communal effort, civic responsibility, radical self-reliance, participation, and immediacy). These aim to integrate participants while sparking creativity. Similarly, Netflix embodies this method in a document of over a hundred slides, described by Facebook's

Sheryl Sandberg as "the most important document in the history of Silicon Valley." Its significance lies not in its content but in its explicit articulation of a work culture that empowers employees within a minimally cooperative framework. The principles are kept to a few to encourage initiative and adaptability.

From this perspective, projects—as forms of work organization—are central. They can range in scale from large (e.g., setting up a camp or managing a major work) to medium (e.g., organizing a party, yoga session, or workshop) to small (e.g., an impromptu nail polish workshop for men or skydiving at dawn during the event). These projects bridge themes and temporalities from Silicon Valley throughout the festival and offer a particularly receptive audience of integrated enthusiasts, creating a unique echo chamber. The Burning Man organization produces and hosts its own TedTalk. It also sets up a seminar program during the event, which featured in 2017 sessions on blockchain, socially responsible business, leadership, and how artificial intelligence could revolutionize humankind. In addition to the artistic projects, technological projects are developed at the festival, driven by strong permeability between art and technology. Drones, urban planning, renewable energy, and equipment manufacturing experts use the festival as a platform for experimentation. In 2017 the festival's Solipmission project placed three people inside a several-foot-square box and gained significant attention in the virtual reality community. Inside this confined space, those in the box used virtual reality tools to re-create the experiences shared with them by attendees.

For code workers and software architects, Burning Man provides a unique platform to showcase their creations. The festival serves as an unconventional exhibition space that is both socially dynamic and trendsetting, allowing these professionals to make their work visible in a highly engaging environment.[30] Those involved in these projects, including the design of the temple, enjoy notable reputational gains within Silicon Valley. Finally, the Burning Man Project fosters networking through volunteerism and individual initiatives. This networking occurs both within the festival and extends beyond it. As the event's umbrella organization, members of the Burning Man Project engage in seminars and conferences, such as the Global Leadership Conference held in San Francisco from 2007 to 2017 and the European Leadership Summit. They participate in events organized by the Burning Man Regional Network, which spans more than a hundred locations worldwide as of 2020. These activities help propagate the values, principles, and spirit of Black Rock City, fostering a community that is both structured and open.

Community Building

The realization of projects requires group involvement several months before and after the festival. These collectives take varying forms and are more or less structured. When these are sufficiently advanced, participants use the term *communities*. Although heterogeneous, they often revolve around a central figure or architect. This individual leads a core group of highly committed members who engage in meetings and collaborate on projects involving the production of versions and the execution of stages. As the group evolves, tasks become more specialized, and additional volunteers are included, extending the reach beyond the original core. One participant who had attended eight festivals describes how participation in these communities fosters a learning dynamic among members:

> We have twenty-seven camps in the village, each consisting of two to thirty-five people. Most of them are very organized, including my own camp, with structures for shade, a common area, a bar, a trailer, a unicorn ranch, etc. But all these subcamps have their own organization. Sometimes it's a community, sometimes not. When it is, the sense of community is pretty strong, because we see each other all year long. We have parties, projects, etc. In my camp there are at least ten people living somewhere in the Valley. And there's a pretty strong feeling of belonging.... People want to be part of the core group, not just a participant.
>
> The people who just participate are tourists, they come on Monday and their scene is smaller than the people who contribute the rest of the year. And you get into it because you work with someone, you meet someone, who knows someone they know.... From the get-go, it creates a strong bond. It erases differences. I started working on a project with engineers. And my roommate, who was an engineer handling the electronics for the project, told me I had to come. She mentioned they had a place not far from where we lived in Oakland. I was doing the painting. That was it. I don't like having responsibilities, and these people are really good. You have to master several domains, hardware, software. You have to know the whole spectrum...
>
> So I have a great deal of respect for the people who do that, they work at Autodesk, at Apple ... I was just a painter and that was fine. When I worked on the temple, which was a very big project, there was real management of volunteers, with a great leader, who made sure that people felt proud of what they were doing and appreciated. You could go to her and ask her for the next

step. She was a great guide. Not everyone is. I've seen people say *Fuck you, I'm doing this for free and pro bono.* I've seen other people break down nervously when they were managing big projects and quit (interview with a PhD candidate, Stanford, October 25, 2015).

As previously mentioned, worker turnover is high in Silicon Valley, and social relations are fluid and heterogeneous. This high geographical mobility creates uncertainty about the durability of relationships. The idea that anyone can leave, almost overnight, is deeply rooted in people's minds, especially since Silicon Valley has had since the 1980s one of the highest divorce rates in the country. Half of married people divorce, and expatriates rarely see their families. This is why Burning Man represents for some participants, in their own words, a surrogate family. In 2008, 67 percent of attendees were in relationships with Burners outside of the festival.[31]

Participants find in Burning Man the opportunity to consolidate and extend social relationships within an affinity group throughout the year. In addition to the projects, a series of more or less formal and supervised events before and after the festival provide regular opportunities for networking in the Bay Area. These include a precompression party at the start of summer, a party organized in Reno the week after Burning Man, and a decompression party in San Francisco at the beginning of October during which an entire neighborhood is closed off. The network extends to parties organized by various camps throughout the year. Burners are active participants in city fairs, such as the Folsom Fair Party, the largest BDSM gathering in the country, the Greengrass Festival, Halloween parties, the Castro Fair party, Gay Pride, and others.

Burners also go on group vacations and retreats. The frequency of these gatherings leads to the formation of friendship circles of Burner veterans based on such factors as proximity, status, and age. These connections are often formed outside of Burning Man but are strengthened through repeated participation in its annual events. These circles often include members from various sectors, including different companies, nonprofits, academic institutions, and government organizations. The core group in each camp, typically comprising five to six people, establishes a social structure with clearly defined roles. These roles include practical tasks, such as logistics, food management, and technical setup, as well as emotional responsibilities like managing feelings, monitoring relationships, and ensuring effective communication within the group. Titles like "mom," "dad," "brother," and "sister" reflect these varied functions, emphasizing both the material and emotional support roles within the camp.

Often far from their families and the close friends from their student years, Silicon Valley residents re-create a chosen family. The chosen family is represented in domestic, professional, and digital spaces, including photos in apartments on the fridge and in the bathroom, photos on work desks, and photos on social media profiles. Organized around a community of practices, language, and communication, Burning Man offers for many participants a surrogate family that nurtures a feeling of being integrated in a larger social world. Sociologist Tomatsu Shibutani describes the term *social world* as one of cultural connection: "Each social world, then, is a culture area the boundaries of which are set neither by territory nor formal group membership but by the limits of genuine communication."[32] For participants the festival reenchants a world, a world that they contribute to disenchanting the rest of the year through the production of digital tools, measuring instruments, methods of calculation, and a broad approach to rationalization. In this way Burning Man is not a party. It serves as the matrix for an ethos centered on change.

EIGHT

Technology, a Religion of the Future

I've no gods, I've no ghosts. I rely on technology. . .
—Online interview with an AI robotician,
San Francisco, October 8, 2024

NEW TECHNOLOGIES HAVE BEEN ASSOCIATED with various symbolic notions, including imagination, utopia, political philosophy, secularization, deification, and religion.[1] Historian David Noble has shown that technologies have awakened religious exaltation since the Middle Ages.[2] In *Religion of Technology*, Noble notes how in the medieval world, Christianity's evangelical mission depended on technological advances in "geography, astronomy, and navigation, as well as shipbuilding."[3] In France this interest in science led Henri de Saint-Simon to call for a "science of society," which his protégé Auguste Comte first labeled *sociology*. Comte went on to call for a "religion of humanity" based on science, reason, and moral values. Later, the Jesuit philosopher and scientist Teilhard de Chardin would posit that evolution resulted in complexities of consciousness that would ultimately lead to a cosmic awakening.[4] Such thinkers made science and technology the foundation of a civil religion. Across the Atlantic, twentieth-century thinkers Norbert Wiener, Gregory Bateson, and Marshall McLuhan described technologies as the vehicle of global science and the opportunity to think about the world as a whole. In their wake the internet has emerged as the embodiment of a spiritual community.[5] More recently, in England, controversial thinkers such as Nick Land, Nick Bostrom, and William MacAskill have renewed the thinking of the way technologies should shape future societies, stressing liberty or charity, sometimes in close dialogue with controversial Silicon Valley figures such as Peter Thiel, Elon Musk, Sam Bankman-Fried, or Marc Andreessen. These ongoing discussions between engineers, scientists, entrepreneurs, and philosophers in Northern California in particular have played a central role in the elaboration of the technological political agenda. They have developed tools grounded in their own values that operate independently from traditional institutions, including religious ones.[6]

I've already mentioned Edward Ross, a professor at Stanford University in the late nineteenth century who followed in the footsteps of European sociologists such as Emile Durkheim and Georg Simmel. In his seminal *Social Control: A Survey of the Foundations of Order*, Ross argues that customs and traditions are maintained through socialization and such institutions as family, weddings, and religion. He claims "great men" brook institutional dominance and social hierarchy. They initiate, lead, assert their opinions and preferences, and often create their own "social religions" that stand apart from, and sometimes in opposition to, existing institutions.[7] By doing so, such "great men" are able to transcend social control. Ross's idea of the "great man" who ascends to power through personal character and intellect is a forerunner of Ayn Rand. In her novels, particularly in *Atlas Shrugged*, Rand depicts entrepreneurs as modern-day heroes, akin to Atlas, the figure in Greek mythology who held up the heavens. Rand's heroes are creative, individualistic, disciplined, intelligent, powerful, and often physically attractive, bearing the weight of economic dynamism and progress on their shoulders. Published in 1957, the book became an immediate bestseller, with readers ranking it their most influential book after the Bible in a 1991 nationwide survey.[8] *Atlas Shrugged* has sold over ten million copies and been translated into thirty-six languages.[9]

Rand's ode to the power of individual genius has inspired many entrepreneurs in Silicon Valley, even when it comes to undertaking seemingly Promethean projects. In the 2010s, Larry Page and Google planned to "solve death"; Elon Musk envisioned Mars as the way out for humankind threatened with extinction; and Sam Altman wants to solve everything with Artificial General Intelligence (AGI). From this perspective new technologies represent the path to salvation. Various currents of thought have been linked to this vision, including techno-libertarianism, technoliberalism, objectivism, cosmism, cyberlibertarianism, technocapitalism, dark enlightenment, crypto-anarchism, anarchocapitalism, singularism, accelerationism, effective altruism, and techno-messianism (Figure 5). Among these ideologies, libertarianism, transhumanism, and long-termism are the most frequently associated with tech billionaires in media discussions.

Virtual communities were envisioned as early as the 1980s as a means to realize the libertarian project, a project that invoked the classical liberalism of the Founders. Since the 1990s, libertarians engaged in the field of new technologies have advocated for augmented humanity. They see biotechnology and artificial intelligence as opportunities for a better life, both individually

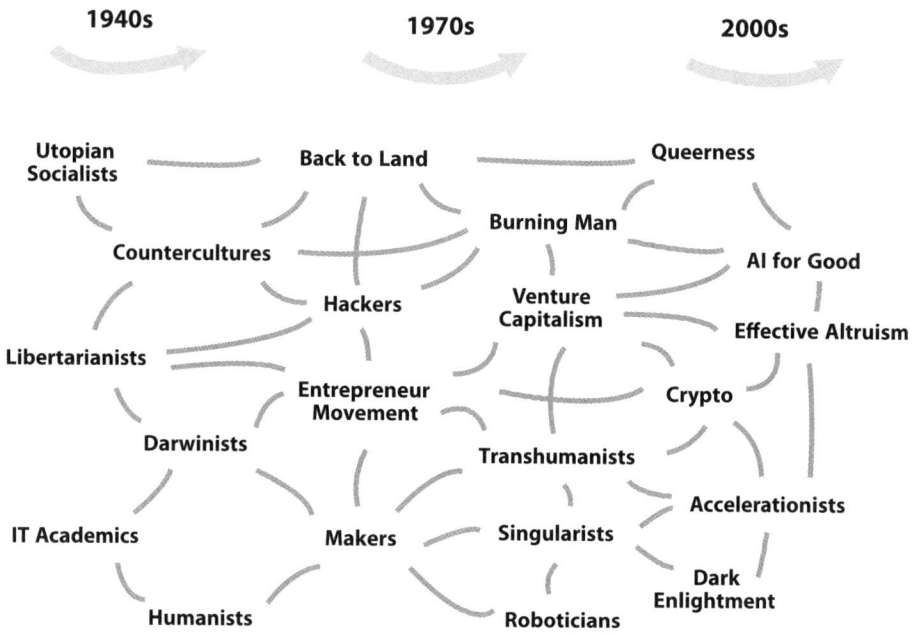

1940s   **1970s**   **2000s**

Utopian Socialists — Back to Land — Queerness — Burning Man — Countercultures — Hackers — Venture Capitalism — AI for Good — Effective Altruism — Libertarianists — Entrepreneur Movement — Crypto — Darwinists — Transhumanists — Accelerationists — IT Academics — Makers — Singularists — Dark Enlightment — Humanists — Roboticians

FIGURE 5. Silicon Valley ideological network, 1940s–2000s. Visualization produced by Céline Vaslin.

and collectively. However, they do not minimize growing technological risks. Thinkers of transhumanism have endeavored, since the year 2000, to provide answers to this challenge. A segment of these thinkers emerged in the 2010s under the umbrella term *long-termism*, a movement focused on anticipating the future of humanity. Several thinkers and tech celebrities have gone from one trend to another. They convene in private meetings, workshops, and conferences. They discuss their agenda through talks, books, and podcasts. They engage with decision-makers in nonprofit organizations, such as think tanks and institutes. And they are active not only in Silicon Valley but also in Washington, DC, the Boston area, and Oxford, England.

Transhumanists can be found at different coordinates of this ideological constellation, including the Esalen Institute, the Bionomics Institute, the Extropy Institute, the Machine Intelligence Research Institute, the Institute for Ethics and Emerging Technologies, the Future of Humanity Institute, the Seasteading Institute, the Future of Life Institute, the Global Priorities Institute, the Forethought Foundation, the Center for Security and Emerging Technologies, and others. These centers are located near leading research institutions, such as Stanford, Berkeley, Georgetown, MIT, Harvard, and Oxford.

The Esalen Institute (1962, Big Sur, California) is dedicated to the reflection on human potential. The Bionomics Institute (1990s, San Francisco) focused on the self-organizing systems of living organisms and their possible applications in the political and social domain. The Extropy Institute (1991–2006, Silicon Valley) focused on technological development and the future of humanity. The Machine Intelligence Research Institute (2000, Berkeley) focuses on the promises and dangers of artificial intelligence. The Institute for Ethics and Emerging Technologies (2004, Boston area) is dedicated to foresight and the future of humanity. The Future of Humanity Institute (2005–24, Oxford) focused on the future of humanity. The Seasteading Institute (2008, San Francisco) is a project for the development of maritime dwellings that due to their location in international waters can escape state regulations. The Future of Life Institute (2015, Boston area) focuses on reducing risks to humanity. The Global Priorities Institute (2018, Oxford) is designed to accompany the action and reflection of decision-makers on the future of humanity. The Forethought Foundation (2018, Oxford) focuses on the long-term future of civilization. The Center for Security and Emerging Technologies (2019, Washington, DC) is a think tank dedicated to policy analysis at the intersection of national and international security and new technologies.

Leading entrepreneur-philanthropists are among the donating members of these institutes and think tanks, starting with Elon Musk and Peter Thiel. In addition, techno-libertarianism, transhumanism, and long-termism have been presented, sometimes even promoted, through two media: the Technology, Entertainment, and Design (TED) conferences and *Wired* magazine. The TED conferences began in 1984 in Northern California in Monterrey. *Wired* launched in 1993 in Silicon Valley. Chris Anderson, though sharing a name, refers to two distinct individuals in this context. One is TED's administrator since 2001, and the other was the editor-in-chief of *Wired* between 2001 and 2012. *Wired*'s Chris Anderson succeeded Louis Rosetto and Katrina Heron and preceded Nicolas Thompson and Katie Drummond. Despite notable Silicon Valley figures aligning with these three technological philosophies—techno-libertarianism, transhumanism, and long-termism—their roots and influences are distinct. This chapter introduces these three intellectual movements. Beyond the specificities of each trend, it is possible to identify common principles of what could be described as "techgnosis."[10] Then, the degree of influence of these ideological currents within Silicon Valley is assessed through an analysis of the discourses of the most followed tech personalities on Twitter/X and LinkedIn.

The tech industry has clear elective affinities with libertarianism, transhumanism, and long-termism. As theorist Karl Mannheim noted, an ideology is not inherently coherent or self-contained; it is defined in relation to other currents of thought.[11] In the same way that capitalism and socialism are connected (though as binary opposites), libertarianism, transhumanism, and long-termism seem to walk hand in hand in Silicon Valley. This is why I use the concept of *elective affinity*, a term originally coined in chemistry and sociology to denote the special connection between two entities, persons, ideas, or cultural forms. The term was first popularized by Goethe's eponymous novel and later conceptualized by Max Weber to describe the unique relationship between Protestantism and capitalism as well as between "the Puritan sect and political democracy" in America, which are both driven by a shared pursuit of freedom.[12] Freedom is indeed central to the libertarian movement.

Libertarianism, the Pursuit of Radical Freedom

In the United States, libertarianism has been adopted by proponents of individual liberties. Libertarians espouse the principles of freedom advocated by the Founders, notably Thomas Jefferson—particularly the unalienable right to "life, liberty, and the pursuit of happiness." The December 16, 1773, Boston Tea Party against British taxation has become emblematic of this American desire for liberty. Opposition to taxes, state regulation, and foreign influence has consistently characterized the libertarian movement.

However, libertarianism was never a linear political movement. It has experienced numerous inflections and internal divisions. The term *libertarianism* has French origins. French libertarian communist Joseph Déjacque (1821–1865) coined the word *libertaire* in a letter to anarchist Pierre-Joseph Proudhon (1809–1865) in 1857. He wanted to describe a left-wing stance that rejected any limitations on individual freedom in social or political matters. In 1858 the term was used as the title of a New York anarchist newspaper. By the mid-twentieth century, the term evolved to represent a different connotation in the American context. Those identifying as libertarians sought to differentiate themselves within the American Right, distinguishing their views from those of both conservatives and social democrats. They criticized state intervention as liberticidal, denouncing it as "statism." Drawing inspiration from the Old Right—a movement that emerged in opposition to FDR's New Deal—libertarians began to systematize their diverse inclinations in the 1970s.

Three currents converged toward a synthesis: anarchism, liberalism, and isolationism. Key figures such as Friedrich Hayek (1899–1992), Ayn Rand (1905–1982), Robert Nozick (1938–2002), Milton Friedman (1912–2006), and Murray Rothbard (1926–1995) became central references in this political movement, which sanctified individual freedom of action and expression. These figures called for the logic of the market to be extended to all spheres of social life as the only way to bring about a "spontaneous order," a libertarian theory that posits "how voluntary actions of discrete individuals produce a predictable order."[13] This "spontaneous order" as a product of individual behavior can be found in the thinking of the Austrian school of economics (founded in 1927), and before them, in eighteenth-century works by French liberal economists such as Jean-Baptiste Say (1767–1832) and Claude Frederic Bastiat (1801–1850).

Members of the Austrian school such as Ludwig Von Mises (1881–1973) and Friedrich Hayek (1899–1992) criticized state interventionism, collectivism, and socialism. They had been part of the Austrian administration and saw fascist regimes arise. Their political views should be read based on this dual experience. In *The Road to Serfdom*, published in 1943, Hayek condemns the notion of social justice, which he perceives as a delusion based on arbitrariness, and he denounces the perverse effects of associated state intervention. To him, Nazism, fascism, communism, and socialism share the same fundamental assumption—namely that the state is superior to the individual. Fervent opponent to John R. Keynes, Hayek condemns all interventions by the public authorities in economic life because of the imbalances they generate. He goes so far as to develop the idea that redistribution of wealth never benefits the weakest and that, through the setting of a minimum wage, state intervention leads to discrimination that ends up excluding from the labor market workers whose productivity is lower than the wage they would receive.

Beyond their intellectual works, Hayek and Von Mises tried to influence policy making through the Mont Pelerin Society, founded in 1947. Named after a small peak in the Alps overlooking Vevey in Switzerland, it has been since then a learned society, aiming to disseminate liberal ideas. The group has woven a closely followed network of academics and decision-makers in the economic field between Europe and the United States. Several members of the Mont Pelerin Society have been awarded the Nobel Prize in Economics, such as Maurice Allais, Gary Becker, James McGill Buchanan, Ronald Coase, Milton Friedman, Friedrich Hayek, George Stigler, and Vernon Smith. Some members have profoundly influenced or directly taken part in the Nixon, Reagan, and Trump administrations (both Trump's first and the second). Its influence has also been felt through more than one hundred think tanks, including the powerful Von Mises Institute, which provides ready-made expert advice for political leaders. This libertarian influence did not only grow through the institutions of the East Coast, but also through the new technology community of Silicon Valley.

Since the 1970s, several currents of thought have developed in Silicon Valley based on the idea of radical freedom, such as cyberlibertarianism, cypherpunk, techno-libertarianism, and so forth. In these currents the focus is on protecting individual liberties, fighting against overregulation, securing the free market, and developing emancipatory new technologies like the internet, cryogenics, cryptography, and so on. Steward Brand's story (discussed in chapter 7) shows that long before Silicon Valley leaders became public figures, the idea of freedom and autonomy motivated the use of new technologies and its spread within back-to-the-land communities in the 1960s.[14] By extension, the computer communities of the 1980s carried this ideal by other means, finding in the online community of the WELL and then the Web a space for the realization of a full and complete kind of freedom. John Perry Barlow (1947–2018) founded, with billionaire entrepreneur and philanthropists Mitch Kapor (1970–) and John Gilmore (1955–), the Electronic Frontier Foundation in 1990 to defend freedom on the internet.

At the Davos World Economic Forum in 1996, Barlow initiated the Declaration of Independence of Cyberspace to oppose a telecoms censorship law proposed by Al Gore. With Louis Rossetto (1949–), Kevin Kelly (1952–), Eric Hughes (author of the 1993 cypherpunk manifesto), and Nicolas Negroponte (1943–), Barlow also participated in the early years of *Wired* magazine. Launched in 1993, it became a beacon for techno-libertarianism in the 1990s. The influence of this counterculture-tinged libertarianism on these two organizations is noticeable. In these forums the development of the internet was presented as the beginning of the end of bureaucracies and also of economic and energy crises. The World Wide Web would break down the frontiers of entrepreneurship, knowledge, and the physical limitations of the known world. This entailed limiting the power of governments and large corporations. Hacker Eric S. Raymond (1957–), WikiLeaks founder Julian

Assange (1971–), and Wikipedia cofounder Jimmy Wales (1966–) have acknowledged the influence of libertarian ideas on their actions.

Several Big Tech leaders have also acknowledged this influence. Elon Musk, Peter Thiel, Jeff Bezos, and Jack Dorsey have all identified themselves as libertarians. Some core ideas can be highlighted: individualism, private property, free market, spontaneous order, authority skepticism.[15] But ultimately this movement encompasses a broad spectrum of political conceptions, ranging from anarchism to anarchocapitalism, from Hayek to Rothbard, from radicals to reactionaries, from Steward Brand to Elon Musk. Nevertheless, the industrial development of tech has increased the visibility of techno-libertarianism. In the late 1990s journalist and cyberactivist Paulina Borsook noted a rise of wealthy libertarian entrepreneurs in Silicon Valley.[16] According to her, their conception of the world was characterized by a lack of empathy, as illustrated by their desire to transcend the boundaries of mind and body. This aspiration is the core of transhumanism.

Transhumanism, toward Augmented Humanity

Transhumanism "affirms the possibility and desirability of fundamentally improving the human condition through applied reason, especially by developing and making widely available technologies to eliminate aging and to greatly enhance human intellectual, physical, and psychological capacities."[17] This trend owes much to the moral entrepreneurship of English-born philosopher Max O'Connor, who calls himself Max More. Born in 1964, More studied philosophy, politics, and economics at Oxford in 1987. He frequented alternative book shops where libertarians and anarchists mingled, including Chris Tame (1950–2006), the most prominent British libertarian of the time. Tame led the Libertarian Alliance, contributed to the Alliance's publications, and participated in seminars on cryonics at Imperial College London.

In 1988, O'Connor changed his family name to More and began to publish a small magazine, *Extropy*, subtitled "a vaccine against the shock of the future."[18] Following in von Hayek's footsteps, the magazine defended the free individual against authoritarian laws and regimes. Despite a lack of financial resources, the magazine enjoyed a certain degree of success and attracted an exponentially growing number of contributors and readers. In 1991, Harry Hawk and Perry Metzger opened the first *Extropian* mailing list on the internet, as soon as the World Wide Web exploded. Max More founded the

TABLE 13. The Extropian Principles

Expansion without limits	Seeking increased intelligence, wisdom and efficiency, unlimited life span, and the removal of political, cultural, biological, and psychological limits to self-fulfillment and self-actualization; constantly overcoming the constraints on progress and our possibilities; expanding into the universe and advancing without end.
Self-transformation	Affirm continuous moral, intellectual, and physical self-improvement through reason and critical thinking, personal responsibility and experimentation; seeking biological and neurological augmentation.
Dynamic optimism	Fuel action with positive expectations; adopt rational, action-based optimism, avoiding blind faith as well as pessimism and inertia.
Smart technology	Apply science and technology creatively to transcend the "natural" limitations imposed by our biological heritage, culture, and environment.
Spontaneous order	Support decentralized and proactive social coordination processes. Encourage tolerance, diversity, long-term thinking, personal responsibility and individual freedom.

SOURCE: Max More, "The Extropian Principles 2.5," 1993, www.aleph.se/Trans/Cultural/Philosophy/princip.html.

Extropy Institute in 1991. And in 1994, Extro 1, the first international symposium devoted to *Extropian* themes, took place in Sunnyvale, California.

O'Connor continued his academic career in the United States, where he completed a thesis at the University of Southern California in 1995. Titled "The Diachronic Self: Identity, Continuity, and Transformation," O'Connor's dissertation explored transhumanist issues, such as life extension and self-transformation. Founded in response to the risks and opportunities presented by new technologies, the Extropy Institute brought together specialists from various fields—biologists, computer engineers, artificial intelligence experts as well as artists, psychologists, and entrepreneurs. It was the main transhumanist hub in Silicon Valley until it closed in 2006. The concept of *extropy*, a term coined by More, represented limitless expansion and the antithesis of entropy (the degeneration and death of any system). More attached five principles to this current of thought: expansion without limits; self-transformation; dynamic optimism; smart technology; and spontaneous order (Table 13).

The influence of several libertarian principles is evident in the statements of transhumanists. For them, the future of humankind is closely tied to the expansion of individual freedoms. They argue that technology will enhance personal liberties and reduce state control. This perspective aligns with the belief that entropy represents the inevitable degradation of closed systems, including biological ones—a concept from information system theories and the work of cybernetics pioneer Norbert Wiener. To counteract this natural law, transhumanists advocate for the promotion of *extropy*, a principle that seeks to reverse entropy by fostering perpetual improvement and expansion. These extropies could occur in several systems. First, space offers a realm shielded from terrestrial sovereignty and ideologies. Second, oceans and seas are similarly untouched. Third, the boundaries of the human body itself can be pushed back. Alongside genetic manipulations and experiments on living beings, extropians openly consider cryonics and brain-computer interfacing as viable paths to immortality. They also see maritime and space colonies, as well as metaverses, as means to circumvent governmental constrains and accelerate humanity's progress.

Through the World Transhumanist Association (WTA) created in 1998, Nick Bostrom (1973–) and David Pearce (1959–) tried to scale this techno-logical utopianism internationally. In the face of growing criticism and political opposition, however, WTA representatives proposed the more open discourse of democratic transhumanism advocated by progressive American sociologist and bioethicist James Hughes (1961–). Hughes's transhumanism champions innovative ecosystems that push back on ecological, demographic, and competition constraints for a techno-optimistic view of a posthuman future.[19] Although the Extropy Institute was closed in 2006, the movement continues, notably through Humanity+, based in California, which advocates ethical use of new technologies. In Silicon Valley several explicitly transhumanist projects have been developed, including at Google. In December 2012 the company hired Ray Kurzweil (1948–), one of the transhumanist movement's main figures, to develop an artificial intelligence program. The following year saw the birth of Calico, a biotech company, aiming to fight human aging.

However, libertarians are not necessarily transhumanists and vice versa. Nonetheless, certain figures, such as Larry Brilliant (1944–), Steward Brand (1938–), or Hal Finney (1956–2014), have found themselves at the crossroads of diverse interests, from the WELL and internet anonymization to cryptocurrencies and cryonics.[20] What was once a niche movement has gained substantial visibility, with its business applications becoming increasingly apparent and its utopian aspects becoming more subdued. Hughes noted in the early 2010s that "libertarians and singularists, supported by

Thiel's philanthropy, have extended their hegemony over the transhumanist community."[21] Singularism is a prominent horizon for this movement and anticipates the surpassing of human intelligence by artificial intelligence.[22] Its proponents aim to ensure that the emergence of superintelligence will benefit humanity. The Singularity University—founded in 2008 by Kurzweil, Peter Diamandis (1961–), and Salim Ismail (1965–)—trains students in Silicon Valley and organizes events and seminars aimed at "educating, inspiring and empowering" people to address this issue.[23] This orientation partly overlaps with long-termism.

Long-termism: Saving Human Potential

Long-termism originates in the work of Nick Bostrom, who founded the Future of Humanity Institute, with Nick Beckstead (1985–), program manager at Open Philanthropy. The book *The Precipice: Existential Risk and the Future of Humanity* (2020) by Toby Ord (1979–) has garnered a significant audience in the context of pandemic and ecological crisis.[24] William MacAskill is one of long-termism's leading proponents. His story began in the early 2000s, while he was studying at Oxford and discovered Australian philosopher Peter Singer (1946–), who was also an Oxford student. Singer is a moral utilitarian, which is an ethical theory that promotes the overall good, defending veganism, antispeciesism, and systematic gifting.[25] He believes that the moral value of an action should be judged by its outcome, rather than by preconceptions about what seems to be good or bad. To Singer, Western people must reduce world poverty. But to reduce world poverty, we must overcome the obstacle of distance that prevents us from being fully aware of poverty.

This was William MacAskill's starting point. The Scottish-born student, born in 1987, decided to donate part of his meagre income to worthy causes. He wanted to convince his peers to do the same. Becoming the youngest professor in Oxford's history, he published *Doing Good Better*.[26] The book outlined a new doctrine called "effective altruism." According to MacAskill, mathematical calculation and rationality, rather than empathy or compassion, should guide the choice of actions. He advocates using indicators to make decisions. This method leads to some counterintuitive conclusions. MacAskill asserts that opting for extremely lucrative careers, such as that of a Wall Street trader, and redistributing most of one's income would be far more effective than becoming a doctor in a poor country. In so doing, effective altruists validate the logic of philanthropy: "earning to give." Even Elon

Musk endorsed MacAskill's philosophy, which he considered "a close match to my philosophy."[27] For MacAskill, philosophy means not only thinking but also being an active entrepreneur. He runs the Forethought Foundation for Global Priorities Research, cofounded the Centre for Effective Altruism and the nonprofit 80,000 Hours (eighty thousand is the expected number of hours worked in an entire career—i.e., forty years × forty weeks × forty hours). 80,000 Hours provides advice on ethical careers, proving that it is possible to be an ethical banker.

In *What We Owe the Future* (2022) MacAskill pushed his thoughts further.[28] According to him, until the industrial and intellectual revolutions of the eighteenth century, humanity's history is characterized by a slow evolution of progress and human knowledge. In the eighteenth century the Enlightenment and Industrial Revolution introduced a rupture that enabled exponential growth of both wealth and knowledge. However, ethics did not follow, which explains the growing dangers threatening humanity. While human potential should continue to develop in the future, the production of artificial viruses, ecological crises, or a computer superintelligence may put an end to it. From this perspective humanity is not considered even as a species. Rather, humanity is considered a potential for progress—speculative and indeterminate—which must be preserved by anticipation. Future generations are the custodians of this potential, but they neither have the right to vote nor the financial or technological resources to make themselves heard. It is therefore necessary to invest in intellectual and economic resources, notably through philanthropy. Elon Musk, Sam Bankman-Fried (before his bankruptcy), and Dustin Moskovitz (cofounder of Facebook and Asana) have made large donations to promote these guidelines.[29] Elon Musk's statement "the *future of civilization* is assured," on January 20, 2025, the day of Donald Trump's inauguration, can be understood from that perspective as well.

These initiatives and statement echo other efforts within Silicon Valley that encourage appreciation of long-term thinking, such as the Long Now Foundation. Founded in 1996 and chaired by Stewart Brand, the foundation is run by Kevin Kelly from *Wired* and financed by Jeff Bezos. One of the foundation's most notable projects is the development of a mechanical clock designed to last ten thousand years. These three movements have obvious elective affinities. Libertarianism places freedom of action, free market, and limited regulation above all. Transhumanism calls for technologies to become a path to salvation. Long-termism is a pro-technology, pro-business, pro-philanthropic movement that is based on quantification, optimization, and projection. These three systems provide a number of moral justifications for Silicon Valley entrepreneurship. Thus these three currents have attracted a great deal of commentary, generating both fascination and concern in the media. However, libertarianism, transhumanism, and long-termism are not homogeneous. They are not even particularly well-structured ideologies. They are closer to movements than schools, and closer to currents of thought than doctrines. Interest can arise from different sensibilities and convictions, and these can also shift over time. For example, transhumanist optimism has undergone a number of inflections. Bostrom, controversial because of his eugenicist stance, has been theorizing existential risks for humanity that include AI, climate, and pandemics. His book *Superintelligence* has been a major influence in Silicon Valley, starting with Musk.[30]

I've met engineers wearing continuously connected glasses and tech monitoring their intestinal flora. I've also met those in Silicon Valley who believe cryogenics will be a viable option at some point. But it's difficult to establish the degree to which Silicon Valley techies subscribe to these three currents of thought. Long-termism is organized as a community, with different chapters, and its leaders organize meetups and vegan retreats, but it has yet to attract a large audience. Likewise, transhumanism has for years been organized around confidential publications like the *Extropy Journal*. A few dozen people make up transhumanism's insider circles, mostly white men with PhDs working as biologists, computer scientists, or physicists. Some of these insiders come from academia, but they are mostly from companies or nonprofits. Even today, the altruism group in San Francisco had around fifteen hundred members as of mid-2024, and the Centre for Effective Altruism had just over five hundred followers on Twitter/X.

Libertarianism is an older and certainly more widespread movement. However, in San Francisco's local elections, where the Democratic Party easily garners nearly 180,000 voters, the Libertarian Party struggles to get 1,000 votes. During my study period, I met a majority of techies who supported or voted for Democratic candidates, and a very small minority of libertarians. These libertarians, while convinced and sometimes extremely influential, were eager to discuss their views openly. This aligns with a local joke: you always know when you're dealing with a libertarian because it's the second thing they'll mention after their first name when introducing themself. That said, libertarianism is not a homogeneous group. Humanist and democratic projects such as those promoted by Steward Brand or John Perry Barlow may have been associated with it. At the same time, other figures claimed a "dark" orientation. This notion, used by thinkers and entrepreneurs such as Nick Land, Steve Sailer, Curtis Yarvin, and Peter Thiel, is used in reference to the early Middle Ages. It designates a current aspiring to overthrow democracy, accused of threatening individual freedoms and holding back progress through high levels of bureaucratization and protection for the weakest. As a result, they call for the advent of a corporate state led by a CEO, able to promote freedom, innovation, and excellence, no matter the consequences in term of inequalities. As we can see, the same label has been used to designate opposing aspirations. Nevertheless, there are similarities between these different currents, which differentiate them from classic political ideologies.

Donald Trump's alliance with tech billionaires in 2024 means the rise to power of schools of thought. Computer scientist Timnit Gebru and philosopher Emile Torres believe that these intellectual movements have a source and a purpose: eugenics and technosolutionism. This would allow them to be merged into one acronym: TESCREAL.[31] But as mentioned, these currents are invested in many ways and are not unified. Moreover, this type of reading tends to identify them with political ideologies, in the sense given to this notion by philosophers and political thinkers since the eighteenth century. However, these currents do not have the same properties as the major political ideologies (socialism, communism, liberalism, fascism, etc.). They are not conceptual systems produced by professional thinkers to equip political leaders intellectually with a view to conquering power, identified with the state via a party. In Silicon Valley the terms *ideologues, intellectuals*, or even *political parties* and *politicians* are quite rare in techies' discussions and preoccupations.

In their life the role of European and West Coast intellectuals is assumed by entrepreneur-influencers. Intellectual peer-reviewed articles are replaced by blog posts and podcasts, political parties by platforms, and the objective of conquering power by influence. The result is greater flexibility, fluidity, and porosity between conceptual systems that professional philosophers would probably judge severely due to their lack of rigor, consistency, and solidity in terms of argumentation. But it would be wrong to look down on these trends, as their promoters have powerful means at their disposal to put them into practice. In the three various currents mentioned in this chapter, entrepreneurs-philosophers, at the crossroads of academia and consulting through institutes, aim to limit the power of the state by substituting individual initiative in the name of freedom. What is at stake is no longer the coherence of conceptual systems but the ongoing endeavor to unleash technology. That's why it's more accurate to speak of movements than ideologies.

Thus you can question both the influence and the coherence of these move-ments. The region is characterized by a majority of pragmatic progressives, pro-government libertarians, and liberals who predominantly vote Democratic. It includes hackers who work for Big Tech, individuals who support the investor state while demanding tax cuts, and those who cham-pion transhumanism for its role in space exploration yet oppose rights for transgender people. Some even identify as loyal Democrats but endorsed Donald Trump in 2024 for economic reasons.[32] Similarly, there are multiple ideological currents that evolve over time through trends, splits, and overlaps. The focus on these ideological currents is partly due to an academic tendency to overemphasize the influence of intellectual movements. This may seem marginal compared to the practical, hands-on nature of the tech industry. However, the significant funding, political influence, and design of technical infrastructures based on these principles warrant closer examination.

Indeed, as historian Fred Turner demonstrated regarding the conflict between the New Left and technologists in the 1960s, technologies have inherently political effects. Science and technology studies have repeatedly shown that even ordinary objects, such as metro systems, bicycles, or shop-ping carts, reflect underlying political choices.[33] Ordinary objects or services such as supermarket caddies or personal computers have reshaped social organization. For this reason some entrepreneurs can see themselves as politi-cians. This is all the truer for techies raised in the United States, where some of the first politicians were entrepreneurs who supported technologies, the free market, and free speech. As tech pioneers of their day, Benjamin Franklin's kite-in-a-thunderstorm led to the development of the lightning rod. Thomas Jefferson created the Cipher Wheel for deciphering secret messages. And George Washington championed new technologies in weaponry, architecture, and canal construction. Max Weber dedicated extensive analysis to the "spirit of capitalism," focusing on Franklin's work ethic, his dramatized conception of time management, and its connection to monetary gain—all of which were influenced by his Puritan upbringing in Boston.[34]

This can explain in part why Musk has been scandalized by the statue removal of the enslaver Thomas Jefferson in New York City, or why a respondent said to me how and why he identifies with the tireless Alexander Hamilton, who was a delegate to the Constitution Convention of 1787, treasury secretary under George Washington, founder of the Federalist Party, and one of the three main authors of *The Federalist Papers:*

> I am never satisfied. Like . . . Hamilton—I strongly identify with him—he was the first to build the Treasury. He spent a lot of time thinking about the country's economy. He was truly passionate about what he did. He was never satisfied, worked very hard, and was known as a great writer. People remember his words, more than anything else. . . . If you think about the Founding Fathers, they were fighting for freedom, for ideas, for the economy, and revolution. And I think in Silicon Valley, we're also fighting for freedom. . . . Your freedom, everybody's freedom, and that's code ownership, the right to modify code, and the freedom to understand how it works. *Open source* is a fight for these rights. It's like a bill of rights. For software (interview with an entrepreneur, San Francisco, September 25, 2016).

Even if libertarians or transhumanists are not the majority in Silicon Valley, they can be extremely influential because of the impact of their choices. A former Google employee notes:

> The level of debate is so granular within Silicon Valley that nothing deviates from techno-messianism. Some people may think differently, but as long as they execute, it doesn't matter. You can be a maverick, saying that it's horrible to work for such a company, but whether you agree or not, it doesn't matter, as long as you work for them. If you're in the Wehrmacht in 1943 but you're not anti-Semitic, it doesn't make much difference at the end of the day (online interview with an entrepreneur, San Francisco, September 28, 2019).

To assess the extent and coherence of their discourse, I conducted a survey with sociologist Samuel Coavoux that focused on the most followed individuals on Twitter/X and LinkedIn among a thousand Silicon Valley tech executives. The data proved somewhat limited or challenging due to survey constraints, such as difficulties accessing sites or individuals, brief interview durations, and redundancies in information collected with public data. To balance these biases, we reviewed forty-two books and twenty-eight TED conferences by those tech executives represented in the survey (see "Investigating the Voices of the Digital Revolution").

Tech Influencers

While, during the 2010s and 2020s, attention has been drawn to algorithms, echo chambers, the attention economy, deepfakes, and "AI slop" (meaning

INVESTIGATING THE VOICES OF THE DIGITAL REVOLUTION

This text is based on a survey conducted with Samuel Coavoux. The data was collected from the most followed executives on LinkedIn: chief executive officers, chief technical officers, or chief financial officers at the top 1,000 Silicon Valley companies by capital raised (selected from the Crunchbase database). By the 2010s, LinkedIn had established itself as the dominant professional social network in Silicon Valley. This survey's initial sample included 237 individuals.

In this first selection we didn't include those whose activity on social networks was almost exclusively related to their company, such as Airbnb's cofounders, Salesforce's CEO, Facebook executives, and others. Since LinkedIn lacked an open, public-facing API (application programming interface), the activity that was tracked on LinkedIn between 2015 and 2022 was the activity automated to be shared on Twitter/X between 2014 and 2016. The sample was refined to those who were sufficiently active on Twitter/X, defined as having posted four hundred original Tweets between 2014 and 2016, resulting in a total of 167 people.

A total of 317,651 observations were made on Twitter/X, corresponding to as many posted messages. The corpus was analyzed through topic modeling, which consisted of selecting terms on different topics and using an algorithm aimed at reconstructing the distribution of topics and terms (i.e., the probability that a topic is chosen and the probability that a particular word is chosen within a topic). Then we established a prosopography database containing information on sociodemographic criteria (such as age, gender, education level, academic institution, degrees, social origin, professional activities, and primary residence) and on professional trajectories (including sectors and types of positions held). The data was sourced from public information on LinkedIn, Wikipedia, and such media as the *New York Times*, *The New Yorker*, *Wired*, *TechCrunch*, *Business Insider*, *Forbes*, *Inc.*, *Fast Company*, *Bloomberg TV*, and *CNBC* as well as from blogs. From 2015 and 2018 sample members were also tracked at conferences (8), networking sessions (12), and interviews (11).

Approximately forty individuals in the database were contacted. Half of the requests went unanswered despite multiple follow-ups. A quarter declined, citing being "too busy." The remaining quarter agreed to participate on the condition of flexibility regarding the conditions, given that their high geographical mobility made the concept of a workplace somewhat relative and the duration sometimes as short as fifteen minutes. Half of the interviews were therefore conducted by phone, during their commute, or at trade shows during their breaks. Two interviews were conducted in the workplace, where interviewees were as focused on extracting high-quality information from interviewers as on providing information. They punctuated the interview with questions on the social, economic, and political situation in France and Europe (Brexit, populism, protests, the question of the European model versus the US model). While this meant interviews were not as fruitful as hoped, they were nonetheless enlightening about a typical Silicon Valley mind-set regarding transforming interactions into opportunities to gather knowledge and information.

low-quality content made using generative artificial intelligence), in the heart of Silicon Valley tech workers have increasingly valued information sorted by influencer-curators. A specialist in the field of artificial intelligence told me in a meeting room of a major tech company in 2024 that he consumes a lot of news and information, but only the ones that have been filtered by influencers he has selected for their expertise and synthesis quality. A thirty-year-old entrepreneur-AI researcher admits in an interview that he worries about the pressure of consuming information:

> Living here, it pushes you to be constantly sharp. You can't afford to miss the latest article, the latest news, etc. Because people are going to tell you about it. But it's hard to keep up. It's super intense. And I really wonder if I'll be able to do it for more than a few years (online interview, San Francisco, October 8, 2024).

Another entrepreneur told me that he follows five or six "influencers, no more" who really "help him to think" and that "the way Elon Musk's brain works fascinates" him. On social networks, in conferences, and in specialized publications they are called *tech gurus, thinkfluencers, thought leaders, global thinkers, world leading speakers, superinfluencers, key opinion leaders*, and *network celebrities*.[35] They have different monikers and also varying levels of visibility. Seasoned and knowledgeable professionals, like former *Wired* editor-in-chief Nicholas Thompson (129,000 followers on Twitter/X in 2024), are featured alongside tech figures such as the former Apple evangelist

Guy Kawasaki, web 2.0 theorist Tim O'Reilly, and Tim Ferris, described by *Wired* as the "greatest self-made man of all time." Ferris had between 1.3 and 1.9 million followers on Twitter/X in mid-2024.

In addition, internationally known entrepreneurs such as Musk (over 191 million followers) and Bill Gates (more than 65.1 million followers) are also on the list. Some accumulate multibillion-dollar fortunes ($236.1 billion in 2024 for Musk, according to *Forbes*), while others have remuneration levels closer to that of experts (an estimated $150,000 for *Wired*'s editor-in-chief). They play various roles that have marked the history of the internet: builders (entrepreneurs, researchers, engineers), investors (VCs, executives, administrators), and experts (journalists, bloggers, commentators, academics). Entrepreneurship is a cross-cutting activity.

The Voice of Entrepreneurship

The first observation is a truism: tech influencers spend about half their time discussing companies and technology. The prevalence of this theme reflects the role that the sample members assume: to inform and guide others toward the best in the technological world. They focus on highlighting promising solutions, recommending efficient work practices, and showcasing effective organizational strategies. This is evident in the proportion of "advice" in the corpus, which accounts for 10.16 percent (Table 14).

The same approach can be found in their books, conferences, posts, and tweets: giving advice, sharing insights, providing reflections ("lessons," "observations"), delivering tips, and relaying quotes. This method is applied extensively and widely. Indeed, solutions are presented as potentially beneficial to all (e.g., "How Google's Clever AI Startup 'DeepMind' Is Helping To Create A Smarter World"), while political and technological news offer business opportunities (e.g., "See New Opportunities By Monitoring New #legislation and #regulations"). In this regard tech influencers bear a resemblance to the late nineteenth-century hygienist movement exemplified by Louis Pasteur, inventor of pasteurization. The hygiene movement was marked by "an accumulation of advice, precautions, recipes, opinions, statistics, remedies, regulations, anecdotes, and case studies."[36] All things being equal, from this point of view Elon Musk and Reid Hoffman function similarly to Louis Pasteur. Voices of tech do not stand out by imposing theoretical frameworks but by producing, selecting, and accumulating information designed to help decipher, analyze, and make sense of the ever-changing landscape of

TABLE 14. Distribution of major communication categories

Category	Number of themes included	Frequency in the corpus (%)[1]
Companies	15	25.13
Technologies	13	20.52
Media	10	16.30
Politics and society	8	14.04
Advice	6	10.16
Personal life	5	8.28
Organization of time	3	5.57

[1] Defined here as the average of the sum of the a posteriori probability of the themes included in the category. These indicators should be treated with caution, as indicators of orders of magnitude rather than precise measures.

innovation. In doing so, they offer their followers "a grasp on the future," with the future a shared object of focus.

SPREADING THE WORD OF TECH

This accumulation is distinguished not only by its themes but also by the conception of the future it conveys—a future that must be anticipated, a universal future, and a positive future for humanity.

Anticipating the Future

Behind the tech discourse lies a philosophy of history, one that views the world as organized through time. The lexicon of time is abundantly used: *new* (the second most used term), *first* (the twenty-first), *next* (the twenty-ninth). These go hand in hand with expressions related to the present, such as *time, today,* and *passing time* (5 percent of the corpus). This future is portrayed as ambivalent, both full of opportunities for those who capitalize on them but risky for people who do not. Tech influencers adopt a providential role: "preparing [the world] for an impending storm"[37]; because "the faster the world changes, the closer the future is"[38] and so "the future is faster than you think."[39]

Despite this, the effect is not necessarily negative, provided you engage with and embrace the momentum of new technologies. After all, "we humans are distinguished from other species by our ability to perform miracles; and these miracles have a name: technology. Technology is miraculous because it allows us to do more with less, taking our basic faculties to a higher level."[40] Embracing technology is seen as synonymous with embracing progress. However, for this to be effective, progress must be anticipated. The associated expressions are positive and proactive, illustrated by the abundance of imperatives, such as "let's build," "let's do," "let's prepare," "let's be," "let's create." Action verbs are as frequent. *Work* is the twelfth most frequent term; *do*, the seventeenth; *take*, the fortieth. These terms have positive connotations and are often paired with terms like *super* (the third), *love* (the eleventh), or *great* (the thirty-second). The uncertainty of innovation is countered by ordinal modes of comparison that serve as a principle of orientation and identification of what deserves attention. Superlatives and comparatives are prominent, via the terms *better* (the fifteenth most frequent term) or *superior* (the thirtieth). In addition, various diagrams, tables, pyramids, or arrows identify growth with chronology horizontally. Progress is identified with verticality. This symbolism of the x-y coordinates (abscissa and ordinate) tends to undermine the random nature of processes. Instead, these graphics focus on an endpoint: success. Failures are depicted as transitory and preliminary stages along the path to achievement.

Starting with the most spectacular successes, these representations stage lines of flight. Flashbacks recall what was said about a company in difficulty a few months or years earlier, highlighting moments when it was at its apex. This process underscores the highly improbable, and by extension, the exemplary nature of the journey taken. Confronted with the roller coaster of entrepreneurial life, such depictions also serve to feed and renew the energy capital of those who follow it. Classic representations of the industry include Steve Jobs recounting how he called Bill Hewlett for spare parts when he was twelve years old; Jeff Bezos alone in a makeshift office during Amazon's early years; and Jack Ma (founder of Alibaba) listing his long series of failed job interviews, from McDonald's to the police of the People's Republic of China. While European philosophers criticize acceleration, speed is a vital principle of selection and election in the tech industry.[41] Terms such as *now* (the sixth most used term), *today* (the ninth), *day* (the eighteenth) reflect this emphasis on immediacy. Speed in creation, execution, hiring, decision-making, and adaptation is seen as essential for maintaining a link between individual success and collective progress.

The titles of publications by members of the sample often carry millenarian overtones. Examples include Guy Kawasaki's *Rules for Revolutionaries*;

Steve Blank's *The Four Steps to the Epiphany*; Alexis Ohanian's *Without Their Permission: How the 21st Century Will Be Made, Not Managed*; Chris Schroeder's *Startup Rising: The Middle East Entrepreneurial Revolution*; Bob Sutton's *Scaling Up Excellence*; Tim O'Reilly's *WTF: What's the Future and Why It Depends on Us*; and Reid Hoffman's *Blitzscaling: The Lightning Fast Path to Building Massively Valuable Companies*.[42] These books share a philosophy in which the distance between experience and the horizon of expectation is not maximal, as was the idea of rational and steady progress before the eighteenth century, but minimal.[43]

A World without Division

The second characteristic of this mode of representation is its universality. While Karl Marx, Joseph A. Schumpeter, and Adam Keynes saw progress as a process that produces inequalities, for tech voices, economic opportunity takes on universal proportions. Descriptions transcend the antagonisms that usually structure social representations as lines of opposition: economic (powerful/modest); social (national/foreign, upper/working class); demographic (young/old); and racial (white/Black, Hispanic, Asian). Such oppositions have few or no occurrences among tech voices—the only exception being gender (men/women) with the call to reduce gender-based wage inequality and to fight against gender and sexual violence. The denunciation of wage inequality is not found evenly across the board, however, occurring twice as often among women (2.9 percent of speeches) as among men (1.3 percent).

Binary and hierarchical categorizations give way to a single shared vision— one that is attainable through action, reflecting the arguments of Ayn Rand and the libertarians. The prevalence of procedural terms is conveyed by the prominence of transitive forms (-*ing*). *Doing* is the seventeenth most used word. The thirty-eighth is *going*. The prevalence of inclusive terms represents a single shared vision, including *people* (the fifth most common word in the corpus), *world* (the ninth), *team* (the twenty-third), and *all* (the fiftieth). In this context relevant social differentiations are temporal and positivized: visionaries, leaders, early adopters, followers, and so forth. Observations regarding the incomplete democratization of entrepreneurship, the internet, and new technologies are characterized as yet to be resolved. The coexistence of marginalized workers with those who have made great fortunes is obscured.[44] In addition, the impact on the environment, as well as general inequalities between generations and social categories, receives scant attention.

Positivity of World History

This historical perspective and its public engagement are relatively unique in the online public space. Indeed, most practices on social networks are characterized by asymmetric participation, limited social networks, and instances of aggressiveness.[45] In other industries, executives and managers often remain silent. In tech, however, there is a vibrant tweet stream by figures like Musk. Twitter/X has been described as a polarized space. Facebook, as a platform that rewards acrimonious feelings. Instagram, as a realm governed by narcissism, the male gaze, and commodification. YouTube and Twitch have been described as spaces dominated by men. Many tech services also appear biased socially, gender-wise, and racially. Nonetheless, tech voices generally maintain a positive outlook, with an optimistic tone and narrative. Freedom, progress, energy, and self-transformation (in line with the credo of transhumanism) are intensely celebrated values.

Criticism has increased over the past few years, both by scholars, often women (danah boyd, Ethan Zuckerman, Alice Marwick, Kate Crawford, Shoshana Zuboff, Joy Buolamwini, and others) and within Silicon Valley itself. Influential figures such as John Perry Barlow, Edward Snowden, and Aaron Swartz have tackled numerous issues, as have former Facebook, Twitter/X, and Google employees like Tristan Harris, Frances Haugen, Rumman Chowdhury, Timnit Gebru, Meredith Whittaker, or even 2024 physics Nobel Prize winner Geoffrey Hinton. Criticism includes the regulation of online speech, the environmental footprint of digital technology, behavioral surveillance, the need for a discrimination and fairness paradigm in the workplace, and the hegemony of the white male coder. Different organizations have been critical as well, including the Electronic Frontier Foundation, the AI Now Institute, the Silicon Valley Toxics Coalition, the Center for Human Technology, and others. Some of these themes are repeated in the corpus, such as the topics of whistleblowers, regulation, wage gaps, economic crises, and so forth. But they are addressed by mentioning avenues for improvement. Broadly speaking, a positive tone dominates messages (63 percent). Negative, acrimonious, or critical statements are reserved for political themes, mainly concerning Donald Trump (the fourteenth most frequent word). Conversely, themes related to business, self-promotion, and technology are all exclusively positive.

Thus the sometimes-anecdotal nature of contributions should not obscure the normative coherence of these discourses. Even if not explicitly mentioned, they overlap with libertarianism, transhumanism, and long-termism principles. They offer a common, pragmatist expression that appears neutral, though it often involves communication acts that celebrate success, individual initiative, and progress. By conveying a range of philosophies (such as individual freedom, free market ideals, techno-optimism, an accelerated future, and self-transformation), they tend to transform the techno-messianism of a few into a civil religion for the many. The messages intertwine the promotion of new technologies with the promotion of the self. The transformation of the self is aligned with the transformation of the world and individual success with collective progress. In this horizon of expectation, technologies do not confront racial, social, or geographical hierarchies but rather historical ones. Tech voices navigate between ideology and utopia, balancing the principle of reality with explorations of what is possible.

NINE

The Wolf of Market Street

At the end of the day, we need to look at the systems that prevent some people, even in a city as progressive as San Francisco, from finding a place and moving forward.

—Interview with a pastor, San Francisco, March 2016

SILICON VALLEY ENTREPRENEURS WANT to have an "impact." From a technological and global point of view. Not a social and local one. However, the presence and impact of the tech industry on San Francisco are real. For better and for worse. The share of IT jobs in the city has grown from 2.7 percent in 1970 to 10.2 percent in 2010 and 18.7 percent in 2021. A comparison with the city of Los Angeles shows LA in a particularly unfavorable light.[1] LA specialized in low-wage export industries, such as apparel, while San Francisco shifted to high-wage export industries, such as software and IT systems. In 2010 eight of the top ten market sectors on the San Francisco Peninsula had average wages above $100,000, while none of greater Los Angeles's strategic market sectors reached that threshold. The Peninsula's median household income was $113,200 in 2019—$33,000 higher than the rest of California and $47,000 higher than the rest of the United States.[2]

But the tech industry's impact comes with a price: increased water and energy consumption, growing remote work community, sudden layoffs and stock market volatility, downtown office crisis, outsourcing to low-wage workers in countries with low living standards and no labor rights protection, dependence on the large fortunes financing or getting involved in the political campaigns and increasing economic inequality. In 2023, San Francisco proper had a GDP of $263.1 billion and a GDP per capita of $325,000, the highest in the country. Between 2010 and 2020 the median income of the richest 10 percent of households in San Francisco increased by 87 percent ($250,000), almost twice the national average. But by 2021 nearly one-third of the region's residents were living below the poverty line.[3] At the height of the pandemic, San Francisco remained at the top of the US housing market, and San Jose was in fourth place. This rise in housing prices is only one aspect of the transformation in the region. Other changes include a rising cost of living, local businesses crises, increase in evictions, drug crisis (recorded 806 drug overdose deaths in 2023), and a surge in homelessness. Issues surrounding class inequality have been exacerbated by the development of a so-called classless industry.

In San Francisco the arrival of dot-comers during the first tech boom of the late 1990s already increased housing pressure on low-income households, particularly in residential areas such as Noe Valley and the Mission District.[4] Several San Francisco neighborhoods have subsequently been subject to a continuous process of gentrification, only slowed down by the COVID pandemic. Since 2012, San Francisco has been outperforming the overall state and national markets. In August 2024, in a supposedly gloomy housing market, the median sale price of a home in San Francisco County was $1.3 million. And at the same time, the city has experienced several phases of office crisis.

In the 2010s and 2020s this cycle repeated itself. Techies—stereotypically white men in their twenties with high incomes—live in shared apartments or, even worse to San Franciscans, whole houses—known as *hacker houses*— taken over by techies through pooled resources. They develop companies, set up in offices, then move further south, to Silicon Valley, Los Angeles, Austin, Miami, or any other area with lower taxation, or even sometimes just give up on office utility, like WordPress did. San Franciscans used to critique these newcomers' rude behaviors, including staring at phones instead of greeting the neighbors, nonparticipation in neighborhood meetings, incivilities in collective buildings, and appropriation of public spaces. Techies were also derided buying and renting housing above market prices, using electric bikes, e-scooters, self-driving cars, tech shuttles, or surveillance technology services. Some artists, activists, and geographers have named them colonial "settlers"—that is, a heteropatriarchy that displaces residents.[5]

They have been called the "delusional tech elite," complicit "with the worst in American politics," namely "millions of underpaid workers[,] a boiling housing crisis, mass displacement, and severe environmental damage."[6] Public action against "exploding inequality,"[7] especially within the city of San Francisco, is said not only to have failed but also to have encouraged the development of poverty pockets, the homeless crisis[8], urban sprawl, NIMBYism, and increasing segregation to the benefit of upper-class populations. Geographer and activist Erin McElroy, who lived many years in San Francisco, has shed light on displacement effects, economic and cultural predation, and racial relegation dynamics coming with a spreading tech industry in the Bay Area.[9] The tech exodus that took place during the COVID crisis and the subsequent office occupancy crisis in the city center have fueled the feeling that techies are not far from the traders portrayed in the Martin Scorsese–directed film *The Wolf of Wall Street*, an opportunistic class of workers that see the city as nothing more than a commodity.

But at the same time, more and more policy makers and residents have seen the tech industry as a booming economy to foster. Some techies have organized themselves to improve the electoral process in San Francisco (like the SF Grow initiative)[10], and investors (such as Ron Conway, Michael Moritz, Marc Benioff, Sam Altman) have given money, supported candidates, or committed themselves to find solutions for the city. In a city both rich and badly damaged by the pandemic, techies have been perceived in San Francisco as ambivalent political figures, being both the hunting and hunted wolves, described as too or too-little-present. This two-fold representation questions the ability of the tech industry to maintain a hyphen between sectorial growth and social progress.[11] This chapter looks at how San Francisco emerged as the world capital of new technologies, how tech is a resolutely urban economy, and how it has been politicized.

THE POLITICAL AMBIVALENCES OF A NEOTECHNOLOGICAL CITY

San Francisco became the epicenter of Silicon Valley. Yet the Golden City was long considered a stranger to Silicon Valley, and vice versa. HP, Intel, Apple, and Google developed nearly forty miles away from the Golden Gate Bridge. For a long time Santa Clara's hardware companies seemed far more eager to push their trade agenda in Washington, DC, against a backdrop of competition with Japan than to rally turbulent San Francisco. The internet boom brought a large influx of tech workers in the 1990s. But the ensuing crash translated into massive departures in the early 2000s. In the 2001–2002 Bay Area the top 150 companies lost $90 billion, the equivalent to the profits made during the previous eight years, opening a downtown economic and office crisis.[12] Twenty years later, history repeated itself with the mass exodus of techies and companies during the pandemic. Between March 2020 and January 2021, residential rents in San Francisco were down 27 percent, and the office vacancy rate spiked to 16.7 percent, the highest figure by far in a decade.[13] Despite the fickle character of the tech industry, the city administration has repeatedly and paradoxically seen tech as a way to revive and bring stability to its economy. To understand this paradox, it is important to keep in mind that San Francisco is a city of crisis.

San Francisco: City of Crises

San Francisco is among the country's largest and most productive superstar cities, with New York and Los Angeles. It is a municipality, a county, and a metropolis all rolled into one, with a history dating back to the gold miners of the mid-nineteenth century.[14] Its architectural embodiment contrasts with many of the cities that surround it, starting with its technological twin, San Jose, a city characterized by gridded and impersonal suburban architecture. At the beginning of the twentieth century, San Francisco was considered the Paris of the Pacific and the Boston of the West. Its residents cultivated romanticization: from Mark Twain's "eternal Spring of San Francisco"[15] to Rebecca Solnit's *Infinite City*, from the psychedelic San Francisco sound of Jefferson Airplane to the Haight Ashbury jams of the Grateful Dead, from the Pacific Ocean backdrop of *Dirty Harry* to the Telegraph Hill of *Basic Instinct*. The hills, the fog, the Victorian houses make it a canvas for projections, reveries, and detours. Landmark bookstores continue to bear witness to the city's literary vitality. There are also numerous guides, novels, and columns devoted to its cultural milieu, feeding a form of idealization regarding the city's influence and history.

But if San Francisco's image is linked to growth, the city's leaders and officials are haunted by the fear of economic downturn. Its city leaders—most of whom were born in the region, studied in the city or at neighboring universities, or at least lived in the city for almost a decade—keep alive the memory of the cycles of crises that have regularly struck San Francisco. Whereas techies describe San Francisco as an expensive "boom town," civil servants see it as a city constantly threatened by recession. The evolution of its population proves them right. Unlike Los Angeles or New York, San Francisco has not experienced stable growth from the 1930s on. Instead, expansions (in the 1950s, 1990s, and 2010) alternate with crises (in the 1940s, 1980s, and 2020s). The city had 643,000 inhabitants in 1940; 775,000 in 1950; and then went into decline until 1980, where it increased to 678,000 inhabitants; around 723,000 inhabitants in 1990; 776,000 in 2000; 805,000 in 2010; and 884,000 in 2020. Its population decreased by 9.42 percent since 2020 to 788,000 in mid-2024. Compare this number to a population of 2.9 million for Chicago, 3.9 million for Los Angeles, and 8.38 million for New York City (1.6 million for Manhattan alone). The resources available to the city, as well as its cultural life, place it in the second tier of international metropolises.

The AIDS pandemic of the 1980s and 1990s led to the deaths of nearly twenty-three hundred people in 1992, making San Francisco the hardest hit city in the country.[16] The year 1989 marked the mortgage and loan crisis. Later, in March 2000, the dot-com bubble burst. Then, following the World Trade Center attacks in New York in September 2001, San Francisco went through a tourism crisis, then a financial household debt crisis in 2007 and 2008. After the lockdowns during the COVID-19 pandemic, the administration had to deal with tech layoffs in 2022–24, Silicon Valley Bank bankruptcy in 2023, and the downtown office crisis. In 2024–25 some Silicon Valley tech companies were accused of being too liberal by tech icons. Elon Musk emptied the offices of Twitter/X in September 2024, and Mark Zuckerberg announced in January 2025 that his moderation teams would be based in Texas, a region considered less "woke" than Northern California. Thus the most experienced policy makers and elected officials in town have learned that the future of their city is always at stake. A civil servant I interviewed described why the city hoped that a knowledge economy would put an end to recession: "The idea of the new economy at the end of the 1990s was that there would never be another recession because there would be no manufacturing, no factories, but services, products of a knowledge economy, that would not experience a crisis. Everyone bought this speech."[17] But the new economy turned out to be as unstable as the old one. Since then, local authorities looked cyclically to the tech industry to revitalize the economy, and at the same time, to view it as a bad and volatile partner.

The ability to make the most of this industry has been complicated by another instability: the political one. While still mayor of San Francisco, Gavin Newsom became lieutenant governor of the State of California in 2011. An unelected official bureaucrat, Ed Lee, became acting mayor and pledged not to run for the office. However, Lee, a Berkeley graduate, lawyer by training, and advocate for minority rights, went back on his promise and ran for office during the November 2011 municipal elections, becoming the first Asian American mayor of a major American city. During Lee's first term, major protests broke out over the rise of inequality, particularly in the real estate market. He was criticized for his inaction in the face of the deaths of young unarmed African Americans who had been shot by the city's police.

Despite Lee's unpopularity, he ran for reelection in 2016. And was reelected. But he died of a heart attack in December 2017 at the age of sixty-six.

In January 2018, Mark Farrell was appointed by the Board of Supervisors as interim mayor. Then London Breed was elected in a new municipal election in July 2018. Back then, she presented herself as pro-business but also as a San Francisco native, having grown up in public housing. Justice reform, homelessness, and housing were at the top of her agenda. At the beginning of the "tech exodus," Breed's office was even (off record) enthusiastic about seeing techies moving out from the city, letting space for artists, teachers, and fire-fighters. But in 2023–24 her agenda was again mainly about revitalizing the San Francisco economy. Tech wasn't present as a political enemy in City Hall anymore. The new San Francisco mayor Daniel Lurie, philanthropist and heir to the Levi Strauss fortune, named right after his election in 2024 Sam Altman (OpenAI CEO) as cochair of the mayor-elect team, whereas Bilal Mahmood and Danny Sauter, two former software entrepreneurs, were elected to the city's Board of Supervisors. While at the same time Elon Musk was starting an unprecedented reform of the federal state, this growing presence of techies is not an exit from politics, as Peter Thiel aspired, but tech (and technosolutionism) entering and restructuring the political arena.[18]

Because San Francisco's politics extends beyond the mayor and the mayor's office. It includes the justice and transportation administration. The city's political and administrative organization is among the oldest and most complex in California. Power is exercised by a series of agencies and the Board of Supervisors (where careers are often launched). Founded in 1856, the board consists of eleven members elected for four-year terms on the basis of a citywide district system, which corresponds only in part to residential neighborhoods and zoning. Almost entirely dominated by the Democratic Party, there is a structural opposition between progressives and moderates, the latter being considered pro-business. Each member has a staff of three, with the eleven-member board having three partially independent agencies under their authority: the Environmental Appeal Board, the Youth Commission, and the Transportation Authority. Each agency runs several programs, along with other partly autonomous agencies. Other intermediary organizations influence certain measures, such as the Chamber of Commerce, the San Francisco Bay Area Planning and Urban Research Association (SPUR),[19] corporate unions (including the real estate developers' union), and sf.citi (the tech lobby established in 2012 and run in the 2010s by investor Ron Conway). Although the city is identified with new technologies, its services and infrastructures are often criticized for dysfunction and obsolescence. According to interviewees working in new technologies, the political organization is sometimes described as "unintelligible," "completely archaic," or "poorly run," far from the "smart city" label, positioning the tech sector as the solution.

Technological regions have been able to emerge globally thanks to national administrative coherence, like the Ile de France, Bavaria in Germany, or the Italian Lombardy region in Europe. Not so for Silicon Valley. It stretched over nine counties, encompassing more than seventy cities, mostly residential and relatively anonymous communities, although some (like San Francisco, Oakland, Palo Alto, or Berkeley) have international reputations. Some have historical rivalries, like Oakland and San Francisco. For instance, Oakland built its City Hall in 1914 as the first high-rise government building in the United States, geographically turning its back on San Francisco while ensuring the building would be higher than San Francisco's City Hall. All these cities compete to attract capital to their territory and benefit from the growth of the new technology industry, without coordinated policies. Municipalities, counties, the State of California, and the federal government all have cumulative powers. A stroll through the streets of Berkeley gives an idea of the complexity of the region's political organization, where one sign follows another in support of candidates, all different, for equally diverse elections. While transportation or energy are subject to partly common policies, collegiality remains the exception. Geographer Alex Schaffran refers to this as an "unrealized coalition."[20] For all these reasons some policy makers have seen tech industry as the way to salvation. And this is nothing new.

Economic Recovery through New Technologies

Ed Lee's first steps in the mayoral office in 2011 were marked by the desire to revive San Francisco's economy. A civil servant I interviewed explained Lee's policies as "jobs, jobs, jobs": "In 2010, there was 10 percent unemployment. Gavin Newson got elected in California. Ed Lee arrived at the head of the city to develop employment. *Jobs, jobs, jobs*, those were his three words. And everyone agreed on that, even the most leftist members of the Board of Supervisors."[21] The city administration focused on downtown revitalization, where many offices and warehouses were vacant, as well as the industrial and port areas undergoing reconversion. To boost activity, decision-makers sought to attract and retain new technology companies through a series of measures. The three main ones were the Twitter tax break in 2011, the business payroll tax reform, and a stock-option tax reform, adopted in 2013.

Each of these measures was slightly different but pursued the same goal. The first measure was to keep Twitter and other big and medium tech companies in the city. The second was to stimulate business creation and development. The third was to retain mature companies in the sector as they approach their IPO. The Twitter tax break, the most emblematic of these measures, is held to this day by antigentrification activists as the founding event in San Francisco's housing crisis. It involved local progressives such as Jane Kim and David Chiu. Kim, who had also served on the Board of Supervisors, finished third in the 2018 mayoral elections, and was Bernie Sanders's political director for California in the 2020 presidential elections. Chiu held several elective offices in the City of San Francisco and for the State of California (as mentioned) before becoming San Francisco city attorney in 2021. A civil servant recalled:

> It was 2010, Twitter was the biggest company in town. There was this fear with the tech industry: were they going to stay or not? Unlike banking or finance, which have been around for a long time, with tech, you don't know.... The question everyone was asking was, how do you keep Twitter in town? The building they were occupying had not been occupied for twenty years. For a company to turn it into modern offices, there's a cost. They were threatening to move [to southern Silicon Valley], saying it would save them $35 million, the equivalent of the taxes levied in San Francisco. We didn't want our taxes to look like they're driving away Big Tech companies. So we had to do something. And a tax break seemed like the least terrible solution. The idea was to use Twitter as a lure to attract other companies in the same area, like Uber, or Biotech companies... and to break the antibusiness image of San Francisco to get companies to stay and not leave for Silicon Valley (interview with a civil servant, San Francisco, October 11, 2016).

In the wake of Twitter, Uber, Zendesk, Airbnb, and Dropbox took up offices in this area. The central mid-market hub in the mid-2010s was home to nearly two thousand employees in new technologies.

At the same time, to stir up the development of companies, a second measure was adopted, a tax exemption on hiring:

> Payroll tax is 1 percent of what you pay, regardless of your business or how much business you do. There are ninety thousand businesses reported in San Francisco, but only ten thousand that pay the tax. That put a very heavy

burden on a limited number of businesses. So our goal was to equalize all that … to have more stability … because we were looking to create jobs at all costs. We wanted to encourage the creation of businesses, by adopting [the gross receipts model]. That is to say: *No problem if you want to hire; on the other hand, you will be taxed on your income* (with a differentiated level depending on the sector) (interview with a city's department director, October 5, 2016).

Revitalizing the downtown area was economically supported by the growth of new businesses. Nevertheless, dependence on tech would become a liability on the city council's balance sheet if startups that had become firms left the city with their employees. The ecosystem of Stanford University and Palo Alto's laboratories and partner companies could easily attract startups to the southern part of Silicon Valley, and proximity to the airport along with more spacious offices for hundreds of employees could have easily sealed the deal.

To secure the presence of technology companies, which city leaders considered a dynamic contribution to the city's economy, a third reform was instituted—a tax exemption on stock options. A city administrator described the stakes:

We were in the middle of negotiating payroll taxes at the California level in 2012. So we had another measure added: blowing up the compensation tax on stock options. A lot of startups were leaving the city before their IPO for this reason: they would start in San Francisco, then move to the Peninsula, to avoid the 1 percent tax on compensation. That's a lot of money for a company. We got the measure passed, which encouraged companies to stay (online interview with an administrative officer, San Francisco, November 12, 2020).

These measures reflect the belief in tech's ability to represent a key development axis for the city. This view has gained credibility within the municipality's management teams over the years.

Long a satellite city of Silicon Valley, San Francisco became its epicenter in the 2010s. In early 2020, five thousand out of a sample of twelve thousand tech companies were located in San Francisco County. Startup companies have led to a five-fold increase in the share of the city's workforce. Between 2010 and 2020 employees in the new technology sector rose from 22,000 to 115,000 employees.[22] A correlation thus looks as if it could be made between these three tax breaks and the growing presence of the new technology sector in San Francisco. However, the recovery phase in San Francisco actually began before the reforms were implemented. Skeptics thus question the impact of these policies:

I'm not sure if anyone knew what it was going to do at the beginning. . . . It even took the city by surprise, starting with the city planning development department. . . . Every year we do a report on the Twitter tax break, to evaluate its effects; and we still don't know if it's actually beneficial or not. Some people swear to me that it's the reason for the renaissance of San Francisco, others that it's the source of all these ills. . . . It only represented 5 percent of job creation until 2014. So . . . (interview with a director of a city agency, San Francisco, August 25, 2017).

Given the time lag between the implementation of these measures and San Francisco's economic growth, it is unclear how these measures have affected the sustainable establishment of companies in San Francisco.

Still, the tech sector was seen as a growing issue in town. Between 2018 and 2022 six tax increases directly targeted tech and downtown real estate: a gross receipts tax for homelessness (supported by Salesforce CEO Marc Benioff); a tax on commercial rents (passed on to tech companies); a tax on Uber and Lyft; a tax on the sale of commercial properties; and two gross receipts tax increases targeting tech companies and the compensation of the company's CEO. It didn't cause a tech exodus. Whether we look at municipal measures to attract or tax the tech sector, the impact seems minimal or nonexistent. Paradoxically this ineffectiveness can be explained by the growing weight of tech in urban areas as a global and partly uncontrol phenomenon.

THE TECH INDUSTRY AS AN URBAN ECONOMY

IT services are supposed to be free of space constraints. A new category of workers has even emerged—the digital nomads—who work from anywhere, looking, like surfers, for their next spot, which might be Costa Rica or maybe Bali. The development of outsourcing and crowdsourcing, plus the rise of the work-from-home paradigm, have likely accelerated this trend.[23] The COVID pandemic made it seem like the time of cities might be over. The office occupancy crisis in San Francisco seems to leave this question open. And yet, over the past few years, workers in the new technology industry have become increasingly concentrated in urban centers. When they leave Silicon Valley, it's for Seattle, Austin, Denver, or New York in the United States and London, Paris, Berlin, Lisbon, or Barcelona in Europe. In Africa tech is concentrated in Lagos, Nairobi, and Cairo. In Asia, China's tech workers gather in Shenzhen (Nanshan District) and Beijing (Zhongguancun), India's tech workers are in Hyderabad and Bangalore, and Japan's tech workers are in Tokyo and Fukuoka. There are a number of reasons for this trend toward modern urban *technopolises* marked by the preeminence of software and AI services. Corporate real estate strategies and a high-wage workforce are eager to take advantage of big city opportunities.

Technopolis

Like other tech cities, "Silicon San Francisco" is mainly based on software editing and AI services.[24] In 2023 investments in generative AI companies increased by 220 percent in the area.[25] By mid-2024, almost half of Silicon Valley companies specializing in new technologies produced software. A third specialized in AI solutions. Software and AI services have quicker development cycles than hardware, biotech, or infrastructure. They do not require large offices, access to laboratories, warehouses, or abundant raw materials, nor, consequently, the proximity of a population of technicians, lab assistants, or handlers. In the field of computer software and machine learning, a team equipped with terminals is enough, thanks to the decentralization of infrastructures, such as supercomputers, data centers, and cloud services. This reduces the historical dependence of new technology companies on industrial zones, university campuses, residential suburbs. But to be efficient, to have ideas, and to waste less time, managers prefer having their employees in the same workplace and time zone. Admittedly, remote work has increased since the pandemic. "Office vacancy rates across the region rose to nearly 19 percent by the end of 2023" and "the volume of commercial leases declined by 22 percent over the previous year, leaving thirty-one million square feet unoccupied" in Silicon Valley.[26] Yet a majority of tech companies still locate their offices in cities, even if workers don't come to work every day. Managers and executives believe that a greater range of restaurants, social activities, and entertainment make cities more appealing to tech workers, especially as workers from China, India, and Europe are also used to the urban environment.

Global migration scholar Saskia Sassen observed at the end of the 1980s that decision-makers were converging in large urban centers with an international dimension, which is why cities known both for their cultural life and technological activity have risen, such as Austin, Seattle, San Francisco, and others.[27] This was certainly the case during the internet boom of the 1990s, as new information and communication technologies changed the work landscape. A civil servant I interviewed explained: "In the mid-1990, I'd ask the tech workers I met: 'Why come to San Francisco and not go to the suburbs, to Silicon Valley?' They'd say to me: 'We do video games, software, graphics. . . . We need designers, developers and there are far fewer of them in Mountain View than in San Francisco.'"[28] And unlike their parents' generation, tech workers no longer see suburbia and the suburban lifestyle as a way to secure their jobs, access housing, and fulfill a promise of a better future for their children.[29] To them, the environmental crisis is a good reason to give up the car culture. The desirability of a carless lifestyle is reflected in the fact that Silicon Valley's asking office rents are 61 percent higher at locations near public transit. A union leader who grew up in the city puts that trend into perspective:

When I finished law school in the 1970s, everyone around me had a car. My son today, at the same age, lives in the center, in a shared house, with a bunch of friends. Only one or two have a car. Their lifestyle is no longer car-centered. In 1950, San Francisco had eight hundred thousand inhabitants. Then it dropped to six hundred thousand, then slowly rose again. Few cities in the country have more inhabitants than in 1950: only New York, Seattle, and San Francisco. San Francisco has become attractive because of an appreciation of the urban lifestyle (interview, San Francisco, August 1, 2016).

So companies implemented specific real estate strategies to secure access to tech workers as factor of production.

Big Tech as Urban Developers

Indeed, in a particularly tight job market where companies are struggling to recruit engineers, employers have touted the San Francisco scene—its architecture, murals, dive bars, restaurants, and skyline—as a comparative advantage. Big tech companies located in the southern part of the Valley also offer free shuttle services at regular intervals, following the routes of city buses, to transport their workers. This type of service has existed at Google since 2004, eBay since 2007, and Juniper Networks since 2008. Back in 2007, Google's security director considered that his service "runs the equivalent of a small municipal transportation agency."[30] According to a 2015 survey by the city, eighty-five hundred employees were using commuter shuttles from a dozen companies (Google, Facebook, Netflix, Apple, eBay, EA, Yahoo, and others). In 2020 fifty-two thousand tech workers used these services daily. This transportation system of more than a thousand buses works on a budget of $250 million.[31] Developments such as these have put upward pressure on real estate, both within the city and in the region. Between 2012 and 2022 the median price per square foot according to the region's leading real estate agency increased threefold in Oakland and twofold in San Francisco.[32] In 2023, despite tech companies shedding 7 percent of their workforce, the sector still constitutes 28 percent of total employment in Silicon Valley.[33]

This housing crisis has been exacerbated by Airbnbs.[34] Tech workers are often on the go, traveling to other company locations, to professional conferences, for holidays, and to visit their family in their home states or countries. To the pressure on buying property and renting, the impact of short-term rental stays is added. In 2019, Airbnb listed seventy-eight hundred such offers in San Francisco, with rentals representing nearly $20,000 in after-tax household income per year.[35] Some landlords took advantage of the situation to rent out their properties at a premium. Others removed their properties from the rental market and resold them, sometimes evicting families who had lived there for generations. This gentrification process pairs with another phenomenon. Over the past decade big tech companies have become major players in the real estate market. In 2018, Google purchased an office complex on nearly twenty acres for $1 billion—the largest land market deal in the nation. In 2021, in the midst of the COVID-19 crisis, the company acquired a building in New York City for $2.1 billion to expand its operations, despite the debate around remote work. The construction, modernization, and expansion of large corporate campuses have become a leading area of real estate in Silicon Valley, with several large-scale projects, such as Apple's campus, estimated to cost $5 billion, and the Salesforce Tower in downtown San Francisco, named after the CRM software company Salesforce. The Salesforce Tower cost more than $1 billion to build.

At Google the firm's physical capital represented 15 percent of its assets in 2021, compared with 4 percent when it went public in 2004. The launch in 2017 of the California Forever project to build a city of up to four hundred thousand people on farmland about sixty miles from San Francisco backed by a roster of tech billionaires confirmed the fact that the tech industry has also to be considered as a real estate player. Companies offering so-called dematerialized services feed an economy of physical capital through the acquisition of buildings for offices and headquarters and the development of data centers, to which can be added the private real estate operations of tech billionaires. Bill Gates, for example, was the largest landowner in the United States in 2021. Jeff Bezos ranked twenty-fifth. Mark Zuckerberg owns one house in the heart of San Francisco, another in Palo Alto, one on the shores of Lake Tahoe, and land on the island of Hawaii. Owning such prized property has become emblematic of the lifestyle of Silicon Valley billionaires.[36] This led to the "techie" becoming a "class enemy" for many San Franciscans in the 2010s.

The Private World of Techies

During this decade employees of tech companies have been portrayed many times in the media, on social networks, and in protests, murals, songs, and locally produced plays as the cause of deteriorating living conditions for residents, as well as the reason for profound cultural changes within San Francisco neighborhoods. The four axes that feed the dynamics of gentrification— consumption, education, income, and housing—are reflected in these local condemnations. Indeed, in San Francisco, developers, data analysts, designers, and sales managers enjoy average compensation levels that are double those of teachers, journalists, and civil servants. These employees of large companies bring in incomes of more than $100,000 per year, compared with $50,000 to $60,000 for a teacher. Since 2010, Silicon Valley's income divide has grown twice as quickly as that of the state and nation. Those professionals outside the tech industry have had to spend nearly 60 percent of their income on housing. The top 10 percent of households hold 70 percent of collective wealth, and the poverty rate for the 17 percent of Black residents is more than triple that of white residents. This inequality is not only economic but also temporal.

The region has fifty-two thousand "megacommuters" who travel more than three hours every day to and from work. Megacommuters are disproportionately Hispanic and African American.[37] Tech companies drew a line between the tech sector and the rest of San Francisco's inhabitants, offering their tech workers free shuttles, catering, and recreational activities. These perks aim to keep workers in their workspace for longer periods. An engineering team leader at Uber, who is paid nearly $200,000 a year, said in an interview that he goes to Uber on Sundays just to pick up the soda that is provided for free in the company's offices. An entrepreneur who sold his company to Big Tech then worked there said:

> In the big companies they know they're overpaid. They can see that they're much better paid than the guy doing the same job in another company, that they're paid more than the rest of the population in a completely unreasonable proportion. They're completely out of touch with reality, and what's more, they don't have a way out, because if they want to move, they're going to have to change radically, because they won't have free food, gym, massages,

perks, their bonuses, and six-figure salaries. . . . In short, they're going to have to come down from their Olympus, for working harder. And so, these guys are ready to be very aggressive in imposing their company and to protect their status (online interview, San Francisco, March 14, 2021).

New tech workers, who are frequently newcomers to the city, are seen as bad neighbors.[38] This might mean arrogant and entitled gentrifiers who are ignorant of the history of the city and its communities, indifferent to local politics, lacking empathy despite increasing homelessness and evictions, and oblivious to the growing inequalities. However, most of the time they actually value the diversity of their newfound homes in San Francisco as much as they do in New York or London.[39] Interviewees said they are deeply attached to San Francisco's richness and defend its countercultural heritage. Some companies, like Zendesk, ask their employees to volunteer locally. However, their wages and lifestyles make them appear as cultural consumers and urban passengers. According to the residents interviewed, the fact that techies seemed to live in their own world fuels ambient resentment. Observing the queues that form at the arrival of the free shuttles shows the gaps in sociability, as I recorded in my field notes:

> Employees line up scrupulously in order of arrival, at fixed hours, without greeting each other, in silence, headphones on, sunglasses on, eyes glued to their phone screen, before settling into their seats where they sleep, work on their computers, watch Netflix, without speaking to each other, even though they are part of the same company, live in the same neighborhood, and see each other almost every day (field notes, September 6, 2017).

This is a far cry from the "village" spirit and sense of community often highlighted by activists, residents, and artists in the city. For these reasons tech employees are described as outsiders, people who have little interest in the political life of the city, are not registered to vote, do not wish to vote, and do not read the local press. Instead, they read the national press, or news from their country, and prefer publications that focus on the world of technology. In this respect the techie stereotype is valid insofar as it accounts for variations in their identification with where they live.

San Francisco and its neighborhoods have their own almost autonomous identity, character, color, history, and will. City nicknames abound, such as SF, Frisco, San Fran, the City, the Tattooed City. This territorial identity is reproduced at the neighborhood level. The Marina, Chinatown, the Tenderloin, Union Square, the Castro, and the Mission, to name a few, all have distinct names and neighborhood characters. But these identities can change over time. For instance, San Francisco was once controlled by conservative white communities that wanted to turn it into a twin of Boston, dominated by the WASP establishment.[40] But successive economic and real estate crises led to the protests and liberation movements that are currently identified with San Francisco culture.

> The city lived for half a century under the influence of the Republicans, and remained under the control of the conservative party, the construction unions, shipbuilding, police … until the 1960s, when the Democrats took power, with the first elected Democratic mayor in 1966. The only stable component in the city since its founding is the Asian community, which represents a third of the population. At the beginning of the counterculture movement, the city was still 55 percent Irish. Twenty years later, the Irish moved to the suburbs, which is why progressives, students, artists, representatives of the gay, queer, and lesbian communities were able to make it their city (online interview with an administrative official, San Francisco, January 20, 2020).

Social movements were regularly met with official control and law enforcement actions. In the late 1960s arrests were common for hippie communities living off small-scale sales of cannabis and psychedelic drugs. In the 1970s raids on bars and lounges were common in the Tenderloin District, where crossdressers and trans people gathered. In the late 1980s police intervened to stop Burning Man and then banned the festival in San Francisco. In 1978 a former city supervisor, Dan White, murdered Mayor George Moscone alongside supervisor Harvey Milk, the first openly gay elected official in California.

These examples show how San Francisco does not always fit the narrative of tolerance that has been constructed to represent city culture today. There's no such thing as the essence of San Francisco: the city is the product of a series of political conflicts, negotiations, and investments, going from violence to symbolic challenges, all in a spirit of territoriality.[41] Similar ideas of territoriality have prompted politicians, journalists, artists, and activists to politicize the growing presence of techies in town.

POLITICIZING TECH

"Techies fuck off," "Queers hate techies," "Death to Techzilla," and so forth—these messages cover walls and have been relayed on social media. While San Francisco is considered a bastion of tolerance, many artists and activists forcefully confront the representatives of the tech industry they hold accountable for the city's transformations. During the 2010s a coalition of activists and artists attempted to politicize tech's economic, social, and demographic impact on the city. Their opposition to tech intrusion is delivered through visual tactics described by French cultural theorist Michel de Certeau as "a movement *within the enemy's field of vision* . . ., and in the space controlled by him."[42]

Making Gentrification Visible

Gentrification is a complex dynamic involving multiple stakeholders. Artists, activists, and politicians aim to make its consequences visible and sensitive, even if they have to simplify a complex dynamic. They did this in particular through the production of what they call *memorials*—that is, murals that recall the history of a group within the public space.[43] During the 2010s many representations show the impact of "the techies," an expression used as if they were a homogenous population. An artist and the author of some of the most imposing street murals in San Francisco declares:

> My murals make fun of tech. I do it for free, and I do it so that people don't forget, that it's set in stone, to remind people that even if you come here and have money, you have to respect the people who came before you, and the people who were here before, the people who live here; that even if you can afford to live here, and you have the right to live here, you have to respect what's going on around you, and realize that if you keep pushing like that, you risk eradicating the special culture that's here and the reasons why you wanted to live here in the first place. It's like Pac-Man, they're going to eat it all up and realize there's nothing around them anymore, and say, *What the hell did I come here for?!* (interview with a painter-muralist, San Francisco, October 26, 2016).

A San Francisco–born painter and muralist who grew up in the Mission neighborhood explains the meaning of one of her most famous murals dealing with gentrification:

> There have been groundbreaking paintings in this alley since the 1970s. . . . I've lived most of my life in the Mission. My father is Mexican, so I've seen a lot of changes in the neighborhood. I concluded that it was all related to gentrification. The mural is divided in two sections, on the left the Mission I know, and on the right what it has become. To represent inequality, there's the jungle versus Wall Street, the NYSE [New York Stock Exchange]. The

three monkeys are the politicians, playing, acting, and not caring about what's going on underneath, the influx of money, fueling the police, and the military. The woman on the left represents Latino culture, which protects itself from the money coming in. The large skeleton is a techie. He has a zipper for a mouth, because these people don't talk. It's just: go to work and work like a robot. On the right, people are being deported, and in the middle, there is a little girl, holding a sign that says: *We're not going anywhere.* The whole point of the painting is to say that gentrification is not something that makes the city better but instead pushes people out. Putting more money in makes things worse (interview with a painter-muralist, San Francisco, July 29, 2016).

Since the 2000s, activists have used quantifying as a tactic, which is partly inspired by the supposedly objective communication strategies typical of the tech industry—that is, using data to build up a problem then present a solution. An activist who worked in tech and has defended the right to housing for homosexuals with AIDS invokes this connection between evictions and the blinders of those in the tech industry:

The real people in the tech industry . . . aren't looking to do harm. In fact, they're out to do good, at least the way they see it, especially the old developers. But they're just a cog in a larger system. One of the best things about this industry is working with very smart people on projects that you're totally dedicated to. When you work like that, there's something that happens . . . that makes you forget everything else. It's like a war . . . it causes people to develop a psychology where they lose sight of what's around them. It could be wonderful. But if you become short-sighted, you can't see anything outside your field of vision because you're immersed in it. So they're not against housing rights. It's just that it's not part of their consciousness . . .

When we started this organization, I was fortunate enough to have experienced things that opened my eyes regarding the corrupting influence of money. So we don't do high-priced galas, I don't go to wealthy family foundations, corporations, or anything else to raise money. . . . And I ended up having a flash of inspiration when I started creating these signs. . . . Because I wanted to have some tools for decision-making, kind of like on a road. You drive down this lane and think carefully before you get out and go down another road. The idea was to inform . . . *I was the thirteenth gay man with AIDS to be kicked out of my neighborhood in two years.* I saw how they were mowing down the community, so I started mapping all the evictions in 2004, and I would color code when it was an elderly or disabled person being evicted, and I found out that 80 percent of Ellis Act[44] evictions were in buildings with people with disabilities, and by my estimate, 25 percent of them were in the Castro, and they still are.

So we can infer that the vast majority of them were gay men with AIDS who were being evicted from the Castro. . . . In the past I've been in the tech industry, I know how people in tech think. I have my own way of doing things. I don't lie. I don't cheat. I don't manipulate. . . . For them, it was disarming to put all my cards on the table and act like we were solving a problem. Like it was my problem, and I was telling them: *Here, now it's yours too, how can we solve it?* (interview with an activist, San Francisco, July 20, 2016).

The members of the Anti-Eviction Mapping Project (AEMP) used data collection, visualization, and design to extend this work during the 2010s to make people aware of the impact of gentrification. A dozen queer-identified members based in the San Francisco Bay Area who also have graduate degrees, mostly in geography, document "dispossession and resistance in gentrifying landscapes" via "digital maps, software and tools, narrative multimedia works, murals, reports, and community events."[45] AEMP has now expanded to Los Angeles and New York, among other places. The collective makes visible the evictions via an online site, a mural in San Francisco, interventions to the Board of Supervisors, and various other actions.

These memorials circulate in three dimensions of public space: physically in the streets, online, and in the political arena. This work of remembering is a process of building up public problems and collective emotions. On the AEMP website, evictions are graphically represented by black dots accumulating chronologically on a map of San Francisco. Each new eviction is depicted as a bomb hitting the ground from an aerial viewpoint, leaving a black hole circled in red that spreads to its surroundings. This stylized representation symbolizes the human consequences in the city through a battlefield aesthetic. One of the members, who is also a housing rights activist, expressed her commitment: "Being locally based in San Francisco, it allows us to maintain a memory, the memory of the people who lived here, to bring back their history . . . which is very important when there are so many newcomers, people who want to build housing, who are evicting inhabitants."[46]

An artist who has conducted several actions looks back on one of her performances in which she used bricks from a destroyed building in the Hispanic Mission District and sentences from the building's inhabitants, who were invited to express what this lost dwelling meant to them. She offered these bricks for sale at the main technological entrepreneurship conference organized in San Francisco, selling them according to a price indexed to participants' income:

In tech they are very good at appropriating things, ideas, data. . . . It's really a neoliberal mentality: they take what seems progressive and turn it into a commodity. I think they're capitalists who should be controlled, because their utopia is just . . . a supremacist dream. So we took bricks from a house that had been destroyed to build a shopping mall and asked the people who lived there to tell their story and say what they had lost. Then we took sentences from these stories and wrote them on the bricks. And we went and sold them at SF Disrupt. We used irony, playing on the term *disrupt*, which has become a buzzword, but here the idea was to show how they were disrupting people's lives in the city. It was about inequality, their access to wealth. . . . So we put the bricks up for sale, and when people wanted to buy one, we asked them: "How much do you earn?" And the price would go up with the amount. Because if you're Mark Zuckerberg, it's not the same impact as the entrepreneur who's starting out (interview with an artist, San Francisco, October 7, 2016).

These different actions create stylized objects that represent inequalities to raise awareness about the harmful consequences of the tech industry on the city. They make visible and concrete phenomena that are partly diffuse, abstract, or relational, such as the role of companies and their employees on gentrification, the loss of a neighborhood's memory, and the history of groups negatively affected by ongoing community mutations. Consequently the process of representation has a political dimension. It aims to document, evoke emotions, and increase awareness. This effort continues through the creation of tech emblems that are both morally and emotionally charged.

Making Tech Emblems

In the Middle Ages, flags, anthems, mottos, and monuments were used to symbolize a political idea.[47] During the 2010s activists and artists similarly worked to produce and circulate emblems of protest against the impact of the tech industry, using free shuttles, electric scooters, wireless headphones, cell phones, and driverless cars as representations of the tech industry. While San Francisco is considered a bastion of tolerance and diversity, many artists and activists have been alarmed by the arrival of a population identified with the "white, upper-middle class, male, heterosexual," constitutive of what the sociologist Erving Goffman called "sexual classes."[48] This figure has long been socially repulsive to a city that's been queer since the 1970s. Women, queer, and middle- and low-wage workers have described white male heteronormative programmers as the cause and the symbol of changes to the population of San Francisco. In 2015 a cabaret artist and housing rights activist close to this collective posted a song online that incorporated these tech emblems of protest called "This Is Not My City Anymore."

The song addresses various dimensions of income inequality, including differences in cultural habits, education levels, and access to housing. Consumption styles are represented by food chains specializing in organic products—and their high prices. Whole Foods, bought by Amazon for more than $13 billion in 2013, is thus an example of the "great divide." Housing ("rents are going up") represents the social relations of domination between the "top of the ladder" and service occupations, structured around those who work in IT and those who serve them—social relations that extend to men and women and heterosexuals and queer people. More specifically, objects crystallize these relationships: "jewelry," "loft," "$6 coffee," and so forth. A metaphor of rape and exploitation constitutes the song's common thread, opposing one symbolic pole (male newcomers driven by a logic of interest and possession) to another pole (the socially and economically dominated females working service jobs). A rhetorical question "Didn't all this happen before?" refers to the long tradition of white male newcomers: the US marines who seized Yerba Buena (San Francisco) in the nineteenth century; the Forty-niners of the Gold Rush era and the sailors who arrived when naval yards were established in 1870; the Dust Bowl refugees from the Midwest; the so-called squares in the 1940s, the WASPs in the 1950s, the hippies in the 1960s, the dominant males in the 1970s, the yuppies in the 1980s, the dot-comers in the 1990s, and the techies in the 2010s.

These emblems rely most of the time on an opposition, tech versus anti-tech. Socioeconomic inequality is protested with graffiti, expressions such as "class war 2.0," and direct insults of *tech exploitation* as backlash for the status imbalance between tech workers and nontech workers. This antagonism has been noted by the media and academic studies, even if some activists interviewed said they are trapped by a dichotomy that they are themselves working to construct: they know that the tech industry isn't a homogeneous sector, that political positions vary, and they recognize that they are using tech services all day long and have friends, family, and sometimes even a past or present professional experience in the sector. Still, they see "symbolic politics" as often the best way to defend their cause in the political arena.[49]

Indeed, the purpose of these actions is to mobilize political measures. As sociologist Harold Garfinkel pointed out, denunciation involves individuals presenting a group, in this case techies, as outsiders who are distinct from the rest of the inhabitants. Such acts of denunciation tend to create a bond of solidarity with the members who carry out the denunciation, uniting them in a common cause despite differences in status, history, and living conditions. The techie representations are used in what Garfinkel called *status degradation ceremonies*.[50] Techies, despite their disparities in background, wealth, activity, and values, are presented as a homogeneous category opposing the "real San Franciscans." The former are presented as "class enemies" opposed by "social figures with paradigmatic value."[51] In the hearings observed at San Francisco City Hall three "characters" regularly appear (none of them minorities): the white-collar pensioner, the journalist, and the teacher. These three figures share a belonging to the higher intellectual categories and possess the capacity to initiate institutional, activist, and media support. They are particularly powerful as symbols because they have been subjected to a deterioration in their living conditions, even though their social group historically enjoys a preferential position within the city.

According to the 2019 census of the city, the majority of residents were white (39.87 percent), ahead of Asians (34.33 percent), Hispanics (5.4 percent), and African Americans (5.14 percent). Native Americans, the area's historical population before the arrival of the first "mission," account for only 0.43 percent of the population. These same groups had significant income disparities: $104,364 per year for the white population, $72,000 for people of Asian descent, $67,000 for Latin Americans, and $29,000 for African Americans. The latter are almost absent from the rallies and speeches, their memory being evoked only through photos or oral references. The absence of minorities has a direct consequence in denunciation situations since those who are not present have fewer opportunities to be recognized as groups that need political defense. Indeed, physical presence during protests and City Hall hearings is a condition for successful status degradation ceremonies. The housing market combined with the COVID crisis have emptied the city of its young activists. Between 2022 and 2024 the number of San Francisco residents in their late twenties declined by about 20 percent.

Then the narrative changed again. In the early 2020s tech wasn't the issue anymore, but once again the solution. Mobilizations became rarer. Bringing financial and technical resources to the table, techies were no longer presented as an enemy but as the solution. As one of the regional economic policy maker observes:

> That happened in 2021, when it was also clear that the city's economy was badly damaged by COVID, and the political mood began to change a lot. The

tech industry became very engaged politically, established a rival newspaper (the SF *Standard*), and mobilized a lot of neighborhood groups around issues like crime, homelessness, and the policies of the progressive school board. That faction appears to have the upper hand politically at the moment in the city, and indeed [Mayor London] Breed's only serious competition for reelection comes from candidates to her right (online interview with a Californian policy maker, San Francisco, October 14, 2024).

But the same tactics of politicizing tech have been extended into other arenas over the past few years. From hearings in the US Senate to sanction procedures in Brussels, the tech industry has been described as endangering youth and society, whereas the premise of Big Tech is quite the opposite: to make the world a better place. Whether in San Francisco, the US Senate, or the European Commission, the tech industry has been described as a political player. Its growing influence, at every layer of society, from the city of San Francisco to the White House, led to questions about the political future of this industry.

Conclusion

TECH'S POLITICAL FUTURE

These DC and Brussels politicians, who want more regulation,
they are dead, and they don't even know it.

—Interview with an entrepreneur-investor-podcaster,
San Francisco, October 20, 2024

BEWILDERMENT. SUCH WAS THE PREVAILING mood in San Francisco
on the evening of Donald Trump's election on November 8, 2016. For months
the Republican candidate had drawn the mockery of Bay Area techies, who
are highly educated and attached to the scientific spirit, half of them born
outside the United States. However, they didn't usually vote and weren't
interested in local politics, which they see as complex, inefficient, or even
corrupt. In the months leading up to the election, entrepreneurs and investors would take breaks from tech news at lunchtime and late-night meetups
to wonder how such a figure could have been nominated. Small gatherings
were organized to mock him on the evenings of the presidential debates, the
way people used to watch their favorite reality TV shows. But, in 2024, iconic
tech billionaires stepped up their support for Donald Trump, a xenophobic,
misogynistic, climate-change skeptic convicted of sexual assault. Numerous
entrepreneurs and leaders known for their Democratic and progressive commitments throughout the past two decades were on the stage, close to Donald
Trump during the inauguration ceremony on January 20, 2025. At an event
after the ceremony Elon Musk performed what almost the entire community
of fascism historians agree was a Nazi salute. Silicon Valley, which was once
considered both progressive and deliberately distant from Washington, DC,
was showing itself in a new light.

At the same time, according to technologists Yann LeCun, Sam Altman, and Elon Musk, AI will "cause a new Renaissance," a "new Age of Enlightenment"[1] that will bring prosperity, "where no one of us will have a job."[2] These technologists are not far from describing a tech utopia, as Karl Marx imagined, without work and dedicated to self-realization. We are thus living in a perfectly schizophrenic period, where politically the tech industry seems to be taking the direction of reaction, while sometimes these same figures have announced that they are preparing for perfect utopia. Who should we believe? The political entrepreneurs ready to sacrifice truth, information, justice, and democracy for the sake of opportunism and supremacism, or the utopian entrepreneurs who continue to hope for a brave new world? We have to reconstruct the events of recent years to try and understand what political future Silicon Valley really promises us.

PATHS TO COUNTERREVOLUTION

As a matter of fact, Silicon Valley still sees itself as a resolutely progressive sector. Historians, journalists, and essayists have highlighted the hippies, academics, and hackers of the 1970s and 1980s in the Silicon Valley origin story. The internet boom of the 1990s, the 2.0 internet, was the perfect continuation of this narrative. The internet embodied and fulfilled the liberal promise of a world without war and economic crisis. Bureaucracies and regulations were set to lose ground to information and free enterprise. At that time, the philosopher Francis Fukuyama celebrated the "end of history" (meaning that the democratic model and market economy promoted by the United States had prevailed over its alternatives, particularly the communist one), and Al Gore called for information superhighways. Thanks to tech, the world was about to enter a period of peace and democracy marked by an unlimited increase in knowledge and wealth.

Since then, the software industry has actually had a historical affinity with the Democratic Party. The tech sector overwhelmingly supported candidates Bill Clinton in 1992 and 1996, Al Gore in 2000, John Kerry in 2004, Barack Obama in 2008 and 2012, Hillary Clinton in 2016, and Joe Biden in 2020. Donations from employees of major technology companies during the presidential campaigns illustrate this. In 2012, 91 percent of employee donations at Apple went to candidate Obama, 97 percent at Google, and 99 percent at Netflix.[3] In 2016, for every dollar that employees at the world's biggest technology companies donated to Donald Trump, sixty dollars went to Hillary Clinton.[4] Back then, thanks to a single dinner with twenty guests organized by Steve Jobs's widow, $20 million was raised for Clinton's campaign. At that time leaders from all over the world came to Silicon Valley to seek inspiration from its social model based on work and meritocracy, where young entrepreneurs developed solutions that were supposedly useful to everyone. Engineers who came from India and China saw it as the path to a better education, more freedom, and real democracy for their own country.

In 2024 nine of the twenty companies whose employees pledged the largest donations to Kamala Harris were tech firms (Google, Microsoft, Apple, Oracle, Netflix, etc.). Tech personalities such as Reid Hoffman (cofounder of LinkedIn) and Reed Hastings (cofounder of Netflix) have been active supporters of the Democrat candidate. For nearly a decade, Eric Schmidt, former CEO of Google, and Hoffman have worked with the Democratic Party to improve the electoral targeting and digital literacy of its candidates. During the campaign more tech billionaires supported Harris than Trump. Vinod Khosla, John Doerr, Sheryl Sandberg, Ron Conway, Bill Gates, Melinda Gates, Steve Wozniak, Mark Suster, Aileen Lee, Katie Stanton, Leslie Feinzaig, and Jesse Draper all took a clear stand for Harris in the tech sector. Meanwhile, far from Silicon Valley, in the Global South, where 90 percent of the world's young people live, the services of Silicon Valley continue to be enthusiastically perceived and seen as the means to a better life, freer and funnier.[5]

So how can we explain the alignment of part of Big Tech with Trump? It is important to keep in mind that the tech sector is not a political monolith. The semiconductor industry had a reputation for being more Republican than the software industry. Carly Fiorina, who was chief executive of Hewlett-Packard, ran for president in 2016 as a Republican candidate and got support from different investors and entrepreneurs including Peter Thiel. Thiel and David Sacks never made a secret of their anti-inclusion commitment. They are readers of Nick Land and Curtis Yarvin, outspoken opponents of democracy, who believe that it can only lead to the decline of the West. During the 1990s some observers warned against reactionary and supremacist trends in Silicon Valley, talking about "techno-fascism" and afraid of the growing influence of George Gilder, a public intellectual, futurist, and supremacist, who has been active since the 1980s.[6] Newt Gingrich, the architect of the so-called Republican Revolution, was introduced in a 1997 *Wired* magazine issue with this headline: "President Gingrich? Maybe."[7] The same year the venture capitalist James Dale Davidson and the journalist William Rees-Mogg published *The Sovereign Individual*, describing a hyper-mobile, highly intelligent global elite that was freeing itself from the constraints of the nation-state thanks to digital technology. As mentioned in chapter 4, there is a long tradition in Silicon Valley dating back to the founding of Stanford University that defends masculinist and eugenicist ideas. So the ideas promoted by Musk and Thiel in DC after Trump's 2024 election are not new. But they have never been so influential. In early 2025, fifteen former Peter Thiel employees were part of the administration.

To understand the apparent political shift in Silicon Valley, it is necessary to focus less on ideas and more on the system of interests, less on political disruption and more on history. From this latter point of view, history corresponds to three time frames: short, medium, and long term. In the very short term, the regulation on AI and venture capital put in place by the Biden administration convinced a number of tech decision-makers to support Trump. In the medium term, other factors have weighed in, such as changes in the economic fundamentals of the tech industry relating to the costs of AI, the environmental crisis, the return of inflation, the rise in interest rates, and industrial rivalry with China. In the longer term, this election can be seen as the continuation of an endeavor dating back to the aftermath of the Second World War aimed at freeing capital and technology from politics.

If we look at the short term, the current group of "tech bros" surrounding Donald Trump is also relatively diverse. The most visible, vocal, and active member of this group is certainly Elon Musk. This South African immigrant, former environmental cause defender, and seasoned scientific mind has taken positions against "illegal and uncontrolled immigration," the "woke virus," and "legacy media" (which he believes is guilty of skewing the news) and has praised Donald Trump as the only candidate "to preserve democracy in America" and "the future of civilization."[8] To the outside observer, it's hard to know whether this is the growing conservative family man, the sad-at-heart father full of resentment (he lost a child in 2002 to sudden infant death syndrome, and he doesn't speak with his daughter since her transition in 2022), the former bullied kid, the committed eugenicist, the long-term entrepreneur, or the opportunist trying to capitalize on politics by reversing the properties of the causes he claims to defend: freedom of expression for everyone by limiting freedom of expression for researchers and federal employees on his platform, the free market to take advantage of its dominant position, libertarianism to gain access to public markets, or nonelected antibureaucrats whereas he has acted as a nonelected bureaucrat.

Thiel and his close associates (David Sacks, Joe Lonsdale, Keith Rabois, and others) have viewed Donald Trump as an opportunity to set their political agenda, defending freedom over equality, capitalism over democracy, growth over solidarity, and so forth. With the return of war in the heart of Europe and in the Middle East, the tech industry has a martial tone, which fits perfectly to Thiel's orientation. In 2004 he cofounded Palantir, a company that publishes two software products dedicated to data matching and visualization: Palantir Gotham and Palantir Foundry. In 2015 the *TechCrunch* news site revealed that the firm's main clients were the CIA, the NSA, the Air Force, West Point, and the US Marines.[9]

Since 2022, the arenas of the military and cybersecurity have been growing investors when other institutional investors have backed off. The relationship between the military and new technologies is nothing new. Computing and artificial intelligence in the Boston and San Francisco areas benefited from World War II and Cold War military programs. Even the pacifist Norbert Wiener worked on automatic firing of antiaircraft during the Second World War. In the 1980s Silicon Valley was home to several defense satellite and weapon control centers. During the internet, social media, and app revolutions, this link to the military-industrial complex stayed under the media's radar. But it was still present. The five largest military contracts awarded to Amazon, Microsoft, and Alphabet between 2019 and 2022 totaled almost $53 billion.[10] Project Nimbus, jointly sponsored in 2021 by Google, Amazon, and Israel, foresaw strategic applications of cloud and AI services. The tensions between the United States and China surrounding Taiwan could also be described through the prism of the semiconductor war.[11] And the Pentagon has long been a major customer of Silicon Valley companies.

In Silicon Valley, for some technologists, starting with Marc Andreessen and Ben Horowitz, AI will rekindle the economic rivalry between the United States and China. In their view, preserving a laissez-faire attitude and limiting regulation are the path to American prevalence over the Chinese regime. In this respect, Donald Trump and JD Vance were a reasonable bet. Under the patronage of Vance, David Sachs (cofounder of PayPal), and Chamath Palihapitiya (whose fortune was made as one of Facebook's first employees), Trump was invited to Silicon Valley for a fundraising event in June 2024, ten years after his last visit. The organizers highlighted Trump's pro-business stance and his support for cryptocurrencies and tax cuts. A former PayPal associate and one of the leaders of the crypto community, the entrepreneur and investor Keith Rabois was happy to find allies against

Democrats at a time when crypto was under increased criticism and regulation by the Biden administration.

On top of that, since 2020, crises have followed one another in tech like falling dominoes. The pandemic crisis beginning in 2020 was followed by the Silicon Valley office real estate crisis. Then the war in Ukraine beginning in February 2022 kickstarted a global energy crisis. Meanwhile, the Federal Reserve increased interest rates eleven times between early 2022 and mid-2023. In March 2023 the Silicon Valley Bank collapsed. All during an urgent environmental crisis. Against this backdrop, investors' balance sheets have steadily grown heavier, with rising prices for the dollar, graphics processing units (GPUs), energy, and water. The AI revolution turns out to be costly, far more than the internet 2.0 and app revolutions. Processing large databases requires the high-speed calculations of GPUs, cloud services, and high-wage "brains" to support supervision and modeling. Large-scale models therefore need substantial investment. It cost OpenAI more than $79 million to train ChatGPT-4 in 2023, and over $191 million for Alphabet to develop its ChatGPT-4 competitor Gemini Ultra.[12] And this rising cost is compounded by inflation.

Finally, initiatives toward tighter regulation have contributed to the sector's political tensions. The increasing number of Senate hearings, the potential enforcement of the Sherman Anti-Trust Act, the warnings from the Securities and Exchange Commission, and the pressure from the Federal Trade Commission Office of Technology (created in 2023) are causing both irritation and concern within the industry. In Europe the regulatory landscape has led to significant financial penalties. Google faced a $500 million fine in 2021 for failing to pay news outlets for use of their content. This followed a $2.42 billion fine in 2017 for violating EU antitrust laws. Meta was fined €1.2 billion by the Irish Data Protection Commission in June 2023 for violating EU privacy laws by mishandling the transfer of personal data. Apple received a €1.8 billion fine in March 2024 for abusing its dominant position in the music streaming app market. Investigations are also under way against Apple, Alphabet, and Meta for noncompliance under the Digital Markets Act. Meanwhile, since 2022, the Biden administration advocated rules that made it easier for retirement plans to invest in socially responsible funds and companies. In addition, a budget proposal in 2024 included a 25 percent tax on unrealized capital gains owned by Americans whose wealth exceeds $100 million. Venture capitalists perceive these reforms as a threat to their model, which is why prominent figures in the tech industry have increasingly adopted more defensive, right-leaning positions.

So behind the rallying of Alphabet, Amazon, Meta, or Apple CEOs, there is a system of interests and circumstances that explain why part of the tech elite have supported Trump. However, this must not prevent a longer-term perspective on the historical trajectory of this sector and its concrete action.

THE FREEDOM OF HEGEMONY

As we have seen in this book, regardless of ideological leanings and electoral choices in the tech sector, in the long term successive generations have been trying to make smartness triumph over stupidity, the best over the mediocre, tech savviness over bureaucratic organization, venture capitalists over bank institutions, entrepreneur charisma against a disenchanted world. In this story two questions remain: Who created the entrepreneurs, and what kind of world do they produce? They often see themselves as the heroes of the story, even of humanity, because they see themselves as people who came from nowhere, made themselves, and reshaped the world based on their work, vision, and superior intelligence. But there is an institutional environment that keeps them alive as well as their beliefs. This environment has been put in place gradually, since World War II. The army, the venture capitalism, the shareholder revolution, the alt-finance, crypto, and NFTs have been the cumulating layers of an institutional financial environment that has become more and more individualized. It was designed against the state and the bureaucracy, and also against unions, small shareholders, judges, and journalists, with the aim of liberating energies, intelligence, and innovation.

But in doing so, this system has swept away the systems of solidarity, essentialized hierarchies, naturalized skills (as illustrated by the animal metaphors used by respondents), justified monopolies, and ignored any philosophy of knowledge other than objectivism. It has called into question long-term thinking and aims only for production at a forced pace. The losers of the system are all at once the products, the intermediate bodies, and those who do not work directly in the vicinity of capital. There is thus a link of solidarity between the antiunion struggles of the tech industry, the limitation of power to small shareholdings, the desire to automate without redistributing, and the rise of a capitalism made up of services programmed for obsolescence. Whatever the political leanings within the tech sector, its production system and financial institutions push in the same direction: an exit from politics and organization based on solidarity and redistribution.[13]

Considering this historical trend, should we consider that the tech industry will be faithful to its promise, by making the world a better place based on information, disintermediation, dematerialization, and increased wealth? In terms of services, Silicon Valley remains a guarantee of freedom and security. These services are used by Ukrainian developers as well as Russian, Chinese, and Turkish dissidents. In the Bay Area every new player in the tech industry has claimed to bring more freedom to the world through technology: Apple liberating computing from IBM, Google liberating operating systems with Android from Apple, Facebook with its "freedom servers" against the old "black boxes and "vanity servers," OpenAI committing to develop open-source solutions, and so forth.[14] But sooner or later, this promise turns into a closing effect and a logic of domination, as exemplified by the very same OpenAI, an originally nonprofit organization, which transitioned in ten years to a very capitalistic and private company.

Programmers from all around the world continue to view Silicon Valley as a guarantee of freedom because of the prevalence of open-source tools.[15] But in recent years open-source stalwarts such as GitHub and Red Hat have joined the core industry. GitHub has been in operation since 2008 as a software hosting and management service. It was acquired by Microsoft for $7.5 billion in 2018. Red Hat is the world's leading provider of open-source software, including the open-source platform Linux and the open-source browser Firefox. Founded in 1993, Red Hat was acquired by IBM in 2018 for $34 billion. Corporate employees have become the main contributors to open-source projects. Only 15 percent of Linux code is still produced by volunteers.[16] Microsoft, once hated by hackers for its closed solutions, has seen its ecosystem triumph through partnerships with LinkedIn, OpenAI, Blizzard, Mistral AI, and others. This reversal originated in the late 1990s, when the company founded by Bill Gates recognized that developing open-source software was the inevitable path to industrial domination in the IT sector.

This hegemonic strategy is now at the heart of service deployment by Meta, Apple, Amazon, and Alphabet. Access to the "premium APIs" that were central to web 2.0 is now restricted or steeply priced, from $1,500 to $5,000 a year. In addition, it costs cloud service developers between $20,000 and $50,000 to set up an internet application, undermining the web's promise of decompartmentalization. While the internet was supposed to triumph in disintermediation, it is now the capitalist corporate model that predominates. The AI boom reinforces the dominance of the Magnificent 7 (the nickname of the former GAFAMs—Google, Apple, Facebook, Amazon, and Microsoft—joined by

Tesla and Nvidia). In the meantime, AI is constrained by expensive access to resources. Tech's environmental costs are rising accordingly, even as the sector continues to cling to the promise of dematerialization. Amazon is aiming for carbon neutrality by 2040. Google declared it had achieved it in 2007. And Microsoft promises to capture more carbon than it emits.

These declarations are made possible only by the massive purchase of carbon credits and offsetting schemes provided by eco-labeled projects. In fact, between 2013 and 2020 the sector's energy consumption increased by 50 percent.[17] In its annual environmental report published in 2024, Google conceded that the company's greenhouse gas (GHG) emissions had increased by 50 percent over the past five years.[18] Sam Altman regularly warns about the urgent need to develop new energy sources to meet the exponential consumption demands of AI. Since 2021, the amount of water used by Big Tech has increased by 15 to 35 percent annually. Several voices have called for controlling this surge in natural resource consumption, notably through the Artificial Intelligence Environmental Impacts Act. But such initiatives toward tighter regulation contribute to the sector's political tension.

Simultaneously, there has been a shift in the status of information on which the tech economy is based. In the 1990s "information" meant "knowledge." Now, the ongoing AI revolution is leading to a decline in the quality of information. Misinformation occurs in various forms, including hallucinations, deepfakes, and errors. In 2025, according to a study from Columbia Journalism Review's Tow Center for Digital Journalism, of the queries tested, Perplexity provided incorrect information in 37 percent of them, ChatGPT Search 67 percent, Grok 3 94 percent. Wikipedia averages just 3.5 errors per page. With every new launch the error ratio is getting lower. Still, in 2023 a study by researchers at Google DeepMind concluded that false information is increasing on the internet, particularly due to the misuse of pictures of people and the falsification of evidence.[19] Notably, 80 percent of image-based misinformation on the internet is generated by AI, with most of these fakes aimed at influencing opinion, swindling individuals, and generating profits.

In this ecosystem the value of data is increasingly detached from its informational quality. Whether true or false, opinion or sourced information, authentic or doctored photos, each can contribute to the value chain. This dynamic sheds light on the shifting stance of tech companies toward journalism. In 2023, Meta began blocking Canadian media on Facebook and Instagram in response to Canada's Online News Act, which requires compensation for news that is made available through social media services. Since the purchase of Twitter, Elon Musk declared many times that every citizen should be able to make their own truth heard, without having to go through journalistic control. OpenAI has signed several agreements with major press groups, including the Associated Press, News Corp, the German Press Agency, the Axel Springer media company, and *Le Monde*, which assert the company will decide what information will be highlighted by its services.[20]

In journalism and other sectors tech companies have demonstrated a limited capacity to address social mobilizations that target them. The uprising of Uber drivers in California, internal opposition to the military contracts signed by Microsoft and Alphabet, regular unionization attempts in Tesla factories and Amazon warehouses, and the Google Walkouts in 2018—when nearly half the employees protested gender inequalities within the company—were all met with a similar response from management: dismissal of the organizers. This approach reflects a consistent historical pattern in addressing critiques of tech's social model.

THE SILICON VALLEY WAY

If we combine the tech sector, the cryptocurrency industry, and tech investors, we get not only the first industry, but also the first political donator and lobbyist. In 2016 the tech industry ousted the oil industry as the leading funder of presidential campaigns. The communications and electronics sector has grown its federal lobbying expenditures each year since 2017, spending $585.7 million in 2024. According to LobbyControl and Corporate Europe Observatory, tech spent €113 million in lobbying in 2023. And as lobbyists, tech's main demand is not better information but lower taxes on corporate wealth. Although big companies such as Alphabet, Meta, and Netflix hold a progressive line on more inclusive, ethical, and carbon-neutral technologies, the tech industry seems to be tilting toward conservatism.

By surpassing real estate, oil, electricity, agri-food, automobile, and insurance companies, the tech sector has redefined the way we live and represent ourselves as a society.[21] In the nineteenth century the energy and transportation revolution went hand in hand with insurance laws designed to cover risks and develop education in industrial countries. In the first half of the twentieth century, the rise of the automobile industry led to the establishment of Fordism, a social model based on the principle that hard-working factory workers would be paid enough to have access to the consumer goods they produced. With the rise of the tech industry the promise inherited from the 1990s was quite different. New players, such as Amazon, Napster, Google, Facebook, and others, promised to free information and give everyone the means to become an entrepreneur. However, this promise came with a price: the casualization of labor where full-time employment with benefits gave way to a gig economy of casual and contract labor. As the hyper-privileged status of Big Tech employees rises, that of precarious workers falls. And this is happening not only in wealthy countries but also in the Global South, where workers are hired under crowdsourcing and outsourcing contracts.[22]

Big Tech companies are concentrating wealth and focusing on lowering tax levels by constantly optimizing their operations for tax purposes. All this is done without proposing any system of redistribution beyond their offices, other than the concept of universal basic income. In Silicon Valley, figures like Mark Zuckerberg, Jack Dorsey, Sam Altman, Larry Page, Tim Cook, and Elon Musk endorsed the idea. Behind this consensus lies a vision of the state and social assistance with historical roots in the 1970s. During the Nixon years advocates of welfare reform saw tax credits as a means of modernization whereby redistribution of income would occur directly rather than through public services deemed bureaucratic, costly, and dysfunctional. This idea was revived in Silicon Valley in the 1990s, at the height of the internet boom, when tech visionaries prophesied the democratization of entrepreneurship.[23] This proposal is back in the spotlight with the rise of generative AI. It tends to validate, on the one hand, the idea that the state should focus on its role as investor (and not protector), and on the other, the principle that individuals should be their own entrepreneurs. Altman declared in May 2024 that "universal basic income" should give way to "universal basic compute"—a programming capacity that each individual could exploit or sell, with computation set to become the most sought-after value. However, the sector is not conducive to employment. It accounts for just 2 to 3 percent of the US workforce. Nevertheless, it is now setting a new standard.

Like Taylorism used to be the dominant paradigm during the twentieth century, the Silicon Valley way is a model that reaches work organizations far beyond the tech industry. Data centrism, performance measurement, algorithmic processing, and agile work organization have become the new professional standards for large public and private bureaucracies in industrialized countries. The digitization of state services in the 2010s was presented as simpler, more efficient, and faster. Digital tools are intended to streamline administrative procedures; however, obtaining appointments and finding the right information has actually become more difficult for many people: in 2020, 18 percent of the population were considered digitally "limited," 13 percent "illiterate."[24] Accessing information and many other services has become complex for geographically, economically, and socially marginalized individuals. The rise of populism and extremism is in a sense the dark side of a model that increases inequalities and benefits urban economies and tech workers above others.

Although cyberpunk author William Gibson declared that the future belonged to everyone, a Silicon Valley elite, divided but still homogeneous, is monopolizing decisions about it, and most of the world has for almost two decades applauded it. The hubris of Silicon Valley is based on a belief in individual genius, the capacity of companies to meet common needs, and the potential of technology to produce unlimited growth. It is therefore not surprising that Silicon Valley does not persevere in addressing the failures of meritocracy, the incompleteness of democracy, and its ecocidal tendencies. Nonetheless, for every promise of the internet revolution of the 1990s (information society, disintermediation, dematerialization, enrichment), there has been a reverse outcome (disinformation, Big Tech domination, environmental costs, growing inequalities). And this is likely to continue as long as this industry ignores its epistemological limitations, environment impact, and social implications.

MAKING TECH UTOPIAN AGAIN

Silicon Valley was born of the dream of making the world a better place thanks to information, intelligence, and working communities. In the minds of nineteenth-century scientists and engineers, better information would reduce the chaos created by geographical distance, poor transportation, economic crises, and wars; the power given to the intellectually gifted would solve the limitations of bureaucratic organizations. Once in charge, they could get the best of two antagonistic political economies inherited from the nineteenth century: capitalism and socialism. Silicon Valley made these dreams come true, beyond its pioneers' wildest hopes. And these Silicon Valley dreams aren't dead yet.

As Marc Andreessen stated with an unshakeable conviction in his "techno-optimist manifesto," accelerating the forward march of technology and devoting more resources to the development of information systems are the only paths to progress and solving the world's problems.[25] Andreessen's position reiterates Silicon Valley's original aspirations: more innovation to solve the world's chaos; more freedom for entrepreneurs against regulators; less taxation and union organization to optimize the social life and economic productivity in the companies; and the development of libertarian cities to tackle bureaucratized societies. The "best" entrepreneurs, the "best" organizations, and the "best" companies—meaning the strongest—will prevail. Although one of Silicon Valley's catchphrases is "Don't drink your own Kool-Aid," this kind of manifesto proves that Silicon Valley has come to fully believe its own mythology. DOGE is an extrapolation of that philosophy.

But this tech utopia has turned into mental stress, social frustrations, and a political nightmare for many people outside the industry. Many countries and social groups no longer see information systems, entrepreneurs, and tech companies as progress. To them, the tech industry means more and more misinformation, cyberattacks, complexity, wealth inequalities, dominant positions, cultural hegemony, unchecked power, threatening artificial intelligence, entrepreneurial hubris, and entitled privileged tech workers who are disconnected from the hard realities of the rest of the world. This is partly due to the simplistic Silicon Valley conception of what the world is. Beyond its impact, we have to admit that the technology industry's focus on information engineering and the needs of solvent urban populations and client industries has done little to solve the planet's problems. Indeed, there is little incentive for technological solutions to address reducing world poverty or limiting inequalities, even while one person in two lives on less than $7 a day and the richest 10 percent capture half of the world's income.[26]

There is also little incentive to contain pollution, combat species extinction, manage the water crisis,[27] or anticipate the energy crisis—even as global GHG emissions increased by 62 percent between 1990 and 2022,[28] 68 percent of vertebrates and 40 percent of insects disappeared between 1970 and 2016,[29] and roughly half of the world's population experienced severe water scarcity in 2022.[30] When faced with these issues, Big Tech spokespersons consider it more important to defend freedom of expression, tax cuts on profits, and limitation of regulations. And when philanthropic actions are carried out, they are characterized by a lack of transparency, a capitalism justification agenda, and a techno-solutionist orientation that is trapped by visions and representations inherited from northern countries, which often make them ineffective and even counterproductive.[31]

These initiatives go hand in hand with Silicon Valley's extractivism, outsourcing, crowdsourcing, and social Darwinism. Rather than considering the contradictions of their industry, tech workers prefer to celebrate the anarcho-capitalist narratives of space conquest, transhumanism, extropism, effective accelerationism, or a providential general artificial intelligence. From this point of view the tech industry sounds socially violent, historically naïve, and philosophically archaic. In fact, the information revolution of the telegraph and postal services of the nineteenth century occurred in a world of growing resources, where information was a scarce commodity, with slow and limited distribution. Today the problem is the exact opposite. Resources are becoming scarce, while information is abundant. The asymmetric diffusion of information intensifies inequality between technology's haves and have-nots. This is why the industry of innovation needs to reinvent itself, based on several principles:

- natural resources limitation;
- heterogeneity of information;
- reduction of low-quality information flows;
- the fact that information valuation depends on local production, distribution, and reception environments;
- limitation of information system ontologies (meaning the representation of categories and proprieties and their connections of a system);
- asymmetry of information systems coming from the technical world, the human world, the living world, and the physical world;
- growing technological negative externalities of these different worlds, such as the overconsumption of natural resources, pollution, and inequality.

The current economic structures of the tech industry make it impossible to take these principles into account. These structures lead players to constantly project themselves into the future. Like the (all-male) heroes of *Tron, Neuromancer,* and *The Matrix,* they seek to get the most out of their evolving and hyper-selective environment. This book puts forward several concepts to understand their mentality. The notions of players, three-dimensional space, financial gatekeepers, entrepreneurial virtues, energy capital, evolutionary companies, projections, metastasis, and tech emblems are likely to offer a conceptual underpinning for those who want to understand this industry and, perhaps, make it better. Because alternatives do exist.

What if financing were based on respect for corporate social responsibility (CSR) standards, such as human rights, labor practices, environmental protection, anticorruption, social impact, consumer protection, support for communities, and corporate governance? What if tech companies had to systematically compensate for the externalities they caused in the fields of the environment, copyright, and mental health? What if this money helped to finance a world technology organization, based on an international coordination along the lines developed by the OECD and UNESCO, for maintaining global commons for information technologies? What if instead of saying that technology should be brought into schools earlier and earlier, engineers received an education that would help them become fully aware of the social, political, and environmental implications of their projects and products? An increase in mixed training programs in universities, drawing on the sciences and technology studies developed since the 1970s, would make it possible to systematize such knowledge at the crossroads of environmental sciences, social sciences, and political sciences. What if we stop believing in the venture capital = innovation = progress formula? What if we collectively worked to institutionalize growth and development indicators that take into account the negative psychological, social, and environmental externalities of technology?

To implement these "what if" solutions we need to realize that the technologies that unite us are based on the financial institutions that divide us. These questions will undoubtedly not be well received in Silicon Valley, a land with a long-standing distrust of norms and discourses about the way technical, organizational, and financial systems create domination. Yet this is the price the new technology industry will have to pay if it really wants to make the world a better place.

NOTES

INTRODUCTION

1. Saxenian, *Regional Advantage*.

2. "The popular recipe for creating the next Silicon Valley looks like this: Build a big, beautiful, fully equipped technology park; *Mix R&D labs and academic centers; *Promote incentives to attract scientists, companies, and users; *Interconnect industry through consortia and specialized suppliers; *Protect intellectual property and technology transfer; and *Establish a supportive business environment and regulations" (Marc Andreessen, "What It Will Take to Create the Next Great Silicon Valleys," Blog Spot, June 20, 2014, https://a16z.com/2014/06/20/what-it-will-take-to-create-the-next-great-silicon-valleys-plural/).

3. Data from TeleGeography, www2.telegeography.com.

4. For Big Tech Silicon Valley criticism, see Morozov, *To Save Everything, Click Here*; Zuboff, *Age of Surveillance Capitalism*; Rushkoff, *Survival of the Richest*; Swisher, *Burn Book*; Lalka, *The Venture Alchemists*; and Golumbia, *The Right-Wing Politics of Digital Technology*. and Schaake, *The Tech Coup*.

5. Bruno Waterfield, "Big Tech Dominates Lobbying in Brussels," *The Times*, September 1, 2021; Cat Zakrzewski, "Tech Companies Spent Almost $70 Million Lobbying Washington in 2021 As Congress Sought To Rein in Their Power," *Washington Post*, January 21, 2022.

6. Chen, *Work, Pray, Code*.

7. Details per the San Francisco Film Commission.

8. According to the San Francisco Film Commission.

9. Malinowski, *Betaball*. See also the development of analytics tracking (known as "sabermetrics") in the early 2000s by the general manager of the Oakland Athletics baseball team described by Michael Lewis, *Moneyball*, which has also been adapted into a movie [Miller, US, 2011].

10. According to Chris Anderson ("The End of Theory: The Data Deluge Makes the Scientific Method Obsolete," *Wired*, June 23, 2008), massive amounts of data processing will change science, medicine, business and the world of technology,

leading to the end of theoretical models. On the implication for the social sciences, see Pentland, *Social Physics*.

11. Journalist Alexandra Wolfe (in *Valley of Gods*) followed the journey of one of Peter Thiel's twenty-something foundation grant recipients, developing a project to drill for rare minerals from asteroids.

12. Like the Google project aiming toward extending life, Project Calico launched in 2013, and Altos Lab was founded in 2021, working on cell rejuvenation, or tech entrepreneur Bryan Johnson's antiaging endeavor.

13. Castells, Rise of the Network Society; Kelly, *New Rules for the New Economy*; Shapiro and Varian, *Information Rules*; Benkler, *Wealth of Networks*; Jenkins, *Fans, Bloggers, and Gamers*; and Rheingold, *Net Smart*.

14. Michael Kanellos, "General Magic: The Most Important Dead Company in Silicon Valley?," *Forbes*, September 18, 2011.

15. *2023 Silicon Valley Index*, p. 6.

16. Silicon Valley represents the main "unicorns" stable in the world. In 2016 there were fifty-four unicorn companies ahead of Beijing (17), New York (7), Stockholm (5), Los Angeles and London (4). See Jean-Paul Simon, "How To Catch a Unicorn: An Exploration of the Universe of Tech Companies with High Market Capitalization," Joint Research Center, Technical Report, 2016. According to Arthur Mouratov, Silicon Valley was the home of 143 unicorns in 2024 (Arthur Mouratov, "Silicon Valley Unicorns: Key Market Trends And Performance In Q3 2024," *Forbes*, November 25, 2024).

17. "Tracking Large-Scale AI Models," Report, *Epoch AI*, April 5, 2024.

18. "2024 Tech Industry Statistics—Forces Advisor."

19. In April 14, 1984, the founders of the radical antiestablishment magazine *Processed World* "toured" Silicon Valley in a bus. Their interest: the Valley's relationship to military establishments, especially those supporting weapons and satellite control centers.

20. Roberto J. González, "How Big Tech and Silicon Valley Are Transforming the Military-Industrial Complex," San Jose State University, April 17, 2024.

21. See Gilson, "Legal Infrastructure of High Technology Industrial Districts." On institutional issues, see also Chong-Moon et al., *Silicon Valley Edge*, and O'Mara, *The Code*.

22. According to data from the US Bureau of Labor Statistics, 2023.

23. *Forbes*, August 15, 1976. The following year, a September 5, 1977, article in *Business Week* mentioned "an incubator of start-up companies, particularly in the high-growth field of high technology."

24. "A specifically citizen [bourgeois] economic ethic had grown up. With the consciousness of standing in the fullness of God's grace and being visibly blessed by Him, the citizen [bourgeois] business man, as long as he remained within the bounds of formal correctness, as long as his moral conduct was spotless and the use to which he put his wealth was not objectionable, could follow his pecuniary interests as he would and feel that he was fulfilling a duty in doing so. The power of religious asceticism provided him in addition with sober,

conscientious, and unusually industrious workmen, who clung to their work as to a life purpose willed by God. Finally, it gave him the comforting assurance that the unequal distribution of the goods of this world was a special dispensation of Divine Providence, which in these differences, as in particular grace, pursued secret ends unknown to men"(Weber, *Protestant Ethic and the Spirit of Capitalism*, chapter 5).

25. Saxenian, *New Argonauts*.

26. Kenney, *Understanding Silicon Valley*; and Turner, *From Counterculture to Cyberculture*.

27. Becker, *Art Worlds*, introduction.

28. Pierre Bourdieu, *The Logic of Practice* (1990, p. 41), quoted in Hendrik Vollmer, "Elaborating the Theory," chapter 6 in *The Sociology of Disruption, Disaster and Social Change, Punctuated Cooperation* (Cambridge, UK: Cambridge University Press, 2013).

29. Bourdieu, *Rules of Art*.

30. Di Maggio and Powell, "Iron Cage Revisited."

31. The reference to *gatekeepers* can be found in media sociology, the sociology of Pierre Bourdieu, as well as in the Digital Market Act, the European regulation of digital media approved by the European Union Council in 2022.

32. Fligstein, "Innovation and the Theory of Fields."

33. Levy, *Hackers*; Coleman, *Coding Freedom*; and O'Neil, Muselli, Raissi, and Zacchiroli, "Open Source Has Won and Lost the War."

34. Relating to the inability of large companies to stay on top when technologies or markets change. They invest in new technologies to avoid this decline. See Bower and Christensen, "Disruptive Technologies."

35. Expression used in 1981 by Bud Tribble, a member of Apple's Macintosh design team, to talk about Steve Jobs's effect on employees. According to Tribble, the term was borrowed from the *Star Trek* episode "The Menagerie" in which aliens create new worlds by mental force. See Raskin, "More Mac Reactions," 20.

36. Paul Ricoeur considers that phenomenological method leads to consider things, not existing things, but things aimed at. Ricoeur, *Memory, History, Forgetting*, chapter 1.

37. Fink, *Play as a Symbol of the World*, 18.

38. Fink, *Play as a Symbol of the World*. In a different perspective, the researcher Tongyi Wu highlights how gamification is a key part of the software development work in Silicon Valley. Engineers have been and are still video gameplayers. Related to that observation, she points out that the software development is organized as a "field of games" which drives productivity, creativity, and collaboration on the one hand and intensifies competition and blurs the boundaries between work and life on the other hand. See Wu, *Play to Submission*.

39. Fink puts it this way: "In the game man 'transcends' himself, he overcomes the determinations with which he has surrounded himself and in which he has 'realized' himself, he makes the irrevocable decisions of freedom revocable, so to speak, he jumps out of himself, he plunges into the vital depths of original possibilities,

leaving behind any fixed situation, he can always start again and throw off the burden of his history" (Fink, *Play as a Symbol of the World*, 228).

40. According to a rational or utilitarian conception of social action, the actor is guided by the rational search for his interests. For constructivists (like Latour), any entity that modifies a given situation participates in the course of the action and is considered an actor: humans and nonhumans, associated through networks. These entities are *actants*. For Bourdieu, the action of agents is determined by force fields operating within a social environment.

41. Data from US Census Bureau, American Community Survey.

42. The notion of "conceptual character" is used by Gilles Deleuze and Félix Guattari (*What Is Philosophy?*), to designate the fictional or semifictional characters created by a philosopher to develop his thought.

43. On the Silicon Valley frenetic pace, see García Martínez, *Chaos Monkeys*. The author has been criticized and accused of sexist and racist comments in his book. See Casey Newton, Zoe Schiffer, and Elizabeth Lopatto, "Apple Employees Circulate Petition Demanding Investigation into 'Mysogynistic' New Hire," *The Verge*, May 12, 2021, www.theverge.com/2021/5/12/22432909/apple-petition-hiring-antonio-garcia-martinez-chaos-monkeys-facebook.

44. Crunchbase is a platform that compiles data on companies in new technologies.

45. Rheingold, *Smart Mobs*.

46. This mobility is above the country's standards. According to a Gallup Institute survey conducted in 2013, only 24 percent of Americans had moved to a different city or geographic "zone" in the previous five years, with US residents being the second most mobile population in the world. According to the US Census Bureau, only 10.1 percent of Americans had moved in 2017–18.

CHAPTER 1

1. The concept of the "industrial district" was coined by the economist Alfred Marshall to analyze the concentration of resources in small territories, which he explained by the search for access and allocation optimization. Marshall's work stems from a long research tradition, with two main currents: the first focused on the static optimization of the allocation of scarce resources, the other focused on the creation of goods and innovation. See Marshall, *Principles of Economics*. For a study of Silicon Valley based on the notion of "district," see Scott, *Cultural Economy of Cities*; and Lécuyer, *Making Silicon Valley*. For a critique of how geography studies downplay growth dynamics, see Storper and Walker, *Capitalist Imperative*. For industrial geography studies that place growth dynamics of urban space at the heart of their analysis, see Pred, *Spatial Dynamics of Urban Growth*; Scott, *New Industrial Spaces*; Storper, *Regional World*; and Engel, *Global Clusters of Innovation*.

2. The article was based on a collaboration between MIT and Harvard researchers in the late 1970s. See Abernathy and Utterback, "Patterns of Industrial Innovation"; and Chesbrough, *Open Innovation*.

3. As Arthur Stinchcombe (*Information and Organizations*, 2) has pointed out: "What resolves the uncertainty of particular actors, then, is the earliest available information that shows in which direction the actor should go because of the way the future of the world looks. Structures that deviate from idealized markets [. . .] must then be explained functionally, by the growth of the organization towards the places where the information to resolve the uncertainty is primarily found. This information must then be processed quickly, both to adapt the previous tentative strategy and to develop the tentative strategy for the next period. The heart of the structure of organizations is thus information processing, and the basic information to be processed is the earliest information that indicates for what kind of world (i.e., the future) decisions are being made."

4. Fligstein, *Transformation of Corporate Control*.

5. Jackson, *PayPal Wars*.

6. George Gilder, "Metcalf's Law and Legacy," Discovery Institute, Technology, September 1, 1993, www.discovery.org/a/41/; George Gilder, "Telecom: Metcalfe's Law and Legacy," *Forbes ASAP*, 152 Supplement, September 13, 1993, pp. 158–66; and Anthony Wing Kosner, "Facebook Values Itself Based on Metcalfe's Law," *Forbes*, May 31, 2012, updated June 2012, www.forbes.com/sites/anthonykosner/2012/05/31/facebook-values-itself-based-on-metcalfes-law-but-the-market-is-using-zipfs/.

7. See Beausoleil, "Moore's Law and Social Theory"; and Lécuyer, "Driving Semiconductor Innovation."

8. In the late 1960s, Xerox dominated the copier market. Its executives wanted to prepare for the future by positioning themselves in the computer field. In 1970 they created the Xerox Palo Alto Research Center, with the ambition of "inventing the office of the future." Teams worked in the footsteps of Vannevar Bush (who designed the Memex, which prefigured the internet, as early as the 1940s) and Douglas Engelbart (who in 1968 publicly presented the mouse, the graphical interface, and e-mail in the "mother of all demos"). They made important breakthroughs in the field of personal computing (Alto computer, machines connected to the central network, file and print services, etc.).

9. Katz and Shapiro, "Network Externalities, Competition, and Compatibility"; Arthur, "Competing Technologies, Increasing Returns"; and Besen and Johnson, *Compatibility Standards, Competition, and Innovation*.

10. Jensen Huang, quoted in Shara Tibken, "CES 2019: Moore's Law Is Dead, Says Nvidia's CEO," CNET, January 9, 2019, www.cnet.com/tech/computing/moores-law-is-dead-nvidias-ceo-jensen-huang-says-at-ces-2019/.

11. See Tibken, "CES 2019: Moore's Law Is Dead, Says Nvidia's CEO"; Tongia and Wilson, "The Flip's Side of Metcalfe's Law"; Simeon Simeonov, "Metcalfe Law: More Misunderstood Than Wrong?," blog post, July 26, 2006, https://blog.simeonov.com/2006/07/26/metcalfes-law-more-misunderstood-than-wrong/; Bob Briscoe, Andrew Odlyzko, and Benjamin Tilly, "Metcalfe's Law Is Wrong," IEEE

Spectrum, 7, 2006, pp. 26–31; and Xingzhou Zhang, Jing-Jie Liu, and Zhi-Wei Xu, "Tencent and Facebook Data Validate Metcalfe's Law."

12. Cf. Danny Rimer, "What US Startups Can Learn from Europe," *Reuters*, September 6, 2013.

13. Pierre Bourdieu spoke of the "sense of positioning"; sociologists Franck Poupeau and geographer Jean-Christophe François (in *Le Sens du placement*) use this notion to designate the way in which parents seek to "position" their children in "good schools," a sense of positioning that is both social and geographical.

14. Saxenian, *Regional Advantage*, 2.

15. Scott, *Global City Regions*, 139.

16. Zhang, *High-Tech Start-Ups and Industry Dynamics*.

17. See "Tracking the San Francisco Tech Exodus," sf.citi.org, https://sfciti.org /wp-content/uploads/2021/01/SF-Tech-Exodus-Infographic-1.pdf; and Roland Li and Susie Neilson, "Richer People Left San Francisco in the Pandemic. And They Took Billions of Dollars with Them," *San Francisco Chronicle*, July 25, 2022.

18. Granovetter, "Strength of Weak Ties."

19. Entrepreneur, San Francisco, August 26, 2017.

20. Paul Graham, social media post on Twitter/X, July 24, 2022.

21. Star and Bowker, *Sorting Things Out*, 285. In the interactionist tradition the "label" or label is a social (self) representation, which serves as a support for interactions and can be the object of mirror effects or social sanctions. See Mead, "The Social Self"; and Becker, *Outsiders*.

22. Gilles, *History of Techniques*.

23. M. Andreessen, 2011, *op. cit.*

24. Jaton, *Constitution of Algorithms*.

25. On digital labor, see Casilli, *Waiting for the Robots*.

26. In computing, a "gateway" designates a device that connects two separate computer networks. Its implementation makes previously separate systems interoperable. The development of programs makes it possible to link machines, databases, or any preexisting computer systems. As Paul N. Edwards et al. have stated: "Because of the relative ease with which they can be built as software, gateways are among the most common mechanisms by which information infrastructures evolve, but even so, the apparent interoperability very often remains elusive." See Edwards et al., "Introduction. An Agenda for Infrastructure Studies." The "red pill" has been a central tenet of the Manosphere since the developer and neoreactionary thinker Curtis Yarvin mentioned it in a blog post in 2007. See Matteo Botto and Lucas Gottzén, "Swallowing and Spitting Out the Red Pill: Young Men, Vulnerability, and Radicalisation Pathways in the Manosphere," *Journal of Gender Studies* 33, no. 5: 596–608, www.tandfonline.com/doi/full/10.1080/09589236.2023.2260318#abstract.

27. Storper and Walker, *Capitalist Imperative*, 47–48.

28. Albert Einstein defined space as a relational structure with several dimensions (space and time) in which bodies linked by a permanent movement evolve. See Einstein, "Zur Elektrodynamik bewegter Körper,"

CHAPTER 2

1. Weber, *Protestant Ethic and the Spirit of Capitalism*, 7.
2. Weber, *Protestant Ethic and the Spirit of Capitalism*, 50.
3. "Remember that time is money . . . . that credit is money . . . [and that] money can beget money, and its offspring can beget more, and so on." Benjamin Franklin, quoted in Weber, *Protestant Ethic and the Spirit of Capitalism*, 48–50.
4. Carreyrou, *Bad Blood*.
5. Jemima McEvoy, "Where the Richest Live: The Cities with the Most Billionaires 2022," *Forbes*, April 5, 2022.
6. Schiller, *Digital Capitalism*; Srnicek, *Platform Capitalism*; Myers West, "Data Capitalism"; Zuboff, *Age of Surveillance Capitalism*; and Cohen, *Between Truth and Power*.
7. Brynjolfsson and MacAffe, *Second Machine Age*.
8. Corrie Driebusch, "Lyft To Price Shares above Targeted Range of $62 to $68 in IPO. Ride-hailing Service To Price Shares Thursday Ahead of Trading Debut Friday," *Wall Street Journal*, April 29, 2019.
9. Hwang, *Subprime Attention Crisis*.
10. According to data from the National Science Foundation.
11. According to the Silicon Valley Competitiveness and Innovation Project.
12. Friedman, *There's No Such Thing as a Free Lunch*.
13. Tim O'Reilly, "What Is Web 2.0," www.oreilly.com/pub/a/web2/archive /what-is-web-20.html, accessed March 25, 2022.
14. According to the Stanford AI Index Report 2024.
15. Eric Johnson, "Full Transcript: *Chaos Monkeys* Author Antonio Garcia-Martinez on Recode/Decode," *Vox*, August 9, 2016, www.vox.com/2016/8/9 /12415696/antonio-garcia-martinez-chaos-monkeys-recode-decode-podcast-transcript. See García Martínez, *Chaos Monkeys*.
16. Founded in 2009, WhatsApp reportedly earned an average of nearly $350 million for its fifty-five employees at the time of its acquisition by Facebook. Cf. Akshat Rathi, "WhatsApp Bought for 19 Billion, What Do Its Employees Get?," *The Conversation*, February 20, 2014.
17. The notion of "market-fit" is credited to Don Valentine, one of the region's first venture capitalists. Marc Andreessen helped popularize the term in the 2000s, through a June 25, 2007, post on his blog (no longer available but picked up here per Stanford University, https://web.stanford.edu/class/ee204/ProductMarketFit. html): "In a large market—a market with many real potential customers—the market drives the start-up's product. The market must be satisfied and the market will be satisfied by the first viable product that comes along. The product doesn't have to be great; it just has to work. And the market doesn't care how good the team is, as long as the team can produce that viable product."
18. Shestakofsky, *Behind the Startup*.
19. "Startup.com," blog post, 2014.

20. According to Ilya Strebulaev, Venture Capital Initiative, Stanford Graduate School of Business, January 2022.

21. Ndlr: "communist capitalism," see Stross, *E-boys*.

22. Social worlds defined as social groups that create meaning and engage in action. Anselm L. Strauss, "A Social *World* Perspective" in Denzin, *Studies in Symbolic Interaction*, 119–28.

23. According to a 2018 Bloomberg valuation, if Bezos's parents had not given up a portion of their shares in the company, they would represent 3.8 percent of the company, a return on investment of nearly 12,000,000 percent.

24. Kevin Farrell, "Venture Capital's Hot New Breed," *New York Times*, November 18, 1984.

25. Stross, *Launch Pad*, 1–2.

26. Sociologist Brian Uzzi has shown, based on a survey of musicians conducted in the early 2000s, how "small worlds" contribute to creativity, both in financial and content terms. See Uzzi and Spiro, "Collaboration and Creativity."

27. Kurt Lewin, an American behaviorist psychologist, first used the concept in the aftermath of World War II to refer to the role of women in the selection and consumption of food. This role is used as a model to analyze the section of information by the media, institutions, and moral authorities, before being applied to other sectors. For an application of this concept to venture capitalists, see Florida and Kenney, "Venture Capital-Financed Innovation and Technological Change."

28. An observation already made in the 1980s by Adler and Adler, *Social Dynamics of Financial Markets*.

29. Stross, *E-boys*, xvii.

30. According to Ilya Strebulaev, Venture Capital Initiative, Stanford Graduate School of Business, March 2022.

31. Granovetter and Ferrary, "Role of Venture Capital Firms."

32. Granovetter and Ferrary, "Role of Venture Capital Firms."

33. Florida and Kenney, "Venture Capital-Financed Innovation and Technological Change."

34. Cf. 2024 National Venture Capital Association (NCVA) Yearbook.

35. According to Crunchbase.

36. Thornton, "Sociology of Entrepreneurship."

37. Stross, *E-boys*, xvii.

38. According to Silicon Valley Indicators, "Venture Capital Investment," https://siliconvalleyindicators.org/data/economy/innovation-entrepreneurship /private-equity/venture-capital-investment/, accessed March 30, 2022.

39. Thornton, "Sociology of Entrepreneurship."

40. Brophy and Guthner, "Publicly Traded Venture Capital Funds."

41. Giraudeau, "The Predestination of Capital."

42. See Rifkin and Harrar, *Ultimate Entrepreneur*.

43. Hsu and Kenney, "Organizing Venture Capital."

44. Galbraith, *American Capitalism*, 80.

45. Florida and Kenney, "Venture Capital-Financed Innovation and Technological Change."

46. See *Spencer E. Ante, Creative Capital.*

47. "Sequoia and Kleiner Perkins Share Financial News 217.5m Profit from Google IPO," *Financial News*, October 24, 2003, www.fnlondon.com/articles /sequoia-and-kleiner-perkins-to-share-profit-from-google-ipo-20031024.

48. Stross, *E-boys.*

49. For an introduction to Hilferding's work and theory, see Bideleux and Jeffries, *History of Eastern Europe*, 351 and so on.

50. Interview with a former executive and entrepreneur, Palo Alto, January 18, 2016.

51. Interview with an investor, San Francisco, October 16, 2016.

52. Hirsh, "An Organization-Set Analysis of Cultural Industries Systems."

53. The notion is used by sociologists Wayne Baker and Robert Faulkner in their study of Hollywood to qualify the interweaving of different activities, that of production and creation. See Baker and Faulkner "Role as Resource in the Hollywood Film Industry."

CHAPTER 3

1. See MacKenzie, "Vectorialist Class"; Tarnoff and Weigel, *Voices from the Valley*; Burrell and Fourcade, "Society of Algorithms"; Crawford, *Atlas of AI*; and Brockmann, Drews, and Torpey, "Class for Itself?"

2. Dealing with inequalities in the tech industry, see Neely, Sheehan, and Williams, "Social Inequality in High Tech"; and Luhr, "Engineering Inequality."

3. Stinchcombe, "Social Structure and Organizations."

4. Penley and Ross, *Technoculture*, xii.

5. See Desrosières, *Politics of Large Numbers*; Rieder, *Engines of Order*; and Benbouzid, "Fairness in Machine Learning from the Perspective of Sociology of Statistics."

6. Mike H. M. Teodorescu and Christos Makridis, "Fairness in Machine Learning: Regulations or Standards," Brookings Institute, February 24, 2024, www.brookings .edu/articles/fairness-in-machine-learning-regulation-or-standards/.

7. Stross, *Practical Education.*

8. Nicholas Negroponte, author of the 1995 bestseller *Being Digital*, is the founder of Massachusetts Institute of Technology's Media Lab and the One Laptop per Child Association.

9. Chris Anderson is the head of the nonprofit TED organization that creates idea-based TedTalks.

10. A former hedge fund manager and derivatives trader, Nassim Nicholas Taleb's book *Black Swan* (2001) is credited with predicting the 2008 financial crisis.

11. Yuval Noah Harari's books include popular science bestsellers *Sapiens, Home Deus*, and *21 Lessons for the 21st Century*. Harari surveys human history from the

evolutionary emergence of Homo sapiens to twenty-first-century political and technological revolutions.

12. De Certeau, *Practice of Everyday Life*.

13. Knight, *Study of Technological Innovation*.

14. Lallement, *L'Âge du faire*.

15. Chen, *Enabling Creative Chaos*, 34.

16. Weber, *Protestant Ethic and the Spirit of Capitalism*.

17. See Bell, *Cultural Contradictions of Capitalism*.

18. See Chen, *Work Pray Code*.

19. Boltanski and Chiapello, *New Spirit of Capitalism*.

20. Ross, *No-collar*.

21. Gina Neff has shown in particular how the multiplication of networking sessions reflects industrial and work organization changes. See Neff, "Changing Place of Cultural Production."

22. Daub as quoted in Puttick, "Human Potential Movement."

23. Kripal, *Esalen*. See Daub, *What Tech Calls Thinking*.

24. "Welcome: Explore the Stanford d.school," d.school, dschool.stanford.edu/, accessed January 9, 2025.

25. See Miller, "Is Design Thinking the New Liberal Arts"; and the documentary dealing with the strategies and effects of social networks relating to user attention, *The Social Dilemma* (Jeff Orlowski, Netflix, 2020).

26. According to data from US Census Bureau, American Community Survey PUMS, Silicon Valley Institute for Regional Studies.

27. "Meetup San Francisco," www.meetup.com/find/us--ca--san-francisco/, accessed March 5, 2024.

28. The Libertarian Party counted 2,600 registered voters out of 468,000 in the city of San Francisco in the early 2010s, according to John Coté and Neil J. Riley, "SF Prop E Payroll Tax Lovefest," *SFGate*, September 20, 2012.

29. Analysis based on *Forbes* magazine's list of the one hundred richest people in the digital industry, in Brockmann, Drews, and Torpey, "Class for Itself?" On authoritarian finance, see Becquet, Bougeron, *Alt-finance*. On the conservative movements through Silicon Valley history, see Lewis, 2024.

30. Piscione, *Secrets of Silicon Valley*, 6.

31. Mayo, Nohria, and Singleton, *Paths to Power*.

32. See Ross, *Social Control*.

33. One of the leading historians of Silicon Valley, Leslie Berlin, has thus devoted a monograph to seven personalities who played a role in founding companies at the turn of the 1970s and 1980s that already featured this type of motivation. See Berlin, *Troublemakers*.

34. Turner, *From Counterculture to Cyberculture*.

35. Baltzell, *Protestant Establishment*.

36. "Religious Landscape Study: Adults in the San Francisco Metro Area," Pew Research Center, 2019, www.pewresearch.org/religious-landscape-study/database

/christians/christian/metro-area/san-francisco-metro-area/, accessed September 26, 2022.

37. For the case of Gulf countries, see Le Renard, *Society of Young Women.*

38. Carreyrou, *Bad Blood.*

39. Meehan and Turner, *Seeing Silicon Valley.*

40. Bilton, *Hatching Twitter.*

41. Wolfe, *Valley of Gods.*

42. High culture is acquired through family, friends, and private schools, then used to analyze pop culture objects both inside and outside the classroom, ranging from heroic fantasy to Hollywood exploitation films. See Khan, *Privilege.*

43. Marwick, *Status Update.*

44. This notion refers to a social organization that is hierarchical but without a system of caste or control by members of a class. In an article reviewing *The Protestant Establishment*, Baltzell wrote: "An *establishment* means that a society is run by a class of men who act according to an agreed code of manners. Certain things are not done; if they are, they are not discussed in public, even if violations of the convention lead to the ostracization of the class. By contrast, in the absence of convention and class ostracism, everything that happens becomes public property and media exposure is the only remedy. The most institutionalized *leaks* in Washington today are symbols of classless elitism." See Baltzell, "Protestant Establishment Revisited."

45. Broockman, Ferenstein, and Malhotra, "Wealthy Elites Policy Preferences and Economic Inequality."

46. Halpin and Nownes, *New Entrepreneurial Advocacy.*

47. Which differs in this respect from the ideals defended by the elites in France or Brazil. See Naudet, *Entrer dans l'élite*, especially "L'idéologie instituée: Un nouveau concept pour répondre aux défis de la comparaison internationale," 257–65.

48. Online interview with an entrepreneur and investor, lives in San Francisco, May 23, 2021.

49. K.J. Conron, W. Luhur, and S.K. Goldberg "LGBT Adult in Large US Metropolitan Areas," Williams Institute UCLA School of Law, 2021.

50. Lécuyer, *Making Silicon Valley*, chapter 5.

51. See Simmel, "Sociology of Secrecy and of Secret Societies."

52. Interview with the director of a coworking space, San Francisco, August 26, 2017.

53. Granovetter, "Strength of Weak Ties."

54. Jovanovic, "Job Matching and the Theory of Turnover."

55. The imprinting thesis was originally developed by Stinchcombe, "Social Structure and Organizations."

56. Stinchcombe, *When Formality Works*, emphasis in the original.

57. Becker, *Art Worlds*, 66.

58. Ferrary, "*Gift* Exchange in the Social Networks of Silicon Valley."

59. Williamson, *Markets and Hierarchies*, 255.

60. On the language or paradigm of variables, see Abbott, *Time Matters.*

CHAPTER 4

1. Sociologist Scott Shane points out that each year in the United States "more people start a business than get married or have children. And up to 40% of the American population will be self-employed for part of their working lives!" An entrepreneur in the United States is usually "a married white male in his 40s who attended but did not finish college. He lives in either Des Moines or Tampa, where he was born and has lived much of his life. His new business is a low-tech business, like a construction company or an auto repair shop." His business is "individually funded by $25,000 of his savings and perhaps a bank loan that he personally guarantees. The typical entrepreneur doesn't intend to employ many people or make a lot of money. They simply want to make a living and provide for their family." Shane, *Illusions of Entrepreneurship*, 3–4.

2. Some of the wealthiest tech people have signed the "Giving Pledge" promoted by Bill Gates and Warren Buffett, pledging to give at least half of their wealth. In 2017 the top fifty individual donors in the United States gave $15 billion. According to *Philanthropy Roundtable* and *Chronicle of Philanthropy* reports, 60 percent of these donations came from the new technology sector. However, while high net-worth individuals are funding philanthropic structures and activities, Silicon Valley as a whole does not demonstrate the same approach. In 2015 charitable contributions in the city of San Francisco accounted for 2.7 percent of local income, well below the level of Salt Lake City (5.5 percent) or Memphis (5.6 percent). IRS statistics compiled in the report "How America Gives" show that techies earning between $100,000 and $200,000 are still significantly less charitable than many others with equivalent incomes. See Karl Zinsmeister, Justin Torres, "The Calculating Philanthropy of Silicon Valley," *Philanthropy Roundtable*, Fall 2018, www.philanthropyroundtable.org/magazine/the-calculating-philanthropy-of-silicon-valley/; and Tyler Davis, Drew Lindsay, and Brian O'Leary, "How America Gives," *Chronicle of Philanthropy*, October 2, 2017, www.philanthropy.com/package/special-report-how-america-gives. Family dynasties are also much rarer in Silicon Valley than in the energy, legal, or banking sectors.

3. The word *entrepreneur* is borrowed from the world of Middle Ages French chivalry, when knights challenged monarchical authority, when after succeeded, ended up exercising it. See Vérin, *Entrepreneurs, entreprises*.

4. Beniger, *Control Revolution*.

5. Wiener, *Cybernetics*; and Turner, *From counterculture to Cyberculture*.

6. Baltzell, *Philadelphia Gentlemen*.

7. Baltzell, *Philadelphia Gentlemen*.

8. According to the data from the Kauffman Index of entrepreneurial activity, 2011.

9. Data according to Crunchbase.

10. Jessica Stillman, "You'll Never Guess the Average Age of Successful Silicon Valley Founders," *Inc.*, December 8, 2017, www.inc.com/jessica-stillman/youll-never-guess-average-age-of-successful-silicon-valley-founders.html. For a comparison with non-technological migration, from Maghreb to California, see Marie-

Pierre Ulloa, "From North Africa to California: Migrant Trajectories, Narratives of Integration," PhD dissertation, EHESS, 2016.

11. Data according to the trade magazine *The Next Web* using data from Compass listing the incomes of entrepreneurs at more than eleven thousand startups worldwide; see "Startup CEO Salary: How Much Do Founders Pay Themselves. Probably Not a Very High One," *The Next Web*, January 14, 2014.

12. In Walter Isaacson's best-selling book *The Innovators*, Steve Jobs and Bill Gates stand next to Alan Turing and Ada Lovelace.

13. The venture capitalist Ali Tamaseb speaks about "super founders"; see Tamaseb, *Super Founders*.

14. According to Ilya Strebulaev, Venture Capital Initiative, Stanford Graduate School of Business, March 2022.

15. Several well-known entrepreneurs have abandoned their studies, such as Steve Jobs (Apple), Michael Dell (Dell), Bill Gates (Microsoft), Mark Zuckerberg (Facebook), Sean Parker (Napster), Elon Musk (Tesla), Jack Dorsey (Twitter), or Matthew Mullenweg (WordPress). Their dropout occurred at very different levels of advancement (from a second year in college to the final stages of a doctorate), from renowned academic institutions. Entrepreneurs leading unicorns, new companies valued at more than $1 billion, are younger (thirty-four years old) and less experienced than the average Silicon Valley entrepreneur. Data according to Ilya Strebulaev, Venture Capital Initiative, Stanford Graduate School of Business, December 2021.

16. Chang, *Brotopia*; D'Ignazio and Klein, *Data Feminism*; Little and Winch, *New Patriarchs of Digital Capitalism*; Monea, *Digital Closet*; and Guyan, *Queer Data*.

17. Luhr, "We're Better Than Most."

18. Data according to Crunchbase.

19. On the first years of Stanford University and the eugenics influence, see Harris, *Palo Alto*.

20. Quoted in Sandmeyer, Anti-Chinese Movement in California, 43.

21. Quoted in Brian Eule, "Watch Your Words, Professor," *Stanford Magazine*, January–February 2015.

22. McNemar and Merrill, *Studies in Personality*, 11.

23. See Wecter, *Saga of American Society*, chapter 2; and Pierce, *Idiot America*.

24. Terman, "Genius and Stupidity."

25. Richard C. Atkinson, "Foreword to Fred Terman at Stanford," Speech, University of California San Diego.

26. Giraudeau, "Processing the Future"; and Zhikharevich, "Heuristics of Capital."

27. Some Nazi organizational theorists were not far from thinking the same thing. See Chapoutot, *Free to Obey*.

28. Thiel and Sachs, *Diversity Myth*. On Peter Thiel, see Chafkin, *The Contrarian*.

29. Elon Musk, quoted in Andrea Castillo, "Elon Musk, America's Richest Immigrant, Is Angry about Immigration. Can He Influence the Election?" *Los Angeles Times*, June 3, 2024, www.latimes.com/politics/story/2024-06-03/elon-musk-immigration.

30. See Reynolds, "New Firm Creation in the United States a PSED, Overview"; and Baron and Shane, "Entrepreneurship: A Process Perspective."

31. Callon, "Some Elements of a Sociology of Translation."

32. The notion of "front" is used by Bruno Latour in reference to Leo Tolstoy's novel *War and Peace*, which tells the story of two sides of Great Russia at the time of the Napoleonic campaigns, that of military life and that of Russian good society. Latour considers that Louis Pasteur and the Pasteurians carried out entrepreneurial work on two fronts in the 1870s—that of bacteriology and that of politics. See Latour, *Pasteurization of France*.

33. Jackson, *PayPal Wars*.

34. Vérin, *Entrepreneurs, entreprises*, chapter 2.

35. Luhmann, *Trust and Power*.

36. On the role of reputation as a means of orientation in artistic circles, see Becker, *Art Worlds*, chapter 11.

37. Online interview with an investor, San Francisco, March 14, 2019.

38. Storper, *Keys to the City*.

39. Quoted in Ferrary, "*Gift* exchange in the social networks of Silicon Valley."

40. Granovetter, "Strength of Weak Ties."

41. Cited in Kawasaki, *Rules for Revolutionaries*.

42. Michel Ferrary (in "*Gift* exchange in the social networks of Silicon Valley") speaks of "academic (Stanford, Harvard, MIT, UCLA . . .), entrepreneurial (former employees of large companies such as Intel, Sun, Fairchild . . .) and ethnic (25% of Californian residents are foreigners) networks."

43. Social link sharing site created on February 19, 2007, as part of Y Combinator, with the aim of creating a community similar to Reddit.

44. Latour, "Le dernier des capitalistes sauvages."

45. According to data analyses from sixty-eight countries, employed men are more likely to turn entrepreneurs than women and the unemployed; see Thornton and Klyver, "Who Is More Likely To Walk the Talk?"

46. Becker, "Theory of the Allocation of Time."

47. Dewey, *Experience and Thinking*, chapter 11.

48. Online interview with an entrepreneur, Mountain View, February 13, 2020.

49. See McClelland, *Power*; and Shaver and Scott, "Person, Process, Choice."

50. Jankélévitch, *Traité des vertus*.

51. Interview with Guy Kawasaki, Redwood, September 27, 2016.

52. Chandler, *Strategy and Structure*.

53. As told in Carreyrou, *Bad Blood*.

54. Ferrary, "*Gift* exchange in the Social Networks of Silicon Valley."

55. Julia Naftulin and Gabby Landsverk, "Seven Health Trends Silicon Valley Obsessed with, from Dopamine Fasting to the Keto Diet," *Insider*, October 29, 2019.

56. See Chen, *Work Pray Code*.

57. Collins, *Interaction Ritual Chains*, chapter 2.

CHAPTER 5

1. Anthony J. Parisi, "Technology—Elixir for U.S. Industry; 1. Apple Computer New Technology: An Elixir for America's Flagging Industry 2. Genentech 3. Solarex," *New York Times*, September 28, 1980.

2. The book is based on the analysis of a sample of sixty-two companies operating in different sectors within the country. See Peters and Waterman, *In Search of Excellence*, 13–16.

3. Ronald J. Coase, "The Nature of the Firm," *economica* 4, no. 16 (1937): 395, quoted in Thomas J. Sargent and John Stachurski, "Coase's Theory of the Firm," *QuantEcon*, https://python-advanced.quantecon.org/coase.html#:~:text = The%20 answer%20Coase%20came%20up).

4. Branson, *Nudist on the Late Shift*; Ross, *No-Collar*; and Indergaard, *Silicon Alley*.

5. Abernathy and Utterback, "Patterns of Industrial Innovation"; Nelson and Winter, *Evolutionary Theory of Economic Change*; and Dosi and Egidi, "Substantive and Procedural Uncertainty."

6. Takeuchi and Nonaka, "New Product Development Game" Ries, *Lean Startup*; and Martin Fowler and Jim Highsmith, "The Agile Manifesto," Agile Alliance.org.

7. Marx, *Capital*, 304.

8. See "The Ugly Truth about Employee Turnover in Silicon Valley," Menlo Partners Staffing, 2024; and Douglas Charles, "Here's the Average Length of Employment at the Biggest Silicon Valley Tech Companies and It Ain't Long," *Brobible*, October 1, 2018.

9. Stinchcombe (in "Social Structure and Organizations") argued that this difference is due to their lack of experience and lack of learning, since new organizations imply new roles that must be learned.

10. Abernathy and Utterback, "Patterns of Industrial Innovation."

11. According to economists Richard Nelson and Sydney Winter (in *Evolutionary Theory of Economic Change*), routines provide predictability in individual behavior, which is crucial for collective action. They also have a cohesive function and foster the development of problem-solving procedures in technical, productive, and strategic areas. The evolution scenarios take into account the company's assets (what it knows how to do) and the way in which these routines conflict.

12. In the United States, 48 percent of starting entrepreneurs work from their home, 40 percent rent an office, only 5 percent buy property. See Shane, *Illusions of Entrepreneurship*, 68.

13. Tilton, *International Diffusion of Technology*.

14. Stinchcombe, *Information and Organizations*, 16–17.

15. Saxenian, *Regional Advantage*.

16. Quoted in Chrysos, *The Developers*, 64.

17. Christophe Lécuyer used the reference in "Manager les employés dans la Silicon Valley" in Alexandre and Dagnaud, eds., *L'entrepreneuriat technologique, ambivalences d'un modèle*. See also Goffman, *Asylum*, 11.

18. Lécuyer, *Making Silicon Valley.*

19. See Ouchi, *Theory Z*; Peters and Waterman, *In Search of Excellence*; and Trice and Beyer, *Cultures of Work Organizations.*

20. Di Maggio and Powell, "Iron Cage Revisited"; and Hannan and Freeman, "Structural Inertia and Organizational Change."

21. White, *Identity and Control.*

22. Stinchcombe, "Social Structure and Organizations."

23. White, *Identity and Control.*

24. Roelof Botha, "Lessons in Leadership and Decisions Making for Engineers," Stanford University School of Engineering, 2018.

25. Frankl, *Man's Search for Meaning.*

26. Polletta, *Was Like a Fever.*

27. Kawasaki, *Art to Start*, 239–44.

28. Becker, *Propos sur l'art*, 25.

29. Goody, *Domestication of the Savage Mind*, 86.

30. Sims, "Green Magic."

31. Sims, "Green Magic."

32. On these different points, see Mujerki, "Space and Political Pedagogy at the Gardens of Versailles"; Le Roy Ladurie and Fitou, *Saint-Simon ou le système de la Cour*, 48–49; and Turner, *Democratic Surround.*

33. Turner, "Arts at Facebook."

34. See Becker and Faulkner, *Do You Know . . . ?*

35. Burt, Structural Holes.

36. Kawasaki, *Rules for Revolutionaries.*

37. Interview with a manager, Los Gatos, July 16, 2016.

38. Interview with an entrepreneur, Palo Alto, February 4, 2016.

CHAPTER 6

1. For example, 40 percent of Seattle's IT workers are foreign born, and over half of Seattle's software developers, according to Gene Balk/FYI Guy, "More Than Half of Seattle's Software Developers Were Born outside U.S.," *Seattle Times*, January 17, 2018, updated January 19, 2018, www.seattletimes.com/seattle-news/data/more-than-half-of-seattles-software-developers-were-born-outside-u-s.

2. See Levy, *Hackers*; and Coleman, *Coding Freedom.*

3. See Knight, *Risk, Uncertainty, and Profit.*

4. White, *Identity and Control*, 1.

5. Clarke, *Profiles of the Future.*

6. Marc Andreessen defended the idea that Big Tech is historically an economically and financially undervalued sector, or following one of his characteristic sentences: "Tech is undervalued"; see Marc Andreessen, "Software Is Eating the World," *Wall Street Journal*, 2011.

7. Following the expression of John von Neumann, see Jaton, *Constitution of Algorithms*, 91.

8. Stinchcombe, *Information and Organizations*.

9. Naur and Randell, "Software Engineering."

10. Haigh, Priestley, and Rope, *ENIAC in Action*.

11. Mahoney, "History of Computing in the History of Technology."

12. The history and the mentality of these computer enthusiasts are notably evoked in two books published in 1984 by the journalist Stephen Levy (*Hackers*) and the psychologist Shirley Turkle (*Second Self*). For a history of computing in the United States, see Mahoney, *Histories of Computing*.

13. Salaries according to Glassdoor.

14. In 2015, Facebook's US staff comprised 66 percent male and 55 percent white employees. Asian employees made up 36 percent, Hispanics 4 percent, and Black individuals 3 percent of the workforce, according to the "Driving Diversity at Facebook" report from June 25, 2015. By 2022, Meta's global workforce had evolved to 62 percent male, with 46.5 percent Asian, 37.6 percent white, 6.7 percent Hispanic, and 4.9 percent Black employees; see Meta, "US Corporate Demography by ethnicity (2014–2022)," Statista.

15. Like with French elite mathematicians, where one can observe "rivalry among comrades to train to conquer a skill graded by motivating learning." See Menger et al., "Formations et carrières mathématiques en France."

16. Alegria, "What Do We Mean by Broadening Participation?."

17. Joshua Bote, "Bay Area Tech Startup Sanas Wants People To Sound Whiter," *SFGate*, August 22, 2022; and Dominic-Madori Davis, Amanda Silberling, and Kyle Wiggers, "Meta's New AI Council Is Composed Entirely of White Men," *TechCrunch*, May 22, 2024.

18. Star, "Power, Technology and the Phenomenology of Conventions."

19. Charlie Warzel, "AI Has Become a Technology of Faith," *The Atlantic*, July 12, 2024.

20. Hughes, "Social Drama of Work."

21. Stinchcombe, *Information and Organizations*, 17.

22. Rieder, "Méchanologies et delegation," 243.

23. Button and Sharrock, "Mundane Work of Writing and Reading Computer Programs."

24. See Paris Chrysos and Olivier Alexandre, "L'empathie au service de l'innovation," chapter 5 in Alexandre and Dagnaud, *Numérique*, 127–46.

25. See the economist Giovanni Dosi's distinction between substantive and procedural uncertainty. The former is related to a lack of information about events in the environment, while the latter concerns the lack of competence in solving problems. Dosi and Egidi, "Substantive and Procedural Uncertainty."

26. García Martínez, *Chaos Monkeys*.

27. Lécuyer and Choi, "Silicon Valley Secrets."

28. Hughes, "Social Drama of Work."

29. Howard Becker (*Art Worlds*) defined support personnel as all the people involved in the production of the work and who bring direct or indirect help.

30. Ferrary, "*Gift* exchange in the social networks of Silicon Valley California."

31. Siles, "Inventing Twitter."

32. Boltanski and Chiapello, *New Spirit of Capitalism*.

33. Brooks, *Mythical Man-Month*. It should be noted that the project on which he was working nearly jeopardized IBM's commercial equilibrium. Brooks was awarded the Turing Award for his achievement.

34. Chandler, *Visible Hand*.

35. Florian Jaton has shown, in the context of the production of algorithms by a team of young researchers in a Swiss computer science laboratory, that the original objectives drift toward the achievement of other objectives during reference database constitution stage, as well as programming and mathematical formulation stages, despite control, evaluation, and scripting work. Jaton, *Constitution of Algorithm*, 169.

36. Which Mark Zuckerberg filled his workbooks with during the early years of Facebook; see Levy, *Facebook*.

37. Rieder, *Engines of Order*, 116–17.

38. Goody, *Domestication of the Savage Mind*.

39. Bourdieu and Passeron, *The Inheritors*.

40. Jacques Kerneis, "Nicolas Auray, *The Alert or the Investigation. A Pragmatic Sociology of Digital Technology*," *Questions de Communication, Open Edition Journal* 31 (2017), https://doi.org/10.4000/questionsdecommunication.11350.

41. See Sedgwick, *Between Men*.

42. To take the example of the Olympiads in mathematics: "The Olympiads are merely the culmination of an intensive and competitive investment by teenagers that involves multiple extracurricular forms of developing young mathematical talent, much like the associations, clubs, and competitions that punctuate early training in chess, the technically demanding arts (classical music and dance), and sports. This associative world of extracurricular mathematical practices is often made up of teachers and former teachers who make efforts comparable to those of amateur sports coaches. The resources it offers form, with those of families and the school system, the triangle of forces of educational production." See Menger et al., "Formations et carrières mathématiques en France."

43. Mickey, "When Gendered Logics Collide," and Mickey, "Organization of Networking and Gender Inequality in the New Economy."

44. Stinchcombe (in *Information and Organizations*) identified "skills" with learning.

45. In Elder, "Life Course as Developmental Theory."

46. Hughes, "Cycles, Turning Point and Career."

47. According to Andrew D. Abbott (in *Time Matters*), "a turning point, not a mere ripple, presupposes that a sufficiently long time has elapsed in the new direction that it has become clear that the direction has truly changed."

48. Abbott, *System of Professions*.

49. Comparable to mathematicians, animated, "according to Roger Caillois's categories of analysis, by the ludus, the pleasure experienced in solving difficulties by the satisfaction of succeeding in doing so," quoted in Menger et al., "Formations et carrières mathématiques en France."

50. Online interview with developer, San Francisco, September 16, 2019.

51. Brooks, *Mythical Man-Month*.

52. Interview with former tech executive, Palo Alto, March 4, 2016.

53. Harrison White in *Chains of Opportunity* speaks of "chains of opportunity" with the mass or limited retirement of certain cohorts determining the start of careers, just as waves of innovation open up new opportunities.

54. Rudolf Hilferding, *Finance Capital*.

CHAPTER 7

1. For this chapter I used archival material, data from the Black Rock City Census (years 2001–16), in-depth interviews with participants (16), and observations during Burning Man and related events (7).

2. Larry Harvey, quoted in Burning Man Project, https://burningman.org /timeline/1986/.

3. Turner, "Burning Man at Google."

4. In 2010, according to a study of several thousand festival-goers (Black Rock City Census, 2010), participants were 54 percent male, 40 percent female, 6 percent nonbinary; 67 percent were between 21 and 40 years old, with only 4 percent under 21, and 2 percent over 61; 69 percent had graduated from college; 16 percent had an income of less than $10,000 per year, 44 percent between $10,000 and $50,000 per year, 18 percent between $50,000 and $80,000, 10 percent between $80,000 and $100,000, 13 percent between $100,000 and $500,000, 2 percent over $500,000. Although the gathering brings together dozens of different nationalities, participants are overwhelmingly North American (over 80 percent, 10 percent European), 60 percent male to 40 percent female, mostly white (80 percent), high income ($60,000 average income per year), highly educated (70 percent have a college degree), nonbelievers (70 percent atheists), and politically active (over 60 percent vote regularly) in a country where these sociodemographic characteristics are in the minority. While families, grandparents, and young children also attend the festival, the majority of participants are between 25 and 40 years old with an average age of 33 to 34.

5. On the logics of commodification based on the case of Twitter employees, see Marwick, *Status Update*.

6. Tradition of boats carved and then burned and put into the sea at the end of the summer by a community of artists established in the region.

7. Kozinets, "Can Consumers Escape the Market?."

8. Chen, *Enabling Creative Chaos*.

9. Turner, "Burning Man at Google."

10. Marwick, *Status Update*.

11. Sarah Buhr, "Elon Musk Is Right, Burning Man Is Silicon Valley," *Tech-Crunch*, September 4, 2014.

12. According to Black Rock City (BRC) Census 2001, 60 percent answered yes to the question "Are you a changed person?"

13. In 1917, Max Weber spoke about the disenchantment of the world, due to rationalization. Scientific progress made the world predictable and intellectualized, without any magic thinking left. See Landy and Saler, Re-Enchantment of the World.

14. Strauss, *Mirrors and Masks*.

15. According to BRC Census 2014. In 2012 the organization's published statistics (2012 BRC Census) on attendees were: 35.8 percent first-time attendees; 20.9 percent attending for the second time; 12.2 percent for the third time; 11.1 percent for the fourth or fifth times; 10.7 percent for sixth, seventh, or eighth times; 4.7 percent for ninth, tenth, or eleventh times; and 4.6 percent for twelve times or more.

16. Wolfe, *Electric Kool-Aid Acid Test*.

17. At the same time, the iconic lifestyle in the neighborhood known as the Haight echoed more and more in the press (*Life, Time, Harper's*). It embraced DIY, Eastern spirituality, alternative medicine, hallucinogenic drugs, psychedelic music, and open classes, with the most renowned being Stephen Gaskin's Monday Night Class.

18. See Oakes, *Slanted and Enchanted*.

19. Turner, "Burning Man at Google."

20. Shel Kaplan knew Steward Brand in high school, working at the Whole Earth Truck Store in Menlo Park, a mobile lending and educational services library. He manned the cash register and packed books and catalogs to ship to customers. See Stone, *The Everything Store*, 27.

21. John Perry Barlow, "A Declaration of the Independence of Cyberspace," Davos, February 8, 1996, www.eff.org/cyberspace-independence

22. Stewart Brand, "Summer of Love: 40 Years Later," *SF Gate*, May 20, 2007.

23. Turner, "Burning Man at Google."

24. The notion of "trial" and "test" covers several meanings in sociology. Sanctioned testing linked to the practices of modern science, developed in the framework of pragmatic philosophy before finding applications in sociology. Challenge testing found its sources in the humanist tradition of spiritual exercise and classical stages of character formation, reformulated by existentialist philosophy. It is in relation to this second tradition that the term is used here.

25. Rheingold quoted in "*Whole Earth Catalog* symposium to trace cyberculture's roots, featuring Stewart Brand, Kevin Kelly, Howard Rheingold and Fred Turner," Stanford University Libraries, October 18, 2006, www.youtube.com /watch?v=B5kQYWLtW3Y.

26. Anselm Strauss (in *Mirrors and Masks*, 11) questioned the selves as objects (yesterday's, today's, tomorrow's, the daily self, the always self, new selves, etc.). These successive questionings presuppose a process of ratification and validation: any modification can be rejected or modified by others or by ourselves.

27. Interview with a developer, San Francisco, October 29, 2015.

28. We find this concept in Plato, where it refers to the movement of bodies, and in treatises on the movement of animals, as well as in rhetorical works to describe techniques aimed at transporting the audience. Quintilian specifically mentions this rhetorical technique of "transposition of times [*tralatio temporum*], whose technical name is μετάστασις [. . .] which was used by classical orators."

29. See Kelty, *Two Bits*; on rule bending, see Coleman, *Coding Freedom*.

30. Turner, "Burning Man at Google."

31. According to BRC Census data.

32. Shibutani, "Reference Groups as Perspectives."

CHAPTER 8

1. Ellul, *Technological Society*; Mumford, *Myth of the Machine*; Teilhard de Chardin, *Phenomenon of Man*; Postman, *Technopoly*; and Chen, *Work Pray Code*.

2. Noble, *Religion of Technology*, 11.

3. L. M. Sacasas, "Revisiting the Religion of Technology," April 28, 2012, https:// thefrailestthing.com/2012/04/28/revisiting-the-religion-of-technology.

4. Heylighen, "Contemporary Interpretation of Teilhard's Law of Complexity-Consciousness," 470.

5. See Krueger, "Gaia, God, and the Internet."

6. Chen, *Work, Pray, Code*.

7. Ross, *Social Control*.

8. Harold Kushner, "Bible Ranks 1 of Books That Changed Lives," *Los Angeles Times*, December 2, 1991, www.latimes.com/archives/la-xpm-1991-12-02-ca-746-story.html.

9. "Novels and Works of Ayn Rand," https://aynrand.org/novels/atlas-shrugged/, accessed December 8, 2022.

10. Davis, *TechGnosis*.

11. Mannheim, *Ideology and Utopia*.

12. Swedberg and Agevall, *Max Weber Dictionary*, 83–84.

13. "Spontaneous order," LIBERTARIANISM.org, www.libertarianism.org /topics/spontaneous-order, accessed December 8, 2022.

14. Turner, *From Counterculture to Cyberculture*.

15. Zwolinski and Tomasi, *The Individuals*.

16. Borsook, *Cyberselfish*. For a genealogy of libertarianism characterized by market mysticism, anti-statism, and opposition to equality, see Slobodian, *The Globalists*; Slobodian, *Crack-up Capitalism*; and Slobodian, *Hayek's Bastards*. For an analysis of cyberlibertarianism and its reactionary tradition, see Golumbia, *Cyberlibertarianism*.

17. "What Is Transhumanism?" http://whatistranshumanism.org/, accessed December 8, 2022.

18. Antonio Casilli, "Le débat sur le nouveau corps dans la cyberculture: Le cas des Extropiens," Olivier Sirost, Le Corps Extrême dans les Sociétés Occidentales (Paris: L'Harmattan, 2005), 297–329; Brunton, *Digital Cash*.

19. "Moral Enhancements Technologies, with James Hughes," *Futures* (podcast), Episode 63, https://futurespodcast.net/episodes/63-jameshughes.

20. Hal Finney, born in 1954, graduated from Caltech, worked on the Atari 2600, and was an early contributor to this privacy-enhancing project; he participated in *The Cypherpunks Mailing List* (with Julian Assange and Phil Zimmermann), with some of its members volunteering to help him create PGP. See https://mailing-list-archive.cryptoanarchy.wiki/. He participated in the development of the first anonymous remailer, a tool for sending emails while concealing the sender's identity, and Finney was the first Bitcoin network recipient in 2009. On the WELL group, see Julie Mommeja, "The WELL and Usenet Alternative Newsgroup," *New Horizons in English Studies*, 2021.

21. Hughes, "Politics of Transhumanism and the Techno-Millennial Imagination," 757–76.

22. Taillandier, "From Boundless Expansion to Existential Threat"; Taillandier, "*Staring into the Singularity* and Other Posthuman Tales"; Taillandier et al., "Effective Altruism, Technoscience and the Making of Philanthropic Value."

23. "What Is Singularity University?," Singularity University, https://help.su.org/what-is-singularity-university, accessed December 6, 2022.

24. Emile P. Torres, "Against Longtermism," *Aeon*, October 19, 2021, https://aeon.co/essays/why-longtermism-is-the-worlds-most-dangerous-secular-credo.

25. Singer, "Famine, Affluence, and Morality."

26. MacAskill, *Doing Good Better*.

27. Musk as quoted in Kelly Main, "Elon Musk Just Shared the Guiding Force behind His Pursuits," *Inc.*, August 9, 2022, www.inc.com/kelly-main/elon-musk-philosophy-optimism-longtermism.html.

28. MacAskill, *Doing Good Better*, and *What We Owe the Future*.

29. Nicholas Kulish, "How a Scottish Moral Philosopher Got Elon Musk's Number," *New York Times*, October 8, 2022.

30. Bostrom, *Superintelligence*.

31. See Gebru and Torres, "The TESCREAL Bundle."

32. See Greg Ferenstein following an investigation of Silicon Valley elites, see "The Age of Optimists: How Silicon Valley Will Transform Political Power," November 5, 2015, https://medium.com/the-ferenstein-wire/silicon-valley-s-political-endgame-summarized-1f395785f3c1#.f9vjvn12c.

33. See Winner, *The Whale and the Reactor*; Latour, *We Have Never Been Modern*; and Bijker, *Of Bicycles, Bakelites, and Bulbs*.

34. Weber, *Protestant Ethic and the Spirit of Capitalism*.

35. Turner and Larson, "Network Celebrity."

36. Latour, Pasteurization of France, 37.

37. Israel and Scoble, *Age of Context*, 19.

38. Thiel, *Zero to One*, 14.

39. Diamantis, *Abundance*.

40. Thiel, *Zero to One*, 10.

41. Rosa, *Social Acceleration*.

42. Kawasaki, *Rules for Revolutionaries*; Blank, *Four Steps to the Epiphany*; Ohanian, *Without Their Permission*; Schroeder, *Startup Rising*; Sutton, *Scaling Up Excellence*; O'Reilly, *WTF: What's the Future*; and Hoffman, *Blitzscaling*.

43. See Olsen, *History in the Plural*.

44. See Mary Beth Meehan and Fred Turner, *Faces of Silicon Valley*; Gray and Siddharth, "Humans Working behind the AI Curtain"; and Tarnoff and Weigel, *Voices from the Valley*.

45. See boyd, *It's Complicated*; boyd, Jenkins, and Ito, *Participatory Culture in a Networked Era*; Hargittai, *Handbook of Digital Inequality*; and Banaji and Bat, *Social Media and Hate*.

CHAPTER 9

1. See Storper, *Keys to the City*, especially chapter 3.

2. Data from Bay Area Council Economic Institute, www.bayareaeconomy.org/, accessed July 8, 2022.

3. See "How Has Income Inequality Changed in the Bay Area over the Last Decade?," Bay Area Council Economic Institute and Joint Venture Silicon Valley, 2022 Silicon Valley Index, 42 and 44.

4. The Mission District has been predominantly working class and Latin American since the 1970s, but following a scenario typical of large metropolises, deindustrialization led to a drop in housing costs, attracting a population of artists. This was followed by building renovation programs that generated an influx of middle-class workers with high salaries. A gentrification policy is defined as a set of public actions mobilized with a view to the appropriation (or reappropriation) of working-class neighborhoods by categories of nonresident inhabitants or users (shoppers, tourists, conventioneers, etc.). See Smith, "New Globalism, New Urbanism"; and Atkinson and Bridge, *Gentrification in a Global Context*.

5. See in particular McElroy, "Postsocialism and the Tech Boom 2.0"; McElroy, *Silicon Valley Imperialism*; and Florian Opillard, "Mobilizations against Gentrification in San Francisco (United States) and against Real Estate Predation in Valparaíso (Chile)," PhD thesis, EHESS, 2018.

6. Walker, *Pictures of a Gone City*. See also Schaffran, *Road to Resegregation*.

7. Walker, *Pictures of a Gone City*. See also Schaffran, *Road to Resegregation*.

8. An estimated population of 8,323 people in 2024. On the night of the 2024 Point-in-Time Count, 3,969 people were living in shelters (39 percent increase since 2019), according to the San Francisco Department of Homelessness and Supportive Housing.

9. McElroy, *Silicon Valley Imperialism*.

10. SF Grow is at https://growsf.org/.

11. The regulatory and institutional framework overlaps between the national level (the investor-state, via agencies and military funding), the regional level (the State of California, whose assembly is in Sacramento), the local level (through coun-

ties, including San Mateo, Santa Clara, and San Francisco), and the municipal level (with the City of San Francisco). For an analysis of the tech industry in New York City, see Zukin, *Innovation Complex*.

12. Richard Walker, "Boom and Bombshell: New Economy Bubble and the Bay Area," FoundSF, 2025, www.foundsf.org/index.php?title=Boom_and_Bombshell:_New_Economy_Bubble_and_the_Bay_Area.

13. Nellie Bowles, "They Can't Leave the Bay Area Fast Enough," *New York Times*, October 11, 2021.

14. Zukin, *Innovation Complex*.

15. Mark Twain, *Roughing It*, chapter 56, https://futureboy.us/twain/roughing/rough56.html.

16. "From 1981, when there were just 84 cases of AIDS diagnosed in the United States, the number has soared to 29,000, with nearly a quarter of them in California," see Brian Deer, "AIDS and HIV on Castro Street," *The Sunday Times*, January 11, 1987. See also Robert Lindsey, "Where Homosexuals Found a Haven, There's No Haven from AIDS," *New York Times*, July 15, 1987.

17. Interview with a civil servant, San Francisco, March 23, 2016.

18. Barton Gellman, "Peter Thiel is Taking A Break From Democracy," The Atlantic, November 9, 2023 https://www.theatlantic.com/politics/archive/2023/11/peter-thiel-2024-election-politics-investing-life-views/675946/

19. Active since 1910, SPUR is a nonprofit think tank focused on regional planning and public policy in the San Francisco Bay Area, with a budget of nearly $7 million in the late 2010s.

20. See Schaffran, *Road to Resegregation*, chapter 8.

21. Interview with a civil servant, San Francisco, November 12, 2016.

22. According to the Bureau of Labor Statistics, Quarterly Census of Employment and Wages.

23. Jose Maria Barrero, Nicholas Bloom, and Steven J. Davis, "Let me work from home, or I will find another job," World Economic Forum, July 18, 2021, https://wfhresearch.com/wp-content/uploads/2021/07/Let-me-work-from-home-19-July-2021.pdf.

24. Schaffran, *Road to Resegregation*.

25. "Record-high $14.3 Trillion Market Cap As Income Gaps, Layoffs, & Adjustments Signal Recalibration," 2024 Silicon Valley Index, Joint Venture Silicon Valley, February 28, 2024.

26. *Idem.*

27. Sassen, *Global City*. This phenomenon is similar to the broader observation made by Neil Smith in 1996, based on the case of New York, of a movement of middle-class reurbanization following the financial crisis of the late 1980s, the development of tourism and the service economies. See Smith, *New Urban Frontier*.

28. Interview with a civil servant, San Francisco, October 11, 2016.

29. On the suburban settlement strategies of World War II generations based on a survey of middle-class employees in suburban San Jose, see Berger, *Working-Class Suburb*.

30. *New York Times*, March 10, 2007.

31. According to San Francisco Bay Area Metropolitan Transportation Commission, accessed July 17, 2022.

32. According to the real-estate listing company Redfin.

33. According to Joint Venture Silicon Valley.

34. "Modern Workplaces: Inside Airbnb's San Francisco Headquarters," *San Francisco Business Times*, July 12, 2019.

35. "An Update about Our Community in San Francisco," Airbnb, February 24, 2019, https://news.airbnb.com/an-update-about-our-community-in-san-francisco/.

36. Sarah Paynter, "Inside Mark Zuckerberg's Houses, Sprawling $320M Real Estate Portfolio," *New York Post*, June 17, 2021.

37. "Record-high $14.3 Trillion Market Cap As Income Gaps, Layoffs, & Adjustments Signal Recalibration," 2024 Silicon Valley Index, Joint Venture Silicon Valley, February 28, 2024.

38. As opposed to the "good neighbors" of Boston's South End studied by Sylvie Tyssot (in *Good Neighbors*).

39. For the case of New York, see Zukin, *Loft Living*; for the case of Boston, see Tyssot, *Good Neighbors*; and for London, see Butler and Robson, *London Calling*.

40. Baltzell, *Protestant Establishment*.

41. For instance, as early as the 1960s, regulars of gay bars challenged heterosexual strangers, foreigners, and newcomers if they crossed the threshold into their neighborhoods. These provocations included questioning them in front of everyone, hugging them, claiming they had been there before, even acts of violence. See Sherri Cavan's ethnography of the city's gay bars, "Interaction in Home Territories."

42. De Certeau, *Practice of Everyday Life*, 50 and so on.

43. I am using here the terms used by the New History project led by Pierre Nora about "lieux de mémoire" through a series of French case studies (the Pantheon, the war memorials, the red white and blue flag, etc.), case studies that gave an account of the links between space and memory through objects and places. See Nora, *Realms of Memory*.

44. The Ellis Act is a 1985 California state law that allows landlords to evict residential tenants on the condition that they withdraw from the rental market. It has since been regularly used to justify evictions for speculative sale. There have been an estimated ten thousand such evictions in the City of San Francisco since its enactment.

45. AEMP web page, https://antievictionmap.com/, accessed September 19, 2022. The collective has grown, is less focused on San Francisco, and includes chapters in New York City and Los Angeles. See Erin McElroy, "Boycotting, Identifying, and Organizing Against Serial Evictors," *e-flux*, June 2024, www.e-flux.com/architecture/spatial-computing/602441/boycotting-identifying-and-organizing-against-serial-evictors/.

46. Interview with an activist, October 16, 2020.

47. Pastoureau, *Heraldry*.

48. Goffman, "Arrangement between the Sexes," 113.

49. Max Weber defines three types of instruments of power: the exercise of public power, rhetorical action, and symbolic policies.
50. Cf. Garfinkel, "Conditions of Successful Degradation Ceremonies."
51. Boltanski and Thévenot, "Comment s'orienter dans le monde social."

CONCLUSION

1. Yann LeCun, Twitter/X, April 1, 2023.
2. Samantha Murphy Kelly, "Elon Musk Says AI Will Take All Our Jobs," CNN, May 23, 2024.
3. Nate Silver, "In Silicon Valley, Technology Talent Gap Threatens G.O.P. Campaigns," *FiveThirtyEight*, November 28, 2012.
4. Ari Levy, "Silicon Valley Donated 60 Times More to Clinton Than to Trump," NBC, November 7, 2016.
5. Arora, *From Pessimism to Promise*.
6. Lewis, "Tech's Right Turn"; and Becca Lewis, "Headed for Technofascism: The Rightwing Roots of Silicon Valley," *The Guardian*, January 29, 2025, www.theguardian .com/technology/ng-interactive/2025/jan/29/silicon-valley-rightwing-technofascism.
7. Wired Staff, "President Gingrich? Maybe," *Wired*, December 19, 1997, www .wired.com/1997/12/president-gingrich-maybe/.
8. Meg Kinnard, "Elon Musk Makes His First Appearance at a Trump Rally and Casts the Election in Dire Terms," *Washington Post*, October 6, 2024.
9. Matt Burns, "Leaked Palantir Doc Reveals Uses, Specific Functions and Key Clients," *TechCrunch*, January 11, 2015.
10. Roberto J. Gonzalez, "How Big Tech and Silicon Valley Are Transforming the Military-Industrial Complex," Watson Institute, April 17, 2024.
11. Miller, *Chip War*.
12. According to Stanford AI Index, May 2024.
13. Historian Quinn Slobodian shows his readers the world dreamed up by neoliberal intellectuals and entrepreneurs, free from democracy and public power. This world is not embodied in a single place but in a multitude of microterritories linked to each other by the mobility of capital and elites, united by a common rejection of the state and democracy. He sheds the light on the alliance in the 1990s between intellectuals, policy makers, and technologists called the "new fusionism," defending libertarian policies through cognitive science, genetics, and biological anthropology. See Slobodian, *The Globalists* and *Crack-up Capitalism*. Marietje Schaake defends the idea that the very structure of Big Tech leads them to sacrifice the public interest. See Schaake, *The Tech Coup*.
14. In 2011, "Facebook began an internal project called 'Project Freedom' which focused on redesigning an efficient data center from the ground up" (Open Compute Project, Meta for Developers). On this topic, see Velkovska and Plantin, "Data Centers and the Infrastructural Temporalities of Digital Media."

15. Coleman, *Coding Freedom.*

16. O'Neil et al., "Subverting or Preserving the Institution."

17. Mélodie Pitre, "Cloud Carbon Footprint: Do Amazon, Microsoft and Google Have Their Head in the Clouds?," *Carbone* 4, November 2, 2022.

18. "Google Environmental Report," July 2024, www.gstatic.com/gumdrop /sustainability/google-2024-environmental-report.pdf.

19. Nahema Marshal et al., "Generative AI Misuse: A Taxonomy of Tactics and Insights from Real-World Data," Google DeepMind, July 6, 2024, https://arxiv.org /pdf/2406.13843?utm.

20. Nicolas Dufour et al., "AMMEBA: A Large-Scale Survey and Dataset of Media-Based Misinformation In-the-Wild," May 21, 2024.

21. Castel, *From Manual Workers to Wage Laborer.*

22. Roberts, *Behind the Screen*; Crawford, *Atlas of IA*; and Casilli, *Waiting for Robots.*

23. Cf. Jager and Zamora Vargas, *Welfare for Markets.*

24. According to the National Skills Coalition. In 2019, in France, 15 percent of people aged fifteen or over did not use the internet during the year; 15 percent and 38 percent of users lack at least basic digital skills. See Stéphane Legleye and Annaïck Rolland, "One in Six People Do Not Use the Internet, More Than One in Three Users Lack Basic Digital Skills," INSEE, October 10, 2019.

25. Marc Andreessen, "The Techno-Optimist Manifesto," October 16, 2023.

26. Half of humanity receives 8 percent of all income. According to data from the World Inequality Database for 2021.

27. According to the United Nations report "Water Crises Threaten World Peace," March 2024: in 2022 roughly half of the world's population experienced severe water scarcity, while one-quarter faced "extremely high" levels of water stress, using over 80 percent of their annual renewable freshwater supply; see www.unesco.org/en/articles/water-crises-threaten-world-peace-report.

28. According to the United Nations Environment Program.

29. According to data from WWF, Biological Conservation, IPBES.

30. United Nations, "Water Crises Threaten World Peace."

31. Al Dahdah, *Mobile (for) Development.*

BIBLIOGRAPHY

Abbate, Janet. *Recoding Gender: Women's Changing Participation in Computing.* Cambridge, MA: MIT Press, 2012.

Abbott, Andrew. *The System of Professions: An Essay on the Division of Expert Labor.* Chicago: Chicago University Press, 1988.

Abbott, Andrew D. *Time Matters: On Theory and Method.* Chicago: Chicago University Press, 2001.

Abernathy, William J., and James M. Utterback. "Patterns of Industrial Innovation," *Technology Review* (June–July 1978): 40–47.

Adler, Patricia A., and Peter Adler. *The Social Dynamics of Financial Markets.* Greenwich, CO: JAI Press Inc., 1984.

Alegria, Sharla N. "What Do We Mean by Broadening Participation? Race, Inequality, and Diversity in Tech Work," *Sociology Compass* 14, no. 6 (2020).

Alexandre, Olivier, and Monique Dagnaud, eds. *L'entrepreneuriat technologique, ambivalences d'un modèle.* Berne: Peter Lang, 2023.

Alexandre, Olivier, and Monique Dagnaud, dir. *Numérique: Le travail réinventé.* Bern: Peter Lang, 2023.

Arora, Payal. *From Pessimism to Promise. Lessons from the Global South on Designing Inclusive Tech.* Cambridge, MA: MIT Press, 2024.

Arthur, Brian W. "Competing Technologies, Increasing Returns, and Lock-In by Historical Events," *Economic Journal* 99, no. 394 (1989): 116–31.

Atkinson, Rowland, and Gary Bridge, eds. *Gentrification in a Global Context: The New Urban Colonialism.* London: Routledge, 2005.

Baker, Wayne E., and Robert R. Faulkner. "Role as Resource in the Hollywood Film Industry," *American Journal of Sociology* 97, no. 2 (1991): 279–309.

Baltzell, Digby E. *Philadelphia Gentlemen: The Making of a National Upper Class.* London: Routledge, 1958.

Baltzell, Digby E. *The Protestant Establishment. Aristocracy and Caste in America.* New York: Random House, 1964.

Baltzell, Digby E. "The Protestant Establishment Revisited," *American Scholar* 45, no. 4 (1976): 499–518.

Banaji, Shakuntala, and Ramnath Bat. *Social Media and Hate*. London: Routledge, 2022.

Baron, Robert A., and Scott Shane. "Entrepreneurship: A Process Perspective." In Robert J. Baum, Michael Frese, and Robert A. Baron, eds. *The Psychology of Entrepreneurship*, 19–39. Mahwah, NJ: Lawrence Erlbaum Associates Publishers, 2007.

Beausoleil, Angèle. "Moore's Law and Social Theory: Deconstructing and Redefining Technology Industry's Innovation Edict," *International Journal of Actor-Network Theory and Technological Innovation* 6, no. 4 (2014): 1–12.

Becker, Gary S., "A Theory of the Allocation of Time," *Economic Journal* 75, no. 299 (1965): 493–517.

Becker, Howard S. *Art Worlds*. Berkeley: University of California Press, 1982.

Becker, Howard S. *Outsiders. Studies in the Sociology of Deviance*. New York: Free Press of Glencoe, 1963.

Becker, Howard S. *Propos sur l'art*. Paris: L'Harmattan, 1999.

Becker, Howard S., and Robert Faulkner. *Do You Know . . . ? The Jazz Repertoire in Action*. Chicago: Chicago University Press, 2008.

Becquet, Bougeron, *Alt-finance*: *How the City of London Bought Democracy*. Las Vegas, NV: Pluto Press, 2022.

Bell, Daniel. *The Cultural Contradictions of Capitalism*. New York: Basic Books, 1976.

Benbouzid, Bilel. "Fairness in Machine Learning from the Perspective of Sociology of Statistics: How Machine Learning Is Becoming Scientific by Turning Its Back on Metrological Realism," *Proceedings of the 2023 ACM Conference on Fairness, Accountability, and Transparency* (FAccT '23) (2023): 35–43.

Beniger, James R. *The Control Revolution. Technological and Economic Origins of the Information Society*. Cambridge, MA: Harvard University Press, 1986.

Benkler, Yochai. *The Wealth of Networks: How Social Production Transforms Markets and Freedom*. New Haven, CT: Yale University Press, 2006.

Berger, Bennett. *Working-Class Suburb: A Study of Auto Workers in Suburbia*. Berkeley: University of California Press, 1960.

Berlin, Leslie. *Troublemakers: Silicon Valley's Coming of Age*. New York: Simon & Schuster Ltd, 2017.

Besen, Stanley M., and Leland Johnson. Compatibility Standards, Competition, and Innovation in the Broadcasting Industry. Santa Monica, CA: Rand Corporation, 1986.

Bideleux, Robert, and Ian Jeffries. *A History of Eastern Europe: Crisis and Change*. New York: Routledge, 1998.

Bijker, Wiebe E. *Of Bicycles, Bakelites, and Bulbs: Toward a Theory of Sociotechnical Change*. Cambridge, MA: MIT Press, 1995.

Bilton, Nick. *Hatching Twitter: A True Story of Money, Power, Friendship, and Betrayal*. New York: Penguin, 2013.

Blank, Steve. *The Four Steps to the Epiphany: Successful Strategies for Products That Win*. Hoboken, NJ: K & S Ranch, 2005.

Boltanski, Luc, and Eve Chiapello. *The New Spirit of Capitalism*. New York: Verso, 2005.

Boltanski, Luc, and Laurent Thévenot. "Comment s'orienter dans le monde social," *Sociologie* 6, no. 1 (1995): 5–30.

Borsook, Paulina. *Cyberselfish: A Critical Romp through the Terribly Libertarian Culture of High Tech.* New York: PublicAffairs, 2000.

Bostrom, Nick. *Superintelligence: Paths, Dangers, Strategies.* Oxford: Oxford University Press, 2014.

Bourdieu, Pierre. *Rules of Art: Genesis and Structure of the Literary Field.* Redwood City, CA: Stanford University Press, 1996.

Bourdieu, Pierre, and Jean-Claude Passeron. *The Inheritors: French Students and Their Relations to Culture.* Chicago: Chicago University Press, 1979.

Bower, Joseph L., and Clayton M. Christensen. "Disruptive Technologies: Catching the Wave," *Harvard Business Review* 73, no. 1 (January–February 1995): 43–53.

boyd, danah. *It's Complicated: The Social Lives of Networked Teens.* New Haven, CT: Yale University Press, 2014.

boyd, danah, Henry Jenkins, and Mimi Ito. *Participatory Culture in a Networked Era.* Hoboken, NJ: Polity Press, 2015.

Brand, Stewart. "Summer of Love: 40 Years Later." *SF Gate*, May 20, 2007.

Branson, Po. *The Nudist on the Late Shift: And Other True Tales of Silicon Valley.* New York: Random House, 1999.

Brockmann, Hilke, Wiebke Drews, and John Torpey. "A Class for Itself? On the Worldviews of the New Tech Elite," *PLoS ONE* 16, no. 1 (2021): e0244071.

Broockman, David E., Greg F. Ferenstein, and Neil A. Malhotra. "Wealthy Elites Policy Preferences and Economic Inequality: The Case of Technology Entrepreneurs," Stanford University Graduate School of Business Research Paper, no. 17-61, 2017.

Brooks, Frederick. *The Mythical Man-Month: Essays on Software Engineering.* 1972; reprint, Boston: Addison-Wesley, 1996.

Brophy, David J., and Mark W. Guthner. "Publicly Traded Venture Capital Funds: Implications for Institutional Fund of Funds Investors," *Journal of Business Venturing* 3, no. 3 (1988): 187–206.

Brunton, Finn. *Digital Cash: The Unknown History of the Anarchists, Utopians, and Technologists Who Created Cryptocurrency.* Princeton, NJ: Princeton University Press, 2019.

Brynjolfsson, Erik, and Andrew MacAffe. *The Second Machine Age, Work, Progress, and Prosperity in a Time of Brilliant Technologies.* New York: W. W. Norton & Company, 2015.

Burrell, Jenna, and Marion Fourcade. "The Society of Algorithms," *Annual Review of Sociology* 47 (2021): 213–37.

Burt, Ronald S. Structural Holes: The Social Structure of Competition. Cambridge, MA: Harvard University Press, 1995.

Butler, Tim, and Gary Robson. *London Calling: The Middle Classes and the Remaking of Inner London.* Oxford: Berg Publishers, 2003.

Button, Graham, and Wes W. Sharrock. "The Mundane Work of Writing and Reading Computer Programs." In Paul T. Have and George Pathas, eds., *Situated*

Order: Studies in the Social Organization of Talk and Embodied Activities, 231–58. Washington, DC: University Press of America, 1995.

Callon, Michel. "Some Elements of a Sociology of Translation: Domestication of the Scallops and the Fishermen of St. Brieuc Bay," *Sociological Review* 32 (1 suppl) (1984): 196–233.

Carreyrou, John. *Bad Blood, Secrets and Lies in Silicon Valley*. New York: Knopf, 2018.

Casilli, Antonio. *Waiting for the Robots: The Hired Hand of Automation*. Chicago: Chicago University Press, 2024.

Castel, Robert. *From Manual Workers to Wage Laborers: Transformation of the Social Question*. London: Transaction Publishers, 2002.

Castells, Manuel. The Rise of the Network Society, The Information Age: Economy, Society and Culture. Cambridge, MA: Blackwell, 1996.

Cavan, Sherri. "Interaction in Home Territories," *Berkeley Journal of Sociology*, no. 7 (1963): 17–32.

Chafkin, Max. *The Contrarian: Peter Thiel and Silicon Valley's Pursuit of Power*. London: Bloomsbury Publishing, 2021.

Chandler, Alfred. *Strategy and Structure: Chapters in the History of the American Industrial Enterprise*. Cambridge, MA: MIT Press, 1962.

Chandler, Alfred. *The Visible Hand. The Managerial Revolution in American Business*. Cambridge, MA: Belknap Press, 1977.

Chang, Emily. *Brotopia: Breaking Up the Boys' Club of Silicon Valley*. New York: Random House, 2018.

Chapoutot, Johann. *Free To Obey: How the Nazis Invented Modern Management*. New York: Europa Compass, 2023.

Chen, Carolyn. *Work, Pray, Code: When Work Becomes Religion in Silicon Valley*. Princeton, NJ: Princeton University Press, 2022.

Chen, Katherine. *Enabling Creative Chaos: The Organization behind the Burning Man Event*. Chicago: Chicago University Press, 2009.

Chesbrough, William. *Open Innovation: The New Imperative for Creating and Profiting from Technology*. Cambridge, MA: Harvard Business Review Press, 2003.

Chong-Moon, Lee, William F. Miller, Marguerite Gong Hancock, and Henry S. Rowen. *The Silicon Valley Edge: A Habitat for Innovation and Entrepreneurship*. Redwood City, CA: Stanford University Press, 2000.

Chrysos, Paris. *The Developers*, Limoges: FYP, 2015.

Clarke, Arthur C. *Profiles of the Future: An Inquiry into the Limits of the Possible*. New York: Harper & Row.

Cohen, Julie. *Between Truth and Power: The Legal Constructions of International Capitalism*. Oxford: Oxford University Press, 2019.

Coleman, Gabriella. *Coding Freedom: The Ethics and Aesthetics of Hacking*. Princeton, NJ: Princeton University Press, 2013.

Collet, Isabelle. *L'informatique a-t-elle un sexe? Hackers, mythes et réalités*. Paris: L'Harmattan, 2006.

Collins, Randall. *Interaction Ritual Chains*. Princeton, NJ: Princeton University Press, 2004, chap. 2.

Crawford, Kate. *The Atlas of AI: Power, Politics and the Planetary Costs of Artificial Intelligence*. New Haven, CT: Yale University Press, 2021.

Criado Perez, Caroline. *Invisible Women: Exposing Data Bias in a World Designed for Men*. New York: Vintage Books.

Daub, Adrian. *What Tech Calls Thinking*. New York: FSG Originals, 2020.

Davis, Erick. *TechGnosis. Myth, Magic and Mysticism in the Age of Information*. Berkeley, CA: North Atlantic Books, 2015.

De Certeau, Michel. *The Practice of Everyday Life*. Chicago: Chicago University Press, 1984.

Deleuze, Gilles, and Félix Guattari. *What Is Philosophy?*. New York: Columbia University Press, 1994.

Denzin, Norman. *Studies in Symbolic Interaction*. Greenwich, CT: JAI Press, 1978.

Desrosières, Alain. *The Politics of Large Numbers: A History of Statistical Reasoning*. Cambridge, MA: Harvard University Press, 1998.

Dewey, John. *Experience and Thinking*. Cambridge, UK: Cambridge University Press, 2017.

Diamantis, Kotler. *Abundance. The Future is Better Than You Think*. New York: Free Press, 2012.

D'Ignazio, Catherine, and Lauren Klein. *Data Feminism*. Cambridge, MA: MIT Press, 2020.

Di Maggio, Paul, and Walter W. Powell. "The Iron Cage Revisited. Institutional Isomorphism and Collective Rationality in Organizational Fields," *American Sociological Review* 48, no. 2 (1983): 147–60.

Dosi, Giovanni, and Massimo Egidi. "Substantive and Procedural Uncertainty: An Exploration of Economic Behavior in Changing Environments," *Journal of Evolutionary Economics* 1, no. 2 (1991): 145–68.

Edwards, Paul N., Geoffrey C. Bowker, Steven J. Jackson, and Robin Williams. "Introduction. An Agenda for Infrastructure Studies," *Journal of the Association for Information Systems* 10, no. 5 (2009).

Einstein, Albert. "Zur Elektrodynamik bewegter Körper," *Annalen der Physik* 322, no. 10 (1905): 891–921.

Elder, G. "The Life Course as Developmental Theory," 69, no. 1 (1998): 1–12.

Ellul, Jacques. *The Technological Society*. New York: Knopf, 1964.

Engel, Jerome S., ed. *Global Clusters of Innovation*. Cheltenham, England: Edward Elgar Publishing, 2014.

Ferrary, Michel. "The *Gift* Exchange in the Social Networks of Silicon Valley," *California Management Review* 45, no. 4 (2003): 120–38.

Fink, Eugen. *Play as Symbol of the World. And Other Writings*. Bloomington: Indiana University Press, 2016.

Fligstein, Neil. "Innovation and the Theory of Fields," *AMS Review* 11 (2021): 272–89.

Fligstein, Neil. *The Transformation of Corporate Control.* Cambridge, MA: Harvard University Press, 1990.

Florida, Richard L., and Martin Kenney. "Venture Capital-Financed Innovation and Technological Change in the USA," *Research Policy* 17, no. 3 (1988): 119–37.

Frankl, Viktor E. *Man's Search for Meaning.* New York: Beacon Press, 1959.

Friedman, Milton. *There's No Such Thing as a Free Lunch: Essays on Public Policy.* Open Court Publishing Company, 1975.

Galbraith, John K. *American Capitalism: The Concept of Counter Vailing Power.* Boston: Houghton Mifflin, 1952.

García Martínez, Antonio. *Chaos Monkeys: Obscene Fortune and Random Failure in Silicon Valley.* New York: Harper, 2016.

Garfinkel, Harold. "Conditions of Successful Degradation Ceremonies," *American Journal of Sociology* 61, no. 5 (1956): 420–24.

Gebru, Timnit, and Emile P. Torres. "The TESCREAL Bundle: Eugenics and the Promise of Utopia through Artificial General Intelligence," *First Monday* 29, no. 4 (2024).

Gillepsie, Tarleton. "The Politics of Platforms," *New Media and Society* 12, no. 3 (2010): 347–64.

Gilles, Bertrand, ed. *The History of Techniques.* New York: Gordon and Breach Science Publishers, 1986.

Gilson, Ronald J. "The Legal Infrastructure of High Technology Industrial Districts: Silicon Valley, Route 128, and Covenants Not To Compete," *New York University Law Review* 74 (1999): 575–629.

Giraudeau, Martin. "The Predestination of Capital: Projecting E. I. Du Pont de Nemours and Company into the New World," *Critical Historical Studies* 6, no. 1 (2019): 33–62.

Giraudeau, Martin. "Processing the Future: Venture Evaluation at American Research and Development Corporation (1946–1973)." In Jens Beckert and Richard Bronk, eds., *Uncertain Futures: Imaginaries, Narratives and Calculation in the Economy,* 259–77. Oxford: Oxford University Press, 2018.

Goffman, Erving. "The Arrangement between the Sexes," *Theory and Society* 5, no. 1 (1978): 113.

Goffman, Erving. *Asylum: Essays on the Situation of Mental Patients.* New York: Anchor Books, 1968.

Golumbia, David. *Cyberlibertarianism: The Right-Wing Politics of Digital Technology.* Minneapolis, MN: University of Minnesota Press, 2024.

Goody, Jack. *The Domestication of the Savage Mind.* Cambridge: Cambridge University Press, 1977.

Granovetter, Mark. "The Strength of Weak Ties," *American Journal of Sociology* 78, no. 6 (1973): 1360–80.

Granovetter, Mark, and Michel Ferrary, "The Role of Venture Capital Firms in Silicon Valley's Complex Innovation Network," *Economy and Society* 38, no. 2 (2009): 326–59.

Gray, Mary, and Suri Siddharth. "The Humans Working behind the AI Curtain," *Harvard Business Review* (2019).

Guyan, Kevin. *Queer Data: Using Gender, Sex and Sexuality Data for Action.* London: Bloomsbury Publishing, 2022.

Haigh, Thomas, Mark Priestley, and Crispin Rope. *ENIAC in Action: Making and Remaking the Modern Computer.* Cambridge, MA: MIT Press, 2018.

Halpin, Darren R., and Anthony J. Nownes. *The New Entrepreneurial Advocacy: Silicon Valley Elites in American Politics.* Oxford: Oxford University Press, 2021.

Hannan, Michael T., and John Freeman. "Structural Inertia and Organizational Change," 49, no. 2 (1984): 149–64.

Haraway, Donna. "A Cyborg Manifesto: Science, Technology and Socialist-Feminism in the Late 20th Century." In *Simians, Cyborgs and Women: The Reinvention of Nature,* 127–48. London: Routledge, 1991.

Harari, Yuval Noah. *Sapiens: A Brief History of Humankind.* Harper Collins, 2011.

Harari, Yuval Noah. *Home Deus: A Brief History of Tomorrow.* Harper Collins, 2016.

Harari, Yuval Noah. *21 Lessons for the 21st Century.* Spiegel & Grau, 2018.

Hargittai, Esther, ed. *Handbook of Digital Inequality.* Cheltenham, England: Edward Elgar Publishing, 2021.

Harris, Malcolm. *Palo Alto: A History of California, Capitalism, and the World.* Boston, MA: Little, Brown and Company, 2023.

Heylighen, Francis. "A Contemporary Interpretation of Teilhard's Law of Complexity-Consciousness," *Religion, Brain & Behavior* 13, no. 4 (2023): 470.

Hilferding, Rudolph. *Finance Capital: A Study in the Latest Phase of Capital Development.* Routledge, 2007.

Hirsh, Paul M. "An Organization-Set Analysis of Cultural Industries Systems," *American Journal of Sociology* 77, no. 4 (1972): 639–59.

Hoffman, Reid. *Blitzscaling: The Lighting Fast Path to Building Massively Valuable Companies.* New York: Harper Collins, 2018.

Hsu, David H., and Martin Kenney. "Organizing Venture Capital: The Rise and Demise of American Research & Development Corporation, 1946–1973," *Industrial and Corporate Change* 14, no. 4 (2005): 579–616.

Hughes, Everett C. "Cycles, Turning Point and Career." In Everett C. Hughes, *The Sociological Eye,* 124–31. Chicago: Aldine, 1971.

Hughes, Everett C. "The Social Drama of Work," *Mid-American Review of Sociology* 1, no. 1 (1976): 1–7.

Hughes, James. "The Politics of Transhumanism and the Techno-Millennial Imagination 1626–2030," *Zygon* 47, no 4 (2012): 757–76.

Hwang, Tim. *Subprime Attention Crisis. Advertising and the Time Bomb at the Heart of the Internet.* New York: Macmillan Publishers, 2020.

Indergaard, Michael. *Silicon Alley: The Rise and Fall of a New Media District.* New York: Routledge, 2004.

Isaacson, Walter. *The Innovators: How a Group of Hackers, Geniuses, and Geeks Created the Digital Revolution.* New York, Simon & Schuster, 2015.

Israel, Shel, and Robert Scoble, *Age of Context: Mobile, Sensors, Data and the Future of Privacy.* Scott Valley, CA: CreateSpace Independent Publishing Platform, 2014.

Jackson, Eric M. *The PayPal Wars, Battles with eBay, the Media, the Mafia, and the Rest of Planet Earth.* Chicago : World Ahead Publishing, 2004.

Jager, Anton, and Daniel Zamora Vargas. *Welfare for Markets: A Global History of Basic Income.* Chicago: University of Chicago Press, 2023.

Jankélévitch, Vladimir. *Traité des vertus*, vol. 1, Paris: Flammarion, 2011.

Jaton, Florian. *The Constitution of Algorithms. Ground-Truthing, Programming, Formulating.* Cambridge, MA: MIT Press, 2021.

Jenkins, Henry. *Fans, Bloggers, and Gamers: Media Consumers in a Digital Age.* New York: NYU Press, 2006.

Jovanovic, Bojan. "Job Matching and the Theory of Turnover," *Journal of Political Economy* 87, no. 5 (1979): 972–90.

Katz, Michael L., and Carl Shapiro. "Network Externalities, Competition, and Compatibility," *American Economic Review* 75, no. 3 (1985): 424–40.

Kawasaki, Guy. *The Art to Start: The Time-tested, Battle-hardened Guide for Anyone Starting Anything.* New York: Portfolio, 2004.

Kawasaki, Guy. *Rules for Revolutionaries: The Capitalist Manifesto for Creating and Marketing New Products and Services.* New York: Harper, 2000.

Kelly, Kevin. *New Rules for the New Economy: 10 Radical Strategies for a Connected World.* New York; Penguin, 1999.

Kelty, Christopher. *Two Bits: The Cultural Significance of Free Software.* Durham, NC: Duke University Press, 2008.

Kenney, Martin. *Understanding Silicon Valley: The Anatomy of an Entrepreneurial Region.* Redwood City, CA: Stanford University Press, 2000.

Khan, Shamus R. *Privilege: The Making of an Adolescent Elite at Saint Paul School.* Princeton, NJ: Princeton University Press, 2010.

Knight, Franck. *Risk, Uncertainty and Profit.* Kissimmee, FL: Signalman Publishing, 2009.

Knight, Kenneth. *A Study of Technological Innovation: The Evolution of Digital Computers.* Pittsburgh, PA: Carnegie Institute of Technology, 1963.

Kozinets, Robert V. "Can Consumers Escape the Market? Emancipatory Illuminations from Burning Man," *Journal of Consumer Research* 29, no. 1 (2002): 20–38.

Kripal, Jeffrey. *Esalen: America and the Religion of No Religion.* Chicago: University of Chicago Press, 2011.

Krueger, Oliver. "Gaia, God, and the Internet: The History of Evolution and the Utopia of Community in Media Society," *Numen-International Review for the History of Religion*, no. 54/2 (2007): 138–73.

Lalka, Rob. *The Venture Alchemists: How Big Tech Turned Profits into Power.* New York: Columbia Business School Publishing, 2024.

Lallement, Michel. *L'Âge du faire.* Paris: Seuil, 2015.

Landy, Joshua, and Michael Saler, eds. *The Re-Enchantment of the World: Secular Magic in a Rational Age.* Redwood City, CA: Stanford University Press, 2009.

Latour, Bruno. "Le dernier des capitalistes sauvages: Interview d'un biochimiste." *Fundamenta Scientiae* 4, no. 3–4 (1984): 301–27.

Latour, Bruno. *The Pasteurization of France*. Cambridge, MA: Harvard University Press, 1993.

Latour, Bruno. *We Have Never Been Modern*. Cambridge, MA: Harvard University Press, 1991.

Latour, Bruno, and David Woolgar. *Laboratory Life. The Social Construction of Scientific Facts*. Los Angeles: Sage, 1979.

Lécuyer, Christophe. "Driving Semiconductor Innovation: Moore's Law at Fairchild and Intel," *Enterprise and Society* 23, no. 1 (2022): 133–63.

Lécuyer, Christophe. *Making Silicon Valley: Innovation and the Growth of High Tech (1930–1970)*. Cambridge, MA: MIT Press, 2006.

Lécuyer, Christophe, and Hyungsub Choi. "Silicon Valley Secrets, or American Microelectronics Firms Facing Technical Uncertainty," *Revue d'histoire moderne & contemporaine* 59, no. 3 (2012): 48–69.

Le Renard, Alice. *A Society of Young Women: Opportunities of Place, Power and Reform in Saudi Arabia*. Redwood City, CA: Stanford University Press, 2014.

Le Roy Ladurie, Emmanuel, and Jean-François Fitou. *Saint-Simon ou le système de la Cour*. Paris: Fayard, 1997.

Levy, Steven. *Facebook: The Inside Story*. New York: Penguin, 2020.

Levy, Steven. *Hackers: Heroes of the Computer Revolution*. Garden City, NY: Doubleday, 1984.

Lewis, Becca. "Tech's Right Turn: The Rise of Reactionary Politics in Silicon Valley and Online." PhD dissertation, Stanford University, 2024.

Lewis, Michael. *Moneyball: The Art of Winning an Unfair Game*. New York: W. W. Norton & Company Inc., 2003.

Little, Ben, and Alison Winch. *The New Patriarchs of Digital Capitalism Celebrity Tech Founders and Networks of Power*. London: Routledge, 2021.

Luhmann, Niklas. *Trust and Power*. Hoboken, NJ: Wiley, 2017.

Luhr, Sigrid W. "Engineering Inequality: Informal Coaching, Glass Walls, and Social Closure in Silicon Valley," *American Journal of Sociology* 129, no. 5 (2024).

Luhr, Sigrid W. "'We're Better Than Most': Diversity Discourse in the San Francisco Bay Area Tech Industry," *Social Problems* (2023).

MacAskill, William. *Doing Good Better: Effective Altruism and a Radical Way to Make a Difference*. London: Guardian Faber, 2015.

MacAskill, William. *What We Owe the Future*. New York: Basic Books, 2022.

MacKenzie, Wark. "The Vectorialist Class," *e-flux Journal*, no. 65 (2015).

Mahoney, Michael S. *Histories of Computing*. Cambridge, MA: Harvard University Press, 2011.

Mahoney, Michael S. "The History of Computing in the History of Technology," *Annals of the History of Computing* 10 (1988): 113–25.

Malinowski, Erik. *Betaball: How Silicon Valley and Science Built One of the Greatest Basket Ball Team in History*. New York: Atria Books, 2017.

Mannheim, Karl. *Ideology and Utopia*. London: Routledge, 1936.

Marshall, Alfred. *Principles of Economics: An Introductory Volume*. New York: Macmillan, 1920.

Marwick, Alice. *Status Update: Celebrity, Publicity, and Branding in the Social Media Age*. New Haven, CT: Yale University Press, 2013.

Marx, Karl. *Capital: The Process of Capitalist Production*, vol. 1. Chicago: Charles H. Kerr and Co., 1909.

Mayo, Anthony J., Nitin Nohria. and Laura G. Singleton. *Paths to Power: How Insiders and Outsiders Shaped American Business Leadership*. Cambridge, MA: Harvard Business School Press, 2006.

McClelland, Clearence. *Power: The Inner Experience*. New York: Irvington Publishers, 1975.

McElroy, Erin. "Postsocialism and the Tech Boom 2.0: Techno-utopics of Racial/ Spatial Dispossession," *Social Identities* 24, no. 3 (2017): 1–16.

McElroy, Erin. *Silicon Valley Imperialism: Techno Fantasies and Frictions in Postsocialist Times*. Durham, NC: Duke University Press, 2024.

McNemar, Quinn, and Maud Amanda Merrill. *Studies in Personality: Contributed in Honor of Lewis M. Terman*. New York: McGraw-Hill Book Company, 1942.

Mead, George H. "The Social Self." *Journal of Philosophy, Psychology and Scientific Methods* 10, no. 14 (1913): 374–80.

Meehan, Mary Beth, and Fred Turner. *Seeing Silicon Valley: Life Inside a Fraying America*. Chicago: University of Chicago Press, 2021.

Menger, Pierre-Michel, Colin Marchika, Yann Renisio, and Pierre Verschueren. "Formations et carrières mathématiques en France: Un modèle typique d'excellence?," *Revue française d'économie* 32, no. 2 (2020): 155–217.

Mickey, Ethel L. "The Organization of Networking and Gender Inequality in the New Economy: Evidence from the Tech Industry," *Work and Occupations* 49, no. 4 (2022): 383–420.

Mickey, Ethel L. "When Gendered Logics Collide: Going Public and Restructuring in a High-Tech Organization," *Gender & Society* 33, no. 4 (2019): 509–33.

Miller, Chris. *Chip War: The Fight for the World's Most Critical Technology*. New York: Scribner, 2022.

Miller, Peter N. "Is Design Thinking the New Liberal Arts." In Peter Marber and Daniel Aray, eds., *The Evolution of Liberal Arts in the Global Age*, 167–73. New York: Routledge, 2017.

Monea, Alexander. *The Digital Closet: How the Internet Became Straight*. Cambridge, MA: MIT Press, 2022.

Morozov, Evgeny. *To Save Everything, Click Here: Technology, Solutionism, and the Urge To Fix Problems That Don't Exist*. New York: Allen Lane, 2013.

Mujerki, Chandra. "Space and Political Pedagogy at the Gardens of Versailles," *Public Culture* 24, no. 3 (1968): 509–34.

Mumford, Lewis. *The Myth of the Machine, Vol. 1. Technics and Human Development*. San Diego: Harcourt, 1967.

Myers West, Sarah. "Data Capitalism: Redefining the Logics of Surveillance and Privacy," *Business & Society* 58, no. 1 (2017): 20–41.

Naudet, Jules. *Entrer dans l'élite*. Paris: PUF, 2012.

Naur, Peter, and Brian Randell, eds. "Software Engineering," Report on a Conference Sponsored by the Nato Science Committee, 1968.

Neely, Megan T., Patrick Sheehan, and Christine L. Williams. "Social Inequality in High Tech: How Gender, Race, and Ethnicity Structure the World's Most Powerful Industry," *Annual Review of Sociology* 49, no. 1 (2023): 319–38.

Neff, Gina. "The Changing Place of Cultural Production: The Location of Social Networks in a Digital Media Industry," *Annals of the American Academy of Political and Social Science* 597, no. 1 (2005): 134–52.

Nelson, Richard, and Sydney Winter. *An Evolutionary Theory of Economic Change*. Cambridge, MA: Belknap Press, 1982.

Noble, David F. *The Religion of Technology. The Divinity of Man and the Spirit of Invention*. London: Penguin, 1999.

Nora, Pierre. *Realms of Memory*. New York: Columbia University Press, 1996–98.

Oakes, Kaya. *Slanted and Enchanted: The Evolution of Indie Culture*. New York: Holt Paperbacks, 2009.

Ohanian, Alexis. *Without Their Permission: How the 21st Century Will Be Made, Not Managed*. New York: Grand Central Publishing, 2013.

Olsen, Niklas. *History in the Plural: An Introduction to the Work of Reinhart Koselleck*. New York: Berghahn, 2012.

O'Mara, Margaret. *The Code: Silicon Valley and the Remaking of America*. New York: Penguin Press, 2019.

O'Neil, Mathieu, Laure Muselli, Fred Pailler, and Stefano Zacchiroli, "Subverting or Preserving the Institution: Competing IT Firm and Foundation Discourses about Open Source," *New Media and Society* (2024).

O'Neil, Mathieu, Laure Muselli, Mahin Raissi, and Stefano Zacchiroli, "Open Source Has Won and Lost the War: Legitimizing Commercial-Communal Hybridization in a FOSS Project," *New Media & Society* 23, no. 5 (2021): 1157–80.

O'Reilly, Tim. *WTF: What's the Future and Why It's Up to You*. New York: Harper, 2017.

Ouchi, William G. *Theory Z*. New York: Avon Books, 1981.

Pastoureau, Michel. *Heraldry: Its Origins and Meaning*. London: Thames & Hudson, 1997.

Penley, Constance, and Andrew Ross, eds. *Technoculture*. Minneapolis: University of Minnesota Press, 1991.

Pentland, Alex. *Social Physics. How Good Ideas Spread: The Lessons from a New Science*. New York: Penguin Press, 2014.

Peters, Tom, and Robert H. Waterman Jr. *In Search of Excellence*. New York: Harper and Row, 1982.

Pierce, Charlie. *Idiot America: How Stupidity Became a Virtue in the Land of the Free*. New York: Knopf Doubleday, 2010.

Piscione, Deborah S. *Secrets of Silicon Valley: What Everyone Else Can Learn from the Innovation Capital of the World*. New York: St. Martin's Press, 2013.

Polletta, Francesca. *Was Like a Fever: Storytelling in Protest and Politics*. Chicago: Chicago University Press, 2006.

Poupeau, Franck, and Jean-Christophe François. *Le Sens du placement: Ségrégation résidentielle et ségrégation scolaire*. Paris: Raisons d'agir, 2008.

Postman, Neil. *Technopoly: The Surrender of Culture to Technology*. New York: Knopf, 1992.

Pred, Allan R. *The Spatial Dynamics of Urban Growth in the United States, 1800–1914*. Cambridge, MA: Harvard University Press, 1966.

Puttick, Elizabeth. "Human Potential Movement." In Christopher Hugh, ed. *Encyclopedia of New Religions*. Oxford: Lion, 2024.

Raskin, Jef. "More Mac Reactions," *BYTE* 9, no. 5 (1984): 20.

Reynolds, Paul D. "New Firm Creation in the United States a PSED, Overview," *Foundations and Trends in Entrepreneurship* 3, no. 1: 1–150.

Rheingold, Howard. *Net Smart: How to Thrive Online*. Cambridge, MA: MIT Press, 2012.

Rheingold, Howard. *Smart Mobs: The Next Social Revolution*. New York: Basic Books, 2002.

Ricoeur, Paul. *Memory, History, Forgetting*. Translated by Kathleen Blamey and David Pellauer. Chicago: University of Chicago Press, 2004.

Rieder, Bernardt. *Engines of Order: A Mechanology of Algorithmic Techniques*. Amsterdam: Amsterdam University Press, 2019.

Rieder, Bernardt. "Méchanologies et delegation: Pour un design orienté-société dans l'ère du web 2.0." PhD dissertation, Université Paris 8, 2006.

Ries, Eric. *The Lean Startup: How Today's Entrepreneurs Use Continuous Innovation to Create Radically Successful Businesses*. New York: Crown Currency, 2011.

Rifkin, Glen, and George Harrar. *The Ultimate Entrepreneur: The Story of Ken Olsen and Digital Equipment Corporation*. Chicago: Contemporary Books, 1988.

Rosa, Harmut. *Social Acceleration: A New Theory of Modernity*. New York: Columbia University Press, 2015.

Roberts, Sarah T. *Behind the Screen: Content Moderation in the Shadows of Social Media*. New Haven, CT: Yale University Press, 2019.

Ross, Andrew. *No-collar: The Humane Workplace and Its Hidden Costs*. New York: Basic Books, 2003.

Ross, Edward A. *Social Control: A Survey of the Foundations of Order*. New York: Macmillan Company, 1901.

Rushkoff, Douglas. *Survival of the Richest: Escape Fantasies of the Tech Billionaires*. Melbourne: Scribe Publications, 2023.

Sassen, Saskia. *The Global City: New York, London, Tokyo*. Princeton, NJ: Princeton University Press, 1991.

Sandmeyer, Elmer C. *The Anti-Chinese Movement in California*. Champaign: University of Illinois Press, 1939.

Saxenian, AnnaLee. *The New Argonauts: Regional Advantage in a Global Economy.* Cambridge, MA: Harvard University Press, 2006.

Saxenian, AnnaLee. *Regional Advantage: Culture and Competition in Silicon Valley and Route 128.* Cambridge, MA: Harvard University Press, 1994.

Saxenian, AnnaLee. *Silicon Valley's New Immigrant Entrepreneurs.* San Francisco: Public Policy Institute of California, 1999.

Schaake, Marietje. *The Tech Coup: How to Save Democracy from Silicon Valley.* Princeton, NJ: Princeton University Press, 2024.

Schaffran, Alex. *The Road to Resegregation: Northern California and the Failure of Politics.* Oakland: University of California Press, 2018.

Schiller, Dan. *Digital Capitalism: Networking the Global Market System.* Cambridge, MA: MIT Press, 1999.

Schroeder, Chris. *Startup Rising : The Entrepreneurial Revolution Remaking the Middle East.* New York: St. Martin's Press 2013.

Scott, Allen J. *The Cultural Economy of Cities.* London: Sage, 2000.

Scott, Allen J. *Global City Regions: Trends, Theory, Policy.* Oxford: Oxford University Press, 2001.

Scott, Allen J. *New Industrial Spaces.* London: Pion, 1988.

Sedgwick, Eve. *Between Men: English Literature and Male Homosocial Desire.* New York: Columbia University Press, 1985.

Shane, Scott. *The Illusions of Entrepreneurship: The Costly Myths That Entrepreneurs, Investors, and Policy Makers Lie.* New Haven, CT: Yale University Press, 2008.

Shapiro, Carl, and Hal R. Varian. *Information Rules: A Strategic Guide to the Network Economy.* Cambridge, MA: Harvard Business Review Press, 1998.

Shaver, Kelly G., and Linda R. Scott. "Person, Process, Choice: The Psychology of New Venture Creation," *Entrepreneurship Theory and Practice* 16, no. 2(1991): 23–45.

Shestakofsky, Benjamin. *Behind the Startup: How Venture Capital Shapes Work, Innovation, and Inequality.* Berkeley: California University Press, 2024.

Shibutani, Tomatsu. "Reference Groups as Perspectives," *American Journal of Sociology* 60, no. 6 (1955): 562–69.

Siles, Ignacio. "Inventing Twitter: An Iterative Approach to New Media Development," *International Journal of Communication*, no. 7 (2013): 2105–27.

Sims, Christo. "Green Magic: On Technologies of Enchantment at Apple's Corporate Headquarters," *Public Culture* 34, no. 2 (2022): 291–317.

Simmel, George. "The Sociology of Secrecy and of Secret Societies," *American Journal of Sociology* 11, no. 4 (1906): 441–98.

Singer, Peter. "Famine, Affluence, and Morality," *Philosophy and Public Affairs* 1, no. 3 (1972): 229–43.

Slobodian, Quinn. *The Craq-up Capitalism: Market Radicals and the Dream of a World Without Democracy.* London: Allen Lane, 2023.

Slobodian, Quinn. *The Globalists: The End of Empire and the Birth of Neoliberalism.* Cambridge, MA: Havard University Press, 2018.

Slobodian, Quinn. *Hayek's Bastards: The Neoliberal Roots of the Populist Right.* Brooklyn, NY: Zone Books, 2025

Smith, Neil. "New Globalism, New Urbanism: Gentrification As Global Urban Strategy." *Antipode* 34, no. 3 (2002): 427–50.

Smith, Neil. *The New Urban Frontier: Gentrification and the Revanchist City.* New York: Routledge, 1996.

Srnicek, Nick. *Platform Capitalism.* New York: Wiley, 2016.

Star, Susan L. "Power, Technology and the Phenomenology of Conventions: On Being Allergic to Onions," *The Sociological Review* 38, no. 1: 26–56.

Star, Susan L., and Geoffrey C. Bowker. *Sorting Things Out: Classification and Its Consequences.* Cambridge, MA: MIT Press, 1999.

Stinchcombe, Arthur L. *Information and Organizations.* Berkeley: University of California Press, 1990.

Stinchcombe, Arthur L. "Social Structure and Organizations." In James G. March, ed., *Handbook of Organizations,* 142–93. Chicago: Rand McNally & company, 1965.

Stinchcombe, Arthur L. *When Formality Works: Authority and Abstraction in Law and Organizations.* Chicago: University of Chicago Press, 2001.

Stone, Brad. *The Everything Store: Jeff Bezos and the Age of Amazon.* Boston: Little, Brown and Company, 2013.

Storper, Michael. *Keys to the City: How Economics, Institutions, Social Interaction, and Politics Shape Development.* Princeton, NJ: Princeton University Press, 2013.

Storper, Michael. *The Regional World: Territorial Development in a Global Economy.* New York: The Guilford Press, 1997.

Storper, Michael, and Richard Walker. *The Capitalist Imperative: Territory, Technology and Industrial Growth.* Cambridge, MA: Blackwell Publishers, 1989.

Strauss, Anselm L. *Mirrors and Masks: The Search for Identity.* New York: Routledge, 1997.

Stross, Randall, *E-boys: The First Inside Account of Venture Capitalists at Work.* New York: Ballantine Books, 2000.

Stross, Randall. *The Launch Pad: Inside Y Combinator.* New York: Penguin, 2013.

Stross, Randall. *A Practical Education: Why Liberal Arts Majors Make Great Employees.* Redwood City, CA: Stanford University Press, 2017.

Sutton, Bob. *Scaling Up Excellence: Getting to More Without Settling for Less.* New York: Crown, 2014.

Swedberg, Richard, and Ola Agevall. *The Max Weber Dictionary: Key Words and Central Concepts.* Redwood City, CA: Stanford University Press, 2005.

Swisher, Kara. *Burn Book: A Tech Love Story.* New York: Simon & Schuster, 2024.

Takeuchi, Hirotaka, and Ikujiro Nonaka. "The New Product Development Game," *Harvard Business Review* 64, no. 1: 137–46.

Taillandier, Apolline. "From Boundless Expansion to Existential Threat: Transhumanists and Posthuman Imaginaries." In Jenny Andersson and Sandra Kemp, eds., *Futures,* 333–48. Oxford: Oxford University Press, 2020.

Taillandier, Apolline. "*Staring into the Singularity* and Other Posthuman Tales: Transhumanist Stories of Future Change," *History and Theory* 60, no. 2 (2021): 215–33.

Taillandier, Apolline, Neil Stephens, and Samantha Vanderslott. "Effective Altruism, Technoscience, and the Making of Philanthropic Value." *Economy and Society* 54, no. 1 (2025): 1–25.

Tamaseb, Ali. *Super Founders: What Data Reveals about Billion-Dollar Startups.* New York: PublicAffairs, 2021.

Tarnoff, Benjamin, and Moira Weigel. *Voices from the Valley: Tech Workers Talk about What They Do and How They Do It.* New York: Macmillan, 2020.

Teilhard de Chardin, Pierre. *The Phenomenon of Man.* New York: Harper Perennial, 1976.

Terman, Lewis. "Genius and Stupidity: A Study of Some of the Intellectual Processes of Seven 'Bright' and Seven 'Stupid' Boys," *Pedagogical Seminary* 13 (1906): 307–73.

Thiel, Peter. *Zero to One: Notes on Startups, or How to Build the Future.* New York: Crown Business, 2014.

Thiel Peter, and David Sachs. *The Diversity Myth: Multiculturalism and the Politics of Intolerance at Stanford.* Oakland, CA: Independent Institute, 1995.

Thornton, Patricia H. "The Sociology of Entrepreneurship," *Annual Review of Sociology* 25, no. 1 (1999): 19–46.

Thornton, Patricia H., and Kim Klyver. "Who Is More Likely To Walk the Talk? The Symbolic Management of Entrepreneurial Intentions by Gender and Work Status," *Journal of Innovation, Organization, and Management* 21, no. 3 (2018): 1–26.

Tilton, John E. *International Diffusion of Technology: The Case of Semiconductors.* Washington, DC: Brookings Institution, 1971.

Tongia, Rahul, and Ernest J. Wilson III. "The Flip's Side of Metcalfe's Law: Multiple and Growing Costs of Network Exclusion," *International Journal of Communication* 5 (2011): 665–81.

Trice, Harrison M., and Janice M. Beyer. *The Cultures of Work Organizations.* Englewood Cliffs, NJ: Prentice Hall, 1993.

Turkle, Sherry. *The Second Self: Computers and the Human Spirit.* New York: Harper Collins Publishers, 1984.

Turner, Fred. "The Arts at Facebook: An Aesthetic Infrastructure for Surveillance Capitalism," *Poetics* 67 (2018).

Turner, Fred. "Burning Man at Google: A Cultural Infrastructure for New Media Production," *New Media and Society*, no. 11 (2009): 73–94.

Turner, Fred. *Democratic Surround: Multimedia and American Liberalism from World War II to the Psychedelic Sixties.* Chicago: Chicago University Press, 2013.

Turner, Fred. *From Counterculture to Cyberculture. Stewart Brand, the Whole Earth Network, and the Rise of Digital Utopianism.* Chicago: Chicago University Press, 2006.

Turner, Fred, and Christine Larson, "Network Celebrity: Entrepreneurship and the New Public Intellectuals," *Public Culture* 27, no. 1 (2015): 53–84.

Tyssot, Sylvie. *Good Neighbors: Gentrifying Diversity in Boston's South End.* London: Verso Books, 2015.

Uzzi, Brian, and Jarrett Spiro. "Collaboration and Creativity: The Small World Problem," *American Journal of Sociology* 111, no. 2 (2005): 447–504.

Velkova, Julia, and Jean-Christophe Plantin, "Data centers and the Infrastructural Temporalities of Digital Media: An Introduction," *New Media & Society* 25, no. 2 (2023): 273–86.

Vérin, Hélène. *Entrepreneurs, entreprises. Histoire d'une idée.* Paris: PUF, 1982.

Walker, Richard A. *Pictures of a Gone City: Tech and the Dark Side of Prosperity in the San Francisco Bay Area.* Oakland, CA: PM Press, 2018.

Weber, Max. *The Protestant Ethic and the Spirit of Capitalism.* Brooklyn, NY: Angelico Press, 2014.

Wecter, Dixon. *The Saga of American Society: A Record of Social Aspiration (1607–1937).* New York: Charles Scribner's Sons, 1937.

White, Harrison C. *Chains of Opportunity, System Models of Mobility in Organizations.* Cambridge, MA: Harvard University Press, 1970.

White, Harrison C. *Identity and Control: How Social Formations Emerge.* Princeton, NJ: Princeton University Press, 2008.

Wiener, Norbert. *Cybernetics: Or Control and Communication in the Animal and the Machine.* Cambridge, MA: MIT Press, 1948.

Williamson, Oliver. *Markets and Hierarchies: Analysis and Antitrust Implications.* New York: Free Press, 1975.

Winner, Langdon. *The Whale and the Reactor: A Search for Limits in an Age of High Technology.* Chicago: Chicago University Press, 1986.

Wolfe, Alexandra. *Valley of Gods.* New York: Simon & Schuster, 2017.

Wolfe, Tom. *The Electric Kool-Aid Acid Test.* New York: Picador, 1968.

Wu, Tongyu. *Play to Submission: Gaming Capitalism in a Tech Firm.* Philadelphia: Temple University Press, 2024.

Xingzhou Zhang, Jing-Jie Liu, and Zhi-Wei Xu. "Tencent and Facebook Data Validate Metcalfe's Law," *Journal of Computer Science and Technology* 30, no. 2 (2015): 246–51.

Zhang, Junfu. *High-Tech Start-Ups and Industry Dynamics in Silicon Valley.* San Francisco: Public Policy Institute of California, 2003.

Zhikharevich, Dmitrii M. "Heuristics of Capital: A Historical Sociology of US Venture Capitalism, 1946–1968." PhD thesis, London School of Economics, 2019.

Zuboff, Shoshana. *The Age of Surveillance Capitalism: The Fight for a Human Future at the New Frontier of Power.* London: Profil books, 2018.

Zukin, Sharon. *The Innovation Complex: Cities, Tech and New Economy.* Oxford: Oxford University Press, 2020.

Zukin, Sharon. *Loft Living: Culture and Capital in Urban Change.* Baltimore, MD: Johns Hopkins University Press, 1982.

Zwolinski, Matt, and John Tomasi. *The Individuals. Radicals, Reactionaries and the Struggle for the Soul of Libertarianism.* Princeton, NJ: Princeton University Press, 2023.

INDEX

Note: Tables and figures are indicated by an italic *t* and *f* following the page number.

Abernathy, William J., 25
abstraction, 96, 164
accelerationism, 5, 211, 212*f*, 270
acqui-hire, 61
active financing, 74
Actor-Network Theory (ANT), 10, 12
administrative autonomy, 4
AIDS pandemic, 238, 251–252
Airbnb, 9, 64, 66*f*, 138–139, 149, 156, 226, 246
Alphabet, 2–4, 10, 88, 141, 261–266
Altman, Sam, 7, 90–91, 166, 211, 239, 267
Amazon, 2–4, 30, 58, 88, 135, 137, 141, 145–146, 180, 254, 261, 263–267
American Research and Development Corporation (ARD), 71
anarchocapitalism, 211, 217
Anderson, Chris, 213
Anderson, Karlan, 71
Andreessen, Marc, 2, 47, 69, 111, 268–269
Andreessen Horowitz, 68–69
Android, 2, 12, 171, 182, 264
Anti-Eviction Mapping Project (AEMP), 252
antitrust penalties, 1
Apple, 2–4, 81, 93, 133, 135, 137, 152–153, 182, 246, 258, 262–264
Arab Spring, 3
architects, 125, 153, 160, 164–165, 206–207, 259

Artificial General Intelligence (AGI), 161, 211
artificial intelligence (AI): companies specializing in, 107; controversy over, 1; at Google, 52; impact of, 159–161, 265; industry hype over, 55; machine learning models, 45; Magnificent 7 companies and, 51, 264; OpenAI, 7, 12, 51, 55, 90, 104, 262, 264, 266; primacy of, 48–49; resurgence of, 25; rising costs of, 264–265; in San Francisco, 244; Silicon Valley connection, 32–33
Assange, Julian, 216–217
atheism, 89–90, 104
Atlas Shrugged (Rand), 211
augmented humanity, 211, 217–220

Baltzell, Digby, 104
bankruptcy, 51, 56, 238
Barlow, John Perry, 197, 216
Bastiat, Claude Frederic, 215
Bateson, Gregory, 84, 210
Battery Ventures, 61
Becker, Gary, 131
Becker, Howard, 11, 152
Beckstead, Nick, 220
Behind the Startup (Shestakofsky), 55
Bell, Daniel, 82
Bezos, Jeff, 53, 58, 230, 246
Biden, Joe, 258
Biggerstaff, Bill, 57

Big Tech: analysis through subcategories, 44; antitrust penalties and, 1, 4; employee office hours, 15; innovation-focused culture, 7, 10, 149; layoffs in, 41; tax levels and, 267; urban development and, 245–247; venture capital firms in, 61. *See also* Silicon Valley; tech companies/industry

Black Lives Matter movement, 156

BlackRock, 69

The Blood of the Nation: A Study in the Decay of Races by the Survival of the Unfit (Jordan), 108

Boltanski, Luc, 82–83

Bostrom, Nick, 111, 219, 220

Botha, Roelof, 150

Bourdieu, Pierre, 11–12, 176

Brand, Stewart, 195, 197, 221

breakthroughs in venture capitalism, 72–77

Brin, Sergey, 7, 53, 59

brogrammer cliché, 165

broligarchy, 51

Brooks, Frederick (Brooks's Law), 173–174

Brown, Wendy, 144–145

builders, 78, 164, 228

Burning Man: body trials, 198–201; civic responsibility and, 189, 205; communal effort and, 189, 205; community building, 206–209; countercultures with, 194–198; decommodification and, 189, 205; defined as arts community, 81; development of skills, 204–205; deviance and norm, 201–204; gifting and, 189, 205; Google and, 188; immediacy and, 189, 205; interactions in, 191–194; introduction to, 15, 187–191; leave-no-trace and, 189; organizational skills, 205–206; participant experiences, 198–204; participation and, 189, 205; radical inclusion and, 189, 205; radical self-reliance and, 189, 205; self-expression and, 189, 205; tech project skills and, 204–209

Bush, Vannevar, 110

Bushnell, Nolan, 136

business to business (BtoB), 53

business-to-consumer area (BtoC), 53

California Public Employees' Retirement System (CalPERS), 76–77

California State Teachers' Retirement System (CalSTRS), 76–77

Cambridge Analytica, 3, 16

capitalism: anarchocapitalism, 211, 217; communist capitalism, 56–57; data capitalism, 51; decentralized capitalism, 51; digital capitalism, 51; economy of failure, 54–57; energy capital, 131–132; entrepreneurs and, 50–77; exchange economy, 54; financial capitalism, 51; free economy, 52–53; historical principles of, 52; informational capitalism, 50–51; new capitalism, 50–51; new economy, 2, 6, 82, 134, 238; platform capitalism, 50–51; surveillance capitalism, 51; technocapitalism, 211; upside-down capitalism, 52–57

capital sources. *See* venture capitalists

Cassady, Neal, 195

Center for Employment Equity, 107

CEOs, 136, 155–158

Certeau, Michel de, 81

Chandler, Alfred, 174

Chardin, Teilhard de, 210

ChatGPT, 5, 56, 262, 265

Chiapello, Eve, 82–83

Choi, Hyungsub, 169

Cisco, 121, 134

civic responsibility, 189, 205

Clark, Jim, 7, 130

Clarke, Arthur C., 161

Clinton, Bill, 258, 261

Clinton, Hillary, 258–259

cloud computing, 47

Coase, Ronald, 133

Coavoux, Samuel, 225, 226

coding elite, 78

collaborative networks, 11, 12

Collins, Randall, 132

communal effort, 189, 205

communicability, 47–49, 96

communication theory, 83–85

communist capitalism, 56–57

community building, 206–209

community networking, 120–125

Compton, Karl, 71

computer tools, 175–178, 177*t*
Comte, Auguste, 210
Conway, Ron, 73
corporate culture, 147–154
corporate social responsibility (CSR), 270
corporatism, 119, 143, 147–154
cosmism, 211
cosmopolitanism, 89
countercultures, 194–198
counterrevolution, 258–263
COVID-19 pandemic, 7, 14, 16, 41, 238, 246
Crunchies Awards, 32
crypto-anarchism, 211
crypto/cryptocurrencies, 13, 211, 216, 219, 261, 263, 266
cyberlibertarianism, 211, 216
Cybernetics: Or Control and Communication in the Animal and the Machine (Wiener), 83–84

dark enlightenment, 211, 261
data capitalism, 51
Daub, Adrian, 84
decentralized capitalism, 51
decommodification, 189, 205
Defense Advanced Research Projects Agency (DARPA), 163
DEI initiatives, 88
Déjacque, Joseph, 214
delusional tech elite, 235
dematerialization, 15, 246, 264–265, 268
Denmark, 4
Department of Government Efficiency (DOGE), 3, 133, 269
developers. *See* programmers/programming
Dewey, John, 126, 192
The Diggers, 195–196
digital ambassador, 4
digital capitalism, 51
Digital Equipment Corporation (DEC), 71–72, 111
digital revolution, 226–227
D'Ignazio, Catherine, 168
Disney. *See* Walt Disney Company
The Diversity Myth (Thiel, Sack), 111
Doerr, John, 118–119, 129
doers, 78, 109
Doing Good Better (MacAskill), 220

Doriot, Georges, 70–71, 72, 110–111
Dorsey, Jack, 156–157
dot-com boom/bust, 3, 70, 97, 122, 235, 238, 254
Dow Jones, 72
Draper, Tim, 69
dreamers, 78
Dropbox, 154, 241

economic reassurance, 127
economy of failure, 54–57
effective altruism, 5, 211, 220–222
egalitarianism, 88–93
elective affinity, 214
Electronic Frontier Foundation, 3, 197, 216, 232
Electronic Warfare Lab, 8
Elk, Daniel, 8
Elwell, Cyril Frank, 108
energy capital, 131–132
Engelbart, Douglas, 7
entrepreneurs: capitalism and, 50–77; energy capital of, 131–132; experiences of, 125–132; multitasking abilities, 112–117; networking, 117–125; problem-solving, 113–115; role in tech, 1–2, 4, 6–9, 11–21, 25–44, 47–48; simplicity and sincerity, 128–130; solo, 68; trust-worthiness, 115–117; voice of, 228–229
Esalen Institute, 84
Ethernet, 28–29
eugenics, 108–111, 222–223, 257, 260
evolutionary companies: corporatism, 119, 143, 147–154; hiring talent, 136–147; introduction to, 133–136, 136*t*; as personified, 136, 155–158; work environment, 152–154
exchange economy, 54
extropy, 212–213, 217–219, 222

Facebook, 2–3, 28, 169
Fairchild Semiconductor, 144
Fairness in Machine Learning (FairML), 79–80
Farrell, Mark, 239
Federal Telegraph Company (FTC), 108
feedback, 35, 96, 113, 125–127, 140, 170–174
Ferris, Tim, 228

Red Hat, 264
Religion of Technology (Noble), 210
Rheingold, Howard, 18
Rieder, Bernhardt, 175
Rosedale, Philip, 188
Ross, Edward, 108, 211
Rothbard, Murray, 215
Rubin, Andrei, 182
Rudy, Rick, 93

Sacks, David, 111, 259, 261
SAGE mainframe, 45
Saint-Simon, Henri de, 210
Salesforce, 246
San Francisco: AI industry and, 244; economic concerns and, 237–240; economic recovery and, 240–243; gentrification and, 235, 241, 246–248, 250–253; political ambivalence of, 236–243; politicizing tech, 249–256; tech emblems and, 253–256; tech industry and, 234–236, 243–249; urban development and, 245–247. *See also* Big Tech; Silicon Valley
Sassen, Saskia, 244
Sauter, Danny, 239
Say, Jean-Baptiste, 72, 215
Schmidt, Eric, 74, 259
Schumpeter, Joseph A., 56, 231
Scorsese, Martin, 236
Second Life (Rosedale), 188
secret societies, 94, 191, 195–196
seed companies, 18, 60
seed-funding, 61, 67, 101
self-expression, 128, 153, 189, 205
self-forgetfulness, 128
self-interest, 98, 128
Semiconductor International, 27
Sequoia Capital, 61, 68, 72–73
sexism, 147, 167
sexual harassment, 167
Shannon, Claude, 84
Shestakofsky, Benjamin, 55
Shockley, William, 28, 144
Shockley Semiconductor, 144
Silicon Africa (Cape Town), 2
Silicon Allee (Berlin), 2
Silicon Graphics, 36
Silicon Sentier (Paris), 2

Silicon Valley: artificial intelligence and, 32–33; barriers to, 14–21; communication theory and, 83–85; counterrevolution and, 258–263; cultures of, 79–85, 93–98; demographics of, 38–42, 40*f*, 85–88, 86*t*; egalitarianism of, 88–93; as enigma, 6–10; expansion of, 43–49; future of, 268–271; geographic landscape of, 34–38, 37*f*; global significance, 10–14; innovation in, 2, 6, 31–32; introduction to, 1–2, 25–27; investment economy of, 50–52, 64; makers in, 78, 80–82, 81*f*, 164, 187; Metcalfe's Law, 28–31; model of, 2–6; Moore's Law, 27–31; progressiveness of, 88–93; rust belt, 37; technological trends, 32–34, 33*t*; tech talent in, 38–39, 67–68, 85; work etiquette, 95*t*. *See also* Big Tech; San Francisco; tech companies/industry
Silicon Valley Bank, 1, 238, 262
Silicon Wadi (Tel Aviv), 2
simplicity virtue, 128–130
sincerity virtue, 128–130
Singer, Peter, 220
singularism, 211, 220
Smith, Adam, 134
Social Control: A Survey of the Foundations of Order (Ross), 211
social organizations, 31, 82, 108, 115, 118, 157–158, 224
social reassurance, 127
social science, 5, 108, 110, 271
software development kits (SDKs), 175
software engineers/engineering, 145, 160, 162, 164, 204
SolarCity, 188
solutionism, 3, 5, 223, 239, 269
sovereign wealth funds, 63, 76–77
Spotify, 8, 91
Square, 156
Stanford, Jane, 109
Stanford, Leland, 102–103, 108
Stanford University, 103, 108, 111, 120–121, 180–181, 242
Star, Susan Leigh, 166
startups: artificial intelligence and, 43, 55; founding by programmers, 183–184; identification processes, 155; introduction and definitions, 7–10

Founded in 1893,
UNIVERSITY OF CALIFORNIA PRESS
publishes bold, progressive books and journals
on topics in the arts, humanities, social sciences,
and natural sciences—with a focus on social
justice issues—that inspire thought and action
among readers worldwide.

The UC PRESS FOUNDATION
raises funds to uphold the press's vital role
as an independent, nonprofit publisher, and
receives philanthropic support from a wide
range of individuals and institutions—and from
committed readers like you. To learn more, visit
ucpress.edu/supportus.